OXFORD GREEK AND LATIN COLLEGE COMMENTARIES

Aristophanes' *Wasps*

OXFORD GREEK AND LATIN COLLEGE COMMENTARIES

THE OXFORD GREEK AND LATIN COLLEGE COMMENTARIES series is designed for students in intermediate or advanced Greek or Latin at colleges and universities. Each volume includes, on the same page, the ancient text, a running vocabulary, and succinct notes focusing on grammar and syntax, distinctive features of style, and essential context. The Greek and Latin texts are based on the most recent Oxford Classical Text (OCT) editions whenever available; otherwise, other authoritative editions are used. Each volume features a comprehensive introduction intended to enhance utility in the classroom and student appreciation of the work at hand.

The series focuses on texts and authors frequently taught at the intermediate or advanced undergraduate level, but it also makes available some central works currently lacking an appropriate commentary. The primary purpose of this series is to offer streamlined commentaries that are up-to-date, user-friendly, and affordable. Each volume presents entire works or substantial selections that can form the basis for an entire semester's coursework. Each commentary's close attention to grammar and syntax is intended to address the needs of readers encountering a work or author for the first time.

Ovid, *Ars Amatoria* Book 3
Commentary by Christopher M. Brunelle

Selected Letters from Pliny the Younger's *Epistulae*
Commentary by Jacqueline Carlon

Aristophanes' *Wasps*
Commentary by Kenneth S. Rothwell, Jr.

Aristophanes' *Wasps*

Commentary by

Kenneth S. Rothwell, Jr.
University of Massachusetts Boston

OXFORD
UNIVERSITY PRESS

Oxford University Press is a department of the University of Oxford. It furthers
the University's objective of excellence in research, scholarship, and education
by publishing worldwide. Oxford is a registered trade mark of Oxford University
Press in the UK and certain other countries.

Published in the United States of America by Oxford University Press
198 Madison Avenue, New York, NY 10016, United States of America.

CIP data is on file at the Library of Congress
ISBN 978–0–19–063971–6 (pbk.)
ISBN 978–0–19–090740–2 (hbk.)

1 3 5 7 9 8 6 4 2

Paperback printed by Webcom, Inc., Canada
Hardback printed by Bridgeport National Bindery, Inc., United States of America

CONTENTS

MAP OF ATTICA

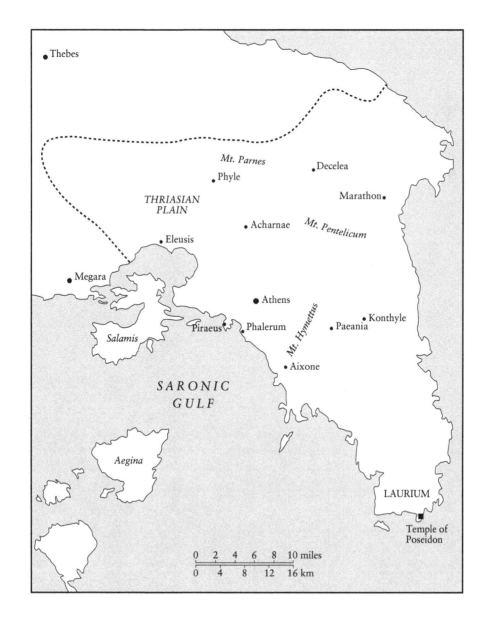

Thebes

Mt. Parnes

Decelea

Phyle

THRIASIAN
PLAIN

Marathon

Acharnae

Mt. Pentelicum

Eleusis

Megara

Athens

Konthyle

Piraeus

Phalerum

Paeania

Mt. Hymettus

Salamis

Aixone

SARONIC
GULF

Aegina

LAURIUM

Temple of
Poseidon

| 0 | 2 | 4 | 6 | 8 | 10 miles |
| 0 | 4 | 8 | 12 | 16 km |

MAP OF GREECE AND THE AEGEAN

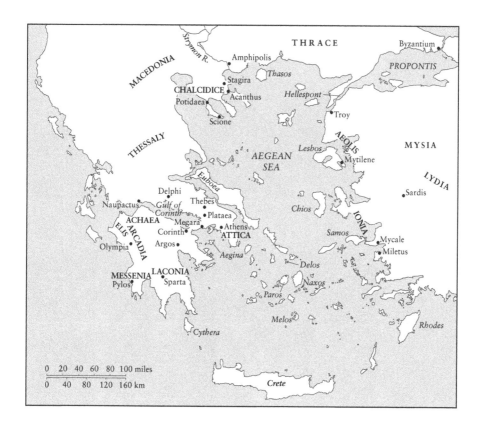

ACKNOWLEDGMENTS

MY FIRST THANKS go to Stephen Esposito, the general editor of Greek commentaries in the OGLCC, who has been unfailingly supportive, prompt, and a font of knowledge about the Greek language. I also appreciate the encouragement and advice of Charles Cavaliere and Stefan Vranka of Oxford University Press. A sabbatical leave granted by the University of Massachusetts Boston allowed me to finish this edition, and I am enormously grateful for that.

It was a teacher's dream to have several of my students read *Wasps* with early drafts of this commentary: Anna Scher, Ian Nurmi, David Chu, Lesleigh Balkum Jones, Andrew Campbell, Aidan Cheney-Lynch, C. J. Ellstrom, David Irvin, Alexandria DeSio, and Daphne Bissette. All helped me see things from a student's perspective. The proposal was generously vetted by Profs. Matthew Farmer, Jeffrey Rusten, Ralph Rosen, Jennifer Starkey, and Andrew Scholtz; their advice was welcome, and I hope this final version meets their hopes. An anonymous reader helped save me from a number of missteps. Prof. Donald Mastronarde rescued me at the last minute with his expertise in GreekKeys. I have benefitted from the insights of Peter Barrios-Lech and Randall Colaizzi, colleagues who have taught comedy for years. Jacqui Carlon, both a colleague and a fellow OGLCC editor, has been a model and inspiration. Pam's love, humor, and patience have made this volume possible.

INTRODUCTION

THE STING OF Aristophanes' *Wasps* (the title is Σφῆκες in Greek and *Vespae* in Latin) is more like a tickle. This delightful comedy plunges readers into the politics of late fifth-century Athens, but shows us that in important ways, such as in the skewering of politicians and charges of corruption, public life has not changed in the last two and a half millennia. Audiences also enjoy watching the messy private lives of any family, and the family in this comedy will not disappoint. Adding to the pleasure is the fact that the central character, Philocleon, and the chorus of wasp-like old men for which the play is named, are some of the great creations of comic drama.

AN OVERVIEW OF *WASPS*

I find it convenient to think of *Wasps* as being composed of a series of four contests.

1–462: Philocleon has developed an obsession with serving on juries in Athens. His son, Bdelycleon, thinks that Philocleon needs to be saved from his impulses, so Bdelycleon and his household slaves try to keep Philocleon at home. At one point the father even tries to escape by lashing himself under a donkey, like Odysseus escaping the Cyclops's cave. A crowd of retired, lower-class Athenian men, the "wasp" chorus, enter and try to help the father escape; this intervention degenerates into a violent attack on Bdelycleon and the slaves, but they resist forcefully and the chorus are beaten back. The son has held his ground.

463–724: Philocleon and Bdelycleon agree to debate the merits of jury service: Philocleon enumerates the benefits and pleasures of judging; Bdelycleon argues that the jurors are actually being exploited by manipulative politicians. The chorus are won over by Bdelycleon, who wins the debate.

725–1008: Philocleon is offered a consolation for his house confinement: he will adjudicate domestic disputes. The household dog Labes ("Grabber"), accused of stealing cheese, is put on trial. The prosecutor is a dog of Kydathenaion; Bdelycleon speaks in Labes's defense. Philocleon would like to convict Labes but is tricked by his son into dropping his "guilty" vote into the "acquittal" urn, and Labes goes free. Bdelycleon wins, having outwitted his father.

1009–1537: After the *parabasis* (an interlude during which the chorus speak out of character and present the author's case for victory in the dramatic festival), Bdelycleon tries to re-educate Philocleon and train him to participate in a high-class symposium, but Philocleon winds up boorishly insulting guests at the party, assaulting innocent bystanders on the way home, and cavorting with a sexy flute-girl named Dardanis. (Some of these events occur off-stage and are related by a slave, in a report reminiscent of messenger speeches in tragedy.) Bdelycleon's attempt to reshape his incorrigible father's behavior is a failure. Thus Philocleon, the "loser" in the first three contests, is the "winner" in the end. (One could add a fifth contest in which, as part of the choral *exodos*, Philocleon dances competitively with the sons of the tragic playwright Carcinus.)

The genius of *Wasps* is that these scrapes and scuffles work on multiple levels: generational (father vs. son), political (supporters of Cleon and of the war against Sparta vs. their opponents), social (upper-class vs. lower-class behavior), and literary (Aristophanes vs. other comic playwrights as they compete in the festivals). Each of these themes deserves examination.

FATHER AND SON

We are meant to understand that Philocleon, in retirement, has ceded legal control of the household to Bdelycleon. The slaves certainly answer to the son, not the father. But Philocleon, rather than assume a position as a benign elder, has instead reverted to adolescent immaturity. Thus the father and son have traded places, a role-reversal that provides the *Wasps* with the topsy-turvy twist that every comedy needs. The dutiful son clearly goes through a lot of trouble to make sure that his high-maintenance father is well cared for, but he is rebuffed; says Philocleon, "He's ready to feast me in luxury, but it's not what *I* want" (341). The comic absurdity reaches its apogee when the father tells the flute-girl Dardanis that he would like to pay for her freedom, but that he is young and needs to wait for his son to die before he can get control of his own property (1352–56).

In truth, though, the father-son relationship itself is only lightly sketched in *Wasps*. The grown, confident son and elderly but vigorous father surely share a lifetime of history, yet we are told very little about it. Nor is much said of other family members; we hear that when Philocleon comes home from jury duty, his daughter welcomes him and his wife brings him puff pastry (607–12), but they are never heard of again. Ultimately *Wasps* offers no nuanced insights into the emotional and psychological dynamics of a relationship of long standing—though one would be hard-pressed to find that in any play of Aristophanes. For that we need to look to tragedy, or wait for New Comedy and Menander.

What Aristophanes' comedy *does* accomplish is to use this family drama as a stage to enact the social and political tensions that Athenians faced during the Peloponnesian War. Philocleon's identity is defined by his bonds with his fellow jurors and by his allegiance to the politician Cleon, who, he asserts, treats him better than his own son does (598).

CLEON, POLITICS, AND THE PELOPONNESIAN WAR IN 422 BC

One of the most significant people in *Wasps*, although he never appears on stage, is Cleon. After all, the two main characters are literally defined by their attitudes toward him: Philocleon's name means "Lover of Cleon," and Bdelycleon's means "Loather of Cleon."

After the death of Pericles in 429, it fell to Cleon to pursue the war against Sparta and her allies. Cleon had become a *strategos* (one of ten annually elected generals) for 424/23, but his strategy suffered a setback when in 424 the Spartans captured Amphipolis, a northern city adjacent to Thrace that had been an Athenian colony and ally. Cleon was evidently not re-elected for 423/22, and the general Laches arranged a one-year truce. But the revolt from Athens in 423 of Scione, an allied city in the Chalcidice region, also in northern Greece (mentioned at *Wasps* 210), forced the Athenians to return to a more aggressive policy. In 422, Cleon, elected general again, took Athenian troops up to the area to recover Scione and to recapture Amphipolis (cf. *Wasps* 288), but he was killed fighting there in the summer of 422, a few months after *Wasps* was performed. His death, and the death of the Spartan commander Brasidas, opened the door for the peace parties at Athens and Sparta. A truce was struck in 421.

More important for *Wasps* than Cleon's military campaigns were his domestic policies. Although Cleon's family had become wealthy from a leather-tanning factory (and references to leather or hides sometimes turn out to be allusions to Cleon, e.g., 38), he was not an aristocrat by birth. By political instinct he was a populist. It was Cleon who in 425 had cemented his reputation as an advocate for the Athenian *demos* by raising jury pay to three obols. (An obol was one sixth of a drachma, a drachma being the approximate daily wage of a skilled worker.) The chorus see Cleon as their patron (*kedemon*, 242; cf. 197, 409). Philocleon says that Cleon "holds them in his arms and keeps off the flies" (597).

Just how effective an advocate he really was is what Bdelycleon questions. In a passage of his speech that has caught the attention of economic historians, Bdelycleon opens up the account books of the Athenian government and explains that total annual income from tribute, taxes, fees, and such amount to 2,000 talents per year (655–65). If juror payments cost only 150 talents (assuming 6,000 jurors were paid three obols a day for 300 days each year), that leaves a whopping 1,850 talents for the politicians.[1]

In fact, the shocking declaration at the core of Bdelycleon's argument (esp. 666–724)—and a source of resentment that animates much of Aristophanic comedy—is that what is in name a democracy is actually a system that has been rigged to exploit the common citizens and enrich the powerful. The citizen-jurors may not have exactly been slaves, but they were certainly dupes. Cleon, says Bdelycleon, is at the core of this rigged system, pretending to

---

1. It is impossible to know whether these numbers are accurate; they seem on the high side but are probably not absurdly exaggerated. A talent would be, perhaps, the equivalent of a million dollars.

promote the interests of the *demos* when in fact the three daily obols they get as jurors are measly scraps (672). Bdelycleon is careful not to denigrate the importance of jury duty, or to question the principle that the democracy should function for the good of the common *demos*, but argues instead that the jurors are being cheated. The politicians, bureaucrats, and generals have cannily convinced the citizen jurors that they are being fairly rewarded. Even the allies of the Athenians have caught onto this and are bribing Athenian politicians so as to win favors for themselves (673–77). This corruption has found its way into the judicial process: a prosecutor, whose daily salary of one drachma is double what jurors get, can earn even more by accepting a bribe from a defendant. As Bdelycleon puts it, "They're like a couple of sawyers, one pulling while the other pushes" (691–94). Once this betrayal is explained to him, Philocleon momentarily becomes a figure in his own tragedy: his eyes have been opened to an appalling reality that he had been blind to.

THE JURY SYSTEM OF THE ATHENIAN DEMOCRACY

Satire only works if the target of the mockery (in *Wasps*, the jury system) is familiar to the audience; a review of legal procedures at Athens is therefore essential. What follows is necessarily schematic, but covers steps relevant for understanding in the *Wasps*. (Please also consult Appendix B for legal terminology.)

When a crime had been committed, the wronged individual would issue to the perpetrator a summons to present himself to a magistrate who, on the basis of witness testimony and affidavits, would decide whether to bring the case to court for a full jury trial. The choice of the courtroom (there were several possibilities) would depend on questions of jurisdiction and the nature of the crime. Announcements of pending trials were posted on notice boards (*sanides*).

All Athenian citizens were eligible to be jurors, and six thousand men were chosen annually to serve. In the fourth century BC, a complicated process involving random lotteries had been developed to ensure that the jurors would be impartial and that no jury could be stacked by either prosecution or defense, but at the time of *Wasps* these measures seem not to have been in place, and it was apparently possible for defendants to meet the jurors and make personal appeals to them before the trial got underway. Then again, the potential for corruption was limited by the fact that juries were extremely large; there were 500 jurors at the trial of Socrates in 399 BC.

Once the proceedings were underway, a water clock would be used to guarantee that both prosecution and defense had equal amounts of time to give their speeches. Unlike our system, in which criminal prosecutions are the responsibility of the state, in Athens it was generally up to individual citizens themselves to perform the prosecution and give speeches in court. (The prosecutor mentioned at 691–94 was enlisted only in specific cases.) Surviving speeches by orators such as Antiphon, Andocides, Lysias, and Demosthenes are filled with examples of specific argumentative techniques that were used in front of a jury. The court system helped shape a culture of debate and oratory at

Athens that left unmistakable imprints on tragedy and historiography. In *Wasps*, not only are there two pairs of opposing speeches (Philocleon vs. Bdelycleon on the jury system, the Kydathenaion Dog vs. Bdelycleon on Labes's guilt), but also numerous references to the culture of debate.

A magistrate supervised the proceedings, but only in a perfunctory way; there was no "judge" in our sense of the word—no one was there to enforce legal procedures, rule on the admissibility of evidence or testimony, or declare a speaker out of order. The verdict was entirely in the hands of the jury. Voting was done when jurors dropped tokens or pebbles (evidently seashells could be used too, 333) into one of two jars—one jar to convict and another to acquit—and the pebbles would be spilled out onto a flat stone (332) and counted. A second vote would be held to determine the punishment or fine.

Wasps itself offers tantalizing if comically distorted evidence for courtroom procedure. We see the first stage of the legal process when Philocleon assaults a bread seller named Myrtia and other bystanders, all of whom then initiate legal action by issuing a summons (1334, 1401, 1441) and by calling on witnesses (1413). The chorus mention specific court locations that jurors might be expected to attend: some judge in "the Archon's court, some with the Eleven, and some in the Odeum" (1108–9). The dog trial also comically recreates a courtroom: the litigants settle on which member of the household will do the speaking (840–42), courtroom railings (*druphaktoi*, 830) are expected, as are notice boards (*sanides*, 848), voting urns (though ladling cups will work, 854–55), a water clock (the chamber pot suffices, 857–59), customary opening prayers (868–90), and formulaic reading of the charges (894–97). The Kydathenaion Dog's prosecution speech (908–30) relies on stock features of courtroom oratory, as does the defense speech given by Bdelycleon (950–80), which even includes the standard appeal for sympathy by bringing one's children up for the jury to pity (975–78). The trial ends with the dropping of voting tokens (*psephoi*) into the jars (986–91).

A legal system in which the verdict was entirely in the hands of citizens was one of the central safeguards of the Athenian classical democracy. In this way, the citizens were able to ensure that legislation was carried out. The abuses seen in *Wasps* may have been real, but the system had the potential to empower citizen jurors and enable them to hold individual politicians accountable: all elected officials were considered "subject to accountability" (*hypeuthunos*) and had to submit to an audit at the end of their term in office. Irregularities could be referred to the court for prosecution.

PHILOCLEON THE JUROR

Unfortunately, justice is the last thing on Philocleon's mind. In fact, the practices that he extols are inexcusably cruel. Cynical self-interest is taken for granted. Philocleon's world is one in which it is plausible to imagine that a cock can be bribed to crow at the wrong time (101), and that a defendant would try to sway jurors by appealing to an assumption that all of them would embezzle a little something if they were holding office (556–57). The Kydathenaion Dog baldly states that Labes's crime is that he did not share the cheese with the prosecutor or anyone else (914, 917). Philocleon is content to quit for the day after hearing only one case, knowing that he will still get the full day's wage (595). A high point in his life is coming home with pay and being pampered by his daughter and wife (605–15). Entertainment was part of the appeal of jury duty: not only do courtrooms stage the drama of the political, social, and private affairs of Athenians, but occasionally a bonus might be thrown in: when the actor Oeagrus was in court, he was forced to recite a speech from the tragedy *Niobe* (579–80). (In a metatheatrical touch, the lively world of dramatic competition thus appears even in the courtroom.)

Bdelycleon was able to convince Philocleon to accept the household trial as an alternative to a real trial by appealing to his selfish needs: being at home means avoiding bad weather (772–75), having food available (777–80), easy access to a toilet (807–10), and a brazier and hot soup to keep him warm (811–14). He will also continue to get his three obols (from Bdelycleon, 784–85).

Philocleon has a sadistic streak and makes no attempt to hide it. Punishment is always severe (106), and he claims that an oracle prophesied that he would shrivel up if he ever acquitted anyone (159–60). Even the chorus say he has been the fiercest juror (*drimutatos*, 278); asking for mercy from him is as useless as "cooking a stone" (280). He freely admits that the reason he wants to escape the house is to harm someone (322). When at the conclusion of the dog trial Philocleon discovers that he has been tricked into dropping his voting pebble into the "acquittal" urn, he practically faints dead (994–95) and has to beg forgiveness of the gods (1001). It is plain to all, especially in his great speech describing the appeal of jury duty (548–630), that Philocleon is less interested in justice than in intimidating and convicting defendants. Humiliating powerful men is a bonus. He gleefully describes the groveling and desperate measures that defendants resorted to in their attempts to sway the jurors (560–75). He says he can make the rich and grand cluck and shit their pants in fear (625–27), but it is not about justice—it is about power for him. The experience of watching people resort to desperate arguments and stratagems to win acquittal would probably darken anyone's view of human nature. One suspects that the courtroom was the one place where a retired old man like Philocleon could maintain autonomy and a sense of purpose. It is sad that this purpose requires that others suffer whether they are guilty or not.

Standard moral judgments do not apply. When Bdleycleon says to his father, "You're a *bad* one [*poneros*], and a professional past master at it" (192), it is not clear that this was an insult; in fact, as Cedric Whitman (1964, 156) showed long ago, "badness" (*poneria*) was if anything a positive quality for him. The term can embrace the cleverness and resourcefulness that Odysseus relied on—and it was of course Odysseus who was Philocleon's model when he tried to sneak out of the house lashed under a donkey (175–95).

The courtroom offers Philocleon a life superior to anything at home. The perks are many: examining the privates of boys being inspected for deme registration, enjoying a free recitation of a tragic speech, dreaming about the sexual availability of an heiress, and of course the three obols of pay. So obsessed was he with courtrooms that he wished to be transformed into the stone on which juror's voting pebbles were counted (332). This escapist fantasy even had a religious component: he claims Lykos, a mythical hero whose shrine was adjacent to the law court, as an ancestral god, one who takes pleasure in the sufferings of defendants (389–90). As his life's denouement, he wants to be buried under the *druphaktoi*, the court railings (386).

Philocleon's disregard for justice is reaffirmed at the end of the play: freed of all inhibitions, seeing himself as a charming old rascal, he knocks loaves of bread off of the tray of the bread seller Myrtia; her legitimate attempts to get compensation are met with complete contempt by Philocleon (1388–1412). He is "not subject to accountability" (*anupeuthunos*, 587). This single word, I suggest, captures the spirit of Philocleon: a man unencumbered by any legal, social, or private constraints.

THE CHORUS OF *WASPS*

One of the conspicuous features of Aristophanic comedy, and of Old Comedy in general, is the remarkable variety of the choruses; frequently a comedy was named for the chorus (this is of course also true of tragedy). Even if the comedies themselves have not survived, we know from their titles of plays whose choruses were composed of women, peasants, foreigners, cities, islands, satyrs, personified abstractions, and animals. Choruses in the fifth-century comedies tended to intervene in the action and set themselves up a counterforce to the protagonist, at least in the first half of the play.

The men of the chorus of *Wasps* are retired citizens who represent the bedrock of the Athenian *demos*. Going to jury duty is like answering a call to military service—at least that is how they see it when Cleon has ordered them to prepare three days' rations (242–43), a command normally given to citizen soldiers as they mobilize for battle. They form up like infantrymen when they attack Bdelycleon and the slaves (422–24).

They come by this sense of duty honestly: they are the generation that fought and built the Athenian empire and the democracy from the time of the Persian Wars. They recall military service going back to the capture of Naxos, ca. 470 BC (354–55), and the revolt of Samos in 440 BC (283). Bdelycleon knows he can appeal to the sense of pride that Philocleon and the chorus have by invoking the victory at the Battle of Marathon (711). Part of the *parabasis* dwells on the prowess they showed fighting the Persians (1060–62, 1078–88, 1091–1101).

But that was years ago. Their reminiscences of earlier martial valor (1060–70) quickly turn to regret at their lost youth. They are slow (230, 236) and picture Philocleon as infirm (276–77). This is evident in their musical tastes, which lean toward the "oldies" of the earlier fifth century. They sing "old honeyed Sidonian" songs of Phrynichus, a tragic playwright active at the beginning of the century (220).

The Wasps are men with unpretentious names (230–34) and of modest means: lamp oil is a luxury item for them (251–53), and dried figs are an indulgence (297–302). They can barely afford to support a family of three. If they are worried that their crops are not getting enough rain (263–65), they must be small farmers. This no-nonsense rural outlook—no city sophisticates among them!—helps explain descriptions of them as having a "heart-of-oak" temperament (383). They are righteous and sharp spirited (455), proud of their anger (*orge*) and wrath (*thumos*, 646, 649).

The men of the chorus have an innate hostility to Sparta or anything that smacks of Laconia. For most of the fifth century, hard-core democrats were suspicious that Spartan sympathizers would try to overthrow the democracy and impose an oligarchy. The chorus assume that Bdelycleon is just such a conspirator (345); they call him a "long-haired [=pro-Spartan?] Amynias" (466), a lover of monarchy who consorts with Brasidas (475), and someone who wants to exercise *turannis* over them (487). When in the end they are persuaded by Bdelycleon's speech, it is because he has convinced them that he loves the *demos* like no one else of his younger generation (888–90).

SOCIAL VALUES IN *WASPS*

The leading characters in *Wasps* are a wealthy, conservative son and a father who identifies himself as a simple citizen of modest circumstances. The discrepancy is never explained, but one could imagine that the son struck it rich, and that the father had been welcomed into the son's household; alternatively, the father's position may be a pose, for there are hints that he has always lived in what is obviously a prosperous household.

However it came to be, the differing statuses of these two men under one roof gives Aristophanes a chance to explore their different values. For all intents and purposes, Philocleon represents the social values and habits of the common Athenian *demos*: he is proud of his frugality, wears modest clothes, and, in the climactic symposium scene, proves himself to be a boorishly lower-class character. Philocleon will not part with his old cloak, a *tribonion* (1122–32), when Bdelycleon tries to get him to wear a much classier, imported Persian *chlaina* (1137), which, as it requires a talent of wool, is very expensive (1145–47). Bdelycleon wants to replace Philocleon's simple shoes (*embades*, 103, 1157) with nice ones, "Laconians" (1157–65), though the name alone is enough to make Philocleon seethe all over again about anything Spartan. When Bdelycleon recommends strategies for making conversation with upper-class Athenians at a symposium, he suggests anecdotes about participating in state delegations, Olympic exploits, or boar hunting (1186–1204), but Philocleon, who has never done any of these things anyway, can only think of crude things to say. Bdelycleon instructs him to recline elegantly on a symposium couch, compliment the host's dining room, pour libations, sing appropriate party songs, and tell witty anecdotes (1208–64).

Another way of understanding the social divide is to see Philocleon and Bdelycleon as facing a dilemma familiar to fifth-century Athenians: whether to engage with, or withdraw from, public life. Philocleon and members of the jury plunge into jury duty and make it their business to know about everything in Athens; they are *polypragmones*, "busy-bodies," to choose the word of the day. This hyperactivity was seen as characteristic of Athens ever since Pericles built up the institutions of the democracy and the Delian League. It was, however, famously critiqued by observers such as the Corinthians in Thucydides (1.70; cf. 6.87), who lashed out against the oppressive nature of Athenian foreign policy, and by the "Old Oligarch" (3.2), who recoiled at the amount of Athenian judicial activity. The response of conservatives to these excesses was to be *apragmones*, keeping clear of public life and the frenzy of political engagement, cultivating instead their private lives and minding their own business. After all, they thought, it was smart politics to keep a low profile when the other side was in control of the government.

This attitude can be detected in Bdelycleon. He explicitly critiques the institutions of government in his speech to the chorus (650–724), though of course he voices not so much his disagreement with the principle of democracy as his concern that the average Athenian citizen is being exploited. A better example of his *apragmosyne* is the simple fact that his efforts are centered on disengaging his father from the public realm and pulling him into a more private world of household concerns and symposia with the aristocratic elite of Athens.

THE CULTURE OF SYMPOSIUM SOCIETY

The final scenes of *Wasps* stage one of the more important institutions of ancient Greece: the symposium. The symposium, which emerged in the archaic period as an occasion for bonding among aristocratic men, had developed its own conventions and etiquette. Symposiasts would meet in a private home, wear imported cloaks, admire the host's dining room and its furnishing, and recline on couches for a meal. Once settled in, they turn to wine drinking and make a libation to the *agathos daimon* ("Good Spirit," cf. 525), put garlands on their heads, sing *skolia* (short drinking songs, cf. 1222), recite poetry (snippets of Sappho and Alcaeus are quoted by Bdelycleon, 1232–35, 1238–39), tell stories, play games with riddles, and be entertained by a girl playing an *aulos* (a flute-like musical instrument, cf. 1477). All of this camaraderie would reinforce social values and a feeling of membership among the elite men in attendance, and it could end with a drunken procession (*komos*) in the streets.

Elite men facing the threat of the egalitarian tendencies of the democracy would have felt a stronger need for an insular institution. Clearly Philocleon was not familiar with the ways of these wealthier men: he needs to change his wardrobe, know what topics of conversation are appropriate, flatter hosts and guests, recline at a couch, sing the right songs, and tell appropriate anecdotes. It is a mark of his lack of education that he never learned to play the lyre (so too Labes, 959, 989). Perhaps the "instruction" scenes were inserted so that the audience could understand, firsthand, how flagrantly Philocleon violated all social protocols by insulting the fellow guests. His instinct as a juror—to humiliate the rich and powerful—is the only thing that stays with him after Bdelycleon has attempted to re-educate him.

THE COMEDY OF *WASPS*

We might not want to admit it, but Philocleon was right: it is fun to watch other people suffer. We smile when our enemies are embarrassed and we laugh out loud when they fall flat on their faces; so of course we enjoy watching someone on stage get his (and it is usually a "he") well-deserved comeuppance. The suffering does not have to be physical, and in fact emotional or psychological cruelty can be just as satisfying. Moreover—and this is one irony of comedy—the victim *does not even need to know* that he has been humiliated. He may go through life completely unaware that he is the butt of laughter, with a "Kick Me" sign Scotch-taped to his rear end. On a gentler and more elevated plane, this same pleasure can be found in Plato's dialogues when "Socrates" reveals his interlocutor's ignorance. In all of these contexts, it is important that there be someone (even if only the spectator or reader) to witness this humiliation; the presence of an audience makes it a comic performance.

Accordingly, one useful approach to any comedy is to see whether we can identify the *eiron* and *alazon* (Aristotle discussed these types in *Nicomachean Ethics* 1008a12). The *eiron* is the underdog, a person who may be an unprepossessing social inferior. Yet appearances are deceiving: this is the character who is able to control the course of events. (Our word *irony* derives from it, and *eironeia* was a quality of seemingly humble Socrates.) This character type is set against the *alazon*, the "boaster," who is pretentious, immodest, and frequently in a high station in life: perhaps a military officer, a father figure, or a politician. Another natural pairing is an overbearing man subverted by a clever woman: women are naturally suited to the asymmetric warfare of the *eiron* against the *alazon*, as *Lysistrata* shows. By the end of a comedy, the *alazon* will have been shown to be an ignorant fool. The two roles would harden into the tricky slave and the braggart soldier in Plautus, and they still survive in comic drama, fiction, and film.

But part of what gives *Wasps* its dynamic is that the characters can reverse positions. It may be easy to think of Bdelycleon as the *alazon*, for he serves as the earnest father-figure, keen to follow social conventions and trying to keep the rambunctious troublemaker at home. And yet in his great speech it is he who pulls away the curtain and reveals the political system to be corrupt. In that moment, it is Philocleon—the one asserting his credentials as a lower-class citizen who can humiliate the fat cats, mocking the pretensions of social superiors—who is shown to be the fool. He has been exploited by a political system that enriches the wealthy but pays the common citizens a pittance. His claims about his power as a juror are exposed as the hollow pretentions of an *alazon*; his inside "knowledge" of the jury system has been unmasked as ignorance. "Knowledge" was, after all, what Aristotle was reflecting on when he contrasted the *alazon* and *eiron* in the *Nicomachean Ethics*: if someone who tells the truth is the intermediate person, the *alazon* is the person who exaggerates it and the *eiron* the one who understates it. Or, as Plato put it, what is laughable is self-ignorance (*Philebus* 49c).[2]

I wrote earlier that Philocleon is the "winner" in the end. In some ways, this is undeniable: he has broken artificial social constraints and indulged his inner rascal. But do we laugh with him or at him? Both—at least I do. Some readers take a negative view of the finale: it stages the sort of "low-brow" humor (*phortike komoidia*, 66) that was criticized in the prologue, almost embodying what Aristophanes found offensive in Cratinus's *Pytine* of 423 (see below on this). Worse, it may be that Philocleon is a self-deluded *alazon* when it comes to his own potency, because it is entirely possible that the audience could see the old man's limp, dangling phallus.

Yet there is no hard evidence about that soft piece of costume; perhaps Philocleon's interest in the girl should be read as a sign of youthful vitality, whether he attains an erect phallus or not. His incorrigibility can be seen as "a mark of his redemption according to Dionysian standards" (Biles and Olson, 2015, xxxiii). No longer a passive spectator in a courtroom, he has been transformed into an invigorated participant in the chorus. In fact, perhaps Philocleon's salient characteristic is his chameleon-like ability to shift over the course of the *Wasps* from one identity to another, untouched by any need for inner consistency and unconstrained by any external necessity.[3]

Many readers find Bdelycleon the more sympathetic character: he is the one who shows concern for his father, gives a reasoned critique of the jury system, and generally exhibits more polite behavior. In truth "loathing," the βδελ-root built into his name, is not a particularly pronounced feature of his character. He may possibly be a crypto-oligarch, and he dislikes Cleon, but he actually has little to say about the man. If Philocleon is an *alazon*, to use Aristotle's term, we might decide that Bdelycleon is not the *eiron* but the intermediate figure who simply tells the truth.

---

2. I am indebted to Hubbard (1991, 1–15), who emphasizes the doctrine of "comedy as a deficiency of self-knowledge." For theories of comedy, see Lowe 2008, 1–20.

3. For a recent discussion of Philocleon's comic freedom, see Nelson 2016, 141–76.

THE FESTIVALS OF DIONYSUS AT ATHENS AND ARISTOPHANIC COMEDY

Comedy is thought to have been first performed at the dramatic contests of the City Dionysia in March/April of 486 BC; comic performances at the Lenaea, which was held in January/February, began in the mid-440s. Over the course of his career Aristophanes had comedies performed in both festivals; *Wasps* was performed at the Lenaea of 422 BC.

It is hard not to read the comedies as products of these festivals.[4] Of course the characters and plots of Old Comedy were, to a considerable extent, freely invented by the playwrights themselves. Tragedy and epic drew on the storehouse of Greek mythology, whereas comic playwrights were limited only by their imaginations. Indeed, the plots contrived by Aristophanes are famously full of ludicrous twists and turns.

That said, one important way of reading Aristophanic comedy is through the lens of Athenians who were well versed in their own myths and religious rituals, and it is entirely possible that they recognized familiar patterns. The abolition of social constraints, the promotion of fertility, the significance of *phalloi*, and wine (the liquid propellant of the final scenes and Dionysus's signature product), were features of the cult of Dionysus that are replicated in comedy. Philocleon seems to enjoy a renewed sexual vigor with the flute-girl Dardanis. Biles and Olson (2015, xxxiv) point to the Dionysiac theme of containment and escape that is evident in Euripides's *Cyclops*; Philocleon can plausibly be compared with satyrs. Bdelycleon attempted to rechannel Philocleon's energies into a private symposium, only to find that he had opened up another outlet for his father's irrepressible vitality.

Other ritual patterns, in addition to those of the Dionysia, also appear in Aristophanic comedy. One relevant practice was *aischrologia*, the use of obscenity and insult in ritual contexts, most famously in the procession of the Eleusinian Mysteries. The verbal abuse of people, even if they are socially or politically prominent people, was sanctioned and expected on ritual occasions. This ritual precedent may explain why characters in Aristophanes feel free to try to humiliate members of the audience or of Athenian society. The number of people insulted in the course of *Wasps* is rather large, and part of Aristophanes' ingenuity is to devise new ways to twist the knife. Even what starts out like a compliment ends up an insult: Ariphrades is talented—at cunnilingus! (1280–83).

WASPS IN ARISTOPHANES' CAREER

If, as seems likely, Aristophanes was born soon after 450 BC, he would have been in his early twenties when his first comedy, *Banqueters*, was performed in 427. We are told that he wrote at least forty plays; eleven have survived, the last being *Plutus* of 388.

---

4. For ritual aspects of Aristophanic comedy, see Bowie 1996.

A poet wrote the script, but he would often also serve as the *didaskalos*, the "teacher" who acted like a modern director (though scholars often describe this position as "producer"), and concern himself with the business of actually putting on the show. He would work with a *choregos*, a wealthy man who was financially supporting the production, like a modern producer or "angel"; specifically, the *choregos* would recruit and underwrite the training of the chorus and musicians, and would also supply costumes and masks.

Aristophanes, however, did not begin his career by serving as his own *didaskalos*; he relied instead on a certain Callistratus for his first three comedies.[5] A disadvantage to this arrangement was that it was the *didaskalos* whose name was announced to the public; the playwright's identity would only be circulated informally. Aristophanes finally served as his own *didaskalos* for *Knights* in 424 and *Clouds* in 423.[6] *Clouds* won third place in 423, defeated by *Pytine* (*Wine Flask*) of the veteran comic poet Cratinus, a loss that troubled Aristophanes so much that in the *parabasis* of *Wasps* he chides the audience for the verdict (1016–18, 1044–50).[7]

For *Wasps*, which won second prize in 422, it appears that Aristophanes was acting as his own *didaskalos*. First prize was given to a now-lost play titled *Proagon* and ascribed to the comic playwright Philonides. (It was a comedy about poets, with Euripides as the main character.) Other evidence, however, suggests that the *Proagon* was actually written by Aristophanes. What seems to have happened, then, is that Aristophanes wrote two plays for the Lenaea of 422 but had the *Proagon* submitted under the name of Philonides as *didaskalos*. If the first-place-winning *Proagon* was Aristophanes', the second-place finish of *Wasps* would have stung a little less.

The main speech in the *parabasis* of *Wasps* (1009–59) is a personal testament of poetic principles. Here he (that is, the chorus leader voicing, in first-person singular, Aristophanes' own views) reproaches the Athenian people for not having supported the *Clouds* in 423: no one, he says, ever heard better comic poetry (1047). What exactly made his poetry so good? It was intellectual and innovative, and he had sown brand-new ideas (*kainotatai dianoiai*, 1044). Poets' ideas should be stored carefully, scented with cleverness (*dexiotes*, 1055–59), like clothes packed away with citrons for the season.

Aristophanes contrasts this intelligence with what is found in comedies written by his rivals. Already in the prologue, in a *parabasis*-like direct address to the audience, Xanthias had belittled

5. *Banqueters* in 427, *Babylonians* in 426, and *Acharnians* in 425. When he says at *Wasps* 1018–22 that at first he assisted others secretly, but later took a chance on competing openly, he may be referring to these first three years, or perhaps to writings before 427.
6. The surviving text of *Clouds* is a version that was revised and published some five years later.
7. *Wasps* can be seen as a response and comeback play to *Pytine*, yet at the same time seems to recapitulate some of its themes. In *Pytine*, Cratinus needs to be rehabilitated from his fondness for drink, assisted by his wife, Komoidia, but in the end reverts to drunkenness. So too Philocleon needs to be cured of his jury obsession, and a family member intervenes to help, but the finale shows that his nature cannot be changed. See Biles 2011, 146–66; and Telò 2016, 56–58.

vulgar stage routines that other comedians resorted to, like the scattering of nuts to the audience, Heracles being shown cheated of dinner, and Euripides being abused (58–61). Xanthias's claim for *Wasps* is that it "makes sense: not more intellectual than you are yourselves, but more artistic than low-brow comedy" (64–66). All of this may strike readers as somewhat odd because, set against the history of comedy ever since, much of what one finds in Aristophanes, with its coarse language, sexual explicitness, and outright physical violence, seems decidedly on the farcical and low-brow end of the spectrum, more *Borat* than Oscar Wilde. We would love to see what these rival comic playwrights were doing to make Aristophanes seem respectable.

Another striking feature of the *parabasis* are the metaphors that Aristophanes uses to highlight the competitive nature of the dramatic festivals. He speaks of himself "holding the reins of a team of Muses" (1022), as if he were in a chariot race; in his ambition he was attempting to overtake his rivals—but wrecked his chariot (1049–50). (The rivals in question were Cratinus and Ameipsias, whose comedies placed ahead of *Clouds* in 423.)

The defeat of 423 notwithstanding, Aristophanes claims to have made a great contribution to Athenian civic life, namely, his attack on Cleon in *Knights* of 424. In *Wasps* Aristophanes likens himself to Heracles attacking a "jag-toothed monster" (1029–39) and says he stood up against a counterattack from Cleon (1284–91). Precisely what counterattack Aristophanes is referring to here is not clear, but the chorus pick up this theme when they describe themselves as dutiful citizen-soldiers who have no use for a younger generation who give speeches and engage in sycophancy (1060–1121, esp. 1095–97). They have synthesized Aristophanes' (and Bdelycleon's) talking points into their nature as resilient wasps.

THE STRUCTURE OF *WASPS*

Despite the apparent spontaneity of Aristophanic comedies, they relied on recurring formal features. We today think in terms of "acts" and "scenes," but Aristophanes had a wider range of options.

The plays begin, of course, with a *prologue*; in *Wasps*, it is the dialogue between the two slaves, Xanthias and Sosias, which gives the exposition of the story and introduces the leading characters (1–229). The chorus then enter in the *parodos* ("entry," 230–333).

The action heats up with the *agon* ("contest"), when the chorus face off against Bdelycleon and the household slaves to see if they can spring Philocleon free. It begins with an *epirrhematic agon*, in which Philocleon and the chorus stir up each other's anger against Bdelycleon (334–402);[8] the scenes that follow consist of a free-for-all that starts with name-calling and degenerates into fists being thrown and stingers stinging (403–525). Another *epirrhematic agon* follows in which Philocleon and Bdelycleon debate the value of jury service (526–728).

---

8. An *epirrhema* is, literally, a "follow-up (ἐπί) speech (ῥῆμα)," spoken after a choral song; "argument" or "debate" might be fair translations of *epirrhema* when it is in an *agon*.

The subsequent dog trial is less formally structured, being made up primarily of dialogue, though punctuated with occasional lines of verse (729–1008).

Perhaps the most distinctive element of Old Comedy is the *parabasis* ("stepping forward," 1009–1121), during which the plot is interrupted, the actors leave the stage, and the chorus speak directly to the audience. This is where they explain that the poet is unhappy with the audience because they rejected his *Clouds* of the year before. Not only does the *parabasis* interrupt the action, it breaks the illusion that theater tries to sustain. During a tragedy, the actors and chorus do not acknowledge the presence of an audience, at least not directly, but that convention is regularly violated in Aristophanic comedy. Already in the prologue Xanthias had been speaking directly to the audience (55–135).

The *parabasis* itself falls into several parts: the *kommation* ("snippet," 1009–14), a short introduction in anapests; then a speech by the chorus leader, in anapestic tetrameters, during which the chorus leader speaks on behalf of the poet (1015–1050; this is sometimes called the "*parabasis* proper"); the *pnigos* ("choker," 1051–59), a short passage spoken rapidly, as if without taking a breath, to finish the chorus leader's statement. The rest of the *parabasis* is devoted to the *epirrhematic syzygy*,[9] which comprises an *ode* (1060–70) followed by a speech (an *epirrhema*, 1071–90) and an *antode* (1091–1100) followed by an *antepirrhema* (1101–21). The *ode* and *antode* are metrically identical, as are the two *epirrhemata*; here the chorus speak about their military service and their waspish nature.

The actors return at 1122 for an episode of dialogue (the symposium-training scene) but leave at 1265–91 when the chorus perform a "second *parabasis*" that entails a short *ode* (1265–74) and *epirrhemata* (1275–91); an *antode* metrically corresponding to the ode, which would have appeared after 1283, has been lost. The remainder of the play contains various lyric songs and episodes, culminating in the *exodos* (1516–37) at the end.

STAGE, COSTUME, AND PERFORMANCE

The performance would have taken place in the Theater of Dionysus on the south side of the Acropolis. The seating area in this period may have accommodated six thousand people; perhaps another two thousand could stand above the seating area.[10] No reliable archaeological remains attest to the seating area, shape of the orchestra, or the stage building, but vases of the late fifth century BC show a stage raised about three feet above the orchestra level. The stage building was probably temporary, made out of wood. *Wasps* requires that Bdelycleon have a house with a door, windows, and points of potential escape for Philocleon such as a chimney

9. A *syzygy* (literally "yoked together") is a combination of related odes and speeches.
10. Csapo 2014, 53; earlier estimates had been higher.

(142) and roof (206). There is a net over the courtyard (131), and Bdelycleon was initially sleeping on the roof.

Vase-paintings, terracotta statuettes, and references within the plays themselves give us some notion of the costumes worn in Aristophanic comedy. All actors had masks; they also wore tights that covered all but their extremities; men wore a phallus hanging from below a short *chiton* (an inner garment or "tunic"). A slave would wear a *chiton* only, but an Athenian citizen usually wore a *himation*, the standard cloak, over the *chiton*. A coarse, everyday type of *himation* was known as the *tribon*; a more expensive and warmer one was the *chlaina*. In the dressing scene (1122–73), Bdelycleon persuades Philocleon to put aside his *tribon* and put on a fancy *chlaina* imported from Persia.[11]

Four actors could play all parts, three if they made extremely quick costume changes. All actors were men, so the actor playing the bread-seller Myrtia would have worn a dress and mask with feminine features. Dardanis, the flute-girl, is surely naked (or else no one would comment on her cleavage and pubic hair, 1373–74), and the nonspeaking extra playing her would have used a body costume of flesh-colored tights with padding where appropriate.

THE LANGUAGE OF ARISTOPHANES

One of the more remarkable chapters of the history of the Greek language was the "Atticist" movement of the second century AD, when writers sought to reach back to the time before Koine, the language of the New Testament, and recover "authentic" examples of Attic Greek as used in classical Athens. Atticists treasured Aristophanes for his extensive vocabulary. Dialogue in Aristophanes, while not quite reproducing everyday speech (after all, dramatic dialogue was in iambic trimeter), retains colloquial features and surely echoes what was heard in the agora. For example, the deictic iota (see on line 67 of Commentary and the Glossary of Grammatical and Rhetorical Terms), which conveys a sense of real people speaking to one another, is absent from higher genres like tragedy but ubiquitous in Aristophanes. The use of particles like δήπου and τοίνυν attest to an overlap with the conversational dialogues of Plato.[12]

Conservatism is a notable characteristic of Aristophanes' Greek. Although Attic would take steps toward becoming Koine in the generation after his death, the process is not evident in the comedies. One finds, for example, that he preserves the older purpose conjunction ὅπως ἄν, which is attested in fifth-century inscriptions and which was being replaced by ἵνα. (The orator Lysias, who was a generation younger, preferred ἵνα evidently on the grounds that ὅπως ἄν was too pretentious.) The older spelling of the preposition ξύν is found alongside the newer σύν, the older 1 pl. –μεσθα with the newer –μεθα, and the older dat. pl. –οισι with the

---

11. On costumes, see Compton-Engle 2015.
12. I am particularly indebted here to Willi 2003.

new –οις. Aristophanes' use of the dual, ὅστις instead of τίς in indirect questions, and the genitive of comparison instead of ἤ are other examples of this conservatism.

The comedies are also linguistically significant in that characters frequently slip into modes of speech drawn from other literary genres. Perhaps the best example is "paratragedy": occasionally a character will suddenly start quoting or paraphrasing verses from a tragedy (often Euripides) to lend pathos or gravity—or humor—to the moment. This would be immediately recognizable by the audience, as if someone today were to start speaking in Shakespearean pentameter. In *Wasps* it is almost exclusively Philocleon who slips into paratragedy, which brings out his occasional tendency to cast himself as a tragic victim.[13]

Choral odes in *Wasps* draw heavily on the vocabulary of Greek poetry. Phrases or words from Homer are brought in as needed. When Philocleon is being prepared for the symposium, Bdelycleon quotes excerpts of poems by Sappho and Alcaeus (with dialectal features changed) as well as popular Attic drinking songs, *skolia*. Other genres of literature hew to their traditional lexicon; the language of Old Comedy is more permeable.

Aristophanes' vocabulary also draws on nonliterary realms and registers (and these are noted in the commentary). Religious language turns up in prayers and hymns. Words and phrases at home in specialized fields such as medicine, bureaucracy, and official decrees appear from time to time. *Wasps* has more legal terminology than almost all other plays of Aristophanes put together (although it is doubtful whether we should think of these terms as "technical," as the words would be easily understood by any citizen). The language of intellectual life also appears in Aristophanic comedy; after all, as an imperial city, Athens was open to influences from around the Greek world and had become a magnet for sophists and intellectuals. One example: Aristophanes participated in the trend of creating technical-sounding adjectives with the –ικός suffix. New verbs were formed by adding endings like –ίζω and –άζω, and he coined a large number of neologisms, including striking polysyllabic compound words. Thus Aristophanes, conservative in syntax and morphology, could be innovative in his lexicon.

WORD ROOTS

To add a further dimension to students' understanding of the Greek vocabulary, the commentary includes brief etymological notes on the Indo-European origins of selected words. For example, *māter* (the asterisk * denotes a word as reconstructed from Proto-Indo-European) is the root of Greek μήτηρ, Latin *māter*, Sanskrit *mātár*, and Old High German *muoter* (from which English *mother* is derived). These are *cognates* ("born together," from a common parent). The case of *māter* is fairly transparent; others are less so, though they

---

13. An obsession with tragedy can be seen as the madness that he needs to be cured of, suggests Farmer 2017.

reveal interesting relationships. The root **kar-*, which means "tough," produced the Greek word κάρυον, "nut," but also κράτος, "might," and is cognate with the Latin *cancer*, "crab." In Old High German, the root became *hart* and led to English *hard* (the Germanic branch of the family changed *k* to *h*).

In this commentary, square brackets [ ] give the reconstructed root, the basic meaning of the root, and then representative cognates. Most of the cited cognates are Latin and English (that is, English derivatives from Germanic or other cognates). Squiggly brackets {} give *derivatives*, English words tracing their origins directly to Greek. Thus *metropolitan* is a derivative (that is, it came directly into English from the Greek μήτηρ). The derivatives are frequently scholarly, medical, or scientific terms {e.g., *poliomyelitis*, coined in 1874}, though many others made their way to English by way of Latin and then French {Greek ἐπιστέλλειν > ἐπιστολή > L. *epistula* > Old French *epistle* > E. *epistle*}. For more, readers are encouraged to consult Watkins 2011.

ABBREVIATIONS USED IN THE COMMENTARY

B-O	Zachary Biles and S. Douglas Olson, eds. *Aristophanes: Wasps*. Oxford: Oxford University Press, 2016.
GP	J. D. Denniston. *The Greek Particles*. 2nd ed. Rev. K. J. Dover. Oxford: Oxford University Press, 1954.
Graves	C. E. Graves, ed. *The Wasps of Aristophanes*. Cambridge: Cambridge University Press, 1894.
Hend.	Jeffrey Henderson, trans. *Aristophanes: Clouds, Wasps, Peace*. Loeb Classical Library. Cambridge, MA: Harvard University Press, 1998.
LA	Andreas Willi. *The Languages of Aristophanes*. Oxford: Oxford University Press, 2007.
LSJ	H. G. Liddell, R. Scott, H. S. Jones. *A Greek-English Lexicon*. 9th ed. with rev. supplement. Oxford: Oxford University Press, 1996.
MacD.	Douglas M. MacDowell, ed. *Aristophanes: Wasps*. Oxford: Oxford University Press , 1971.
Meiggs & Lewis	R. Meiggs and D. Lewis, eds. *A Selection of Greek Historical Inscriptions*. Oxford: Oxford University Press, 1969; rev. 1988.
MM	Jeffrey Henderson. *The Maculate Muse*. New Haven: Yale University Press, 1975.
Parker	L. P. E. Parker, *The Songs of Aristophanes*. Oxford: Oxford University Press, 1996.
S	H. W. Smyth. *Greek Grammar*. Rev. G. Messing. Cambridge, MA: Harvard University Press, 1956.
Sihler	Andrew Sihler. *New Comparative Grammar of Greek and Latin*. Oxford: Oxford University Press, 1995.
Somm.	Alan Sommerstein, ed. and trans. *Aristophanes: Wasps*. Warminster: Aris and Phillips, 1983.
Starkie	W. J. M. Starkie, ed. *The Wasps of Aristophanes*. London: Macmillan, 1897.
Wilson	N. G. Wilson. *Aristophanea. Studies on the Text of Aristophanes*. Oxford: Oxford University Press, 2007.

abs.	absolute	adv.	adverb
acc.	accusative	aor.	aorist
act.	active	aor.[2]	second aorist
adj.	adjective	Ar.	Aristophanes

art.	article, articular	neg.	negative
Bdel.	Bdelycleon	neut.	neuter
cf.	*confer* (compare, consult)	nom.	nominative
cogn.	cognate	opt.	optative
condit.	condition, conditional	part.	partitive
conj.	conjunction	pass.	passive
dat.	dative	pcl.	particle
dim.	diminutive	perf.	perfect
dir.	direct	Phil.	Philocleon
E.	English	pl.	plural
ed.	editor, edition	pred.	predicate
esp.	especially	prep.	preposition
exclam.	exclamatory, exclamation	pres.	present
fem.	feminine	Pres. Gen.	Present General
FMV	future more vivid	priv.	privative
fut.	future	prohib.	prohibition, prohibitive
gen.	genitive	pron.	pronoun
hort.	hortatory	ptcp.	participle
IE	Indo-European	quest.	question
impv.	imperative	redupl.	reduplication
impers.	impersonal	rel.	relative
indef.	indefinite	sc.	*scilicet* (understand)
indic.	indicative	sing.	singular
indir.	indirect	subjv.	subjunctive
inf.	infinitive	superl.	superlative
interrog.	interrogative	suppl.	supplementary
intrans.	intransitive	tr.	translated
L.	Latin	vb.	verb
masc.	masculine	voc.	vocative
mid.	middle	W.	*Wasps*

COMMENTARY

The Greek text followed is that of N. G. Wilson, *Aristophanis Fabulae*. Oxford Classical Texts. Oxford: Oxford University Press, 2007. Although Wilson's text uses a lunate sigma, c, the commentary uses -ς at the end of a word and σ elsewhere.

ON THE NOTATIONS IN THE COMMENTARY

The notation cf. refers readers to other notes that offer fuller explanations of the meaning, usage, or etymology of the word in question.

Nouns: I give nom., gen., and art., though the gen. is usually omitted for straightforward first- or second-declension nouns.

Verbs: I give first principal part and the principal part relevant for the passage, which is labeled if clarity seems necessary, esp. second or root aorists (using the abbrev. aor.[2]), aor. passives, deponent futures, and future passives.

Adjectives: Adjectives of the first/second declension type are given in the masc. nom. sing. form, e.g., δεινός, and then (3) to indicate that all three endings (masc., fem., neut.) are regular. For other adjectives, all three forms are given.

The notations a]...b]... are used in discussions of words or phrases that are open to more than one interpretation. Words that are underlined give meanings that are particularly significant for the passage in question.

A pair of angled brackets < > mark words presumably omitted by *ellipsis*.

Squiggly brackets { } give English words derived from Greek.

Square brackets [ ] give Indo-European roots, in italics (the asterisk * indicates that these are reconstructed), the basic meaning of the root, and representative cognates.

Grammatical and rhetorical terms in *italics* are explained in the Glossary (Appendix A).

ϹΦΗΚΕϹ

ϹΩϹΙΑϹ   Οὗτος, τί πάϲχεις, ὦ κακόδαιμον Ξανθία;

ΞΑΝΘΙΑϹ   φυλακὴν καταλύειν νυκτερινὴν διδάϲκομαι.
Ϲω.   κακὸν ἄρα ταῖϲ πλευραῖϲ τι προὐφείλειϲ μέγα.

LINE 1

1–53: Prologue. The play is set at the house of Bdelycleon and his father Philocleon. It has a door, a high window, and a roof accessible to actors and extras. The door is barred and the courtyard has a net over it to keep Philocleon from escaping. The play opens with the slaves Xanthias and Sosias at the door of the house. They have been ordered to make sure Phil. does not escape, but they were nodding off and now start rambling on about their dreams. Both dreams contain political allegories.

1–229: Meter: iambic trimeters

Σωϲίας, –ου, ὁ	(< ϲῴζω, save, "Savior") Sosias, a slave of Bdel. (declension S #222); named at 136; cf. n. on 433
οὗτος	"Hey, you" (nom. for voc., as often in address: S #1288a, LSJ C.I.S)
τίς, τί	(interr. pron. when accent is acute) Who? What? [< IE *kʷi-, who; cogn. L. *quis*; E. *who*]
πάϲχω	suffer, undergo; τί πάϲχεις; = "What's *the matter with you*?" (LSJ III.4) {> *paschal*}
κακο-δαίμων, –ονος	possessed by evil spirit; miserable, "poor devil," "you damned jinx" (Hend.); declension S #293; cf. 10
Ξανθίας, –ου, ὁ	(< ξανθός, yellow, "Mr. Golden Hair") Xanthias; another slave in Bdel.'s house; named at 136; most common male slave name in Ar.

LINE 2

φυλακή, ἡ	(< φύλαξ, guard) a watch, sentry-duty {> *prophylactic*}
κατα-λύω	dissolve, stop; neglect, abandon (κατά is intensive: S #1690.3) {> *catalyst*}
νυκτερινός (3)	(< νύξ, night + -ινος suffix denoting time: S #858.12) nightly, by night (cf. 91)
διδάϲκω	teach; (mid.) learn (an *inceptive* verb in –ϲκω: S #526d; redupl. pres. δι-δαϲκ-: S #447a) {> *didactic*}

LINE 3

ἄρα	(particle) "Oh, I see; in that case . . . ," "So then . . ."; marks an inference or realization, perhaps expressing surprise or disappointment, often with imperfect verb: *GP* 32–35; S #2795
πλευρά, ἡ	side, ribs {> *pleurisy*, an inflammation of the lungs}
προὐφείλω	(< ὀφείλω, owe; Attic contraction προ-οφείλω, οο > ου: S #50), owe beforehand; "you owe some big evil thing to your ribs," that is, "you deserve to be beaten" (What looks like a smooth breathing over the -ὐ- in προὐφείλω is a *coronis*, which indicates *crasis*: S #62.)
μέγας, μεγάλη, μέγα	great, big (declension: S # 311; μέγα, neut. sing., modifies the substantive κακόν)

ἆρ' οἶσθά γ' οἷον κνώδαλον φυλάττομεν;

Ξα.   οἶδ', ἀλλ' ἐπιθυμῶ ϲμικρὸν ἀπομερμηρίϲαι.　　　　　5

Cω.   ϲὺ δ' οὖν παρακινδύνευ', ἐπεὶ καὐτοῦ γ' ἐμοῦ
κατὰ ταῖν κόραιν ἤδη τι καταχεῖται γλυκύ.

Ξα.   ἀλλ' ἦ παραφρονεῖϲ ἐτεὸν ἢ κορυβαντιᾷϲ;

LINE 4

ἆρ'	(particle) = ἄρα by *elision* (S #70–71). Not easily translatable; it signals a quest. but expects neither neg. nor positive answer: GP 46: S #2650. Do not confuse with ἄρα.
οἶδα	know (old perf. used as pres., without redupl., conjugation: S #794); οἶσθα = οἶδ + θα: S #799 [< IE *weid-, see; cogn. L. *video*; E. *wit, wise*; Celtic, dru*id*]
γ'	(particle) = γε; adds emphasis to preceding word; after ἄρα it sharpens the quest.: GP 50) "Do you *know*?" (γ' also prevents an awkward *hiatus* of οἶσθα οἷον.)
οἷος (3)	what sort of (rel. pron., an alternative to the indir. interrog. ὁποῖος, correlative with dir. interrog. ποῖος: S #340)
κνώδαλον, τό	a wild creature, beast (conveying contempt, hinting at the animal nature of the challenge the two slaves face)

LINE 5

ἐπι-θυμέω	(< ἐπί, on/at + θῡμός, spirit) desire, set one's heart on (ἐπί in composition: S #1689.4)
ϲμικρός (3)	little, a little bit (adv. acc.); (variant of μικρός; on initial σ-, Sihler #171.a) {> *o*micron}
ἀπο-μερμηρίζω,-εμερμήριϲα	
	(< μέρμηρα, poetic for μέριμνα, care + –ιζω, suffix for *denominative* verb denoting action: S #866.6) throw off one's cares, stop worrying

LINE 6

δ' οὖν	(particles) "Well, go ahead, for all I care" (assent with defiant tone: GP 466: S #2959)
παρα-κινδυνεύω	(> 2 sing. act. impv. παρακινδύνευε with final –ε omitted by *elision* < παρά, amiss, reckless: S #1692.4 + κίνδυνος, danger) run the risk (the *risk* is falling asleep on duty)
καὐτοῦ	= καὶ αὐτοῦ (*crasis*; –αι is dropped from καί: S #68.c.1)
καὶ . . . γε	"Over *even my own* eyes"; γε with adv. καί, "even": GP 158; S #2829
κόρη, ἡ	(> fem. dual gen. ταῖν κόραιν: S #332) maiden; <u>pupil of the eye</u> (gen. with κατά) [< IE *ker-, grow; cogn. L. *cresco, Ceres*]
ἤδη	(adv.) already, by this time; just now
κατα-χέω	pour over (κατά in composition = "down from above": S #1690.3). By repeating the prep. κατά Ar. obeys a law that was gradually becoming more stringent in prose: Starkie.
γλυκύς, –εῖα, –ύ	sweet, pleasant (the "something sweet" is sleep) {> *gluc*ose}

LINE 8

ἀλλ' ἦ	(particles) "Whaaat!?"; ἦ asks the quest.; ἀλλά marks surprise, putting an objection into interrog. form: S #2784d, GP 27)
παρα-φρονέω	(< παρά, beside + φρονέω, think < φρήν, mind) be beside one's self, be out of one's mind; be mad {> *fr*antic, *frenzy*}
ἐτεόν	(adv. < adj. ἐτεός, genuine < εἰμί, be, exist) in truth, really (frequently used by Ar. in quests.)
κορυβαντιάω	(< Κορύβᾱς, –αντος, ὁ = Corybant, priest of Cybele in Phrygia + suffix –ιαω denoting desire or a bodily affliction: S #868) celebrate rites of the Corybantes, <u>be filled with Corybantic frenzy</u>; "comically, of a drowsy person nodding off and suddenly starting up": LSJ.

Cω.   οὔκ, ἀλλ᾽ ὕπνος μ᾽ ἔχει τις ἐκ Cαβαζίου.

Ξα.   τὸν αὐτὸν ἄρ᾽ ἐμοὶ βουκολεῖς cὺ δαίμονα.   10
        κἀμοὶ γὰρ ἀρτίως ἐπεστρατεύcατο
        Μῆδός τις ἐπὶ τὰ βλέφαρα νυστακτὴς ὕπνος·
        καὶ δῆτ᾽ ὄναρ θαυμαστὸν εἶδον ἀρτίως.

LINE 9

ἀλλά — (particle) "I'm not crazy, <u>but</u> I'm tired"; *adversative*, "not x but y," rejecting previous speaker's assertion: GP 1

ὕπνος, ὁ — sleep; dream {> *hypnotic*} [< IE *swep-, sleep; cogn. L. *somnus*]

μ᾽ — = με (enclitic for ἐμέ: S #325)

ἐκ — from, thanks to (+gen., indicates agent regarded as source: S #1688.1.c; LSJ III.4)

Cαβάζιος, –ου, ὁ — Sabazius, a Phrygian god whose mysteries resembled those of Dionysus. Possibly connected with wine or beer; to honor him would be to drink alcohol (MacD.). Here, in turn, he also represents the drowsiness that overcomes them (Somm.).

LINE 10

ἐμοί — (dat. with ὁ αὐτός, to denote sameness/agreement: S #1500, LSJ s.v. αὐτός III.1) "the same <u>as I do</u>"

βουκολέω — (< βούκολος, a shepherd < βοῦς, cattle) tend, herd; (of persons) serve, honor: LSJ I.2 {> *bucolic*}

δαίμων, –ονος, ὁ — god, divinity (referring to Sabazius){> *demon*}

LINE 11

κἀμοί — = καὶ ἐμοί (*crasis*: S #62)

γάρ — for, because; "[I say this] because ..."; explains previous sentence: S #2808, GP 56–60

ἀρτίως — (adv. < ἄρτι = just, exactly) just now, newly [< IE *ar-, fit together; cf. ἄριστος, "best fitted"; cogn. L. *artus* (joint)]

ἐπι-στρατεύω — march against, make war upon + dat. (-ευω vbs. *in mid.* signify that subjects are acting in a manner appropriate to their state: S #1728b)

Μῆδος, ὁ — a Mede, a Persian; hostile barbarian. Media had been conquered and incorporated into the Persian empire a century earlier; thus it remained a potent term for an arch-enemy, however anachronistic. This is an (inexact) allusion to the Phrygian origin of Sabazius.

βλέφαρον, τό — (< βλέπω, look at) eyelid; pl. eyes {> *blepharitis*, an eyelid inflammation}

νυστακτής, –ου, ὁ — (< νυστάζω, be half asleep, doze) drowsy

δῆτ᾽ — = δῆτα, "really," "certainly"; "I really had an extraordinary dream"; common in lively dialogue: GP 278, S #2851

ὄναρ, τό — dream (only nom. & acc. sing.; other cases supplied by ὄνειρος: S #285.19)

θαυμαστός (3) — (< θαυμάζω, wonder) strange, amazing; admirable, excellent. Verbal adjs. in –τός are often, but not always, pass.: <u>to be wondered at</u> (S #472)

ὁράω, aor.² εἶδον — see, behold (Greeks "see" dreams). The augment is syllabic; the verb began with a digamma in its early history: εἶδον < ἐ-ϝιδον: S #431, 529.2

Cω.   κἄγωγ' ἀληθῶς οἷον οὐδεπώποτε.
                ἀτὰρ cὺ λέξον πρότεροc.

Ξα.   ἐδόκουν αἰετὸν   15
                καταπτάμενον εἰc τὴν ἀγορὰν μέγαν πάνυ
                ἀναρπάcαντα τοῖc ὄνυξιν ἀcπίδα
                φέρειν ἐπίχαλκον ἀνεκὰc εἰc τὸν οὐρανόν,
                κἄπειτα ταύτην ἀποβαλεῖν Κλεώνυμον.

LINE 14

κἄγωγ' = καὶ ἔγωγε (*crasis*: S # 68.c.1); ἔγωγε = emphatic ἐγώ (sc. εἶδον)

οἷος –α –ον as, such as (sc. ὄναρ) "I too (had a dream) <u>like</u> I've never had . . ."

ἀληθῶς (adv. < ἀ- priv. + λήθη, forgetfulness) truly [< IE *lādh-, hidden; cogn. L. *lateo*]

οὐδεπώποτε (< οὐδέ, and not + πω, yet + ποτε, ever/at any time) never yet at any time, <u>never</u> (usually with past tense vbs.)

LINE 15

ἄταρ (particle) but; indicating a sudden change of topic: *GP* 52; S #2801

λέγω, ἔλεξα (> aor. act. impv. 2 sing. λέξον: S #669) collect; recount; <u>speak</u>. The aor. λέξον appears 8x in Ar., usually when the speaker asks another to give an account. More common (68x) is εἰπέ, usually used in a quick quest., less literary but also common in Plato and orators: *LA* 249.

πρότερος (3) (comparative of πρό: S #320) before, earlier; agrees with subject of λέξον: "speak <u>first</u>"

δοκέω think, imagine (personal construction: S #1983, δοκῶ governs acc. αἰετόν as subject acc. of φέρειν, which governs ἀσπίδα: "I imagined that an eagle bore . . .") {> *dogma*, ortho*doxy*}

αἰετός, ὁ eagle. Xanthias resorts to dreamy, oracular language about an eagle and a serpent—and this dream has Homeric echoes (*Iliad* 12.208–29).

κατα-πέτομαι, aor.²-επτάμην,
    fly down to. On the interchange of vowels, or *ablaut*, of πετ-/πτα-: S #35, #373. The dropping of the interconsonantal -ε- also illustrates *syncope*: S #446, 493b. On the root πτ- cf. <u>πτέρον</u>, wing: Sihler #110, 115.1 {> *ptero*dactyl}

ἀν-αρπάζω, -ήρπασα (< ἁρπαγή, seizure) snatch up {> *harpoon*}

ὄνυξ, -υχος, ὁ talon, claw, nail; onyx (stone) {> *onyx*}

ἀσπίς, –ιδος, ἡ shield; asp, an Egyptian cobra with a shield-like head. Xanthias plays on both meanings. [< IE *asp-, cut (a shield is "cut" from a hide); cogn. L *asper*]

ἐπί-χαλκος, -ον (< χαλκός, ore, copper, bronze) bronze-plated {> *chal*ice}

ἀνεκάς (adv. < ἀνά, up + ? ἑκάς, afar) upward

οὐρανός, ὁ heaven, sky (cf. Uranos, husband of Gaia in mythology)

ἔπειτα (adv. < ἐπί, upon + εἶτα then); κἄπειτα = καὶ ἔπειτα, then, thereupon, thereafter

ἀπο-βάλλω, aor.²-έβαλον
    throw away; "he threw his shield down—becoming Cleonymus"

Κλεώνυμος, ὁ Cleonymus. The name, acc. subject of inf. ἀποβαλεῖν, is postponed as a kind of punchline; only at the end do we discover that the subject of the inf. is not the eagle but Cleonymus. Cleonymus, satirized several times by Ar. for cowardice, was evidently a politician allied with Cleon (cf. 62).

Cω.	οὐδὲν ἄρα γρίφου διαφέρει Κλεώνυμος.	20
Ξα.	πῶς δή;	
Cω.	προερεῖ τις τοῖσι συμπόταις, λέγων	
	ὅτι "ταὐτὸν ἐν γῇ τ' ἀπέβαλεν κἀν οὐρανῷ	
	κἀν τῇ θαλάττῃ θηρίον τὴν ἀσπίδα."	
Ξα.	οἴμοι, τί δῆτά μοι κακὸν γενήσεται	
	ἰδόντι τοιοῦτον ἐνύπνιον;	
Cω.	μὴ φροντίσῃς.	25

LINE 20

οὐδέν	(< adv. acc. from οὐδείς, οὐδεμία, οὐδέν: declension S #349b) in no way, not at all
γρῖφος, ὁ	(<γρῖπος, fishing basket, tangle, something intricate) riddle. Fellow drinkers at a symposium would pose riddles to one another; here, the animal-shield riddle of 22–23. Earliest instance of the word.
δια-φέρω	carry over, carry across; (intrans.) <u>differ from</u> + gen. of distinction (S #1401)
δή	πῶς δή, "Precisely how?"; adds urgency in quests.: S #2843a, GP 210
προ-λέγω, -ερῶ	pick out; foretell; <u>announce</u> (ἐρῶ, Attic fut. from Homeric εἴρω)
συμπότης, –ου, ὁ	(< σύν + πόσις, drinking + -της, suffix denoting agency: S #839a) fellow drinker (σύν- becomes σύμ- before π-: S #91) {> *symposium*}
ὅτι	(conj.) that (oft. inserted pleonastically to introduce a quotation: LSJ II.1, S #2592)
ταὐτὸν	= τὸ αὐτό. Movable –ν (S #134–35) added to avoid *hiatus* (S #46–47, 328.c.N)
κἀν	= καὶ ἐν (crasis). Note *polysyndeton* of repeated καί (S #3043)
θηρίον, τό	wild animal (subject of ἀπέβαλεν), dim. in form, not meaning: S #855

LINE 24

οἴμοι	alas! (excl. of pain, fright, pity, anger, grief, surprise)
δῆτα	τί δῆτα, "What on earth, *then* . . ."; marks an inference: S #2851b, GP 269–70
γίγνομαι, γενήσομαι	come into being; happen; become {> *genesis*} [< IE *genə-, give birth; cogn. L. *gigno, gens*; E. *kin, kind, king*]

LINE 25

ὁράω, aor.² εἶδον	(> aor. ptcp. ἰδών) see (cf. 13)
τοιοῦτος (3)	(demonstrative pron. of quality) such, of such a sort (S #333e)
ἐνύπνιον, τό	(< ὕπνος, dream) dream, vision in sleep
φροντίζω, ἐφρόντισα	(< φροντίς, care and -ίζω denoting action in a *denominative* verb: S #866.6) consider, worry about (μή + 2 sing. aor. subjv. = prohib. subjv.: S #1800)
εἰμί, ἔσομαι	be (fut. in mid.: S #806; conjugation: S #768) [< IE *es-, be; cogn. L. *sum*; E. *is; sie* ("may it be so") > OE *gese* > *yes*]
δεινός (3)	awesome, <u>terrible</u>; ". . . nothing very *awful* will come of it" (By the fifth century, the word's semantic range had also come to include "strange," "marvelous," "clever.") {> *dinosaur*}
μά	(particle) in the name of (+acc. of god by whom one swears: S #1596.b, 2894); in Ar. often in neg. statements (but not always: cf. 134, 181; LSJ III.1.a)
γέ	(particle) "it *is* terrible" (cf. 4; for accent of successive enclitics: S #185)
που	somewhere; I suppose, <u>surely</u> (enclitic adv., adds a note of uncertainty, or perhaps irony, GP 490–92)
πούστ'	= πού ἐστι; crasis of που and 'στ' with *aphaeresis* or *prodelision* of initial ε- : S #76, and *elision* of final -ι: S #73. Pred. adj. δεινόν in neut. sing. refers to a general truth: S #1048: "a man throwing away his weapon is <u>a terrible thing</u>."
ὅπλον, τό	tool, implement; weapon. Perhaps a pun on male genitalia, *MM* p. 123

οὐδὲν γὰρ ἔσται δεινόν, οὐ μὰ τοὺς θεούς.

Ξα.   δεινόν γέ ποῦστ' ἄνθρωπος ἀποβαλὼν ὅπλα.

ἀτὰρ cὺ τὸ cὸν αὖ λέξον.

Cω.   ἀλλ' ἐcτὶν μέγα.

περὶ τῆc πόλεωc γάρ ἐcτι, τοῦ cκάφουc ὅλου.

Ξα.   λέγε νυν ἀνύcαc τι τὴν τρόπιν τοῦ πράγματοc.   30

Cω.   ἔδοξέ μοι περὶ πρῶτον ὕπνον ἐν τῇ Πυκνὶ

ἐκκληcιάζειν πρόβατα cυγκαθήμενα,

LINE 28

σός (3)   your (possessive adj.; τὸ cόν, sc. ἐνύπνιον = "your dream")

αὖ   (adv.) again, on the contrary (with personal pron.: "you, <u>in turn</u>, tell . . .": S #2802)

ἀλλά   (particle) "<u>Oh, well</u>, it's big"; a person asked to speak conveys his readiness to do so: *GP* 18

πόλις, –εως, ἡ   city, city-state {> *politics*}[< IE *pelə-*, citadel; cogn. Sanskrit *–pur*; cf. Singa*pore*]

σκάφος, –ους, τό   hull of ship; ship. Sosias invokes the "ship of state" metaphor.

ὅλος (3)   whole, entire. The adj. ὅλος, which would eventually replace πᾶς in Greek, tends to be used by slaves and women in Ar.: *LA* 192. {> *holo*caust}

LINE 30

νυν   (enclitic adv.) now; used with commands and quests.: "come now!" "why now?," not used of time; contrast accented νῦν, "now," "the present moment."

ἀνύω, ἤνυσα   achieve, complete (aor. ptcp. ἀνύσᾱς used with impv. = "with haste") λέγε . . . ἀνύσᾱς "<u>hurry up</u> and tell me": S #2062; also written with smooth ἀ- {> αὐ<u>θέντ</u>ης, author, "self-achiever" > *author*, *authentic*}

τι   in some way; in any degree (enclitic; neut. acc. sing. of the indef. pron. τις, used as adv.), "hurry <u>as best you can</u>" (contrast interrog. τί, with acute, in 1)

τρόπις, –ιος, ἡ   (< τρέπω, turn) keel (ship of state metaphor); "tell me the *hull* story!" (tr. Hend.)

πρᾶγμα, –ατος, τό   (< πράττω, act; –μα, –ματος, suffix denoting result of an action: S #841.2) affair, business, matter at hand {> *pragmatic*}

LINE 31

δοκέω, ἔδοξα   seem, appear. "Personal" construction of δοκῶ: S #1983: take πρόβατα as subject of ἔδοξε, followed by inf. ἐκκληcιάζειν. Sosias tells his allegorical dream; sheep represent citizens and the whale the demagogue Cleon. All look foolish.

Πνύξ, Πυκνός, ἡ   the Pnyx, the meeting place for the assembly at Athens in the classical period (declension: S #285.23, illustrates *metathesis*, whereby vowel and consonant exchange places in inflection: S #128)

ἐκκληcιάζω   (< ἐκκληcία, the citizen assembly of Athens < ἐκ + καλέω, summon forth + *denominative* verb + -αζω: S #866.6) meet, and speak, at the assembly. This verb gave us the title of Ar.'s play of ca. 392, the *Ecclesiazusae*.

περί   (+acc.) about the time of (LSJ C.II); περὶ πρῶτον ὕπνον, in the early part of the night

πρό-βατον, τό   (< προβαίνω, walk in front) sheep; orig. of small livestock walking in front; elsewhere in poetry used of cattle and herds

cυγ-κάθ-ημαι   (cυν, with + κάθημαι, sit; ν before κ becomes γ-nasal: S #92) sit together, sit in assembly or court; οἱ cυγκαθήμενοι are judges or citizens in assembly (κάθημαι only used in pres and imperfect: S #790).

βακτηρίας ἔχοντα καὶ τριβώνια·
κᾆπειτα τούτοις τοῖσι προβάτοις μοὐδόκει
δημηγορεῖν φάλλαινα πανδοκεύτρια,   35
ἔχουσα φωνὴν ἐμπεπρημένης ὑός.

Ξα.   αἰβοῖ.

Cω.   τί ἐστι;

Ξα.   παῦε παῦε, μὴ λέγε·
ὄζει κάκιστον τοὐνύπνιον βύρσης σαπρᾶς.

Cω.   εἶθ' ἡ μιαρὰ φάλλαιν' ἔχουσα τρυτάνην

βακτηρία, ἡ	walking staff, held by speakers at assembly {> *bacterium*, for its rod-like shape as seen in microscope}
τριβώνιον, τό	(dim. of τρίβων, worn cloak < τρίβω, wear out) threadbare cloak. Later in the play this article of clothing will help define Phil.'s identity as a lower-class Athenian.

LINE 34

κᾆπειτα	= καὶ ἔπειτα (cf. 19 above)
μοὐδόκει	= μοι ἐδόκει (*crasis*)
δημηγορέω	(< δῆμος, people + ἀγορεύω, speak in public) speak in the assembly
φάλλαινα, ἡ	whale; a devouring monster. Cleon is now a "whale." {> *ballene*} [< IE *bhel-, swell; cf. φαλλός; *cogn*. L. *balaena*; E. *bowl, ball*]
παν-δοκεύτρια, ἡ	(< πᾶν, all + δέχομαι, receive) hostess, innkeeper; <u>omnivorous</u>
φωνή, ἡ	voice, speech {> mega*phone*, sym*phony*}
ἐμ-πίμπρημι,-πέπρημαι	
	(> perf. ptcp. ἐμπεπρημένος) catch on fire; be angry. B-O point to evidence that pigs were doused in oil and set aflame, with pitiful wailing.
ὑς, ὑός, ὁ, ἡ	pig

LINE 37

αἰβοῖ	Yech! Ugh! Agh! (exclam. expressing disgust or dismay, often with surprise)
παύω	stop; <u>stop immediately</u>! MacD. sees pres. impv. παῦε as more staccato and urgent than aor. impv. παῦσαι; cf. S #1841 and *LA* 257–58. The pres. impv. predominates in conversation with human beings, aor. impv. with gods: *LA* 258.
μή	(neg. with 2nd person impv: S #1840.B): <u>don't</u>!
ὄζω	smell, smell of something (+gen.) {> *ozone*}
τοὐνύπνιον	= τὸ ἐνύπνιον (*crasis*), cf. 25
βύρσα, ἡ	ox-hide, leather. Ar. contrives an opportunity to take a pot-shot at the source of Cleon's family wealth: a leather tannery. {> *bursar, purse*}
σαπρός (3)	(< σήπομαι, rot) rotten, putrid; worn out

LINE 39

εἶτα	(adv.) next, then, after that. Denotes sequence of one act after another, useful in simple, "homely" narratives: B-O; εἶθ' = εἶτα in *elision* before aspirate: S #124.
μιαρός (3)	(< μιαίνω, stain, pollute) stained, impure; repulsive, disgusting {> *miasma*}
τρυτάνη, ἡ	balance, pair of scales

ἴϲτη βόειον δημόν.

Ξα.   οἴμοι δείλαιοϲ·   40

τὸν δῆμον ἡμῶν βούλεται διιϲτάναι.

Cω.   ἐδόκει δέ μοι Θέωροϲ αὐτῆϲ πληϲίον

χαμαὶ καθῆϲθαι τὴν κεφαλὴν κόρακοϲ ἔχων.

εἶτ' Ἀλκιβιάδηϲ εἶπε πρόϲ με τραυλίϲαϲ,

"ὁλᾷϲ; Θέωλοϲ τὴν κεφαλὴν κόλακοϲ ἔχει."   45

ἴϲτημι	(> 3 sing. imperfect indic. ἴϲτη) stand; make to stand, <u>weigh</u>
βόειος (3)	(< βοῦς, ox) of an ox (cf. 10)
δημός, ὁ	fat. Distinct from, but with a pun on, δῆμος, people, made explicit two lines below.
δείλαιος (3)	(< δέος, fear) sorry, wretched, pathetic (nom. in exclam.: S #1288, as pred. with subject unexpressed). The diphthong -αι- is scanned short due to internal *correption*.
δῆμος, ὁ	land, district; people, the common citizens of Athens {> *demo*cracy} (cf. 34)
βούλομαι	want [< βάλλω, throw, "throwing forward of the mind"]
δι-ίϲτημι	(> pres. inf. διϲτάναι) divide, set acc. at odds with gen. The pun on ἴϲτη in 40 suggests that weighing beef is like causing rifts among the citizenry.

LINE 42

Θέωρος, ὁ	(< θεωρός, spectator, envoy) Theorus, a follower of Cleon
αὐτῆς	= the whale
πλήσιος (3)	near, close to (adv. acc., + gen.)
χαμαί	(adv.) on the ground. A fossilized noun functioning as adv.: Sihler #336a. [< χθών, earth < IE *dhghem, earth; cogn. L. *humus, homo*; E. *human*]
κάθ-ημαι	(> pres. inf. καθῆϲθαι) sit
κεφαλή, ἡ	head {> en*cephalo*gram} [< IE *ghebhel, head; cogn. E. *gable*]
κόραξ, -ακος, ὁ	raven; anticipating pun on κόλαξ, flatterer, fawner

LINE 44

εἶτα	then (cf. 39)
Ἀλκιβιάδης, ὁ	Alcibiades; a young man of promise in 422 BC, soon to be a notably controversial figure in Athenian politics and military
λέγω, aor.² εἶπον	(< ἔπος, word) speak, talk (εἶπον actually redupl., from an earlier form with a digamma, ἔϝειπον: S #549, Sihler 61.1a; cf. 15)
τραυλίζω, ἐτραύλισα	(< τραυλός, lisping + -ιζω to denote action) lisp, mispronounce a letter; <u>with a lisp</u> (circumstantial ptcp. of manner: S #2062)
ὁλᾷϲ; Θέωλοϲ . . . κόλακοϲ	
	The joke unfolds: Alcibiades was said to have a lisp and pronounced the letter "ρ" as "λ."

Ξα.   ὀρθῶς γε τοῦτ' Ἀλκιβιάδης ἐτραύλισεν.

Σω.   οὔκουν ἐκεῖν' ἀλλόκοτον, ὁ Θέωρος κόραξ
    γενόμενος;

Ξα.   ἥκιστ', ἀλλ' ἄριστον.

Σω.   πῶς;

Ξα.   ὅπως;

    ἄνθρωπος ὢν εἶτ' ἐγένετ' ἐξαίφνης κόραξ.

    οὔκουν ἐναργὲς τοῦτο συμβαλεῖν, ὅτι   50

    ἀρθεὶς ἀφ' ἡμῶν ἐς κόρακας οἰχήσεται;

LINE 46

ὀρθῶς   (adv.) rightly, correctly {> *orthodoxy*}

γε   "He got it dead right" (Somm. tr.); emphatic, even exclam.: *GP* 127

οὔκουν   (particle) therefore not (οὐκ + οὖν, emphasizing οὐκ; contrast οὐκοῦν, 221 below); in excited or surprised quests.: "Well, now, isn't that unusual?" *GP* 431.

ἐκεῖνος (3)   that (demonstrative pron.); ἐκεῖνο and ἀλλόκοτον are subject & pred.; omission of copulative εἶναι: S #944; Θέωρος . . . γενόμενος are nom. in apposition to the subject.

ἀλλόκοτος, -ον   (< ἄλλος, other/different + κότος, ill-will) strange, unnatural, of unusual form (compound adj. with two endings: S #288)

γίγνομαι, aor.² ἐγενόμην
    become, happen; be. The verb is used of metamorphoses in myth; this is the first of several such transformations of identity in *W.* (cf. 24)

ἥκιστα   (adv. < ἥκιστος, least, superl. of ἦκα, slightly) least, not at all (reply to quest.)

ἄριστος (3)   best (nt. sing. agrees with ἐκεῖνο in 47; superl. adj. for ἀγαθός); cf. ἀρτίως, 11

ὅπως   (adv.) How? Indir. interrog.: Sosias asks, πῶς; ("How?") to which X. replies, ὅπως; ("[You ask,] 'How'?"), LSJ III.9; see correlative advs.: S #346. Ar.'s contemporary Lysias was freer in usage and would simply repeat πῶς: *LA* 263.

LINE 49

εἰμί   (> pres. ptcp. ὤν; declension S #305) be

ἐξαίφνης   (adv.) (ἐξ- in composition implies resolution: S #1688.2 + αἴφνης, suddenly) suddenly, instantaneously

ἐν-αργής, -ές   (< ἀργός, bright) clear, obvious, manifest

συμ-βάλλω, aor.² -έβαλον
    put together; conclude, infer, figure out (*epexegetical* inf. with adjs.: S #2002); "it is obvious to infer"

ὅτι   (conj.) that (dependent statement, explaining τοῦτο: S #2577); "to infer this, namely, that . . ." (συμβαλεῖν, a verb of intellectual perception, governs the clause: S #2581)

αἴρω, ἤρθην   (> aor. pass. ptcp. ἀρθείς) raise, waft aloft {> *aorta, artery*}

ἀφ'   = ἀπό. Note *elision* of final –ο; π > φ before rough breathing of ἡμῶν: S #124.

ἐς κόρακας   go "to the crows"; Aristophanic equivalent of telling someone to go "to hell." Comedy generally uses the prep. εἰς; ἐς is a fossilized idiom: *LA* 234–35.

Cω.   εἶτ' οὐκ ἐγὼ δοὺς δύ' ὀβολὼ μιcθώcομαι
                οὕτωc ὑποκρινόμενον cοφῶc ὀνείρατα;

Ξα.   φέρε νυν κατείπω τοῖc θεαταῖc τὸν λόγον,

                ὀλίγ' ἄτθ' ὑπειπὼν πρῶτον αὐτοῖcιν ταδί,   55

                μηδὲν παρ' ἡμῶν προcδοκᾶν λίαν μέγα,

                μηδ' αὖ γέλωτα Μεγαρόθεν κεκλεμμένον.

LINE 52

δίδωμι, ἔδωκα	(> aor. ptcp. δούς: S #307) give; pay {> *dose*, anti*dote*, anec*dote*}
ὀβολός, ὁ	(> dual nom./acc. ὀβελώ: S #229) obol, a coin worth 1/6th of a drachma. A drachma was a typical daily wage for a skilled worker, today perhaps $200.00, so an obol might be $30.00 or more. Of course, establishing currency equivalencies is deeply hazardous.
μισθόω	(< μισθός, pay + -οω, verbal suffix: S #866.3) let out for hire, offer services; (mid.) hire for oneself (mid. fut. μισθώσομαι with understood obj. σε; in neg. quest. after οὐκ, "Shouldn't I . . ?")
ὑπο-κρίνομαι	(< ὑπὸ, gradually + κρίνω, choose; distinguish) reply, expound, interpret (acc. ptcp. agrees with understood σε) {> *crisis, critic, criterion*}
ὄνειρον, –ατος τό	dream (cf. 13) {> *oneiromancy*}

LINE 54

54–67: The meandering conversation between the two slaves comes to a close. Xanthias, breaking the theatrical "fourth wall" and directly addressing the audience, promises that the comedy will be reasonably sophisticated and not indulge in vulgar jokes.

φέρε νυν	come now (φέρε introducing hort. subjv.: S #1797b)
κατα-λέγω, aor.² -εῖπον	recount, relate (in composition κατά intensifies verb: S #1690.3)
θεᾱτής, –οῦ, ὁ	(< θέα, sight) spectator {> *theater*}
λόγος, ὁ	word, account, story; <u>plot</u>. Xanthias now explains the circumstances: Phil. has been locked up for his own good.
τις, τι	anyone, anything; someone, something. Indef. pron.; neut. pl. is τινά but is sometimes spelled ἄττα; here the final –α is lost due to *elision*; because the following word has a rough breathing, the second –τ- becomes –θ'.
ὑπ-εῖπον	(aor.² with no pres.) say as foundation, as preface; give explanation
ὅδε, ἥδε, τόδε	this here, L. *hic* (old demonstrative pron. ὁ, ἡ, τό + enclitic suffix –δε designating what is present; the *deictic* iota, ταδί (note long -ῑ), added for emphasis: S #333a, g; on stage the actor surely points or gestures. The *deictic* iota was common in Ar. (over 600x) and colloquial Attic, but is virtually absent from inscriptions, tragedy, and Thucydides: *LA* 244–45.
μηδέν	nothing (μηδέν not οὐδέν, since μή is neg. with inf.: S #2715)
προσ-δοκάω	expect (inf. as impv.: S #2013)
λίᾱν	(adv., postpositive) too, excessively (a petrified acc. adv., like πλήν: Chaintraine)
γέλως, γέλωτος, ὁ	laughter, joke
Μεγαρόθεν	Megara, city west of Athens, sanctioned by the "Megarian Decree" of 432 and known for feeble jokes (+suffix –θεν denoting direction from: S #342)
κλέπτω, κέκλεμμαι	(perf. mid./pass.) steal {> *klepto*mania, *klepto*cracy}

ἡμῖν γὰρ οὐκ ἔστ᾽ οὔτε κάρυ᾽ ἐκ φορμίδος
δούλω διαρριπτοῦντε τοῖς θεωμένοις,
οὔθ᾽ Ἡρακλῆς τὸ δεῖπνον ἐξαπατώμενος,   60
οὐδ᾽ αὖθις ἐνασελγαινόμενος Εὐριπίδης·
οὐδ᾽ εἰ Κλέων γ᾽ ἔλαμψε τῆς τύχης χάριν,
αὖθις τὸν αὐτὸν ἄνδρα μυττωτεύσομεν.

LINE 58

οὔτε ... οὔτε ... οὐδὲ ... οὐδὲ

(Whereas οὔτε ... οὔτε tend to be a simple "neither ... nor," οὐδέ is often a stronger "and not *even*": S #2930–50. When a simple neg. like οὐκ precedes a compound neg. like οὔτε, the second simply confirms the first: S #2761. For the *anaphora*: S #3010)

κάρυον, τό
nut. Nuts and figs were tossed to spectators at performances. [< IE *kar-, tough; cf. κράτος, might; cogn. L. *cancer* (crab); E. *hard*]

φορμίς, –ίδος, ἡ
(dim. of φορμός, basket < φέρω) small basket

ἔστ᾽
= ἔστι, with *elision*. When following οὐκ, ἔστι is *orthotone* (accented on penult, unlike enclitic ἐστί; cf. Glossary). Although the verb is sing., the subject δούλω is dual: S #961, and ἡμῖν is dat. of possession: S #1476.

δοῦλος, ὁ
slave

δια-ρριπτέω
throw about (usually spelled διαρρίπτω; note doubling of ρ in composition: S #80)

θεάομαι
(< θέα, cf. 54) view, gaze at; οἱ θεώμενοι are "the viewers," "spectators"

Ἡρακλῆς, ὁ
Heracles, the most popular hero of Greek mythology; in comedy he was a low-brow character famous for his appetites.

ἐξ-απατάω
deceive, cheat; (pass.) to be cheated of + acc.

αὖθις
again, in turn (a lengthened form of αὖ). This was not the first time Euripides was a target.

ἐν-ασελγαίνω
(< ἀσελγής, elated, wanton) treat lewdly, abuse

Εὐρῑπίδης, ὁ
Euripides, the tragic poet (ca. 485–ca. 406 BC); his tragedies, which upended traditional portrayals of mythological heroes, were parodied and ridiculed by Ar., especially in the *Thesmophoriazusae* and *Frogs*.

LINE 62

Κλέων, ὁ
Cleon, the politician of the radical democracy, nemesis of Aristophanes and patron of Athenian jurors, for whom he enacted a three-obol payment for daily jury service.

γε
οὐδ᾽ ... γε = "nor yet"; in continuous speech: GP 156

λάμπω, ἔλαμψα
light, shine; achieve glory {> *lamp*}

τύχη, ἡ
(< τυχεῖν, aor.[2] of τυγχάνω, hit upon) fortune, luck

χάριν
(< χάρις, grace, favor; cf. 186) for the sake of, thanks to (prep. with gen.)

ὁ αὐτός
the same (αὐτός with art.: S #1173)

μυττωτεύω
(< μυττωτός, a blend of cheese, garlic, and honey) hash up, "make mincemeat of." In fact, Cleon, or at least the constituency and institutions he has twisted to serve his pruposes, *do* come in for criticism in *W*.

ἀλλ' ἔστιν ἡμῖν λογίδιον γνώμην ἔχον,
ὑμῶν μὲν αὐτῶν οὐχὶ δεξιώτερον,   65
κωμῳδίας δὲ φορτικῆς σοφώτερον.
ἔστιν γὰρ ἡμῖν δεσπότης, ἐκεινοcὶ
ἄνω καθεύδων, ὁ μέγας, οὑπὶ τοῦ τέγους.
οὗτος φυλάττειν τὸν πατέρ' ἐπέταξε νῷν,
ἔνδον καθείρξας, ἵνα θύραζε μὴ 'ξίῃ.   70

LINE 64

ἔστιν	*orthotone*, expressing existence
λογίδιον, τό	(dim. of λόγος: S #852.2) little story, modest plot
οὐχί	an emphatic οὐ, used before both vowels and consonants: S #137a
δεξιώτερος (3)	(< comparative of δεξιός) shrewder, wiser
κωμῳδία, ἡ	(< κῶμος revel + ᾠδή, song—the traditional derivation) comedy (in gen. with comparative σοφώτερον)
φορτικός (3)	(< φόρτος, burden < φέρω) lowbrow, raunchy. The suffix –ικός was used, esp. in the late fifth century, to create *denominative* adjs. from nouns: S #858.6; words like these may have seemed pretentious: *LA* 140.

LINE 67

67–114: Xanthias explains that he and Sosias have been ordered by Bdel. to keep Phil. at home. Phil. is afflicted with a disease: a compulsion to participate in jury duty.

δεσπότης, –ου, ὁ	master. The master here is Bdel.; a central joke of the play is that of role-reversal, whereby the son controls (or tries to control) his father.
ἐκεινοcί	demonstrative pron. ἐκεῖνος with *deictic* iota: S #333g
ἄνω	(adv.) upward, aloft; ἄνω by *crasis* = ὁ ἄνω, the man above
καθ-εύδω	(κατά, down + εὕδω, sleep) lie down to sleep
οὑπὶ	= ὁ ἐπί by *crasis*
τέγος, –ους, τό	roof {> *stego*saurus}

LINE 68

ἐπι-τάττω, -έταξα	order, command {> *taxi*dermy}
νῷν	(> 1 person dual gen./dat. pron.: S #325) the two of us
ἔνδον	(adv. < ἐν + –δον suffix: S #344) within, inside
καθ-είργνῡμι, -εῖρξα	(< κατά in composition, suggesting action that is adverse or complete + εἵργνῡμι, shut in or out) confine, shut in
ἵνα	in order that (conj. for purpose clause, with subjv. in primary tense; neg. is μή)
θύραζε	to the door (the suffixes –ζε, –δε indicate direction toward: S #342)
ἔξ-ειμι	(< εἶμι) go out (> pres. subjv. 3 sing. 'ξίῃ; note *aphaeresis*, the *elision* of initial ἐ- following μή or ἤ: S #76 and cf. 27) (subjv. used in place of opt. after a secondary tense verb: S #2197)

νόϲον γὰρ ὁ πατὴρ ἀλλόκοτον αὐτοῦ νοϲεῖ,
ἣν οὐδ' ἂν εἷϲ γνοίη ποτ' οὐδ' ἂν ξυμβάλοι
εἰ μὴ πύθοιθ' ἡμῶν· ἐπεὶ τοπάζετε.
Ἀμυνίαϲ μὲν ὁ Προνάπουϲ φήϲ· οὑτοϲὶ
εἶναι φιλόκυβον αὐτόν.

Ϲω.   ἀλλ' οὐδὲν λέγει,   75
μὰ Δί', ἀλλ' ἀφ' αὑτοῦ τὴν νόϲον τεκμαίρεται.

LINE 71

νόϲος, –ου, ἡ   sickness, illness (internal "cognate" acc.: S #1564); > verb νοϲέω, be sick

ἀλλόκοτος, –ον   weird, different from (+gen.), cf. 47

ἥν   which (rel. pron.; fem. because the antecedent νόϲον is fem.)

ἄν   untranslatable particle; here with apodosis of a Future Less Vivid condit. rel. clause: S #2566

γιγνώϲκω, aor.² ἔγνων
          (> aor. 3 sing. opt. γνοίη) know, recognize, know by observation (contrast οἶδα, "know by reflection"; for redupl. of -ϲκω vbs.: S #526a) [< IE *gnō-, know; cogn. L. (g)nosco; E. know, can, ken, kith, kin, couth]

ξυμ-βάλλω   figure out (cf. 50). The prefix ϲυν- was three or four times more frequent in Ar. than the older Attic spelling ξυν- and would replace ξυν- toward the end of the fifth century. ξυν- may have been retained in speech as a fossil: LA 237–38. Mss. transmit both spellings and editors have kept the inconsistency; occasionally ξυν- is metrically required.

πυνθάνομαι, aor.² ἐπυθόμην
          inquire, find out from a gen.

ἐπεί   since (conj.); elliptical: "Since <you don't know>, you have to guess"

τοπάζω   (< τόπος, place) literally "to put in a place"; guess. A "Can you name it?" guessing game continues up to line 88.

LINE 74

Ἀμῡνίας, ὁ   (< ἀμῡ́νω, defend) Amynias, a general satirized elsewhere in comedy and in W.; he may have impoverished himself by gambling.

Προνάπης, –ους, ὁ   Pronapes, father of Amynias

φημί   say, explain (introducing indir. statement with inf. εἶναι)

οὑτοϲί   this one right here (demonstrative pron. with deictic iota; cf. 55, 67; Xanthias apparently points out Amynias in the audience)

φιλόκυβος, –ον   (adj.) (< φίλος + κύβος, die) fond of dice, a gambler (the first of several humorous guesses about the nature of Phil.'s obsession, each of them a φιλό- compound)

ἀλλ'   = ἀλλά, but

τεκμαίρομαι   (< τέκμαρ, token, sure sign) judge from signs, conjecture; Amynias diagnoses the illness "from himself" (ἀφ' αὑτοῦ)

Ξα.   οὔκ, ἀλλὰ "φιλο" μέν ἐστιν ἀρχὴ τοῦ κακοῦ.
              ὁδὶ δέ φησι Cωcίαс πρὸς Δερκύλον
              εἶναι φιλοπότην αὐτόν.

Cω.   οὐδαμῶς γ', ἐπεὶ
              αὕτη γε χρηστῶν ἐστιν ἀνδρῶν ἡ νόcος.   80

Ξα.   Νικόcτρατος δ' αὖ φησιν ὁ Cκαμβωνίδηc
              εἶναι φιλοθύτην αὐτὸν ἢ φιλόξενον.

Cω.   μὰ τὸν κύν', ὦ Νικόcτρατ', οὐ φιλόξενος,
              ἐπεὶ καταπύγων ἐcτὶν ὅ γε Φιλόξενοc.

LINE 77

οὔκ	a free-standing "No"; followed by punctuation, receives accent: S #180a
ἀρχή	= ἡ ἀρχή by *crasis*; beginning, onset
κακός (3)	here used substantively, τὸ κακόν = the evil (i.e., the disease)
ὁδί	(< ὅδε, demonstrative adj. with *deictic* iota; cf. 55) "Sosias here . . ."
Σωσίας, -ου, ὁ	Sosias: not the slave but a prominent Athenian in the audience whom Xanthias calls attention to
Δερκύλος, ὁ	a prominent Athenian, evidently sitting next to Sosias
φιλοπότης, -ου, ὁ	(< φίλος + ποτόν, drink) a lover of drink
οὐδαμῶς γ'	(adv. < οὐδαμός, not any one) "Absolutely no way <is he a drinker>"; one function of γε is to indicate an *ellipsis*; here, of verb: S #2827
χρηστός (3)	(< χρή, need) good; worthy, of high social status—which entails a good deal of drinking (gen. of quality: S #1320)

LINE 81

Νῑκόστρατος, ὁ	An Athenian general
Σκαμβωνίδης, -ες	(adj.) belonging to the *deme* of Skambonidai, in the northern part of Athens
φιλοθύτης, -ου, ὁ	(< φίλος + θύω, sacrifice) fond of sacrifices
φιλόξενος, -ον	(< φίλος + ξένος, stranger, host) loving strangers, hospitable {> *xeno*phobia} [< IE *ghosti-, stranger; cogn. L. *hostis*; E. *guest*]
κύων, κυνός, ὁ or ἡ	dog; μὰ τὸν κύνα, a familiar oath in Athens {> *cynic*}
καταπύγων, -ονος, ὁ or ἡ	
	(< κατά + πῡγή, rump, buttocks) catamite, fag (a generic term of abuse: *MM* p. 210). The joke is that Philoxenos, who was attacked in comedy as a passive homosexual, is so "loving of strangers" that he allows others to penetrate him.
ὅ γε Φιλόξενος	Philoxenus, about whom nothing certain is known. The particle γε normally follows the word it stresses but, as here, can occupy an attributive position between the art. and noun: *GP* 146.

Ξα.　　　　ἄλλως φλυαρεῖτ’· οὐ γὰρ ἐξευρήσετε.　　　　　　　　　85
　　　　　εἰ δὴ ’πιθυμεῖτ’ εἰδέναι, σιγᾶντε νῦν.
　　　　　φράσω γὰρ ἤδη τὴν νόσον τοῦ δεσπότου.
　　　　　φιληλιαστής ἐστιν ὡς οὐδεὶς ἀνήρ,
　　　　　ἐρᾷ τε τούτου, τοῦ δικάζειν, καὶ στένει
　　　　　ἢν μὴ ’πὶ τοῦ πρώτου καθίζηται ξύλου.　　　　　　　90
　　　　　ὕπνου δ’ ὁρᾷ τῆς νυκτὸς οὐδὲ πασπάλην.

LINE 85

ἄλλως	(adv. < ἄλλος) otherwise; <u>without purpose</u> (dismissive) {> allegory, par*allax*, par*allel*}
φλυᾰρέω	talk nonsense
ἐξ-ευρίσκω, -ευρήσω	find out, discover {> *eureka*, *heuristic*}
εἰ δή	if indeed; "if you really want…"; δή follows word it stresses; used in protases: GP 223–24
οἶδα	(> inf. εἰδέναι) know (cf. 4)
σῑγάω	(< σῑγή; most –αω vbs. are *denominative*: S # 866.1) be quiet
ἤδη	(adv.) already; ἤδη can also express other notions of time relative to the present moment: <u>now, forthwith</u>.

LINE 88

φιληλιαστής, –οῦ, ὁ	(< φίλος + ἡλιαία, chief court at Athens) one who enjoys the Eliaea (an important court with large juries and jurisdiction over a wide variety of legal issues). The guessing game is over: it is jury duty that Phil. is addicted to.
ὡς	like
ἐράω	love, be in love with, desire (+ gen. of person or thing) {> *erotic*, *pederast*} [< ἔρασθαι = "be separated from"< IE *erə-, separate; cogn. L. *rarus* ("full of empty spaces")]
δικάζω	(< δίκη + -αζω for *denominative* verb: S #866.6) judge, give judgment (δίκη is *zero-grade* for δείκνῡμι, show, point out: Sihler #115.2) {> para*digm*, *deictic*} [< IE *deik-, show; cogn. L. *dico, dicio, iudex* ("one who shows the law"); E. *teach*]
στένω	groan, bewail
ἤν	(=ἐάν) if (+subjv., here in Pres. Gen. condit.); ἤν is twice as common in Ar. as ἐάν: LA 235
ἐπί	upon (+gen.); ’πί loses initial ἐ- by *aphaeresis* (cf. 70)
καθ-ίζω	make sit; (mid. sometimes intrans.) sit (subjv. in Pres. Gen. condit.: S #2337) {> syn*izesis*, "settle down"}
ξύλον, τό	timber, plank; <u>bench in courtroom</u> or theater. Xanthias proceeds to list courtroom-related tools and practices that Phil. obsesses about: the benches, water clock, voting token, ballot box, and the satisfaction of convicting defendants (whether guilty or not).

LINE 91

ὁράω	see; on "seeing" dreams, cf. 13.
νύξ, νυκτός, ἡ	night (gen. of time within which: S #1444)
πασπάλη, ἡ	(< παιπάλη, fine flour) morsel; tiny bit (with ὕπνου)

ἢν δ' οὖν καταμύϲῃ κἂν ἄχνην, ὅμως ἐκεῖ
ὁ νοῦς πέτεται τὴν νύκτα περὶ τὴν κλεψύδραν.
ὑπὸ τοῦ δὲ τὴν ψῆφόν γ' ἔχειν εἰωθέναι
τοὺς τρεῖς ξυνέχων τῶν δακτύλων ἀνίσταται,   95
ὥϲπερ λιβανωτὸν ἐπιτιθεὶς νουμηνίᾳ.

LINE 92

κατα-μύω, -έμυσα	(< μύω, close eyes) shut eyes; sleep {> *mystery, myopia*}
κἄν	= καὶ ἄν, redundant after ἤν: S #1765 (subjv. καταμύσῃ + ἄν in FMV condit.)
ἄχνη, ἡ	foam, chaff, anything rubbed off a surface; "the smallest bit" (adv. acc.)
ὅμως	nevertheless, for all that (conj., here, as often, used in apodosis of condit.; distinguish from ὁμῶς, equally)
ἐκεῖ	(adv.) there, in that place (a locative, with final iota: S #341)
πέτομαι	fly, flutter (cf. 16)
κλεψύδρα, ἡ	(< κλέπτω, steal + ὕδωρ, water) water clock, for timing speakers in the courtroom. A jug was perforated, allowing water to trickle at a fixed rate.

LINE 94

ὑπό	under; <u>because of</u> (+gen.)
ψῆφος, ἡ	pebble, voting token; vote. Jurors voted by dropping a pebble into an urn. The verb for "vote," ψηφίζομαι, is built from this.
ἔθω, perf. εἴωθα	(> perf. inf. εἰωθέναι) to be in the habit of, be accustomed to (prep. ὑπό governs an articular inf., τὸ . . . εἰωθέναι, which governs the inf. ἔχειν) {> *ethical, ethos*}
ξυν-έχω	hold together. Phil. has been holding the pebbles in his sleep.
λιβανωτός, ὁ	(< λίβανος, frankincense-tree) frankincense, incense [Semitic loan word]. Jury duty is likened to a religious ritual.
ἐπι-τίθημι	(> pres. act. ptcp. ἐπιτιθείς) lay upon, put upon (used of placing offerings on an altar or brazier) {> *epithet*}
νουμηνία, ἡ	(< νέος + μήν, moon) new moon, first day of the month

καὶ νὴ Δί' ἥν ἴδῃ γέ που γεγραμμένον
υἱὸν Πυριλάμπους ἐν θύρᾳ Δῆμον καλόν,
ἰὼν παρέγραψε πλησίον "κημὸς καλός."
τὸν ἀλεκτρυόνα δ', ὃς ᾖδ' ἀφ' ἑσπέρας, ἔφη   100
ὄψ' ἐξεγείρειν αὐτὸν ἀναπεπεισμένον,
παρὰ τῶν ὑπευθύνων ἔχοντα χρήματα.

LINE 97

καί . . . γε	"Yes, and what's more . . ."; a climactic addition; so too δὲ . . . γε in 94: *GP* 157, S # 2830
Ζεύς, Δίος, ὁ	Zeus (for the irregular declension: S #285.12) [< IE *dyeu-, bright; cogn. L. *deus*, I*u*ppiter; E. Tues*day*]
νή	by, in the name of (+ acc.; only in strong affirmations: S #2923)
ὁράω, aor.² εἶδον	(> aor. act. subjv. ἴδῃ) see (in Pres. Gen. protasis, here with aor. indic. apodosis, an empiric or *gnomic aorist*: S #1930–31, equiv. to pres. indic.: S #2337–38) {> pano*rama*}
γράφω, γέγραμμαι	write, inscribe (for nonrecessive accent on γεγραμμένον: S #425.b2). A lover would inscribe the name of a beloved on a vase, with the adj. καλός; doors and walls could also be so inscribed. {> -*graphy, grammar > glamour*}
Πυριλάμπης, –ους, ὁ	Pyrilampes, father of Demos, a friend of Pericles; naming his son Demos must have demonstrated his democratic political outlook.
Δῆμος, –ου, ὁ	Demos, a young Athenian noted for his good looks. His lover would write "Demos is beautiful" (Δῆμος καλός).
εἶμι	(> pres. ptcp. ἰών) go; "he goes right up and . . ."
παρα-γράφω, -έγραψα	write beside, next to (a *gnomic aorist*, describing what often occurs: S #1931)
πλησίος (3)	near; "nearby" (adv. acc.)
κημός, ὁ	the funnel or spout on top of the urn into which jurors dropped their ψῆφοι, voting pebbles. The καλός joke becomes clear: Phil.'s obsession with voting has an erotic intensity.

LINE 100

ἀλεκτρυών, –όνος, ὁ	cock [< IE *ǝleks-, defend]
ὅς, ἥ, ὅν	who, which
ἄδω	(imperfect ᾖδε) sing {> com*edy*, mel*ody*}
ἑσπέρα, ἡ	evening; ἀφ' ἑσπέρας, <u>after evening began</u> (S #1694b) {> *Hesperus, Hesperides*} [< IE *wes-pero-, west; cogn. L. *vesper*; E. *west*]
φημί	(> imperfect ἔφην) say (ind. statement with acc. αὐτὸν subject of inf. ἐξεγείρειν)
ὄψε	late
ἐξ-εγείρω	arouse, wake someone up
ἀνα-πείθω, -πέπεισμαι	(> perf. pass. ptcp. ἀναπεπεισμένον) persuade; seduce, <u>bribe</u>
ὑπεύθυνος, –ον	subject to accountability. Magistrates leaving office underwent audits (εὔθυναι) and were thus considered ὑπεύθυνος. If guilty, they might want a juror like Phil. to oversleep and miss the trial.
χρῆμα, –ατος, τό	(< χρή, need; cf. 80) thing; (pl.) property, money

εὐθὺς δ' ἀπὸ δορπηϲτοῦ κέκραγεν ἐμβάδαϲ,
κἄπειτ' ἐκεῖϲ' ἐλθὼν προκαθεύδει πρῷ πάνυ,
ὥϲπερ λεπὰϲ προϲεχόμενοϲ τῷ κίονι.   105
ὑπὸ δυϲκολίαϲ δ' ἅπαϲι τιμῶν τὴν μακρὰν
ὥϲπερ μέλιττ' ἢ βομβυλιὸϲ εἰϲέρχεται
ὑπὸ τοῖϲ ὄνυξι κηρὸν ἀναπεπλαϲμένοϲ.
ψήφων δὲ δείϲαϲ μὴ δεηθείη ποτέ,
ἵν' ἔχοι δικάζειν, αἰγιαλὸν ἔνδον τρέφει.   110

LINE 103

ἀπό	(prep. + gen.) after
δορπηϲτός, ὁ	dinner time
κράζω, κέκραγα	croak, shriek, call out for (perf. *frequentative* with pres. sense)
ἐμβάς, –άδος, ἡ	(< ἐμ-βαίνω, step into) a cheap leather shoe. Contrast the expensive λακωνικαί that Phil. must wear at 1157.
κἄπειτ'	= καὶ ἔπειτα (cf. 19)
ἐκεῖσε	(adv. < ἐκεῖ + suffix –σε, toward: S #342) to there
ἔρχομαι, aor.² ἦλθον	(> aor. ptcp. ἐλθών) go
προ-καθ-εύδω	sleep before, sleep first
πρῴ	(adv.) early in the morning
λεπάς, –άδος, ἡ	limpet, a mollusk that clings to a rock (λέπας, τὸ)
προσ-έχω	bring to; (mid.) attach self to (+dat.)
κίων, -ονος, ὁ or ἡ	pillar (evidently part of courtroom architecture)

LINE 106

δυσκολία, ἡ	(δυσ-, hard, difficult + κόλον, nurture?) discontent, peevishness
τῑμάω	(> pres. act. ptcp. τιμῶν) honor, value; <u>assess the punishment due</u> {> timocracy}
μακρός (3)	long (sc. γραμμήν, line). Jurors drew a long line on a wax tablet to inflict a heavy penalty, short for a light one; Phil. used his fingernail. {> macro-}
μέλιττα, ἡ	(< μέλι, honey) honeybee (Attic spelling for μέλισσα) {> Melissa, "Bee"} [< IE *melit-, honey; cogn. L. mel]
βομβυλιός, ὁ	(< βόμβος, humming, buzzing) bumblebee, buzzing insect [< onomatopoeia]
ὄνυξ, –υχος, ὁ	talon, nail (cf. 17); evidently he returns home at the end of the day with wax built up under his nails.
ἀνα-πλάσσω,–πέπλασμαι	
	plaster, cake {> plastic, plasma}
κηρός, ὁ	beeswax

LINE 109

δείδω, ἔδεισα	fear. When μὴ serves as conj. in a fear clause, tr. as "lest" or, for simplicity and clarity, "that": S #2221; after secondary tenses, it is followed by opt.
δέομαι, ἐδεήθην	need (+ gen.) {> deontology}
ἔχω	have; <u>to be able</u> (+inf.) (ἔχοι is opt. in purpose clause; the main verb, τρέφει, is pres., but describes an attitude of long standing: S #2200.)
αἰγιαλός, ὁ	beach, seashore (which is of course filled with pebbles)
τρέφω	nourish, maintain

> τοιαῦτ' ἀλύει· νουθετούμενος δ' ἀεὶ
> μᾶλλον δικάζει. τοῦτον οὖν φυλάττομεν
> μοχλοῖσιν ἐγκλήσαντες, ὡς ἂν μὴ 'ξίῃ.
> ὁ γὰρ υἱὸς αὐτοῦ τὴν νόσον βαρέως φέρει.
> καὶ πρῶτα μὲν λόγοισι παραμυθούμενος   115
> ἀνέπειθεν αὐτὸν μὴ φορεῖν τριβώνιον
> μηδ' ἐξιέναι θύραζ', ὁ δ' οὐκ ἐπείθετο.
> εἶτ' αὐτὸν ἀπέλου κἀκάθαιρ', ὁ δ' οὐ μάλα.
> μετὰ τοῦτ' ἐκορυβάντιζ', ὁ δ' αὐτῷ τυμπάνῳ
> ᾄξας ἐδίκαζεν εἰς τὸ Καινὸν ἐμπεσών.   120

LINE 111

ἀλύω	wander in mind, rave. The verb is poetic; lines 111–12 parody Euripides's *Stheneboia*.
μοχλός, ὁ	a wooden bar placed across a door, secured by a peg (βάλανος; cf. 154)
ἐγ-κλείω, -έκλησα	(< ἐν + κλείς, bar, bolt; older Attic spelling κλῄς) shut in, confine (ἐν- > ἐγ- before κ-, γ-, χ-, ξ- by nasalization: S #92)
ὡς + ἄν	(conj.) that (rare in purpose clauses in Ar. [14x] compared with ἵνα [183x]; more common in tragedy; ἵνα is more conversational and prosaic: LA 265.)
ἐξ-έρχομαι	go out (indic. forms of εἶμι are used in Attic for the fut.; oblique moods of εἶμι [subjv., etc.] are used for the pres. tense. For *aphaeresis* of 'ξίῃ cf. 70.)
βαρέως	(< adj. βαρύς, heavy) heavily. βαρέως φέρειν τι = take something badly. {> *baritone*, *charivari*, "heavy head"}
πρῶτος (3)	(< superl. adj. of πρό, cf. 15 on πρότερος) first (neut. pl. πρῶτα is adv. acc.)

LINE 115

115–35: Xanthias describes the different strategies they have attempted to cure Phil. Once they even tried taking him to Aegina for medical treatment at the temple of Asclepius.

παρα-μῡθέομαι	encourage; pacify, assuage (cf. 566)
μή ... μηδέ	negs. for infs. with ἀναπείθω
φορέω	bear; wear (of clothes; *frequentative* of φέρω, implying habitual action)
τριβώνιον, -ου, τό	old cloak (cf. 33); Bdel. wants Phil. to dress more respectably.
ὁ, ἡ, τό	he, she, it (usually def. art. but here, without a substantive, a demonstrative pron.); ὁ δέ is repeated in the following lines as Xanthias relates Phil.'s antics.
ἀπο-λόω	(> imperfect 3 sing. ἀπέλου, a contraction of ἀπέλοε: S #398a, p. 705) wash, wash off, bathe (λόω is a Homeric form of λούω)
καθαίρω	(< καθαρός, clean, pure; κἀκάθαιρε = καὶ ἐκάθαιρε by *crasis*) cleanse, purify. Many of the imperfect vbs. in this passage are surely *conative* (S #1895): the men of the house may *try* to reform Phil., but failure is inevitable. {> *katharsis*}
μάλα	(adv.) very; very much

LINE 119

μετά	after (+ acc.); μετὰ τοῦτο = <u>next</u>
κορυβαντίζω	(< Κορύβας, cf. 8 + ίζω suffix, cf. 5) purify by corybantic rites
τύμπανον, τό	kettledrum; drum (αὐτῷ τυμπάνῳ, dat. of accompaniment without σύν; cf. LSJ s.v. αὐτός I.5); drums were part of Corybantic rites.
ᾄττω, ᾖξα	(> aor. ptcp. ᾄξας) move quickly, shoot forth
καινός (3)	new. τὸ Καινὸν is apparently elliptical for τὸ Καινὸν <δικαστήριον>, "the New Courtroom," of which little is known. {> *cenozoic*}
ἐμ-πίπτω, -έπεσον	fall upon; burst into (+dat.) (for shift of ἐνεπ- to ἐμπ-: S #449a; reduplication in pres.: S #447) {> *symptom*}

ὅτε δῆτα ταύταιϲ ταῖϲ τελεταῖϲ οὐκ ὠφέλει,
διέπλευϲεν εἰϲ Αἴγιναν, εἶτα ξυλλαβὼν
νύκτωρ κατέκλινεν αὐτὸν εἰϲ Ἀϲκληπιοῦ,
ὁ δ' ἀνεφάνη κνεφαῖοϲ ἐπὶ τῇ κιγκλίδι.
ἐντεῦθεν οὐκέτ' αὐτὸν ἐξεφρίεμεν,   125
ὁ δ' ἐξεδίδραϲκε διά τε τῶν ὑδορρόων
καὶ τῶν ὀπῶν· ἡμεῖϲ δ' ὅϲ' ἦν τετρημένα
ἐνεβύϲαμεν ῥακίοιϲι κἀπακτώϲαμεν,

LINE 121

δῆτα	"And, next, when . . ."; a rare connective use: *GP* 278
τελετή, ἡ	(< τελέω, fulfill, initiate) ritual of initiation (dat. of means) {> tele*ology*}
ὠφελέω	be of service, help (ὠφέλει is imperfect; by contrast pres. is ὠφελεῖ; vbs. with initial ω- show no augment and remain unchanged: S #436)
δια-πλέω, -έπλευσα	sail across
Αἴγῖνα, ἡ	Aigina, an island across the Saronic Gulf from Athens, site of a sanctuary of Asclepius
ξυλ-λαμβάνω, -έλαβον	
	collect; seize, arrest, take with one (for συλ-/ξυλ- cf. 72) {> epil*epsy*, syll*able*}

LINE 123

νύκτωρ	(adv. < νύξ, νυκτ- + –ωρ, a unique adv. suffix) at night
κατα-κλίνω	make someone recline, lay down {> *clinic, climate*}
Ἀσκληπιός, ὁ	Asclepius, god of medicine. The phrase εἰϲ Ἀϲκληπιοῦ is elliptical for εἰϲ <ἱερὸν> Ἀϲκληπιοῦ, "to <the temple> of Asclepius."
ἀνα-φαίνω, -εφάνην	bring to light, show; (pass.) be shown, appear {> *fantasy, pheno-*}
κνεφαῖος (3)	(< κνέφας, evening + –αιος, adj. suffix: S #858.2) in the dark, early in the morning
κιγκλίς, –ίδος, ἡ	latticed gate at the barrier (δρύφακτοι, cf. 386) of the law courts

LINE 125

ἐντεῦθεν	(< ἔνθα, there + suffix –θεν denoting direction from: S #342, 346) hence or thence; (here, adv. of time) <u>after that</u>, henceforth, thereupon
ἐκ-φρέω	(> imperfect 1 pl. ἐξεφρίεμεν) let out (cf. 147, 162, and 891; Wilson and B-O assume it follows conjugation of ἵημι). An unusual verb in Greek, but not unimportant in this escape drama.
ἐκ-διδράσκω	(< δρόμος, running) run away, escape. One of several vbs. with redupl. and –σκω in pres. stem, like διδάσκω, γιγνώσκω: S #526c. Surely a *conative* imperfect, "he was trying to . . ."
ὑδρορρόα, ἡ	conduit; gutter, spout (for doubling of ρρ: S #80)
ὀπή, ἡ	opening; hole in roof, chink {> met*ope*}
τετραίνω, τέτρημαι	pierce, open (for *periphrastic* in pluperfect: S # 599)
ἐμ-βύω, -έβῡσα	stuff in
ῥάκος, –εος, τό	rags, tattered garments
πακτόω, ἐπάκτωσα	fasten, close; stop up, caulk

ὁ δ’ ὡσπερεὶ κολοιὸς αὑτῷ παττάλους
ἐνέκρουεν εἰς τὸν τοῖχον, εἶτ’ ἐξήλλετο.　　　　　　130
ἡμεῖς δὲ τὴν αὐλὴν ἅπασαν δικτύοις
καταπετάσαντες ἐν κύκλῳ φυλάττομεν.
ἔστιν δ’ ὄνομα τῷ μὲν γέροντι Φιλοκλέων,
ναὶ μὰ Δία, τῷ δ’ υἱεῖ γε τῳδὶ Βδελυκλέων,
ἔχων τρόπους φρυαγμοσεμνάκους τινάς.　　　　　　135

LINE 129

ὡσπερεί	(< ὥσπερ + εἰ) just as if
κολοιός, ὁ	jackdaw; the bird was known for hopping from one peg to the next
πάτταλος, ὁ	peg (Attic spelling for πάσσ-)

LINE 130

ἐγ-κρούω	knock in, hammer in
τοῖχος, ὁ	wall of a house
ἐξ-άλλομαι	(> imperfect 3 sing. ἐξήλλετο) jump out from, hop out {> *halter*}

LINE 131

αὐλή, ἡ	hall, courtyard (evidently not visible to the audience)
δίκτυον, τό	casting net, hunting net
κατα-πετάννῡμι, -επέτασα	cover over
κύκλος, ὁ	circle, ring (ἐν κύκλῳ, or κύκλῳ alone, <u>all around</u>) {> *cycle, cyclo-*} [redupl. < IE *k^wel-, turn; cogn. E. *wheel*]

LINE 133

ὄνομα, –ατος, τό	name (the name, Φιλοκλέων, agrees with ὄνομα though logically it might agree with dat. γέροντι: S #1478) {> *anonymous*, patro*nymic*}
Φιλοκλέων, –ωνος, ὁ	(< φίλος + Κλέων: "Lover of Cleon") Philocleon, father of Bdelycleon, protagonist of *W.*; a follower of the democratic politician Cleon, the champion of jurors and opponent of Sparta.
δὲ . . . γε	"And what's more . . ." (cf. 97)
ναί	yes; ναὶ μὰ Δία, "Yes, by Zeus!"
υἱός, ὁ	(> fifth-century Attic dat. sing. υἱεῖ: S #285.27) son
Βδελυκλέων, –ωνος, ὁ	(< βδελυρός, loathsome, "Hater of Cleon") Bdelycleon. Both names scan ⏑ ⏑ ⏑ –, requiring *resolution* in the last metron of these trimeters. [βδελυρός βδέω < IE *$pezd$-, fart; cogn. L. *pedo*; E. *feist*]
τρόπος, ὁ	turn; custom, character (esp. in pl.) {> *trope, troubadour*}
φρυαγμοσεμνάκος, –ον	(< φρύαγμα, violent snorting or neighing of animal + σεμνός, majestic, pompous—Ar.'s own coinage) haughty, arrogant, "proud-snortical" (B-O), "high-horsical" (Hend.)

ΒΔΕΛΥΚΛΕΩΝ

	ὦ Ξανθία καὶ Cωcία, καθεύδετε;	
Ξα.	οἴμοι.	
Cω.	τί ἐcτι;	
Ξα.	Βδελυκλέων ἀνίcταται.	
Βδ.	οὐ περιδραμεῖται cφῷν ταχέως δεῦρ' ἅτεροc;	
	ὁ γὰρ πατὴρ εἰc τὸν ἰπνὸν ἐξελήλυθε	
	καὶ μυcπολεῖ τι καταδεδυκώc. ἀλλ' ἄθρει	140
	κατὰ τῆc πυέλου τὸ τρῆμ' ὅπωc μὴ 'κδύcεται·	
	cὺ δὲ τῇ θύρᾳ πρόcκειcο.	
Ξα.	ταῦτ', ὦ δέcποτα.	

136–229: Bdel. wakes up and alerts the slaves that Phil. is trying to sneak out of the house. He tries escaping through the chimney and even by clinging to the bottom of a donkey, as had Odysseus when escaping the Cyclops's cave.

LINE 136

οἴμοι	"Uh-oh!"; reaction of an inferior to the approach of superior: MacD. (cf. 24)
περι-τρέχω, –δραμοῦμαι	run around. Bdel. is on the roof, supervising the efforts to prevent Phil.'s escape (cf. 125).
cφῷν	gen./dat. of dual pron. cφώ, you two (contrast cφῶν, 3 pl. of cφεῖς: S #325)
ταχέωc	(adv.) quickly
δεῦρο	(adv. < demonstrative suffix –δε) to here, hither
ἅτεροc	= ὁ ἕτεροc by *crasis*, <u>one or the other</u> of you {> *hetero-*}

LINE 139

ἰπνόc, ὁ	oven, kitchen [< IE, *auk^w*- cooking pot; cogn. E. *oven*]
μυcπολέω	(μῦc, mouse, rat + πολέω, go about, range over) run around like a mouse (*hapax* compound) {> *muscle*}
κατα-δύω, -δέδῡκα	go down, sink, stoop down
ἀθρέω	gaze at, watch; <u>see to it</u> (introduces the ὅπως clause in the next line). This is addressed to Xanthias; Sosias evidently exits the stage and will not reappear: the actor will play the part of Phil., requiring a costume change of near-miraculous speed.

LINE 141

πυέλοc, ὁ	tub, sink in the kitchen
τρῆμα, –ατοc, τὸ	perforation, drain hole in the sink (cf. 127)
ὅπωc	see to it <u>that</u> (+fut. indic. for urgent exhortations and prohibitions; neg. is μή: S #1920, 2213)
ἐκ-δύω, -δύcω	strip off; go out of, escape
πρόc-κειμαι	(> pres. act. impv. 2 sing. πρόcκεισο) lie upon, keep close to (+dat.)
ταῦτα	"Yes," "Very well," "Aye, aye sir" (LSJ s.v. οὗτος VII.1)

Βδ.　　　　　　ἄναξ Πόςειδον, τί ποτ' ἄρ' ἡ κάπνη ψοφεῖ;
　　　　　　　οὗτος, τίς εἶ ςύ;

ΦΙΛΟΚΛΕΩΝ

　　　　　　　　　　　　　καπνὸς ἔγωγ' ἐξέρχομαι.
Βδ.　　　　　　καπνός; φέρ' ἴδω, ξύλου τίνος ςύ;
Φι.　　　　　　　　　　　　　　　ςυκίνου.　　　　　　145
Βδ.　　　　　　νὴ τὸν Δί', ὅςπερ γ' ἐςτὶ δριμύτατος καπνῶν.
　　　　　　　ἀτὰρ οὐκέτ' ἐκφρήςει γε· ποῦ 'ςθ' ἡ τηλία;
　　　　　　　δύου πάλιν· φέρ' ἐπαναθῶ ςοι καὶ ξύλον.

LINE 143

ἄναξ, ἄνακτος, ὁ　　　lord, master. Ar.'s most frequent epithet for divinities: *LA* 20, though MacD. detects surprise or annoyance when it precedes a god's name.

Ποςειδῶν, –ῶνος, ὁ　　(> voc. Πόςειδον) Poseidon (note omission of ὦ: S #1284)

τί　　　　　　　　　　(adv. acc.) "In what way?" "Why?": S # 1262–65

ποτε　　　　　　　　　(indef. adv., enclitic: S #181b) at some time, once; intensifies quests.: τίς ποτε, "Who in the world?" [< IE *$k^w o$-, which; cogn. L. *quando*]

ἄρα　　　　　　　　　"What on earth?"; adds liveliness and is used in anxious quests.: *GP* 39–40, Starkie

καπνή, ἡ　　　　　　　chimney, smoke vent

ψοφέω　　　　　　　　(< ψόφος, noise) make a noise

LINE 144

οὗτος　　　　　　　　addressed to Phil (cf. 1)

ἔγωγε　　　　　　　　strengthened form of ἐγώ; "I, for my part . . ." Phil. now appears for the first time, his head popping up through a hole on the roof.

ὁράω, aor.² εἶδον　　　(> aor. subjv. 1 sing. ἴδω) φέρ' ἴδω = "Well, let's see . . ." (used only with quests. in Ar.)

ξύλον, τό　　　　　　wood (gen. of material: S #1323), cf. 89

ςύκινος (3)　　　　　(adj. < ςῦκον, fig + –ινος, suffix of *denominative* adj. of material: S #858.12) made of fig-wood, with a pun on ςυκοφάνται, "*sycophants*," who made scurrilous prosecutions; Ar. suggests that jurors are gullible to them.

LINE 146

νὴ τὸν Δί'　　　　　　cf. 97

ὅςπερ, ἥπερ, ὅπερ　　(rel. pron.; antecedent is καπνός) the very person who, the very thing which, the same as. "The enclitic particle –περ may be added to emphasize the connection between the relative and its antecedent": S #338c, 2495.

γε　　　　　　　　　"Yes, because it is the sharpest"; causal γε following rel. pron. ὅςπερ: S #2826

δρῑμύς, –εῖα, –ύ　　　piercing; sharp. Fig-wood smoke is esp. pungent, just as the results of false prosecutions are bitter. The same can be said of Phil. himself: piercing and pungent.

ἐκ-φρέω, -φρήςω　　　(> fut. mid. 2 sing. ἐκφρήςει) let out, bring out; "you will not slip out"

ποῦ　　　　　　　　　(interrog. adv.) where?

τηλία, ἡ　　　　　　　chimney cover. Bdel., being on the roof, can at least close this escape route.

δέω　　　　　　　　　(> pres. impv. mid. 2 sing. δύου) go in, sink down; go in again

πάλιν　　　　　　　　(adv.) back, again {> *palindrome, palimpsest*}

ἐπ-ανα-τίθημι, aor.² -έθηκα

　　　　　　　　　　(> aor. act. subjv. 1 sing. ἐπαναθῶ) lay upon, put on top. A piece of wood on top of the chimney cover would keep it in place.

ἐνταῦθά νυν ζήτει τιν' ἄλλην μηχανήν.
ἀτὰρ ἄθλιός γ' εἴμ' ὡς ἕτερος οὐδεὶς ἀνήρ,   150
ὅστις πατρὸς νῦν Καπνίου κεκλήσομαι.

Φι.   παῖ.

Ξα.   τὴν θύραν ὠθεῖ·

Βδ.   πίεζέ νυν σφόδρα,
εὖ κἀνδρικῶς· κἀγὼ γὰρ ἐνταῦθ' ἔρχομαι.
καὶ τῆς κατακλῇδος ἐπιμελοῦ καὶ τοῦ μοχλοῦ,
φύλαττέ θ' ὅπως μὴ τὴν βάλανον ἐκτρώξεται.   155

LINE 149

ἐνταῦθα	(adv.) here, there, in this circumstance; "there now" (with νυν and impv.)
ζητέω	(> pres. act. impv. 2 sing. ζήτει) seek, examine. This sentence is delivered, not without sarcasm, to Phil.
μηχανή, ἡ	contrivance, scheme {> *mechanic, mechanism*}
ἄθλιος (3)	(< ἄθλον, prize; "running for a prize") struggling; miserable, wretched

LINE 151

ὅστις, ἥτις, ὅ τι	(rel. pron.) anyone who, whoever (τις when combined with ὅς generalizes, marking a class or quality; comedy prefers ὅστις over ὅς: *LA* 264)
Καπνίας, –ου, ὁ	(< καπνός, smoke) "Smoky," a nickname perhaps given to braggarts
καλέω, κέκλημαι	(> fut. perf. pass. 1 sing. κεκλήσομαι) call; (pass.) "I shall bear the name of . . ."

LINE 152

παῖς, παιδός, ὁ, ἡ	(> voc. παῖ) boy. The voc. παῖ was often addressed to a slave and implies superiority of speaker; it was never used by women: *LA* 187. {> *pediatrics*}
πιέζω	(< ἐπί, on + ἵζω, sit) squeeze, press, push
ἀνδρικῶς	(adv. < adj. ἀνδρικός, manly, masculine < ἀνήρ, ἀνδρός, man) like a man; κἀνδρικῶς = καὶ ἀνδρικῶς by *crasis*
κἀγω	= καὶ ἐγώ by *crasis*

LINE 154

κατακλής, –ῆδος, ἡ	(< κλής, bar, key; cf. 113) lock, fastening
ἐπι-μελέομαι	(> pres. impv. 2 sing. ἐπιμελοῦ < μέλω, care for) take charge of, care for (+ gen.)
μοχλός, ὁ	wooden bar (cf. 113)
ὅπως	+ fut. indic. (cf. 141)
βάλανος, ὁ	acorn; pin in the shape of an acorn used to hold the μοχλός in place
ἐκ-τρώγω, -τρώξομαι	eat up, nibble off (deponent fut.) {> *trout*} Use of this verb is one of many ways in which Phil. is likened to a small, pesky animal.

Φι.   τί δράϲετ'; οὐκ ἐκφρήϲετ', ὦ μιαρώτατοι,
          δικάϲοντά μ', ἀλλ' ἐκφεύξεται Δρακοντίδηϲ;
Ξα.   ϲὺ δὲ τοῦτο βαρέωϲ ἂν φέροιϲ;
Φι.   ὁ γὰρ θεὸϲ
          μαντευομένῳ μοὔχρηϲεν ἐν Δελφοῖϲ ποτέ,
          ὅταν τιϲ ἐκφύγῃ μ', ἀποϲκλῆναι τότε.   160
Ξα.   Ἄπολλον ἀποτρόπαιε, τοῦ μαντεύματοϲ.
Φι.   ἴθ', ἀντιβολῶ ϲ', ἔκφρεϲ με, μὴ διαρραγῶ.

LINE 156

ἐκ-φρέω — let out (cf. 125, 147)

δικάζω — fut. act. ptcp. δικάϲοντα to denote purpose: S #2066 (cf. 89)

ἐκ-φεύγω, -φεύξομαι — escape; <u>be acquitted</u> in court (deponent fut.)

Δρακοντίδηϲ, –ου, ὁ — (< δράκων, serpent + –ιδηϲ, *patronymic* suffix.: S # 845.4) the name of a defendant awaiting trial. The name was common, and there may have been a particular individual intended.

LINE 158

βαρέωϲ φέρω — cf. 114

φέροιϲ ἄν — "Would you endure . . . ?" (potential opt. with ἄν: S #1824–34)

γάρ — "Oh yes, for . . ."; in answers, γάρ marks assent: *GP* 73, S #2806

LINE 159

μαντεύομαι — (< μάντιϲ, seer) consult an oracle (dat. ptcp. μαντευομένῳ agrees with μοι). Phil. now claims divine sanction for his compulsion to convict defendants.

μοὔχρηϲεν — = μοὶ ἔχρηϲεν by *crasis*

χράω, ἔχρηϲα — proclaim, utter an oracle

Δελφοί, –ῶν, οἱ — (< δελφύϲ, womb) Delphi, home of the oracle of Apollo

ὅταν — (temporal conj. < ὅτε + ἄν) whenever, with subjv.: S #1768

ἐκφύγῃ — escape me = <u>be acquitted</u> by me (cf. 157)

ἀπο-ϲκέλλω, aor.² -έϲκλην —
    (> aor. act. inf. ἀποϲκλῆναι) dry up, parch, wither (inf. here in indir. statement, in a prophecy) {> *sclerosis*}

LINE 161

Ἀπόλλων, –ωνοϲ, ὁ — (> voc. Ἄπολλον) Apollo, god of prophecy

ἀποτρόπαιοϲ, –ον — (< ἀπό, away + τρέπω, turn) apotropaic, averting evil (an epithet of Apollo)

μάντευμα, –ατοϲ, τό — (< μάντιϲ, seer + –μα, –ματοϲ, suffix denoting result of an action: S #841.2) oracle (gen. of cause, used in exclam.: S #1407)

LINE 162

εἶμι — (> pres. impv. 2 sing. ἴθι) go, come; <u>please</u> (introducing a request)

ἐκ-φρέω — (> aor.² impv. 2 sing. ἔκφρεϲ; cf. 125, 147) let out

μή — + subjv. in neg. purpose clause; μή alone stands for ἵνα μή: S #2193

δια-ρρήγνῡμι, –ερράγην —
    (> aor. pass. subjv. 1 sing. διαρραγῶ) burst, explode

Ξα.   μὰ τὸν Ποσειδῶ, Φιλοκλέων, οὐδέποτέ γε.

Φι.   διατρώξομαι τοίνυν ὀδὰξ τὸ δίκτυον.

Ξα.   ἀλλ' οὐκ ἔχεις ὀδόντας.

Φι.   οἴμοι δείλαιος·   165
        πῶς ἄν σ' ἀποκτείναιμι; πῶς; δότε μοι ξίφος
        ὅπως τάχιστ', ἢ πινάκιον τιμητικόν.

Βδ.   ἄνθρωπος οὗτος μέγα τι δρασείει κακόν.

Φι.   μὰ τὸν Δί' οὐ δῆτ', ἀλλ' ἀποδόσθαι βούλομαι
        τὸν ὄνον ἄγων αὐτοῖcι τοῖc κανθηλίοιc·   170

LINE 163

Ποσειδῶν, –ῶνος, ὁ	(> acc. Ποσειδῶ) Poseidon (cf. 143). Poseidon's name is chosen for metrical conven- ience, suggest B-O.
οὐδέποτε	(adv., usually with pres. or fut. vbs.; contrast οὐδεπώποτε, 14) not ever
γε	emphatic in neg. answers: *GP* 132
δια-τρώγω, -τρώξομαι	gnaw through (deponent fut.) {> *trout*}
τοίνυν	"Well, then, in that case . . ."; in dialogue, introducing an answer as springing from the attitude of the previous speaker: *GP* 569–70
ὀδάξ	(adv. < ὀδούς, ὀδόντος tooth) by biting with the teeth (cf. similarly formed advs. λάξ, with the foot; πύξ, with the fist: S #341 Nom.) {> mas*todon*}

LINE 166

ἀπο-κτείνω, -έκτεινα	(> potential opt. ἄν . . . ἀποκτείναιμι) kill
ὅπως	(+ superl., usually with ὡς or ὅτι: S #1086) *as quickly as possible*
τάχιστα	(superl. adv. acc. < ταχύς, fast) quickest (cf. 138)
πινάκιον, -ου, τό	(dim. of πίναξ, board, writing tablet) small tablet on which jurors wrote verdict—for Phil. a better weapon than a sword
τῑμητικός (3)	(< τῑμάω, cf. 106 + -ικος suffix, cf. 66) for assessing punishment

LINE 168

ἄνθρωπος	= ὁ ἄνθρωπος by *crasis* [< ἄνθρωπος < νρ- < IE *ner-*, manly, + ὤψ = "having a man's face"]
οὗτος	when adjectival in Ar. it generally takes the art., as in prose: S #1171, 1178
δρᾱσείω	(< desiderative of δρᾱω: S #868) have in mind to do (the verb hints at tragic parody)
μὰ τὸν Δί'	"No, by Zeus"; μά + acc. for a strong oath; can be affirmative but in Attic generally neg. (cf. 26)
δῆτα	"*Surely* not"; used in dramatic dialogue; οὔκουν . . . δῆτα is an emphatic neg. answer to a statement: *GP* 272
ἀπο-δίδωμι, -έδωκα	(> aor. mid. inf. ἀποδόσθαι) return, yield; (mid.) sell (also aor. mid. opt. 1 sing. ἀποδοίμην, 172 below)

LINE 170

κανθήλια, τά	panniers, pack-saddle (αὐτοῖς τοῖς κανθηλίοις = "panniers and all"; for omission of σύν with αὐτοῖς, cf. 119)

νουμηνία γάρ ἐϲτιν.

Βδ.　　　　　　　οὔκουν κἂν ἐγὼ

αὐτὸν ἀποδοίμην δῆτ’ ἄν;

Φι.　　　　　　　　　　οὐχ ὥϲπερ γ’ ἐγώ.

Βδ.　μὰ Δί’, ἀλλ’ ἄμεινον.

Φι.　　　　　　　ἀλλὰ τὸν ὄνον ἔξαγε.

Ξα.　οἵαν πρόφαϲιν καθῆκεν, ὡϲ εἰρωνικῶϲ,

ἵν’ αὐτὸν ἐκπέμψειαϲ.

Βδ.　　　　　　　ἀλλ’ οὐκ ἔϲπαϲεν　　　　　　175

ταύτῃ γ’· ἐγὼ γὰρ ᾐϲθόμην τεχνωμένου.

ἀλλ’ εἰϲιών μοι τὸν ὄνον ἐξάξειν δοκῶ,

LINE 171

νουμηνία, ἡ	new moon. The first day of the month was market day (cf. 96).
οὔκουν	(< οὐκ + οὖν) "couldn't I?"; particle in impatient quests.; S #2953d (cf. 47)
κἄν	= καὶ ἄν by crasis. For repetition of ἄν: S #1765; an extra ἄν is placed early in a sentence to flag the construction to follow; here used with potential opt.
δῆτα	"Surely, then, I could . . ."; used by Ar. in quests., sometimes following other particles (cf. 24)
ὥϲπερ γ’ ἐγώ	"<You would not sell it> *the way I* would"; γε marking *ellipsis* of verb: S #2827
ἀλλά	"Not as well <u>but</u> better"; *adversative*: GP 1. Contrast the use of ἀλλά in the following line, in which the speaker's ἀλλά breaks off objections and issues an impv.: "Anyway, bring out the donkey": GP 8, 17–19.
ἀμείνων, ἄμεινον	better (comparative of ἀγαθός: S #319; frequently follows a neg.)

LINE 174

πρόφαϲις, –εωϲ, ἡ	(< πρό + φαίνω, reveal) alleged reason, excuse
καθ-ίημι, –ῆκα	let fall, dangle (used of bait on a fishhook) {> *catheter*}
ὡϲ	"how" with advs.
εἰρωνικῶϲ	(adv. < εἴρων, dissembler) insincerely, mockingly, craftily {> *irony*}

LINE 175

ἐκ-πέμπω, -έπεμψα	(> aor. act. opt. 2 sing. ἐκπέμψειαϲ) send out, <u>let go out</u>
ϲπάω, ἔϲπαϲα	draw, pull out; catch; pull it off (used of hauling up fish)

LINE 176

ταύτῃ	a] sc. προφάϲει; b] as adv., "in this way": LSJ s.v. οὗτος C.VIII.4.c
αἰϲθάνομαι, aor.² ᾐϲθόμην	perceive, see (takes a gen., like other vbs. of perception: S #1367) {> *aesthetic*, *anesthesia*}
τεχνάομαι	(< τέχνη, skill) make by art; contrive; devise cunningly {> *technology*}

LINE 177

εἴϲ-ειμι	go in (indic. serves as fut. of εἰϲέρχομαι; other moods, including ptcp., signify pres.; cf. 113)
ἐξ-άγω, -άξω	lead out
δοκέω	I have a mind to, I think I'll, <u>I am determined to</u> (personal construction with μοι: S #1983 + inf.: S #1998, LSJ I.3; fut. inf. indicates action follows without delay)

ὅπως ἂν ὁ γέρων μηδὲ παρακύψῃ πάλιν.
κάνθων, τί κλάεις; ὅτι πεπράσει τήμερον;
βάδιζε θᾶττον. τί στένεις, εἰ μὴ φέρεις
'Οδυσσέα τιν';   180

Ξα.   ἀλλὰ ναὶ μὰ Δία φέρει
κάτω γε τουτονί τιν' ὑποδεδυκότα.

LINE 178

ὅπως ἄν   so that (purpose clause with subjv.). ὅπως with ἄν was an older conj. that was standard in inscriptions, Thucydides and Xenophon: S #2201; it was also frequent in Ar.'s *Lys.*, parodying official style, notes Starkie on 113. It would eventually be replaced in Attic by ἵνα: *LA* 176–78, 264–65.

παρα-κύπτω, -έκυψα   peep out of. At this moment, Bdel. goes into the house and re-emerges with a donkey.

LINE 179

κάνθων, –ωνος, ὁ   pack ass, donkey. Also known in Greek as ὄνος; the following five vbs. are addressed to it.

κλάω   cry, wail (Attic spelling of κλαίω)

ὅτι   (causal conj.) because. This conj. was favored by writers of simpler prose, such as Lysias, but was avoided in formal genres like tragedy: *LA* 266.

πέρνημι, πέπρᾱμαι   (> fut. perf. 2 sing. πεπράσει) sell

τήμερον   (adv. < ἡμέρα, day) today {> eph*emer*al}

LINE 180

βαδίζω   (< βαίνω, cf. 230) walk, march

θάττων, –ον, -ονος   (> neut. acc. θᾶττον < comparative of ταχύς: S #125f) faster (adv. acc., Ar.'s only use of the adj.)

στένω   groan (cf. 89; also used of animals)

'Οδυσσεύς, –έως, ὁ   (> acc. 'Οδυσσέᾱ) Odysseus. Phil., thinking of Odysseus's escape from Polyphemus by hanging on underneath a ram in *Odyssey* 9.425–65, thinks he can sneak out of the house by hanging on to a donkey.

ἀλλά   "Why, of course"; assentient: a second speaker confirms something imagined by the first speaker: *GP* 20.

ναί   yes

κάτω   (adv.) beneath, down below

γε   "He is carrying (φέρει) . . ."; in assent, echoing previous speaker's words: *GP* 136

τουτονί   *deictic* iota: S #333g (cf. 74)

ὑπο-δύω, -δέδῡκα   slip under, crawl under (-δέδῡκα intrans., –δέδῡκα transitive.: S p. 694; ὑπό can suggest furtiveness: S #1699.4)

Βδ.   ποῖον; φέρ' ἴδωμαι.
Ξα.   τουτονί.
Βδ.   τουτὶ τί ἦν;
        τίς εἶ ποτ', ὤνθρωπ', ἐτεόν;
Φι.   Οὖτις, νὴ Δία.
Βδ.   Οὖτις σύ; ποδαπός;
Φι.   Ἴθακος Ἀποδρασιππίδου.   185
Βδ.   Οὖτις μὰ τὸν Δί' οὖτι χαιρήσων γε σύ.
        ὕφελκε θᾶττον αὐτόν. ὦ μιαρώτατος,
        ἵν' ὑποδέδυκεν· ὥστ' ἔμοιγ' ἰνδάλλεται
        ὁμοιότατος κλητῆρος εἶναι πωλίῳ.

LINE 183

ποῖος (3)	of what sort? "What do you mean?" (used to repeat a word, often expressing surprise), "nonsense!"
φέρε	with subjv., cf. 54
ἴδωμαι	for use of mid. in act. sense: LSJ s.v. ὁράω II.4
τουτὶ τί ἦν	"Good heavens, what's this?" (ἦν imperfect of truth just recognized, elsewhere with ἄρα: S #1902)
ὤνθρωπ'	= ὦ ἄνθρωπε
ἐτεόν	really (cf. 8)
Οὖτις	Nobody; the name Odysseus gave when speaking to Polyphemus (< οὔτις, pron. "no one," "nobody"; οὐδείς was generally used only in prose)
ποδαπός (3)	(interrog.) from what country?
Ἴθακος (3)	(adj.) of Ithaca
Ἀποδρᾱσιππίδης, –ου, ὁ	(< ἀποδιδράσκω, run away + ἵππος, horse + –ιδης, "son of," *patronymic*) "Son of Runaway-horse"

LINE 186

οὖτι	(adv. acc. < οὔτις) in no way
χαίρω, χαιρήσω	enjoy, act with impunity (in neg. and in fut.: "you will not go unpunished," LSJ II; for idiom with ptcp. cf. *Ach.* 562, *Frogs* 843)
ὑφ-έλκω	pull, draw away from under (addressed to a slave)
θᾶττον	faster (cf. 180)
μιαρώτατος (3)	(superl. < μιαρός, cf. 39) Scoundrel! Skunk! (a "genuinely rude" insult: *LA* 186)
ἵνα	(adv. of place) where; (used with exclam.) what a place where
ὥστε	(conj.) so that, with the result that (with indic., of actual result: S #2274, cf. 2257–59)
ἔμοιγε	to me at least (the emphatic pron. ἐμοί strengthened by enclitic γε)
ἰνδάλλομαι	seem, appear. The verb is drawn from the vocabulary of epic; almost only used in pres. tense.
ὁμοιότατος (3)	(superl. < ὅμοιος, like, resembling) most similar to
κλητήρ, –ῆρος, ὁ	(< καλέω, call, summon) a summoner, or a witness who attests that a legal summons has been served; by extension, a braying donkey
πώλιον, τό	foal. By comic logic a κλητῆρος πώλιον is the animal offspring of a legal witness.

Φι.	εἰ μή μ᾽ ἐάϲεθ᾽ ἥϲυχον, μαχούμεθα.	190
Βδ.	περὶ τοῦ μαχεῖ νῷν δῆτα;	
Φι.	περὶ ὄνου ϲκιᾶϲ.	
Βδ.	πονηρὸϲ εἶ πόρρω τέχνηϲ καὶ παράβολοϲ.	
Φι.	ἐγὼ πονηρόϲ; οὐ μὰ Δί᾽, ἀλλ᾽ οὐκ οἶϲθα ϲὺ	
	νῦν μ᾽ ὄντ᾽ ἄριϲτον· ἀλλ᾽ ἴϲωϲ, ὅταν φάγῃϲ	
	ὑπογάϲτριον γέροντοϲ ἡλιαϲτικοῦ.	195
Βδ.	ὤθει τὸν ὄνον καὶ ϲαυτὸν εἰϲ τὴν οἰκίαν.	
Φι.	ὦ ξυνδικαϲταὶ καὶ Κλέων ἀμύνατε.	
Βδ.	ἔνδον κέκραχθι τῆϲ θύραϲ κεκλημένηϲ.	

LINE 190

μ᾽	= με
ἐάω, ἐάσω	allow (εἰ + fut. indic. + fut. indic. apodosis: FMV or "Emotional Future" condit., often conveying a threat or warning: S #2328)
ἥσυχος (3)	quiet
μάχομαι, μαχοῦμαι	fight {> titano*machy*}
τοῦ	= τίνος (interrog.)
νῷν	(gen. and dat. dual, 1 person pron.) evidently referring to Bdel. and Xanthias
δῆτα	"About what, <u>then</u>, will you fight?"; in quests. arising from something just said (cf. 24)
σκιά, ἡ	shadow. Phil. repeats a common proverb: a donkey's shadow is worthless; the previous twenty-five lines may have been simply leading up to this punchline. {> *squirrel* < σκιά, shadowy + οὐρά, tail}

LINE 192

πονηρός (3)	(< πόνος, toil) toilsome; worthless, good for nothing {> geo*ponic*}
πόρρω	(adv., with gen.) far advanced in; far from
τέχνη, ἡ	skill; πόρρω τέχνης = "a past master" (cf. 176)
παράβολος, -ον	(< παρα-βάλλω, throw beside, expose) exposing oneself, reckless
οἶσθα μ᾽ ὄντα	"you know that I am" (ptcp. used in ind. statement after vbs. of knowing and showing: S #2106)
ἔφαγον	(used as aor.² of ἐσθίω) eat, devour {> eso*phagus*}
ὑπογαστήριον, τό	(< γαστήρ, belly) belly of seafish; a choice cut {> *gastro-*} Phil. is saying that if Bdel. were, like Poyphemus, to taste the flesh of this man under a donkey's belly, he would find it was high-quality meat.
ἡλιαστικός (3)	of a juror in the Eliaea courtroom (cf. 88, 206)

LINE 196

σαυτόν	= σεαυτόν: S #329
οἰκία, ἡ	house, home {> *diocese, economy, paro*chial (> *parish*)} [< IE *weik-*, clan, abode; cogn. L. *villa, vicus*]
ἀμύνω, ἤμῡνα	keep off; help
ἔνδον	within (cf. 70)
κράζω, κέκρᾱγα	(> perf. act. impv. 2 sing. κέκρᾱχθι) cry, screech; "go ahead and shout" (for –μι forms using aor. personal endings: S #698) [< *onomatopoeia*]
κλήω, κέκλημαι	(> perf. mid./pass. ptcp. κεκλημένης) close (gen. abs.: S #2070)

ὤθει cὺ πολλοὺς τῶν λίθων πρὸς τὴν θύραν,
καὶ τὴν βάλανον ἔμβαλλε πάλιν εἰc τὸν μοχλόν,   200
καὶ τήν δοκὸν προσθεὶc τὸν ὅλμον τὸν μέγαν
ἀνύcαc τι προσκύλιcον.

Ξα.   οἴμοι δείλαιοc·
πόθεν ποτ' ἐμπέπτωκέ μοι τὸ βωλίον;

Βδ.   ἴcωc ἄνωθεν μῦc ἐνέβαλέ cοί ποθεν.

Ξα.   μῦc; οὐ μὰ Δί', ἀλλ' ὑποδυόμενόc τιc οὑτοcὶ   205
ὑπὸ τῶν κεραμίδων ἡλιαcτὴc ὀροφίαc.

Βδ.   οἴμοι κακοδαίμων, cτροῦθοc ἀνὴρ γίγνεται·
ἐκπτήcεται. ποῦ ποῦ 'cτί μοι τὸ δίκτυον;

LINE 199

πολύς, πολλή, πολύ	much, many (with part. gen.: LSJ II.1)
πρός	direction toward, against (with acc.)
βάλανος, ὁ	pin. Cf. B-O, here and at 154–55, for a full description of the bar and pin mechanism.
μοχλός, ὁ	bar (cf. 113)

LINE 201

δοκός, ἡ	board, wooden plank to be placed against the door (evidently = the μοχλός)
προσ-τίθημι, -έθηκα	(> aor.² act. ptcp. προσθείς) apply, add on
ὅλμος, ὁ	round stone, millstone
τι	(adv. acc.; S #2062) in any way, at all
προσ-κυλίνδω, –εκύλῑσα	(> aor. act. impv. 2 sing. προσκύλιcον) roll to, roll up
πόθεν	when, from where (interrog. with accent; contrast enclitic ποθεν below)
ἐμ-πίπτω, -πέπτωκα	fall on (cf. 120)
βωλίον, τό	lump of dirt

LINE 204

ἄνωθεν	(< ἀνά up + –θεν, suffix denoting place whence: S #342) from above, from on high
μῦς, μυός, ὁ	mouse or rat; any small rodent (cf. 140)
ποθεν	(adv., enclitic) from somewhere
ὑπο-δύω	(> pres. mid. ptcp. ὑποδῡόμενος) "slip under" in mid. (cf. 182)
τις	can be used euphemistically of particular person whom one wishes to avoid naming, or of someone bad: LSJ A.II.3
κεραμίς, –ίδος, ἡ	(< κέραμος, potter's clay, tiles of baked clay) roof tile {>*ceramic*}
ἡλιαστής, –οῦ, ὁ	juror in the Eliaea court (cf. 88)
ὀροφίας, –ου, ὁ	(< ὀροφή, roof) living under a roof

LINE 207

στρουθός, ὁ, ἡ	sparrow. For the use of γίγνεται to describe metamorphoses, cf. 48.
ἀνήρ	= ὁ ἀνήρ
ἐκ-πέτομαι,-πτήσομαι	
	fly out (for the *syncope* of the fut. [shift from πετ- to πτ-], cf. 16 on aor.)
ποῦ	(interrog. adv.) Where? Note repetition, conveying excitement or haste.
'στί	= ἐστί, by *aphaeresis*

coῦ, coῦ, πάλιν, coῦ. νὴ Δί' ἤ μοι κρεῖττον ἦν
τηρεῖν Cκιώνην ἀντὶ τούτου τοῦ πατρóc.   210

Ξα.   ἄγε νυν, ἐπειδὴ τουτονὶ cεcοβήκαμεν,
κοὐκ ἔcθ' ὅπωc διαδὺc ἂν ἡμᾶc ἔτι λάθοι,
τί οὐκ ἀπεκοιμήθημεν ὅcον ὅcον cτίλην;

LINE 209

coῦ coῦ	(< cεύω, drive) Shoo! Shoo!
ἤ	(particle) "Really"; "Yes, I really should!"; affirmative, strengthens the oath νὴ Δί': S #281 and *GP* 280, 584
κρείττων, –ον, –ονοc	(< κρατύc, strong, though used as comparative of ἀγαθόc) better, stronger {> -*cracy*} [< IE **kar*-, hard; cogn. E. *hard*; cf. κάρυον, 58]
ἦν κρεῖττον	"it would be better" (ἄν can be omitted with the imperfect indic. in impers. expressions denoting propriety or possibility: S #1774)
τηρέω	watch over, guard (inf. as subject of impers. expression: S #1984)
Cκιώνη, ἡ	Scione, a city in the Chalcidice peninsula that had rebelled from the Athenians and was being besieged at the time of the performance of *W.* If Bdel. would rather be at Scione, guarding Phil. must be a grim chore indeed.
ἀντί	(prep. + gen.) instead of (an alternative to the more common comparative using ἤ, "than")

LINE 211

ἄγε νυν	"come now" (though sing., the verb is usually used with pl., "as if an adv.": Graves)
ἐπειδή	(causal conj. < ἐπεί and δή, cf. S #2240) since, seeing that
coβέω, cεcόβηκα	drive off, shoo away, make to go away (one of a class of *causative* vbs. using –εω: Sihler #456b); often used of animals
κοὐκ	= καὶ οὐκ
ἔcθ'	= ἔcτι, *orthotone*
οὐκ ἔcθ' ὅπωc	"it is not possible that" (often followed by fut. indic., sometimes opt. with or without ἄν; ἄν is not used after the positive form ἔcθ' ὅπωc: S #2551–52 & 2515). *Hiatus* is often avoided by using ν-moveable (S #134), but in poetry the final vowel of ἔcτι is lost by *elision*; the aspirate of the following ὅπωc necessitates changing ἔcτ' to ἔcθ': S # 124.
δια-δύω, aor.² διέδῦν	(> aor.² act. ptcp. διαδύc) slip away, evade (for conjugation of this aor.: S #418)
λανθάνω, aor.² ἔλαθον	(< λήθη, forgetfulness, cf. 14) escape notice; διαδὺc ἂν ἡμᾶc λάθοι, "he evaded us by stealth" (with suppl. ptcp.: S #2096), cf. 14
ἀπο-κοιμάομαι, -εκοιμήθην	(ἀπό, implying relief from toil + κοιμάω, put to sleep) get a little sleep (used of troops on duty). The aor. following a quest. introduced by τί οὐκ indicates surprise at something that has not been done: S #1936. {> *cemetery*} (cf. 142)
ὅcον ὅcον	"only just"; doubled ὅcον only here in Attic Greek; Starkie suggests Xanthias is yawning (cf. 125)
cτίλη, ἡ	a drop; a moment (acc. of extent of time: S #1582). An expression of minimal quantity, often spoken by unpretentious speakers like slaves: *LA* 181

Βδ.　　　　ἀλλ', ὦ πόνηρ', ἥξουϲιν ὀλίγον ὕϲτερον
　　　　　　οἱ ξυνδικαϲταὶ παρακαλοῦντεϲ τουτονὶ　　　　　　　　　215
　　　　　　τὸν πατέρα.
Ξα.　　　　　　　　　　τί λέγειϲ; ἀλλὰ νῦν γ' ὄρθροϲ βαθύϲ.
Βδ.　　　　νὴ τὸν Δί', ὀψέ γ' ἄρ' ἀνεϲτήκαϲι νῦν.
　　　　　　ὡϲ ἀπὸ μέϲων νυκτῶν γε παρακαλοῦϲ' ἀεί,
　　　　　　λύχνουϲ ἔχοντεϲ καὶ μινυρίζοντεϲ μέλη
　　　　　　ἀρχαιομελιϲιδωνοφρυνιχήρατα,　　　　　　　　　　　　220

LINE 214

ἥκω, ἥξω	to have come, be present (properly ἥκω is perf.; thus ἥξω fut. perf., "I shall have come" = "I shall be present")
ὀλίγοϲ (3)	little {> oligarchy}
ὕϲτεροϲ (3)	later (ὕϲτερον, like ὀλίγον, is adv. acc.)
παρα-καλέω, -καλῶ	call on, summon (fut. ptcp. to express purpose: S #2065)

LINE 216

ἀλλὰ νῦν γε	"<Perhaps they may call later on,> but *now* ..."; γε marks *ellipsis*: S #2627
ὄρθροϲ, ὁ	dawn, the twilight before dawn
βαθύϲ, –εῖα, –ύ	deep; far-advanced; "<u>very early</u> dawn"

LINE 217

ὀψέ	(adv.) after a long time; late
ἄρα	"It just hit me!" "Now I realize"; although usually used in quests., ἄρα, like ἆρα, can mark a realization of a truth: GP 45, S #2800 (cf. 4)
ἀν-ίϲτημι	(> perf. ἀνεϲτήκᾱϲι) rise, get out of bed (intrans. in perf. tense)
ὡϲ	(conj.) since, because (explaining previous sentence: S # 3000, LSJ B.IV)
ἀπό	(prep.) from; <u>after</u>: S #1684b
μέϲοϲ	(3) middle {> meso-}
ὡϲ ... γε	"They are calling on him from the *middle of the night*"; γε focuses attention on the preceding words: GP 143.
μινυρίζω	(< μινυρόϲ, whimpering or chirping + –ίζω, suffix for *denominative* verb) sing in low, soft tone; hum; warble
μέλοϲ, –εοϲ, τό	song; used of lyric or choral songs, not of epic or dramatic verse [< IE *mel-, limb, member; "connected melody"]

ἀρχαιομελιϲῑδωνοφρῡνιχήρατα

　　　　(< ἄρχαιοϲ, ancient; μελί, honey; Ϲῑδών, Sidon; Φρύνιχοϲ, Phrynichus, a tragic poet of earlier fifth century who had written a *Phoenissae* about women of Sidon; –ήρατοϲ, lovely) "old, sweet, lovely Sidonian (songs) of Phrynichus." Preposterously long compound words like this were an Aristophanic trademark, the longest being *Ecclesiazusae* 1169–75; on Ar.'s creativity in forming compounds: *LA* 124–25. The lyrical meter at 273–89 appears to mimic the style of Phrynichus, who is the "argumentative heart" (B-O) of the word. This puts us on notice that the chorus will have old-fashioned tastes.

οἷc ἐκκαλοῦνται τοῦτον.

Ξα.   οὐκοῦν, ἢν δέῃ,
ἤδη ποτ' αὐτοὺς τοῖc λίθοιc βαλλήcομεν.

Βδ.   ἀλλ', ὦ πόνηρε, τὸ γένος ἤν τιc ὀργίcῃ
τὸ τῶν γερόντων, ἔcθ' ὅμοιον cφηκιᾷ.
ἔχουcι γὰρ καὶ κέντρον ἐκ τῆc ὀcφύοc   225
ὀξύτατον, ᾧ κεντοῦcι, καὶ κεκραγότεc
πηδῶcι καὶ βάλλουcιν ὥcπερ φέψαλοι.

Ξα.   μὴ φροντίcῃc· ἐὰν ἐγὼ λίθουc ἔχω,
πολλῶν δικαcτῶν cφηκιὰν διαcκεδῶ.

LINE 221

οἷς — dat. of means

ἐκ-καλέω — call forth, summon out (in mid., as often)

οὐκοῦν — therefore, accordingly; <u>surely, then</u> (< οὐκ + οὖν, but unlike οὔκουν, e.g., 47, the neg. force has been lost; this is the only instance of οὐκοῦν in *W.*)

δέῃ — it is necessary, one must (pres. subjv. of δεῖ in FMV condit.: S #2323)

ἤδη ποτ' — at once, right away (ποτε adds emphasis to an adv. of time: MacD.)

βάλλω, βαλλήσω — throw; strike, hit (with acc. of person aimed at). The more common fut. βαλῶ would eventually drive βαλλήσω out of the Greek language: *LA* 250; Ar. used it for continued action: S p. 689.

LINE 223

γένος, –ους, τό — race, tribe

ἤν — = ἐάν (Pres. Gen. condit.: ἤν/ἐάν + subjv., pres. indic. apodosis: S #2336)

σφηκιά, ἡ — (< σφήξ, wasp) wasps' nest (note similar ending of other animal names: μύρμηξ, ant; σκώληξ, worm)

LINE 225

κέντρον, τό — goad, stinger (Starkie points to the force of the καί: "they have a *sting*!") {> center, amnio*centesis*}

ὀσφῦς, –ύος, ἡ — lower back, rump. A stinger was attached to the rump of the costume.

ὀξύτατος (3) — very sharp (an *absolute superlative*; not compared with other stingers: S #1085) {> oxygen, *Oxy*Contin}

κράζω — (< perf. act. ptcp. κεκρᾱγότες) clamor; "buzz" (intensive perf. denoting an ongoing action, e.g., of a sustained sound: S #1947)

πηδάω — jump around

φέψαλος, ὁ — spark

LINE 228

φροντίζω, ἐφρόντισα — consider, worry about (cf. 25)

δια-σκεδάννῡμι, –σκεδῶ — scatter, disperse

ἐὰν ἔχω, διασκεδῶ — FMV condit.: S #2323. B-O identify the danger: "Wasps' nests were best destroyed by fire, since the smoke made the insects sluggish ... whereas stones are likely to provoke an attack."

ΧΟΡΟΣ

χώρει, πρόβαιν' ἐρρωμένως. ὦ Κωμία, βραδύνεις.   230
μὰ τὸν Δί' οὐ μέντοι πρὸ τοῦ γ', ἀλλ' ἦσθ' ἱμὰς κύνειος·
νυνὶ δὲ κρείττων ἐστί σου Χαρινάδης βαδίζειν.

LINE 230

230–72. The Parodos (πάροδος), the first entrance of the chorus. Bdel. and Xanthias have moved back against the front of the house and have fallen asleep, waking up again only at 394. The chorus, composed of twenty-four old jurors, enter. They are accompanied by several young boys, their sons, who are carrying lamps. The chorus are dressed to resemble wasps, with stingers protruding from their rear ends, though the stingers are only visible when they remove their cloaks at 408. The leader of the chorus shares memories of military campaigns decades earlier and briefly talks with his son about trimming the lamp.

230–47: Meter: iambic tetrameters catalectic (see appendix D), a meter that has few *resolutions* and imparts the feel of a steady but lumbering gait. Ar. generally uses this meter when a chorus composed of old men enters.

Χόρος, ὁ	Chorus
χωρέω	move forward, move on
προ-βαίνω	step forward {> basis, acro*bat*}
ἐρρωμένως	(adv. < perf. pass. ptcp. of ῥώννῦμι, strengthen) stoutly, vigorously
Κωμίας, –ου, ὁ	(< κῶμος, revelry, the same root as κωμῳδία, *comedy*) name of a chorus member. The names given here were rare in Athens but not complete comic fabrications.
βραδύνω	(< βραδύς, slow) delay, walk slowly. This first line of the chorus has the greatest number of long syllables permitted in iambic tetrameters, imparting a sense of a measured pace.

LINE 231

μέντοι	"Really, you know"; emphatic: "μέν denotes objective certainty, while τοι brings the truth home to another person": *GP* 399; often associated with prons. σύ, οὗτος, τοιοῦτος; so also at 426; but B-O suggest it is *adversative*, "and yet": *GP* 405, 409
πρὸ τοῦ	before this, <u>earlier</u>: "<You weren't so slow> earlier"; on πρό: S #1694b; on the use of the art. as demonstrative pron.: *LA* 255
γ'	= γε; emphatic, following πρὸ τοῦ: *GP* 405
εἰμί	> imperfect indic. 2 sing. ἦσθα
ἱμάς, ἱμάντος, ὁ	leather strap, thong, leash
κύνειος (3)	(< κύων, dog, cf. 83) of a dog; a "dog's leash" might imply that Komias used to be tough and supple
νῦνί	(adv.) now, at this very moment (stronger than νῦν: S #2925), cf. 30
σοῦ	(pron., gen. of ἐγώ) than you (gen. of comparison: S #1402)
Χαρινάδης, –ου, ὁ	(< χάρις, favor, gratitude + –αδης, *patronymic* suffix: S #845) the name of a chorus member, apparently known for being a slow walker
βαδίζειν	walk (*epexegetical* inf., further defining the meaning of adj. κρείττων: S #2001–2)

ὦ Cτρυμόδωρε Κονθυλεῦ, βέλτιcτε cυνδικαcτῶν,
Εὐεργίδηc ἆρ' ἐcτί που 'νταῦθ' ἢ Χάβηc ὁ Φλυεύc;
πάρεcθ' ὃ δὴ λοιπόν γ' ἔτ' ἐcτίν, ἀππαπαῖ παπαιάξ,   235
ἥβηc ἐκείνηc, ἡνίκ' ἐν Βυζαντίῳ ξυνῆμεν
φρουροῦντ' ἐγώ τε καὶ cύ· κᾆτα περιπατοῦντε νύκτωρ
τῆc ἀρτοπώλιδοc λαθόντ' ἐκλέψαμεν τὸν ὅλμον,

LINE 233

Cτρυμόδωρος, ὁ	(< Cτρυμών, a river in Thrace + δῶρον, gift) name of chorus member
Κονθυλεύς, –έως	(adj.) of the *deme* Konthyle, in eastern Attica
βέλτιστος (3)	best (a superl. of ἀγαθός: S #319) [< IE *bel-, strong; cogn. L. debilis (with de- priv.); Russian Bolshevik < Bolshoi (large)]
cυνδικαστής	The ξ- of ξυν-, a double consonant, would necessitate an inconvenient metrical lengthening of the final syllable of βέλτιστε; hence edd. read cυν- (contra 197, 215).
Εὐεργίδης, –ου, ὁ	(> εὖ, good, well + ἔργον, deed + –ιδης, *patronymic* suffix) "Son of Do-Good," name of an absent fellow juror
ἄρα	in quests. (cf. 4)
που 'νταῦθ'	= που ἐνταῦθα, somewhere around here (*prodelision* or *aphaeresis*: S #76)
Χάβης, –ου, ὁ	(perhaps < χαβός, bent) name of an absent fellow juror
Φλυεύς, –έως	(adj.) of the *deme* Phlya, five miles outside the city

LINE 235

πάρ-ειμι	(> pres. 3 sing. πάρεσθ') be present
ὃ δή	"the very thing which"; δή following a rel. pron. emphasizes the antecedent, calling attention to something regretfully well known: *GP* 218–19
ἀππαπαῖ παπαιάξ	"oh my!" "alas!" (exclam., here of sorrow; the "sounds represent the mumbling of the toothless old men": Graves); the interjection interrupts the syntax of the sentence (λοιπόν . . . ἥβης).
ἥβη, ἡ	youth, youthful vigor {> eph*ebe*}
ἡνίκα	(conj.) when, at the moment when (used with indic., more precise than ὅτε: S #2383 n.2)
Βυζάντιον, τό	Byzantium, the Greek colony. Athenians joined Spartans in recapturing Byzantium from the Persians in 478 BC.
ξύν-ειμι	(> imperfect 1 pl. ξυνῆμεν) be together (accent is not recessive beyond augment: S #426)
φρουρέω	(< φρουρός, guard < πρό + οὖρος, watcher > pres. act. ptcp. dual φρουροῦντε) keep guard. The first of three dual ptcps.; B-O point out that we should imagine two old comrades-in-arms reminiscing.
τε καὶ	both . . . and (τε may be redundant, but binds the two elements together and emphasizes parallelism; it also inserts a metrically short syllable: *GP* 511–12)
κᾆτα	= καὶ εἶτα
περι-πατέω	(< πάτος, path) walk up and down, pace {> peri*patetic*}
νύκτωρ	(adv.) at night (cf. 123)
ἀρτόπωλις, –ιδος, ἡ	(ἄρτος, bread + πωλέω, sell + –ις, –ιδος suffix indicating fem. agency: S #839b1) bread woman {> mono*poly*}
λανθάνω, aor.² ἔλαθον	escape notice (LSJ A.2; λαθόντε as circumstantial ptcp. of manner, "secretly," reversing usual suppl. ptcp. construction: S #2062a; contrast 212)
ὅλμος, ὁ	kneading bowl (cf. 201). That they take pride in having stolen the bread woman's bowl alerts us to their roguish self-image.

κᾷθ᾽ ἤψομεν τοῦ κορκόρου κατασχίσαντες αὐτόν.
ἀλλ᾽ ἐγκονῶμεν, ὤνδρες, ὡς ἔσται Λάχητι νυνί·
σίμβλον δέ φασι χρημάτων ἔχειν ἅπαντες αὐτόν.
χθὲς οὖν Κλέων ὁ κηδεμὼν ἡμῖν ἐφεῖτ᾽ ἐν ὥρᾳ
ἥκειν ἔχοντας ἡμερῶν ὀργὴν τριῶν πονηρὰν
ἐπ᾽ αὐτόν, ὡς κολωμένους ὧν ἠδίκησεν. ἀλλὰ

240

LINE 239

κᾷθ᾽	= καὶ εἶτα (with *elision* and -θ᾽ preceding aspirated ἤψ-)
ἕψω	boil, cook (temporal augment for imperfect ἤψομεν: S #435)
κόρκορος, ὁ	pimpernel (usually spelled κόρχορος; part. gen. S #1341: "boil <u>some</u> pimpernel"); pimpernel is barely edible and boiling it would be a sign of desperation.
κατα-σχίζω, -έσχισα	split up {> *schizo-*, *schism*}
αὐτόν	= the kneading bowl, which was made of wood and useful as firewood

LINE 240

ἀλλά	"[Never mind that]—but let's hurry"; speaker leaves off his thought to give an order: *GP* 13–15
ἐγ-κονέω	(< κονέω, raise dust < κόνις, dust) be quick (hort. subjv.: S #1797)
ὤνδρες	= ὦ ἄνδρες
ὡς	(conj., causal) because, since
εἰμί, ἔσομαι	(> fut. 3 sing. ἔσται) be; "There will be <trouble> for Laches" (*ellipsis* of pred.) One would expect the form to be ἔσεται but for *syncope*: Sihler #80.
Λάχης, –ητος, ὁ	Laches, an Athenian general and political adversary of Cleon (Λάχητι dat. disadvantage: S #1481; idiomatic: "Laches will get it today.") To judge from this passage and the mock trial in *W.*, Laches was prosecuted, or threatened with prosecution, for corruption in the wake of a failed expedition to Sicily in 427. He was killed at Mantineia in 418. Like Phil., the chorus members are bent on convicting him.
σίμβλος, ὁ	beehive, hoard
φημί	say (introduces ind. statement, governing acc. + inf.: S #2016; αὐτόν is Laches)

LINE 242

χθές	(adv.) yesterday
Κλέων	cf. 62
κηδεμών, –όνος, ὁ	(< κήδομαι, care for + suffix –ων of persons possessing some physical or mental quality: S #861.18) protector, guardian, patron
ἐφ-ίημι	(> aor. mid. indic. 3 sing. ἐφεῖτο) send, incite; (mid.) command (+ dat. + inf.). The command is given to "us" (ἡμῖν, dat.), but the construction shifts and the acc. ptcp. ἔχοντας (sc. ἡμᾶς) is the subject of inf. ἥκειν.
ἐν ὥρᾳ	in good time, in due time
τρεῖς, τρία	three. Citizen soldiers were typically ordered to bring three days' rations for an expedition.
ἐπί	against (+ acc. to indicate hostility: S #1689.3d)
ὡς	with ptcp., indicates what was intended by the subject: S #2086
κολάζω, κολῶμαι	punish (takes gen. object of the crime: S #1375): "to punish Laches for gen." (The fut. ptcp. denotes purpose: S #2065. κολάσομαι was the usual fut. mid. in Attic, but yielded ground to contracted futs. like κολῶμαι: *LA* 249)
ὧν	the object of the verb ἠδίκησεν should properly be the acc. ἅ, but it has been attracted into gen., the case of the obj. of κολωμένους: S #2522

cπεύcωμεν, ὤνδρεc ἥλικεc, πρὶν ἡμέραν γενέcθαι.   245
χωρῶμεν, ἅμα τε τῷ λύχνῳ πάντῃ διαcκοπῶμεν,
μή που λίθοc τιc ἐμποδὼν ἡμᾶc κακόν τι δράcῃ.

ΠΑΙC

ὤ.
τὸν πηλόν, ὦ πάτερ πάτερ, τουτονὶ φύλαξαι.
Χο.   κάρφοc χαμᾶθέν νυν λαβὼν τὸν λύχνον πρόβυcον.
Πα.   οὔκ, ἀλλὰ τῳδί μοι δοκῶ τὸν λύχνον προβύcειν.   250

LINE 245

σπεύδω, ἔσπευσα	urge on; hurry (hort. subjv.)
ἧλιξ, –ικος, ὁ, ἡ	of same age, comrade
πρὶν ἡμέραν γενέσθαι	
	before it gets to be day (a nice illustration of the rule that the aor. refers to the past only in the indic.: the inf. here clearly refers to the fut.; what counts is the aspect: S #1865; aor. inf. is standard in πρίν cls.: S #2453.c)
ἅμα	(adv.) at the same time; (as prep., with dat.) together with
τε	and (as conj., joining two cls.: χωρῶμεν . . . διασκοπῶμεν)
πάντῃ	(adv.) in every way, in every direction
δια-σκοπέω	examine, consider well; look about (hort. subjv.)
μή	in case; lest (διασκοπῶμεν in effect introduces a fear clause, cf. 109)
ἐμποδών	(adv. < ἐν + πούς, ποδός, foot) at the feet, in the way {> *podium*, octo*pus*, *-pod*}
δράω	make, do (governs two accs. here) {> *drama*, *drastic*}

LINE 248

248–72: Meter: iambic tetrameters syncopated (also called "Euripideans"). The loss of a syllable by *syncope* results in a slight increase in tempo over the previous meter, coinciding with when the boy speaks up. The boy is unlikely to be a member of the chorus. There seem to be several boys (pl. ἡμᾶς, 254) who leave the stage at 258.

ὤ	(interj.) "Oh!" "Hey!" (Note that this is extrametrical.)
πηλός, ὁ	mud {> *polio*myelitis}
φυλάττω	(> aor. mid. impv. 2 sing. φύλαξαι) guard; (mid.) be on guard for, watch out for, avoid
κάρφος, –εος, τό	stick, twig, chip of wood. Another expression of minimal quantity, used in Ar. by unpretentious persons: *LA* 181 (cf. 213). Indeed, this passage is significant for showing the poverty of the members of the chorus.
χαμᾶθεν	(χαμαί, on the ground, cf. 43 + –θεν, suffix denoting place whence: S #342) from the ground
λαμβάνω, aor.² ἔλαβον	
	take (aor. ptcp. λαβών almost like a prep. meaning "with": *LA* 256)
προ-βύω, -βύσω	push up [wick of lamp] (cf. 128)

LINE 250

ἀλλά	"No—instead I'll . . ."; objecting to a previous speaker: *GP* 7
ὁδί, ἡδί, τοδί	this one here (*deictic* iota, cf. 55; with τῳδί sc. δακτύλῳ)

Χο. τί δὴ μαθὼν τῷ δακτύλῳ τὴν θρυαλλίδ' ὠθεῖς,
   καὶ ταῦτα τοὐλαίου cπανίζοντος, ὠνόητε;
   οὐ γὰρ δάκνει c', ὅταν δέῃ τίμιον πρίαcθαι.

Πα. εἰ νὴ Δί' αὖθις κονδύλοιc νουθετήcεθ' ἡμᾶc,
   ἀποcβέcαντεc τοὺc λύχνουc ἄπιμεν οἴκαδ' αὐτοί·   255
   κἄπειτ' ἴcωc ἐν τῷ cκότῳ τουτουὶ cτερηθεὶc
   τὸν πηλὸν ὥcπερ ἀτταγᾶc τυρβάcειc βαδίζων.

LINE 251

δή	"What *ever* induced you . . ."; follows interrogs.: *GP* 210
μανθάνω, aor.² ἔμαθον	
	learn (τί μάθων = "having learned what?" = "what induced you to . . .?": S #2064a) {> *mathematics*}
δάκτυλος, ὁ	finger. Trimming wick with the finger burns oil more quickly.
θρυαλλίς, –ίδος, ἡ	wick of lamp
καὶ ταῦτα	"and at that" ("adding a circumstance heightening the force of what has been said," LSJ s.v. οὗτος C.VIII.2)
ἔλαιον, ὁ	(< ἐλάα, olive tree) olive oil
cπανίζω	(< cπάνιc, scarcity) be rare, scarce (ἐλαίου cπανίζοντος, gen. abs.: S #2070)
ἀνόητος, –ον	ὠνόητε = ὦ ἀνόητε (< ἀ- priv. + νοῦς, sense) unintelligent, foolish, "you fool"
δάκνω	bite; cause worry
δέῃ	it is necessary (cf. 221)
τίμιος (3)	valued, honored; <u>costly</u> (cf. 106)
ὠνέομαι, ἐπριάμην	buy (Attic uses ἐπριάμην as aor. of ὠνέομαι)

LINE 254

αὖθις	in turn, on the other hand (cf. 61)
κόνδυλος, ὁ	knuckle [etymology debated, but cf. other body words: δάκτυλος, σφόνδυλος (vertebra), 1489]
ἀπο-σβέννῡμι, –έσβεσα	
	extinguish, put out {> *asbestos*}
ἄπ-ειμι	(> pres. indic. 1 pl. ἄπιμεν) go (indic. serves as fut.: "we will go"). The burst of re-solved short syllables (ἄπῐμἔν) suggests speed.
οἴκαδε	(< οἶκος, home + –δε, suffix denoting place whither: S #342) to home, homeward
αὐτός	by myself, alone (LSJ I.3)
εἰ νουθετήσετε . . . ἄπιμεν	
	(FMV condit.; for threat conveyed, cf. 190)
κἄπειτ'	= καὶ ἔπειτα
σκότος, ὁ	darkness {> *scotophobia*} [< IE *skot-, dark; cogn. E. *shade*, *shadow*]
τουτουί	the reference is to the lamp. Diphthong -ου- before *deictic* -ί is scanned short; cf. 262, 807
στερέω, aor. pass. ἐστερήθην	
	deprive; (pass.) deprived of (+ gen.)
ὥσπερ	like, just as
ἀτταγᾶς, –ᾶ, ὁ	a bird, perhaps a partridge; known for frequenting marshes
τυρβάζω, τυρβάσω	(< τύρβη, confusion) trouble, stir up

Χο.   ἦ μὴν ἐγώ cου χἀτέρουc μείζοναc κολάζω.
ἀλλ' οὑτοcί μοι βόρβοροc φαίνεται πατοῦντι·
κοὐκ ἔcθ' ὅπωc οὐχ ἡμερῶν τεττάρων τὸ πλεῖcτον   260
ὕδωρ ἀναγκαίωc ἔχει τὸν θεὸν ποιῆcαι.
ἔπειcι γοῦν τοῖcιν λύχνοιc οὑτοιὶ μύκητεc·
φιλεῖ δ', ὅταν τοῦτ' ᾖ, ποιεῖν ὑετὸν μάλιcτα.
δεῖται δὲ καὶ τῶν καρπίμων ἅττα μή 'cτι πρῷα
ὕδωρ γενέcθαι κἀπιπνεῦcαι βόρειον αὐτοῖc.   265

LINE 258

ἦ μήν	"I warn you"; "I'll have you know"; pcls. used esp. in oaths and pledges, introducing "a strong and confident asseveration": *GP* 350
cου	gen. of comparison with μείζοναc
χἀτέρουc	= καὶ ἑτέρουc (καί = "even," "also")
μείζων, –ον, –ονοc	(< comparative of μέγαc) greater, bigger
κολάζω	punish (cf. 244). The other punished victims must be defendants in court.
βόρβοροc, ὁ	mud
φαίνομαι	appear, seem to be (cf. 124)
πατέω	tread, walk (cf. 237)
κοὐκ ἔcθ' ὅπωc	"it's not possible that" (cf. 211)
τέτταρες, –α	four (ἡμερῶν τεττάρων, gen. of time within which: S #1444) [< IE *k^wetwer-, four; cogn. L. *quattuor*; E. *four*]
πλεῖcτοc (3)	(< superl. of πολύc) most, greatest; (adv. acc.) <u>at the most</u>
ὕδωρ, –ατοc, τό	water, <u>rain</u> (acc. object of ποιῆcαι); cf. 126
ἔχω	(transitive.) have; (intrans.) hold oneself, be; with adv. of manner ἀναγκαίωc = "it is necessary": S #1438
ποιέω, ἐποίηcα	make, produce. Some editors here print ποῆcαι; by *correption*, the diphthong -οι- would be considered short anyway when followed by a vowel. {> *poetic*}

LINE 262

ἔπ-ειμι	be set upon, be attached to (+ dat., LSJ B.II.2)
γοῦν	(< γε + οὖν) "At any rate," "For instance," "At least"; introduces evidence for preceding statement: "It looks like rain." "Yes—at least, there is fungus": *GP* 451–52
μύκηc, –ητοc, ὁ	mushroom; excresence, fungus, mold; snuff of lamp-wick
φιλέω	love, love to do (+ inf.).
ὅταν	that is, <u>whenever</u> there is fungus
ὑετόc, ὁ	rain
δέομαι	need (+ inf.; sc. subject "whichever of those crops")
κάρπιμοc, –ον	fruit-bearing (τὰ κάρπιμα are "crops"; part. gen. with ἅττα)
ἅττα	whatever, whichever (nt. pl. nom. of ὅcτιc, ἥτιc, ὅ τι, also spelled ἅτινα: S #339)
μή	in rel. clauses with indef. antecedent: S #2705d
'cτι	= ἐcτι (nt. pl. ἅττα is subject of sing. verb)
πρῷοc (3)	early in the season
ἐπι-πνέω, -έπνευcα	blow upon {> *pneuma-, apnea*}
βόρειοc (3)	of the North wind {> *Hyperboreans*, "living beyond the mountains"}

τί χρῆμ᾽ ἄρ᾽ οὐκ τῆς οἰκίας τῆσδε συνδικαστὴς
πέπονθεν, ὡς οὐ φαίνεται δεῦρο πρὸς τὸ πλῆθος;
οὐ μὴν πρὸ τοῦ γ᾽ ἐφολκὸς ἦν, ἀλλὰ πρῶτος ἡμῶν
ἡγεῖτ᾽ ἂν ᾄδων Φρυνίχου· καὶ γάρ ἐστιν ἀνὴρ

LINE 266

Note that Biles & Olson follow an earlier suggestion that lines 266–89 be moved and inserted after line 316. The arguments in favor of this transposition are persuasive: the conversation with the boys (290–316) makes more sense if it precedes the approach to the house (266–89), and the mix-up can be explained as a misplacement of a single page in the ms. tradition. Although the present edition follows the OCT, which has the traditional order of lines, future translators and directors should consider adopting this change. (That said, a logical and unified plot has never been considered one of Ar.'s strong points, and readers need to be prepared to make mental adjustments for discontinuities.)

χρῆμα, –ατος, τό	thing, matter; τί χρῆμα = "what?"
ἄρα	"What <u>on earth</u> has happened . . . ?"; adds liveliness and anxiety to a quest.: S #2793 (cf. 143). The chorus leader now turns his attention to Phil.'s absence, and the plot can finally proceed.
οὐκ	= ὁ ἐκ (the prep. phrase is in the attributive position, between the art. ὁ and noun συνδικαστής)
ὡς	since, because, seeing that (prob. causal conj. with indic., but see S #3001; B-O read ὥστε)
δεῦρο	"to [come hither and] appear here" ("in pregn. sense with vbs. of rest": LSJ I)
πλῆθος, –ους, τό	the crowd, throng (of fellow jurors)

LINE 268

οὐ μήν	"and yet . . . not"; an *adversative*, drawing a contrast with what precedes: *GP* 335
πρὸ τοῦ γ᾽	earlier (cf. 231)
ἐφολκός, –ον	(< ἐπί + ἕλκω, draw) drawing on; a laggard
ἡγέομαι	(> imperfect indic. 3 sing. ἡγεῖτο) lead {> hegemony, exegesis}
ἄν	"he always <u>used</u> to . . ." (with indic. expresses customary past action: S #1790)
Φρύνιχος	cf. 220 (gen. of possession, with *ellipsis* of, e.g., μέλος, song, as an obj. for ᾄδων)
καὶ γάρ	"for truly"; γάρ is explanatory; καί is not the conj. but the adv., "in fact," "truly": *GP* 108, S #2814–15
ἀνήρ	= ὁ ἀνήρ

φιλῳδός. ἀλλά μοι δοκεῖ στάντας ἐνθάδ᾽, ὦνδρες,   270
ᾄδοντας αὐτὸν ἐκκαλεῖν, ἤν τί πως ἀκούσας
τοὐμοῦ μέλους ὑφ᾽ ἡδονῆς ἑρπύσῃ θύραζε.
τί ποτ᾽ οὐ πρὸ θυρῶν φαίνετ᾽ ἄρ᾽ ἡμῖν ὁ γέρων οὐδ᾽ ὑπακούει;   [στρ.
μῶν ἀπολώλεκε τὰς

LINE 270

φιλῳδός, –ον	(< φίλος + ᾠδή, song) song-loving
ἀλλά	"Well, anyway"; breaking off reflections to announce a plan of action: *GP* 8
μοι δοκεῖ	it seems to me; it seems best = <u>we should</u>
ἵστημι	(> aor. act. ptcp. στάντας) stand
ἐνθάδε	(adv. < ἔνθα, here or there + –δε; despite the suffix, cf. S #342, this adv. rarely denotes motion) "here" or "there" depending on context
ὦνδρες	= ὦ ἄνδρες
ἐκ-καλέω	summon out (sc. ἡμᾶς as acc. subject of inf.)
ἤν	in case (note *ellipsis* of an implied apodosis, e.g., "<We will see him> if he crawls out," LSJ s.v. εἰ VII.1)
πως	(adv.) somehow (further qualified by enclitic τι)
ἀκούω, ἤκουσα	hear (+ gen. of person or thing heard: S #1361) {> *acoustic*}
τοὐμοῦ	= τοῦ ἐμοῦ (< adj. ἐμός) my, mine
ἡδονή, ἡ	pleasure {> *hedonism*}[< ἡδύς, sweet < IE *swad-, sweet; cogn. L. *suadeo*; E. *sweet*]
ὑφ᾽	= ὑπό (+ gen. indicating cause: S #1698b)
ἕρπω, εἵρπυσα	creep, crawl (*syllabic augment* in aor.: S #145) {> *herpes*}

LINE 273

273–89: The chorus wonder why Phil. has not come out; they urge him to get up and join them at the court.

273–89: Meter: ionics and dactyloepitrites. Until now the speaking parts could be described as chant or "*recitative*," neither prosaic everyday speech nor fully lyrical. A consistent feature is the ionic metron (◡◡−−), with many variations in the first half of a verse, including the possibility of scanning lines as dactylo-epitrites (−◡◡−◡◡−). This variety means that *response* between *strophe* (273–80) and *antistrophe* (281–89) is inexact, yet there is some art in it: Parker suggests that "this song aims to reproduce the elegant tragic style of Phrynichus, with which the content and diction would contrast to excellent comic effect" (p. 218).

τί	why? (adv. acc.; acute accent indicates interrog., though in this instance even an enclitic τι would receive an accent from the following enclitic ποτε: S #185)
ὑπ-ακούω	give ear to, comply, listen
μῶν	= μὴ οὖν, in quests. expecting neg. answer: S #2651
ἀπ-όλλῡμι, ἀπολώλεκα	destroy; lose. The perf. denotes "a completed action the effects of which still continue in the present": S #1945; thus the chorus suppose Phil. is now in a state of shoelessness. Yet ἀπολώλεκε is an also example of the transitive act. perf., which Ar. expanded and which in later centuries would encroach on the aor.: *LA* 126–33.

ἐμβάδας, ἢ προσέκοψ’ ἐν   275
τῷ cκότῳ τὸν δάκτυλόν που,
εἶτ’ ἐφλέγμηνεν αὑτοῦ
τὸ cφυρὸν γέροντος ὄντος;
καὶ τάχ’ ἂν βουβωνιῴη.
ἦ μὴν πολὺ δριμύτατός γ’ ἦν τῶν παρ’ ἡμῖν,
καὶ μόνος οὐκ ἀνεπείθετ’, ἀλλ’ ὁπότ’ ἀντιβολοίη
τις, κάτω κύπτων ἂν οὕτω
"λίθον ἕψειc" ἔλεγεν.   280

LINE 275

ἐμβάς, –άδος, ἡ   shoe (cf. 103)
προσ-κόπτω, –έκοψα
          strike against, stumble against, stub {> syn*cope*, apo*cope*, *comma*}
cκότος, ὁ   darkness (cf. 256)
δάκτυλος, ὁ   finger; <u>toe</u> (cf. 251 and 254)
φλεγμαίνω, ἐφλέγμηνα
          (< φλέγμα, phlegm, flame + –αινω, a suffix for *denominative* vbs.: S #866.7) be
          inflamed, swell {> *phlegm*}
cφυρόν, τό   ankle
γέροντος ὄντος   gen. abs., perhaps causal: "as he is an old man": S #2070, though also in agreement
          with the gen. αὑτοῦ (cf. 178) {> geriatric, gerontology}
βουβωνιάω   (> pres. act. opt. 3 sing. βουβωνιῴη < βουβών, groin) suffer from swelling in groin (Ar.
          used –αω and –ιαω suffixes to describe medical conditions: *LA* 85)

LINE 278

ἦ μήν   "The fact is . . ."; a confident statement: *GP* 350; cf. 258
πολύ   (adv. acc.) much
δρῖμύς, –εῖα, –ύ   piercing; shrewd (cf. 146, where it was used of fig-wood smoke)
οἱ παρ’ ἡμῶν   "those among us," virtually = "of us" (gen. with superl.: S #1434; an example of the
          power of the art. to create a substantive: S #2383)
ὅποτε   when, whenever (with opt. to express an event that occurred often)
ἀντι-βολέω   (> pres. act. opt. 3 sing. ἀντιβολοίη) supplicate
κάτω   (adv.) downward
κύπτω   stoop down; hang head (cf. 178)
λίθον ἕψειν   "boil a stone"; proverbial for "trying to persuade the unpersuadable"
ἕψω   boil, seethe (cf. 239)
ὅποτε ἀντιβολοίη, ἄν . . . ἔλεγεν
          (a Past General condit. rel. clause: ὅποτε + opt. in protasis, imperfect indic. in apod-
          osis with ἄν to create an *iterative* imperfect: S #2568)

τάχα δ' ἂν διὰ τὸν χθιζινὸν ἄνθρωπον, ὃς ἡμᾶς διέδυ πως,   [ἀντ.
ἐξαπατῶν καὶ λέγων
ὡς φιλαθήναιος ἦν καὶ
τἀν Cάμῳ πρῶτος κατείποι,
διὰ τοῦτ' ὀδυνηθεὶς
εἶτ' ἴσως κεῖται πυρέττων.
ἔcτι γὰρ τοιοῦτος ἀνήρ.   285
ἀλλ', ὦγάθ', ἀνίcτασο μηδ' οὕτω cεαυτὸν
ἔcθιε μηδ' ἀγανάκτει. καὶ γὰρ ἀνὴρ παχὺς ἥκει
τῶν προδόντων τἀπὶ Θράκης·

LINE 281

χθιζινός (3)	(< χθές, yesterday, cf. 242) of yesterday (referring to a defendant on trial yesterday)
δια-δύω, aor.² -έδῡν	slip through, slip by = <u>was acquitted</u> (cf. 212; on form of aor.: S #418)
ὡς	that (introduces ind. statement after verb of saying: S #2614)
φιλαθήναιος, -ον	Athenian-loving. The defendant must be a non-citizen who is allied with Athens.
τἀν Cάμῳ	= τὰ ἐν Cάμῳ, the events in Samos, referring to the revolt from Athens in 440 BC, when a sympathizer revealed the Samian plot to the Athenians. Evidently someone on trial claimed to be that sympathizer.
κατα-λέγω, aor.² -εῖπον	recount (The verb of the main clause, διέδυ, is aor., so the indir. statement introduced by λέγων ὡς is in secondary sequence. Usually an indic. in the direct form becomes opt., as does κατείποι, but an indic. may be *retained* for vividness, as is ἦν: S #2614–15.)
διὰ τοῦτο	because of this (that is, the fact that a defendant was acquitted and slipped past the jurors)
ὀδυνάω, aor. pass. ὀδυνήθην	(< ὀδύνη, pain + suffix –ιαω; cf. 278) (act.) cause pain; (pass.) suffer pain {> an*odyne*} [considered a "gnawing care" < IE *ed-*, eat]
πυρέττω	(< πυρετός, fever) suffer fever {> *pyro-*, em*pyreal*}

LINE 285

ἔcτι	*orthotone* as first word in sentence: S #187b
ἀν-ίcτημι	(> pres. mid. impv. 2 sing. ἀνίcταcο) get up. Ar. avoids an alternative, contracted, poetic form ἀνίcτω, perhaps a sign of his linguistic conservatism: *LA* 247.
μηδὲ … μηδὲ	μή is the usual neg. in impvs.: S #2709
ἀγανακτέω	feel irritation, be vexed
καὶ γάρ	for in fact (cf. 269)
παχύς, -εῖα, -ύ	fat, plump; "wealthy" {> *pachy*derm} This defendant will be a juicy target.
προ-δίδωμι, -έδωκα	(> aor. act. ptcp. οἱ προδόντες, "the traitors") betray
Θράκη, ἡ	Thrace; τὰ ἐπί = "the region toward Thrace," "the Thracian front." Adjacent to Thrace was the city of Amphipolis, which Athens had recently lost to the Spartans.

ὃν ὅπωc ἐγχυτριεῖc.
ὕπαγ’, ὦ παῖ, ὕπαγε.   290

Πα.   ἐθελήceιc τί μοι οὖν, ὦ   [cτρ.
πάτερ, ἤν coύ τι δεηθῶ;

Χο.   πάνυ γ’, ὦ παιδίον. ἀλλ’ εἰπέ, τί βούλει με πρίαcθαι
καλόν; οἶμαι δέ c’ ἐρεῖν ἀ-
cτραγάλουc δήπουθεν, ὦ παῖ.   295

Πα.   μὰ Δί’, ἀλλ’ ἰcχάδαc, ὦ παπ-
πία· ἥδιον γάρ—

Χο.   οὐκ ἂν
μὰ Δί’, εἰ κρέμαιcθέ γ’ ὑμεῖc.

LINE 289

ὅπωc	"be sure to …" (+ fut. indic., with *ellipsis* of a impv. such as ἄθρει, "see to it," for an exhortation: S #2213; cf. 140–41)
ἐγ-χυτρίζω	(< ἐν + χύτροc, pot) put in a pot and cook {> al*chemy*}
ὑπ-άγω	bring up, move along. Line 290 is a kind of cultic cry that stands outside the meter.

LINE 291

291–316: Conversation with the chorus leader's young son resumes; it reinforces the notion that the chorus members come from modest circumstances. Metrically this "duet with paratragic overtones" (Parker) is composed primarily of ionics. A *strophe* (291–302) responds to an *antistrophe* (303–316).

ἐθέλω, -ήcω	wish (sc. inf., e.g., διδόναι)
τί μοι	τι is enclitic, "something," receiving accent from following enclitic μοι (cf. 273)
ἤν	= ἐάν + subjv. in protasis, fut. indic. apodosis = FMV condit.: S #2323
coυ	δέομαι + gen. or acc. of thing wanted and gen. of the person: S #1398

LINE 293

πάνυ γε	by all means, certainly (in answers)
παιδίον, τό	(dim. of παῖc, cf. 152) small boy, lad
εἰπέ	note that impv. is accented on ultima; so too ἐλθέ, εὑρέ, ἰδέ, λαβέ: S #4246
ἐρῶ	I will say (used as fut. of λέγω; cε is acc. subject of inf. ἐρεῖν)
ἀcτράγαλοc, ὁ	one of the vertebrae; (pl.) knucklebones, dice
δήπουθεν	(< δήπου, presumably (cf. 663) + –θεν) I suppose, doubtless (with a touch of irony)

LINE 297

μὰ Δί’	"No, by Zeus" (cf. 169)
ἰcχάc, –άδοc, ἡ	dried fig. Figs were cheap; if the father cannot afford them, he is quite poor.
παππίαc, ὁ	(dim. of πάππαc, father) dear little papa
ἥδίων, –ον, –ονοc	(comparative of ἡδύc, sweet) sweeter, nicer (cf. 272)
οὐκ ἄν	(*ellipsis*; a verb must be imagined) "I wouldn't <give you figs> even if …"
εἰ … γε	even if (after a neg.: GP 126)
κρέμαμαι	(> mid. opt. 2 pl. κρέμαιcθε) hang; "hang yourselves" (κρέμαμαι is intrans., used as pass. of κρεμάννῡμι; εἰ + opt. is protasis of a Future Less Vivid condit.)

Πα. μὰ Δί' οὔ τἄρα προπέμψω cε τὸ λοιπόν.

Χο. ἀπὸ γὰρ τοῦδέ με τοῦ μιcθαρίου   300

  τρίτον αὐτὸν ἔχειν ἄλφιτα δεῖ καὶ ξύλα κὤψον·

  ⟨ἒ ἔ.⟩

  cὺ δὲ cῦκά μ' αἰτεῖc.   [ἀντ.

Πα. ἄγε νυν, ὦ πάτερ, ἢν μὴ

  τὸ δικαcτήριον ἄρχων

  καθίcῃ νῦν, πόθεν ὠνη-   305

  cόμεθ' ἄριcτον; ἔχειc ἐλ-

  πίδα χρηcτήν τινα νῷν ἢ

  πόρον Ἕλλαc ἱρὸν ⟨εὑρεῖν⟩;

LINE 299

τοι	"certainly," "you know," "I tell you"; strengthens a neg., often with a fut. verb
τἄρα	= τοι + ἄρα, "So, in that case . . ."; τοι brings the point home to the person addressed, ἄρα retains its force: *GP* 555.
προ-πέμπω, -πέμψω	send on; conduct, escort, guide

LINE 300

γάρ	speaker continues train of thought, ignoring interruption: *GP* 64
μιcθάριον, τό	(dim. of μιcθόc) little fee, pittance of a salary (the three-obol payment for jury duty)
τρίτοc (3)	third. If the speaker is third (με . . . τρίτον αὐτόν), then two others need support, presumably his wife and son (cf. 243).
ἄλφιτον, τό	groats, usually made from ground barley that could be mixed with water, wine or oil—an inexpensive household staple
ὄψον, τό	κὤψον = καὶ ὄψον; cooked meat or fish, relishes, delicacies (food eaten with bread and wine) ["extra on the side" < IE *epi-, near, on side; cogn. L. *ob*]
ἒ ἔ	woe!
cῦκον, τό	fig (cf. 145)

LINE 304

δικαcτήριον, τό	(< δικαcτήc, juror + -τηριον, suffix denoting place: S #851.2) courtroom
ἄρχων	= ὁ ἄρχων, the Archon, presiding judge who decided whether to seat a jury
καθ-ίζω, aor. ἐκάθιcα	cause to sit; hold court (note *syllabic augment* preceding prep. of compound vb.: S #450; cf. 90, but here transitive and *causative*)
πόθεν	from where (interrog., cf. 203)
ἄριcτον, τό	lunch, or a morning meal (contrast ἄριcτοc [ᾰ-], best)

LINE 307

ἐλπίc, –ίδοc, ἡ	hope [< IE *wel-, will; cogn. L. *volo, voluptas*; E. *will*]
χρηcτόc (3)	(< χρή, need; cf. 80) useful, good
νῷν	(> dual, gen. & dat., of personal pron.) the two of us
πόροc, ὁ	strait, ford; passageway; resource {> aporia, emporium}
Ἕλλη, –ηc, ἡ	Helle, daughter of Athamas in myth (Doric spelling Ἕλλᾱ); the strait of Helle is the Hellespont ("Sea of Helle"), or Dardanelles. The boy is quoting Pindaric verse (fr. 189).
ἱρόc (3)	holy (Ionic; the normal Attic spelling is ἱερόc [ῐ-]; the reading ἱρόc is suspect) {> hieroglyphic}

67

Χο.	ἀπαπαῖ φεῦ, ⟨ἀπαπαῖ φεῦ,⟩	
	μὰ Δί᾽ οὐκ ἔγωγε νῷν οἶδ᾽	310
	ὁπόθεν γε δεῖπνον ἔσται.	
Πα.	τί με δῆτ᾽, ὦ μελέα μῆτερ, ἔτικτες;	
Χο.	ἵν᾽ ἐμοὶ πράγματα βόσκειν παρέχῃς.	
Πα.	ἀνόνητον ἄρ᾽, ὦ θυλάκιόν, σ᾽ εἶχον ἄγαλμα. ἒ ἔ.	315

LINE 309

ἀπαπαῖ — Alas! (cf. 235)

φεῦ — alas! [< *onomatopoeia*]

ὁπόθεν — from where (an indef. interrog., correlative with πόθεν, used in ind. quest.: "I don't know from where . . .")

γε — "Where on earth . . .?"; γε stresses preceding word, here interrog.: *GP* 125

LINE 312

τί — (adv. acc.) why? "Exactly *why* . . .?"; strengthened by δῆτα (cf. 24)

μέλεος (3) — useless, unhappy. In 312, 314 the boy quotes lines from Euripides's *Theseus* spoken by a youth who was about to be eaten by the Minotaur, which gives the boy's plea a histrionic touch.

μήτηρ, μητρός, ἡ — (> voc. μῆτερ) mother {> *metropolis*}

τίκτω — give birth to

LINE 313

βόσκω — feed (often used of animals); *epexegetical* inf. βόσκειν, further defining πράγματα: "troubles to feed": S #2004 [< βοῦς, ox]

παρ-έχω — provide, offer (although the main verb ἔτικτες is imperfect, the subjv. παρέχῃς is *retained*, indicating that the action is still in the pres. for the older man: *LA* 259, S #2197)

ἀνόνητος, -ον — (ἀ- priv. + ὀνίνημι, profit) unprofitable, useless. The boy continues the tragic parody from Euripides; an empty shopping bag is useless.

ἄρα — ". . . as I now see"; with imperfect, of something just realized: *GP* 36–37 (cf. 3)

θυλάκιον, τό — (dim. of θύλακος, sack) little bag (for carrying groats)

σ᾽ — = σε

ἄγαλμα, -ατος, τό — (< ἀγάλλομαι, exult in + -μα, -ματος, suffix denoting result of an action: S #841.2) ornament, delight (a pred. substantive: S #910a)

Φι.   πάρα νῷν cτενάζειν.

φίλοι, τήκομαι μὲν   317a

πάλαι διὰ τῆc ὀπῆc   317b

ὑμῶν ἐπακούων.   318a

ἀλλ'—οὐ γὰρ οἷόc τ' εἴμ'   318b

ᾄδειν—τί ποιήcω;   319a

τηροῦμαι δ' ὑπὸ τῶνδ', ἐπεὶ   319b

βούλομαί γε πάλαι μεθ' ὑ-   320

μῶν ἐλθὼν ἐπὶ τοὺς καδίc-

κους κακόν τι ποιῆcαι.

LINE 316

ἒ ἒ	woe! (exclam. of grief)
πάρα	= πάρεcτι, it is possible (contrast the prep. παρά, accented on ultima)
cτενάζω	groan; sigh deeply (*frequentative* of cτένω: LSJ; with tragic coloring: B-O); cf. 89

LINE 317

317–95: Phil. now appears at the window; he bewails his plight and implores the chorus to help him escape. They settle on a plan to have him gnaw through the net and let himself down by a rope.

317–33: Meter: Phil. sings a solo song, a *monody*, which is cast in choriambs (– ⏑ ⏑ –, lines 317–23) and anapests (324–33).

τήκω	(act.) melt; (pass.) melt away, waste away, pine. The word has a poetic, tragic tone to it.
πάλαι	(adv.) long ago (pres. τήκομαι used in sense of perf.: S #1885) "I have long pined …" (the -ι of πάλαι is *locative*; cf. ποῖ, ἐκεῖ: S #341)
ὀπή, ἡ	opening; chink (cf. 127; here, more likely the window)
ἐπ-ακούω	listen to (+ gen.: S #1361)
οἷός τ' εἰμί	I am able (οἷός is like other adjs. of ability that take an inf.: S #2001)
ποιέω	(aor. subjv. ποιήσω, deliberative) do (cf. 261)
τῶνδε	that is, Bdel. and Xanthias
καδίcκος, ὁ	(< κάδος, jar + –ιcκος, dim. suffix: S #852.6) voting urn. Once again (cf. 90) Phil.'s obsession takes the form of desire for specific trappings of the courtoom.

ἀλλ᾽, ὦ Ζεῦ μεγαβρόντα,
ἤ με ποίηcον καπνὸν ἐξαίφνηc
ἢ Προξενίδην ἢ τὸν Cέλλου   325
τοῦτον τὸν ψευδαμάμαξυν.
τόλμηcον, ἄναξ, χαρίcαcθαί μοι,
πάθοc οἰκτίραc· ἤ με κεραυνῷ
διατινθαλέῳ cπόδιcον ταχέωc,
κἄπειτ᾽ ἀνελών μ᾽ ἀποφυcήcαc   330
εἰc ὀξάλμην ἔμβαλε θερμήν·

LINE 323

ἀλλά	"Ah, now: Zeus . . ."; transitional; shifting from the language of tragedy to that of prayer: *GP* 16
μεγαβρόντης, –ες	(adj. < βροντή, thunder) great-thundering
ποιέω	(< aor. act. impv. 2 sing. ποίησον) make (the first of five aors. addressed to Zeus in 324–32, characteristic of prayers to the gods: *LA* 31)
ἐξαίφνης	(adv.) suddenly (cf. 49)
Προξενίδης, ὁ	Proxenides, an Athenian mocked for boastfulness in *Birds*
ὁ Cέλλου	"the son of Sellus," perhaps the Amynias of 74. He and Proxenides are simply full of hot air.
ψευδαμάμαξυς, –υος, ὁ	(< ψευδ-, false + ἀμάμαξυς, a vine wrapped around a tree) a sham vine (in some sense the man is a phony or social climber); Ar.s' comic coinage; a *hapax* in Greek.

LINE 327

τολμάω	dare, have the courage, deign (+ inf.)
ἄναξ, ἄνακτος, ὁ	lord, king (cf. 143)
χαρίζομαι, ἐχαρισάμην	
	(< χάρις, favor, cf. 186) do a favor, gratify (+ dat.)
πάθος, –εος, τό	incident; suffering {> *pathetic, apathy* }
οἰκτίρω	(> aor. act. ptcp. οἰκτίρᾱς < οἶκτος, pity) pity
κεραυνός, ὁ	thunderbolt
διατινθάλεος (3)	(< δια-, denoting intensity: S #1685.3 + τίνθος, the steam from a kettle) boiling hot (the compound, a *hapax* in Greek, is a "mock heroic word": Graves)
σποδίζω	(> aor. act. impv. σπόδισον < σποδός, embers) burn, bake in ashes (a "homely word": Starkie)

LINE 330

ἀν-αιρέω, aor.² -εῖλον	(> aor. act. ptcp. ἀνελών) take up and carry off
ἀπο-φῡσάω, -εφύσησα	
	blow away (sc. the ashes) {> em*physema*}
ὀξάλμη, ἡ	(< ὄξος, vinegar + ἅλμη, brine) vinegar and brine sauce. Phil. seems to have forgotten that he is describing the destruction of his own body and now thinks of what roasted meat might be dipped in.
θερμός (3)	hot {> hypo*thermia*}

ἢ δῆτα λίθον με ποίηcον, ἐφ' οὗ

τὰς χοιρίνας ἀριθμοῦcι.   [cτρ.

Χο.   τίς γὰρ ἐcθ' ὁ ταῦτά c' εἴργων

κἀποκλείων τῇ θύρᾳ; λέξον· πρὸς εὔνους γὰρ φράceις.

Φι.   οὑμὸς υἱός. ἀλλὰ μὴ βοᾶτε· καὶ γὰρ τυγχάνει   336

οὑτοcὶ πρόcθεν καθεύδων. ἀλλ' ὕφεcθε τοῦ τόνου.

LINE 332

ἢ δῆτα	"or, <u>better by far</u> . . .": Starkie; δῆτα emphatic after ἤ: *GP* 279. This is the climax of the list of torments that Phil. asks Zeus to inflict on him: if he is to be a stone, at least let it be the one on which jurors' votes are counted.
ἐφ' οὗ	on which (sc. stone)
χοιρίνη, ἡ	small seashell, used instead of a pebble by jurors as a voting token
ἀριθμέω	count {> *arithmetic*}

LINE 334

334–45: Meter: Ar. returns to meters that are more characteristic of comedy; the exchange between Phil. and the Chorus is primarily trochaic until 345. The chorus will urge Phil. to attempt to escape and "the excitement is enhaced by the metre, with its rapid trochees and vigorous anapaests" (MacD.). Here begins an *epirrhematic agon*.

γάρ	"In light of what you've just said, I want to know more"; in quests. when a speaker "wishes to learn something further": *GP* 81
εἴργω	shut in, confine (cf. 70)
ταῦτα	(adv. acc.) in this way
ἀπο-κλείω	κἀποκλείων = καὶ ἀποκλείων by *crasis*; shut off (cf. 113)
θύρα, ἡ	door (cf. 70)
λέγω	(> aor. act. impv. 2 sing. λέξον) tell, say (λέξον is more "literary" than εἰπέ; cf. 15)
εὔνους, –ον	(> acc. pl. εὔνους < εὐ + νοῦς, mind, sense) well-disposed, friendly

LINE 336

οὑμός	= ὁ ἐμός
ἀλλά	"Never mind that: this is what's really important . . ."; breaking off thought and transition to impv.: *GP* 13–15
βοάω	shout (μή + pres. impv: probably "don't continue shouting," i.e., they have already started; contrast μή + aor. impv.: "don't start"; but see S #1841a)
καὶ γάρ	for in fact (cf. 269)
πρόσθεν	in front
καθ-εύδω	sleep (suppl. ptcp. with τυγχάνω: S #2096), cf. 67
ὑφ-ίημι	(< ὑπό + ἵημι > aor. mid. impv. 2 pl. ὕφεσθε) lower; (mid.) slacken from (+ gen.)
τόνος, ὁ	(< τείνω, stretch) rope, stretching; intensity, <u>tension</u>. The metaphor may be taken as that of the strings of musical instruments: B-O. {> en*tas*is, peri*ton*eum, hypo*ten*use}

Χο.	τοῦ δ’ ἔφεξιν, ὦ μάταιε, ταῦτα δρᾶν ϲε βούλεται;	
	τίνα πρόφαϲιν ἔχων;	
Φι.	οὐκ ἐᾷ μ’, ὤνδρεϲ, δικάζειν οὐδὲ δρᾶν οὐδὲν κακόν,	340
	ἀλλά μ’ εὐωχεῖν ἕτοιμόϲ ἐϲτ’· ἐγὼ δ’ οὐ βούλομαι.	
Χο.	τοῦτ’ ἐτόλμηϲ’ ὁ μιαρὸϲ χα-	342
	νεῖν, ὁ Δημολογοκλέων ⟨ὅδ’,⟩	
	ὅτι λέγειϲ ⟨ϲύ⟩ τι περὶ τῶν νε-	343
	ῶν ἀληθέϲ. οὐ γὰρ ἄν ποθ’	
	οὗτοϲ ἀνὴρ τοῦτ’ ἐτόλμη-	344
	ϲεν λέγειν, εἰ	
	μὴ ξυνωμότηϲ τιϲ ἦν.	345

LINE 338

ἔφεξιϲ, –εωϲ, ἡ	(< ἐπί + ἔχω) excuse, pretext (in acc., as prep. + gen.: τοῦ ἔφεξιν, "On what pretext?" in which τοῦ = τίνοϲ, interrog.)
μάταιοϲ (3)	(< μάτη, folly) vain, thoughtless. The chorus are impatient with Phil., or incredulous at the fix he has wound up in.
πρόφαϲιϲ, –εωϲ, ἡ	alleged reason, pretext (cf. 174)

LINE 340

οὐκ . . . οὐδέ	neither . . . nor
ἐάω	(> pres. act. indic. 3 sing. ἐᾷ) allow; with οὐκ = "prevent" (cf. 190)
οὐδὲ δρᾶν οὐδέν	"nor to do anything" (compound, not double neg.: οὐδέν confirms οὐδὲ: S #2761)
εὐωχέω	(< εὖ, well + ἔχω, hold = "regale") entertain, feast, wine and dine
ἕτοιμοϲ (3)	ready to do (+ inf.)
τολμάω, ἐτόλμηϲα	dare (cf. 327)

LINE 342

χάϲκω, aor.² ἔχανον	(< χάοϲ, chaos, gaping space + –ϲκω: S #527a) gape; utter, mouth off (τοῦτ’ is acc. obj.) {> gas}
Δημολογοκλέων, ὁ	(< δημολογικόϲ, suited to public speaking, though with a disparaging connotation) Demagogue-Cleon. Would the chorus really want to insult Cleon? Perhaps the word means a "second-rate" Cleon: MacD.
ὅτι	since, because (causal conj. + indic.)
ναῦϲ, νεώϲ, ἡ	ship. Perhaps a reference to a politically sensitive issue pertaining to the navy. {> nautical, nausea}
ἀληθήϲ, –εϲ	true (cf. 212)
ξυνωμότηϲ, –ου, ὁ	(< ξυν- + ὄμνῡμι, swear) fellow conspirator
εἰ μή . . . ἦν, οὐκ ἂν ἐτόλμηϲεν	
	(mixed Contrary-to-Fact condit.: εἰ + imperfect indic. is protasis of present Contrary-to-Fact, aor. indic. + ἂν is apodosis of past: S #2302–10)

ἀλλ' ἐκ τούτων ὥρα τινά coι ζητεῖν καινὴν ἐπίνοιαν,
ἥτις ce λάθρᾳ τἀνδρὸς τουδὶ καταβῆναι δεῦρο ποιήcει.

Φι.   τίc ἂν οὖν εἴη; ζητεῖθ' ὑμεῖc, ὡc πᾶν ⟨ἂν⟩ ἔγωγε ποιοίην·
οὕτω κιττῶ διὰ τῶν cανίδων μετὰ χοιρίνηc περιελθεῖν.

Χο.   ἔcτιν ὀπὴ δῆθ' ἥντιν' ἂν ἔνδοθεν οἷόc τ' εἴηc διαλέξαι,   350
εἶτ' ἐκδῦναι ῥάκεcιν κρυφθεὶc ὥcπερ πολύμητιc Ὀδυccεύc;

Φι.   πάντα πέφαρκται κοὐκ ἔcτιν ὀπῆc οὐδ' εἰ cέρφῳ διαδῦναι.
ἀλλ' ἄλλο τι δεῖ ζητεῖν ὑμᾶc· ὀπίαν δ' οὐκ ἔcτι γενέcθαι.

LINE 346

346–402: Meter: The chorus and Phil. switch to anapestic tetrameters (346–57), anapestic dimeters (358–64), trochees (365–78, as *antistrophe* to 334–45), and back to anapestic tetrameters (379–402).

ἀλλά	"But, be that as it may . . ."; speaker breaks off reflections and moves on: *GP* 8
ἐκ	in view of, under the circumstances (+ gen.)
ὥρα, ἡ	time; "it is time" (sc. ἐcτίν) {> *hour, horoscope*} [< IE * *yōr-a-* < **yĕr-*, year, season; cogn. E. *year*]
ἐπίνοια, ἡ	(ἐπί, on + νοῦς, mind, purpose) thinking on; thought, <u>invention</u>
λάθρᾳ	(adv. < λανθάνω, cf. 212) secretly; (as prep. with gen.) without knowledge of

LINE 348

εἰμί	(> pres. opt. 3 sing. εἴη; ἄν with potential opt.) be
οὖν	then (often follows τίc; S #2962; draws inference, "If so, what next . . .?" *GP* 425–26)
ὡc	since (causal conj., usually with indic. but can take potential opt.: S #2243)
πᾶν	everything; <u>anything</u> {> *pan-*}
κιττάω	(< κίccα, jay or magpie, bird noted for appetite) crave for, long to do (+ inf.)
cανίc, –ίδοc, ἡ	tablet for writing on (used as a notice board announcing trials)
μετά	with (+ gen.)
χοιρίνη, ἡ	shell used as voting token (cf. 333)
περι-έρχομαι, -ῆλθον	go around, stroll among

LINE 350

ὀπή, ἡ	opening (cf. 127)
δῆτα	then, in that case: *GP* 271 (cf. 24 and 191)
ἔνδοθεν	(< ἔνδον, within + –θεν, suffix denoting place whence: S #342b) from within
δια-λέγω, -έλεξα	pick out, pick open a hole (Mss. read διορύξαι, dig through)
ἐκ-δύω, -έδῦν	slip out, escape
ῥάκοc, -εοc, τό	rags, tattered garment. Odysseus secretly entered Troy disguised as a beggar.
κρύπτω, ἐκρύφθην	hide, disguise {> *crypt, grotto*}
πολύμητιc, –ιοc	(< πολύc, much + μῆτιc, wisdom) of many counsels, an epithet of Odysseus in Homer. Once again, Phil. follows a heroic model suited to him.

LINE 352

φράccω, πέφαργμαι	fence in, block
κοὐκ ἔcτιν ὀπῆc	"there isn't enough of a chink" (gen. does duty as subject—perhaps an archaism: *LA* 252; for orthotone ἔcτιν after οὐκ, cf. 212)
cέρφοc, ὁ	gnat; *ellipsis* in the sense: "not even for a gnat to slip through, if <I were a gnat>"
ἀλλ'	= ἀλλά but
ἄλλο	(< ἄλλοc) other
ὀπία, ἡ	a cheese made with fig juice (ὀπόc); runny whey; ὀπίαν γενέcθαι (sc. μέ) = "that [I] may become runny whey" (and punning on ὀπη, opening)

73

Χο.   μέμνηςαι δῆθ', ὅτ' ἐπὶ ςτρατιᾶς κλέψας ποτὲ τοὺς ὀβελίςκους

          ἵεις cαυτὸν κατὰ τοῦ τείχους ταχέως, ὅτε Νάξος ἑάλω.   355

Φι.   οἶδ'· ἀλλὰ τί τοῦτ'; οὐδὲν γὰρ τοῦτ' ἐςτὶν ἐκείνῳ προςόμοιον.

          ἥβων γὰρ κἀδυνάμην κλέπτειν, ἴςχυόν τ' αὐτὸς ἐμαυτοῦ,

          κοὐδείς μ' ἐφύλαττ', ἀλλ' ἐξῆν μοι

          φεύγειν ἀδεῶς. νῦν δὲ ξὺν ὅπλοις

          ἄνδρες ὁπλῖται διαταξάμενοι   360

          κατὰ τὰς διόδους cκοπιωροῦνται,

LINE 354

μιμνήςκω, perf. μέμνημαι

          remember (perf. used in pres. sense) {> *amnesty*}

δῆτα   used with quests.; interrog. sense could be conveyed by the tone of voice: *GP* 27

ὅτ'   = ὅτε, when

ἐπί   when, at the time of (+ gen.)

ςτρατιά, ἡ   campaign, active service (cf. 11)

κλέπτω   (> aor. act. ptcp. κλέψᾶς) steal (cf. 57)

ὀβελίςκος, ὁ   (< ὀβελός, spit + –ιςκος, dim. suffix: S #852.6) small spit, skewer

ἵημι   (> imperfect act. 2 sing. ἵεις) send, launch (contrast pres. act. 2 sing. ἱεῖς: S #777)

κατά   down from (+ gen.)

τεῖχος –ους, τό   city wall, fortification (cf. 130)

Νάξος, ἡ   Naxos, island subjugated by Athens ca. 470 BC (islands are grammatically fem., no matter what declension: S #199b)

ἁλίςκομαι, aor.² ἑάλων

          (> aor. act. indic. 3 sing. ἑάλω; conjugation like ἔγνων: S #682) be conquered, be captured. ἁλίςκομαι served as the pass. of αἱρέω. The aor. ἑάλων has a *syllabic augment* because the stem formerly began with a digamma (ϝαλ-); it *also* has a temporal augment in the lengthened -ᾱ-; moreover, it was sometimes written ἥλων: S #431.

LINE 356

οὐδέν   (adv. acc.) in no way

προςόμοιος, –ον   very much like, similar to (+ dat.); cf. 189

ἡβάω   be young (cf. 236)

κἀδυνάμην   = καὶ ἐδυνάμην (< δύναμαι, be able)

ἰςχύω   (> imperfect indic. act. 1 sing. ἴςχῦον) be strong, be in control of (+ gen.)

κοὐδείς   = καὶ οὐδείς

ἔξεςτι   (> imperfect indic. ἐξῆν) it is possible (impers. + dat. + inf.)

ἀδεῶς   (adv. < ἀ- priv. + δείδω, fear, cf. 109) carefree, with impunity

LINE 360

ὁπλίτης, ὁ   (< ὅπλον, weapon + –της, suffix denoting agent: S #839.1) armored infantryman (cf. 27; ξὺν ὅπλοις = "under arms")

δια-τάττω, -έταξα   station, draw up in battle order (cf. 69)

κατά   at, opposite (+ acc.)

δίοδος, ἡ   (< διά + ὁδός, road) pass, defile, exit point {> *odometer*}

cκοπιωρέομαι   (< cκοπή, lookout place + οὖρος, watcher?) look out for, watch (cf. 246)

τὼ δὲ δύ' αὐτῶν ἐπὶ ταῖσι θύραις
ὥσπερ με γαλῆν κρέα κλέψασαν
τηροῦσιν ἔχοντ' ὀβελίσκους.   364

Χο. ἀλλὰ καὶ νῦν ἐκπόριζε   [ἀντ.
μηχανὴν ὅπως τάχισθ'· ἕως γάρ, ὦ μελίττιον.

Φι. διατραγεῖν τοίνυν κράτιστόν ἐστί μοι τὸ δίκτυον.
ἡ δέ μοι Δίκτυννα συγγνώμην ἔχοι τοῦ δικτύου.

Χο. ταῦτα μὲν πρὸς ἀνδρός ἐστ' ἄνοντος εἰς σωτηρίαν.
ἀλλ' ἔπαγε τὴν γνάθον.   370

LINE 362

τώ — dual of def. art. ὁ, ἡ, τό
γαλῆ, –ῆς, ἡ — weasel, ferret [< IE *glэis-, mice and such; cf. L. *glis, gliris* (dormouse), *galea* (helmet, made of weasel skin?)]
κρέας, κρέως, τό — meat (pl. κρέα)
τηρέω — watch, observe (cf. 210)
ἔχοντ' — = ἔχοντε, dual, although the verb is pl.
ὀβελίσκος — skewer (cf. 354)

LINE 365

ἐκ-πορίζω — (< πόρος, passage, means of provision, cf. 308) invent, provide
μηχανή, ἡ — device, plan (cf. 149)
ὅπως — "as ___ as possible" (cf. 167)
ἕως, ἕω, ἡ — dawn (Ionic spelling ἠώς; distinguish from conj. ἕως, until) [< IE *aus-, dawn; cogn. L. *aurora*; E. *east*]
μελίττιον, τό — (dim. of μέλιττα, bee, perhaps < μέλι, honey + λείχ-, lick) little bee (cf. 106)

LINE 367

δια-τρώγω — gnaw through (cf. 164)
τοίνυν — "In that case, then . . ."; responding to the previous speaker's suggestion: GP 568–70
κράτιστος (3) — (superl. of κρατύς, cf. 209) strongest, best
Δίκτυννα, ἡ — Dictynna, a goddess of hunting and of nets (cf. δίκτυον, net, 131)
συγγνώμη, ἡ — (< σύν + γνώμη, judgment) fellow feeling; pardon, forgiveness (with δικτύου, gen. of cause: S #1405)
ἔχω — opt. of wish, ἔχοι: S #1814
πρός — characteristic of (+ gen.)
ἄνω — (> pres. act. ptcp., masc. gen. sing. ἄνοντος) accomplish, finish; make way to
σωτηρία, ἡ — (< σῶς, safe) salvation
ἐπ-άγω — set on, apply; apply the jaw, get the jaw working = "start chewing"
γε — emphatic, after pron.: GP 123
γνάθος, –ου, ἡ — jaw [< IE *genu-, jaw; cogn. L. *gena; genuinus (dens)*; E. *chin*]

Φι.   διατέτρωκται τοῦτό γ'. ἀλλὰ μὴ βοᾶτε μηδαμῶς,
        ἀλλὰ τηρώμεσθ' ὅπως μὴ Βδελυκλέων αἰcθήcεται.

Χο.   μηδέν, ὦ τᾶν, δέδιθι, μηδέν·
        ὡc ἐγὼ τοῦτόν γ', ἐὰν γρύ-
        ξῃ τι, ποιήcω δακεῖν τὴν
        καρδίαν καὶ τὸν περὶ ψυ-   375
        χῆc δρόμον δραμεῖν, ἵν' εἰδῇ
        μὴ πατεῖν τὰ
        ταῖν θεαῖν ψηφίcματα.

LINE 371
δια-τρώγω, -τέτρωγμαι

        gnaw through (cf. 164)

ἀλλὰ . . . ἀλλά   first ἀλλά introduces impv.: *GP* 13–15; the second is *adversative*: *GP* 1.

μὴ βοᾶτε   for neg. impv. in pres. cf. 336

τηρέω   take care that (with ὅπως + fut. indic. for an "urgent exhortation": S #1920, 2211;
                hort. subjv.: S #1797). The 1 pl. –μεθα was probably more common in conversation;
                Ar. uses –μεσθα in lyric passages and for metrical reasons S #465d: *LA* 245.

LINE 373
μηδέν   μή is neg. for impvs.

ὦ τᾶν   my good friend (only in voc.; suggests familiarity, sometimes condescending)

[δείδω], δέδοικα   (> impv. perf. δέδιθι: S #703) fear (Attic uses perf. in pres. sense), cf. 109

ὡς   (causal conj.) for, because

γρύζω, ἔγρυξα   (< γρύ, a grunt, a syllable, a morsel, a bit: *LA* 181) "say γρύ"; grunt, grumble (ἐάν +
                subjv., fut. indic. = FMV: S #2323). Bdel. is subject of γρύξῃ; it is *he* who should worry.

δάκνω, aor.² ἔδακον   bite (cf. 253)

LINE 375
καρδία, ἡ   heart

δρόμος, ὁ   running, footrace (cogn. acc.: S #1564) {> palin*drome*}

τρέχω, aor.² ἔδραμον   run (τρέχ- stem only used in pres.; ἔδραμον in aor.) "Running a race for one's life"
                echoes the description of Achilles' pursuit of Hector at *Il.* 22.161; the chorus see an
                enmity of epic scope.

οἶδα   (> subjv. 3 sing. εἰδῇ: S #794) know

πατέω   tread on (cf. 237)

θεά, ἡ   (> dual gen./dat. ταῖν θεαῖν) of the two goddesses (= Demeter and Persephone) {>
                theo-, atheism, Dorothy, *Theodore*}

ψηφίcμα, –ατος, τό   (< ψῆφος, vote + –μα, –ματος, suffix denoting the result of an action: S #841.2) de-
                cree, legislation, enactment (cf. 94)

ἀλλ' ἐξάψας διὰ τῆς θυρίδος τὸ καλῴδιον εἶτα καθίμα

δήσας σαυτὸν καὶ τὴν ψυχὴν ἐμπλησάμενος Διοπείθους.   380

Φι. ἄγε νυν, ἢν αἰσθομένω τούτω ζητῆτόν μ' εἰσκαλαμᾶσθαι

κἀνασπαστὸν ποιεῖν εἴσω, τί ποιήσετε; φράζετε νυνί.

Χο. ἀμυνοῦμέν σοι τὸν πρινώδη θυμὸν ἅπαντες καλέσαντες,

ὥστ' οὐ δυνατόν σ' εἴργειν ἔσται· τοιαῦτα ποιήσομεν ἡμεῖς.

Φι. δράσω τοίνυν ὑμῖν πίσυνος. καὶ μανθάνετ'· ἢν τι πάθω 'γώ,   385

ἀνελόντες καὶ κατακλαύσαντες θεῖναί μ' ὑπὸ τοῖσι δρυφάκτοις.

LINE 379

ἐξ-άπτω, -ῆψα	fasten from
θυρίς, –ίδος, ἡ	(< θύρα, door + –ις, –ιδος, dim. suffix: S #853) small window
καλῴδιον, τό	(dim. of κάλως, rope) cord
καθῑμάω	(> pres. act. impv. 2 sing. καθῑμᾶ < κατά + ἱμάς, strap, rope) let down by rope
δέω, δήσω, ἔδησα	tie, bind (do not confuse with δέω, δεήσω, lack, and its impers. δεῖ)
ἐμ-πίμπλημι, -έπλησα	fill; (mid.) fill for yourself
Διοπείθης, –ους, ὁ	(< Διο-, Zeus + πείθομαι, trust) Diopeithes proposed a decree against atheists and was seen as a religious fanatic; his name is appropriate. (gen. with verb of filling: S #1369)

LINE 381

ἄγε νυν	come now (cf. 211)
αἰσθομένω τούτω	dual: Bdel. and Xanthias
ζητέω	(> pres. act. subjv. dual ζητῆτον) seek, seek to do (+ inf.)
εἰσ-καλαμάομαι	(< κάλαμος, fishing rod) haul in
ἀνασπαστός	(< ἀνασπάω, draw up) dragged up (a pred. with με)

LINE 383

ἀμύνω, ἀμῠνῶ	ward off, defend (+ dat. of person for whom danger is averted) (cf. 197)
πρινώδης, –ες	(< πρῖνος, holm oak + –ωδης, suffix denoting fullness or similarity: S #858.16) tough as oak
δυνατός (3)	strong, possible (δυνατόν ἐστι + inf. = it is possible to)
εἴργω	shut in, confine (cf. 70)

LINE 385

τοίνυν	"In that case, then . . ." (cf. 164)
πίσυνος, –ον	(< πείθομαι, trust + –νος, suffix denoting what can be done: S #858.11) depending on, trusting in (+ dat.); cf. 101
πάσχω, aor.² ἔπαθον	(> aor. subjv. 1 sing. πάθω) suffer (cf. 1, 328)
ἀν-αιρέω, -εῖλον	gather up; take up a body for burial
κατα-κλάω, -έκλαυσα	bewail loudly, mourn
τίθημι	(> aor. act. inf. θεῖναι) place, <u>bury</u> (inf., used as imptv: S #2013, conveys an air of formal solemnity and is used in oracles: *LA* 259)
δρύφακτος, ὁ	(< δρῦς, wood + φράσσω, fence in) railing, bar in court. The expected form δρύφρακτος, which has the letter -ρ- twice, loses one by *dissimilation* (cf. 1279).

Χο.   οὐδὲν πείσει· μηδὲν δείςῃς. ἀλλ', ὦ βέλτιστε, καθίει
             cαυτὸν θαρρῶν κἀπευξάμενος τοῖcι πατρῴοιcι θεοῖcιν.

Φι.   ὦ Λύκε δέσποτα, γείτων ἥρως· cὺ γὰρ οἷςπερ ἐγὼ κεχάρηcαι,
             τοῖc δακρύοιcιν τῶν φευγόντων ἀεὶ καὶ τοῖc ὀλοφυρμοῖc·   390
             ᾤκηcας γοῦν ἐπίτηδες ἰὼν ἐνταῦθ' ἵνα ταῦτ' ἀκροῷο,
             κἀβουλήθηc μόνος ἡρώων παρὰ τὸν κλάοντα καθῆcθαι.
             ἐλέηcον καὶ cῶcον νυνὶ τὸν cαυτοῦ πληcιόχωρον·
             κοὔ μή ποτέ cου παρὰ τὰς κάννας οὐρήcω μηδ' ἀποπάρδω.

Βδ.   οὗτος, ἐγείρου.

Ξα.   τί τὸ πρᾶγμ';

LINE 387

πάσχω	(> fut. mid. indic. 2 sing. πείσει) suffer
δείδω, ἔδεισα	(> aor. act. subjv. 2 sing. δείςῃς) fear (prohib. subjv.; neg is μή: S #1800); cf. 109
βέλτιστος (3)	best (cf. 233)
καθ-ίημι	(> pres. act. impv. 2 sing. καθίει) send down, let down
θαρρέω	(< θάρσος, courage) be of good courage
ἐπ-εύχομαι, -ηυξάμην	pray to
πατρῷος (3)	hereditary, ancestral

LINE 389

Λύκος, ου, ὁ	Lykos, Athenian mythical hero whose shrine was next to any lawcourt
γείτων, –ονος, ὁ	neighbor
ἥρως, –ωος, ὁ	(> gen. pl. ἡρώων) hero
γάρ	"<You are a hero/I address you> underline because of . . ."; *ellipsis* of preceding thought
ὅσπερ, ἥπερ, ὅπερ	the very thing which (the antecedent is δακρύοιcιν); cf. 146
δάκρυον, τό	tear [< IE *dakru-*, tear; cogn. L. *lacrima*; E. *tear*]
ὀλοφῦρμός, ὁ	lamentation

LINE 391

οἰκέω, ᾤκηcα	(< οἰκία, cf. 196) live, dwell
ἐπίτηδες	(adv.) on purpose
εἶμι	(> pres. act. ptcp. ἰών) go (take with ἐνταῦθ' ἵνα "there, where")
ἵνα	so that (purpose clause + subjv., opt. after secondary sequence verb: S #2196; yet ἵνα simultaneously means "where")
ἀκροάομαι	(> pres. mid. opt. 2 sing. ἀκροῷο < ἄκρος, tip + οὖς, ear) "prick the ears," listen to
παρά	(+ acc.) next to

LINE 393

ἐλεέω, ἠλέηcα	(> aor. act. impv. 2 sing. ἐλέηcον) pity, have pity on
cῴζω, ἔcωcα	(> aor. act. impv. 2 sing. cῶcον) save (cf. 369)
πληcιόχωρος, –ον	(< πληcίος, near + χῶρος, space) neighboring
οὐ μή	an emphatic neg., used with subjv. or, as in 397, fut. indic.: S #1919, 2756
κάννα, ἡ	pole; (pl.) railing, wicker fence surrounding the shrine of Lykos
οὐρέω, οὐρήσομαι, ἐούρηcα	
	urinate: *MM* p. 194 (fut. is dep.; thus οὐρήcω must be aor. subjv.)
ἀπο-πέρδομαι, aor.² -έπαρδον	
	fart: *MM* pp. 194–99 [< IE *perd-*, fart; cogn. E. *fart*]

Βδ.	ὥσπερ φωνή μέ τιϲ ἐγκεκύκλωται.	395
	μῶν ὁ γέρων πῃ διαδύεται ⟨αὖ⟩;	
Ξα.	μὰ Δί' οὐ δῆτ', ἀλλὰ καθιμᾷ	
	αὐτὸν δήϲαϲ.	
Βδ.	ὦ μιαρώτατε, τί ποιεῖϲ; οὐ μὴ καταβήϲει.	
	ἀνάβαιν' ἀνύϲαϲ κατὰ τὴν ἑτέραν καὶ ταῖϲιν φυλλάϲι παῖε,	
	ἤν πωϲ πρύμνην ἀνακρούϲηται πληγεὶϲ ταῖϲ εἰρεϲιώναιϲ.	
Φι.	οὐ ξυλλήψεϲθ' ὁπόϲοιϲι δίκαι τῆτεϲ μέλλουϲιν ἔϲεϲθαι,	400

LINE 395

395–456: Bdel., who has been asleep since 229, wakes up and realizes that an escape attempt is underway. The chorus members attack attack him, believing he is a traitor who favors tyranny; they reveal their stingers. Bdel. calls out to the household slaves for backup support, and they prepare for battle.

οὗτοϲ	cf. 1
ἐγείρω	(> pres. mid. impv. 2 sing. ἐγείρου) wake; (mid.) wake up (cf. 101)
ἐγ-κυκλόω, -κεκύκλωμαι	
	(< εν + κύκλοϲ, circle) encircle, echo around (cf. 132)
μῶν	= μή + οὖν, expecting neg. answer (cf. 274)
πῃ	(adv. enclitic) in some way
καθῑμάω	let down (cf. 379)

LINE 397

δέω	bind, tie (sc. "with a rope")
κατα-βαίνω, -βήϲομαι	(> deponent fut. 2 sing. -βήϲει) climb down
κατὰ τὴν ἑτέραν	"the other <way up>" (sc. e.g., ἀνάβαϲιν or ὁδόν; for such *ellipses*: S #1027)
φυλλάϲ, –άδοϲ, ἡ	(< φύλλον, leaf) foliage, leafy branches
παίω	strike, beat (impv. παῖε; contrast voc. ὦ παῖ; impvs. here are for Xanthias) {> ana*pest*}
ἤν πωϲ	in case, to see if
πρύμνη, ἡ	(< πρυμνόϲ, hindmost) stern
ἀνα-κρούω	push back; back water; ἀνακρούεϲθαι πρύμνην = "put ship astern" (cf. 130)
πλήττω, aor. pass. ἐπλήγην	
	(> aor. pass. ptcp. πληγείϲ) strike {> *plectrum*, apo*plexy*}
εἰρεϲιώνη, ἡ	(< εἶροϲ, wool) harvest wreath. A branch of olive or laurel, decorated with wool, hung on door in autumn and dedicated to Apollo; Bdel. will strike Phil. with these. B-O suggest a pun on εἰρεϲία, rowing.

LINE 400

ξυλ-λαμβάνω, -λήψομαι	
	collect together, assist (addressed to audience members)
ὁπόϲοϲ (3)	as many as, all who (dat. of possession: S #1476; sc. antecedent ὑμεῖϲ)
τῆτεϲ	(adv. < demonstrative "this," cf. ἐκεῖνοϲ + ἔτοϲ, cf. 490) this year
εἰμί, ἔϲομαι	(> fut. inf. ἔϲεϲθαι) be

ὦ Cμικυθίων καὶ Τεισιάδη καὶ Χρήμων καὶ Φερέδειπνε;
πότε δ', εἰ μὴ νῦν, ἐπαρήξετέ μοι, πρίν μ' εἴcω μᾶλλον ἄγεcθαι;

Χο.   εἰπέ μοι, τί μέλλομεν κινεῖν ἐκείνην τὴν χολήν,
ἥνπερ ἡνίκ' ἄν τις ἡμῶν ὀργίςῃ τὴν cφηκιάν;
νῦν ἐκεῖνο νῦν ἐκεῖνο   405
τοὐξύθυμον, ᾧ κολαζό-
μεcθα, κέντρον ἐντατέον ὀξέωc.

LINE 401

Cμῑκυθίων, –ιονος, ὁ	Smikythion; he and the other three men named may be prosecutors who were conceivably in the audience, though Chremon and Pheredeipnos are probably comically contrived names.
Τεισιάδης, –ους, ὁ	(< τίνω, τείσω, repay + –ιδης, *patronymic*: S #845.5 = "Son of Settle-Up"?) Teisiades
Χρήμων, ονος, ὁ	(< χρή, need = "Needy") Chremon
Φερέδειπνος, –ου, ὁ	(< φέρω, bring + δεῖπνον, dinner = "Dinner-Bringer") Pheredeipnos
πότε	(interrog. adv.) when? (only instance in *W.*)
ἐπ-αρήγω, -αρήξω	come to aid, help (+ dat.)

LINE 403

403–62: Meter: Mixed trochees and trochaic tetrameters (403–19) followed by trochaic tetrameters (420–62), suggesting the spirited action taking place as the chorus of waspish men swarm and attack the slaves and Bdelycleon, evidently charging up onto the stage platform. MacD. suggests that reduced metra are used in some of the lines spoken by the chorus, e.g., 413–14, as an indication that they are out of breath.

μέλλω	hesitate to, wait to (+ pres. inf.: S #1959, a construction that is new in Greek: *LA* 257–58)
κῑνέω	stir up {> *kinetic, cinema*}
χολή, ἡ	wrath, anger {> *cholera*, melan*choly*}
χολὴν ἥνπερ	"the wrath which <we stir up> when"
ἥνικα	whenever (with ἄν + subjv. for indef. time: S #2394)
ὀργίζω, ὤργιsα	(< ὀργή, anger + -ιζω of *denominative* vbs.) make angry
sφηκιά, ἡ	wasp's nest (take with ἡμῶν); cf. 224

LINE 405

νῦν ἐκεῖνο	repeated in agitation, referring to the κέντρον
ὀξύθῡμος, –ον	(< ὀξύς, sharp + θῡμος, spirit) quick to anger, sharp-spirited (τοὐξύθῡμον = τὸ ὀξύθῡμον)
ἐν-τείνω, -τάθην	strain, stretch tight (verbal ἐντατέος, sc. ἐστι, expressing necessity: S #2149); cf. 337
ὀξέως	(adv. < ὀξύς, sharp, keen) sharply

ἀλλὰ θαἰμάτια λαβόντες ὡς τάχιστα, παιδία,
θεῖτε καὶ βοᾶτε, καὶ Κλέωνι ταῦτ' ἀγγέλλετε,
καὶ κελεύετ' αὐτὸν ἥκειν   410
ὡς ἐπ' ἄνδρα μῑσόπολιν
ὄντα κἀπολούμενον, ὅτι
τόνδε λόγον εἰσφέρει,
μὴ δικάζειν δίκας.
Βδ.   ὦγαθοί, τὸ πρᾶγμ' ἀκούσατ', ἀλλὰ μὴ κεκράγετε.   415
Χο.   νὴ Δί', εἰς τὸν οὐρανόν γ'.
Βδ.   ὡς τοῦδ' ἐγὼ οὐ μεθήσομαι.

LINE 408

θαἰμάτια	= τὰ ἱμάτια (for *crasis* with rough breathing: S #64)
ἱμάτιον, τό	(dim. of εἷμα, garment < ἕννῡμι, clothe) cloak; standard outer garment of Athenian citizens. As the boys remove the cloaks of the chorus, the wasp stingers become visible.
παιδίον, τό	small boy, lad (cf. 293)
θέω	(> pres. act. impv. 2 pl. θεῖτε) run
ἀγγέλλω	announce {> *angel, evangelist*}
κελεύω	order, urge (+ acc. + inf.: S #1992a)
ὡς ἐπί	before a prep. ὡς can express purpose: "to come to confront" (LSJ s.v. ὡς C.II, S #2996)
ἐπί	+ acc. expresses hostility: S #1689.3.d
μῑσόπολις, –ιος, ὁ, ἡ	(< μῑσέω, hate + πόλις, city) hating the city

LINE 412

εἰμί	(> pres. ptcp. acc. ὄντα) be
ἀπ-όλλῡμι, ἀπολοῦμαι	destroy, kill; (mid.) perish, be ruined, (fut.) "doomed to die" (ἀπ- in composition intensifies a word: S #1684.2); cf. 274 (κἀπολούμενον = καὶ ἀπολούμενον)
ὅτι	(conj., causal) because
λόγος, –ου, ὁ	idea, proposal (of not holding trials)
εἰσ-φέρω	introduce, bring in

LINE 415

ὦγαθοί	= ὦ ἀγαθοί
πρᾶγμα, –ατος, τό	(with aor. impv. ἀκούσατε) "listen to what I'm doing," "consider the facts"
κράζω, κέκρᾱγα	croak, clamor (perf. has pres. meaning and, unusually, has a simple, non-*periphrastic* impv.: S #697–98; contrast κεκράγετε here with athematic ending κέκραχθι, 198); cf. 103
νὴ Δί'... γε	"Oh yes we *will* [shout]"; affirmative γε, following ναί: GP 131
εἰς τὸν οὐρανόν	"[We will shout] all the way to heaven"
ὡς	a] (conj., ind. statement) "[you should know] that I won't let go"; b] (conj., causal) "[listen] because I won't let go" (giving reason for the statement in 415; νὴ Δι' ... is an interruption)
μεθίημι, –ήσω	release; (mid.) cease from, let go of (+ gen.)

Χο.   ταῦτα δῆτ' οὐ δεινὰ καὶ τυραννίς ἐστιν ἐμφανής;
                ὦ πόλις καὶ Θεώρου θεοιςεχθρία,
                κεἴ τις ἄλλος προέςτηκεν ἡμῶν κόλαξ.
Ξα.   Ἡράκλεις, καὶ κέντρ' ἔχουςιν. οὐχ ὁρᾶς, ὦ δέςποτα;   420
Βδ.   οἷς γ' ἀπώλεςαν Φίλιππον ἐν δίκῃ τὸν Γοργίου.
Χο.   καὶ σέ γ' αὐτοῖς ἐξολοῦμεν· ἀλλὰ πᾶς ἐπίςτρεφε
                δεῦρο κἀξείρας τὸ κέντρον εἶτ' ἐπ' αὐτὸν ἵεςο,
                ξυσταλείς, εὔτακτος, ὀργῆς καὶ μένους ἐμπλήμενος,

---

LINE 417

δῆτα	"Is this not appalling?"; "a note of surprise or indignation . . . is accentuated when ταῦτα, εἶτα, ἔπειτα precedes the particle, as often in Aristophanes": *GP* 272
ἐμφανής, –ές	(< ἐν + φαίνω, reveal) clear, evident
Θέωρος, –ου, ὁ	Theorus (cf. 42)
θεοιςεχθρία, ἡ	hated by the gods; "god-forsaken Theorus" or "detested Theorus" (a *flectional compound* in that θεοίς remains in dat. case as if in an independent clause: S #879)
κεἴ	= καὶ εἰ, which can mean "even if," "although": S #2372; or "and if": S #2373
προ-ίστημι, –έστηκα	set over (+ gen.); be chief power over; support, champion

LINE 420

Ἡρακλῆς, –έους, ὁ	(> voc. Ἡράκλεις) Heracles (an exclam. expressing surprise)
καί	really, actually
οἷς γ'	"Yes—by the very ones which . . ."; antecedent is κέντρα; γε is used in affirmative answers: *GP* 134
ἀπ-όλλυμι, –ώλεσα	destroy
Φίλιππος, ὁ	Philippus, a son or disciple of Gorgias (one expects ὁ Γοργίου to mean "son of Gorgias" but Philippus's identity is unclear); he must have somehow been "stung" with defeat in court.
ἐν δίκῃ a]	a common phrase meaning "justly"; b] in this context, perhaps "in a lawsuit"
Γοργίας, –ου, ὁ	Gorgias, the rhetorician from Sicily who influenced Athenian oratory at the end of the fifth century; Plato devoted a dialogue on rhetoric to him

LINE 422

αὐτοῖς	that is, the stingers
ἐξ-όλλῦμι, –ολῶ	destroy utterly
ἐπι-στρέφω	turn around
ἐξ-είρω, -εῖρα	put forth, extend (κἀξείρᾱς = καὶ ἐξείρᾱς by *crasis*)
ἵημι	(pres. mid. impv. 2 sing. ἵεςο) send, rush; charge

LINE 424

ξυ-στέλλω, aor. pass. -εστάλην	
	(< ξυν + στέλλω, make ready, gather up) draw together, draw in; ξυσταλείς = "with closed ranks," "ready for action" {> apo*stle*, epi*stle*}
εὔτακτος, –ον	(< εὐ + τάττω, order) well-ordered
μένος, –ους, τὸ	might; fierceness, passion
ἐμ-πίμπλημι, mid. aor.² -επλήμην	
	fill up; aor. mid. ἐμπλήμενος = "after filling yourself up" (with gen.: S #1369); cf. 380

ὡς ἂν εὖ εἰδῇ τὸ λοιπὸν cμῆνος οἷον ὤργιcεν.   425

Ξα. τοῦτο μέντοι δεινὸν ἤδη, νὴ Δί᾽, εἰ μαχούμεθα·
ὡς ἔγωγ᾽ αὐτῶν ὁρῶν δέδοικα τὰς ἐγκεντρίδας.

Χο. ἀλλ᾽ ἀφίει τὸν ἄνδρ᾽· εἰ δὲ μή, φήμ᾽ ἐγὼ
τὰς χελώνας μακαριεῖν σε τοῦ δέρματος.

Φι. εἶά νυν, ὦ ξυνδικαcταί, cφῆκες ὀξυκάρδιοι,   430
οἱ μὲν εἰς τὸν πρωκτὸν αὐτῶν εἰcπέτεcθ᾽ ὠργιcμένοι,
οἱ δὲ τὠφθαλμὼ κύκλῳ κεντεῖτε καὶ τοὺς δακτύλους.

Βδ. ὦ Μίδα καὶ Φρύξ, βοήθει δεῦρο, καὶ Μαcυντία,
καὶ λάβεcθε τουτουὶ καὶ μὴ μεθῆcθε μηδενί·

LINE 425

ὡς ἄν   so that (purpose clause: S #2201)
οἶδα   (> subjv. 3 sing. εἰδῇ) know (cf. 376)
τὸ λοιπόν   (adv. acc.) in the future
cμῆνος, –εος, τό   beehive
οἷος (3)   what sort of (rel. pron., here modifying cμῆνος)

LINE 426

μέντοι   "Really, you know" (cf. 231)
ἤδη   (< ἤ, really + δή, even) although ἤδη normally conveys notions of time in relation to the present moment ("already" or "now") it can also express urgency: "<u>really</u> awful"
ὡς   "how . . . !" (exclam.)
ὁράω   (> pres. act. ptcp. ὁρῶν) see
ἐγκεντρίς, –ίδος, ἡ   (< ἐν + κέντρον, goad + -ις, -ιδος, dim. suffix: S #853) stinger

LINE 428

ἀφ-ίημι   (> pres. act. impv. 2 sing. ἀφίει) release, let go
χελώνη, ἡ   tortoise
μακαρίζω, μακαριῶ   deem happy, envy (inf. in ind. statement after φημί; acc. σε as subject)
δέρμα, –ατος, τό   skin, hide; shell (gen. of cause: S #1405) {> epi*dermis, derm*-}

LINE 430

εἶά νῦν   "Come on now!"
ὀξυκάρδιος, –ον   (< ὀξύς, sharp + καρδία, heart) quick to anger, irascible
οἱ μέν . . . οἱ δέ   The chorus break into two different squads for the assault.
εἰσ-πέτομαι   fly into, against (cf. 16)
ὀφμαλμός, ὁ   (< ὀφθῆναι < ὁράω, see; τὠφθαλμὼ = τὼ ὀφθαλμώ, by *crasis*, dual: S #231) eye

LINE 433

Μίδας, –ου, ὁ   (> voc. Μίδα) Midas. Three slaves are called upon for help. Slaves in comedy generally have ethnic names (after their country of origin), such as Μίδας (a notable Phyrgian name); Φρύξ, "Phrygian"; Θρᾷττα, "Thracian girl," 828; Δαρδανίς, "Dardanian girl," 1371; or are given nicknames: Sosias, "Savior," and Xanthias, "Golden Hair."
Φρύξ, –γος, ὁ   (voc. = nom.) Phrygian
βοηθέω   (< βοή, call + θέω, run) help
Μαcυντίας, –ου, ὁ   (> voc. Μαcυντίᾱ < perhaps μαcάομαι, chew = "Chewer"?) Masyntias
λαμβάνω   take; (mid.) take hold of (+ part. gen.: S #1345)
μεθ-ίημι, –ῆκα   (aor. mid. subjv. 2 pl. μεθῆcθε) release, let go of
μη . . . μηδενί   "not . . . to anyone" (compound neg. reinforces prior simple neg.: S #2761)

83

εἰ δὲ μή, ᾿ν πέδαις παχείαις οὐδὲν ἀριστήσετε,　　　　　　435
ὡς ἐγὼ πολλῶν ἀκούσας οἶδα θρίων τὸν ψόφον.

Χο.　　εἰ δὲ μὴ τοῦτον μεθήσεις, ἔν τί σοι παγήσεται.

Φι.　　ὦ Κέκροψ ἥρως ἄναξ, τὰ πρὸς ποδῶν Δρακοντίδη,
περιορᾷς οὕτω μ᾿ ὑπ᾿ ἀνδρῶν βαρβάρων χειρούμενον,
οὓς ἐγὼ ᾿δίδαξα κλάειν τέτταρ᾿ εἰς τὴν χοίνικα;　　　440

LINE 435

εἰ δὲ μή	"but if not" = "otherwise"; *ellipsis* of verb of protasis
᾿ν	= ἐν
πέδη, ἡ	fetter; (pl.) shackles
παχύς, –εῖα, –ύ	thick, stout (cf. 287)
ἀριστάω, -ήσω	have lunch (cf. 306)
ὡς	(conj., causal) because
ἀκούω, ἤκουσα	hear (+ gen. of person + acc. of the sound: S #1361); the ptcp. may be circumstantial ("having heard, I know") or suppl. ("I know that I heard")
θρῖον, τό	fig-leaf
ψόφος, ὁ	empty sound, noise. The "sound of fig-leaves" was meaningless noise (cf. 143)

LINE 437

ἐμ-πήγνῦμι, aor. pass. -ἐπάγην	
	plant in (prefix ἐν separated from verb by *tmesis*: S #1650–51)
Κέκροψ, –οπος, ὁ	Cecrops, mythical king of Athens and defender of Athenians, conventionally depicted as a serpent from waist down
τὰ πρὸς ποδῶν	"with respect to the things toward the feet" = "below the waist" (τά = acc. of respect)
Δρακοντίδης, –ους, ὁ	(> voc. –ίδη) Dracontides (cf. 157)
περι-οράω	overlook, allow
χειρόω	(< χείρων worse, comparative of κακός) overpower, man-handle
᾿δίδαξα	= ἐδίδαξα (*aphaeresis*)
τέτταρα	four (acc. object of κλάειν); cf. 260
χοῖνιξ, –ικος, ἡ	*choinix*, a dry measure of grain: about a quart, composed of four κοτύλαι (cups): "cry four to the quart" (εἰς + acc., used in measurements "four to …": S #1686c)

Χο. εἶτα δῆτ' οὐ πόλλ' ἔνεστι δεινὰ τῷ γήρᾳ κακά;
     δηλαδή· καὶ νῦν γε τούτω τὸν παλαιὸν δεσπότην
     πρὸς βίαν χειροῦσιν, οὐδὲν τῶν πάλαι μεμνημένοι
     διφθερῶν κἀξωμίδων, ἃς οὗτος αὐτοῖς ἠμπόλα,
     καὶ κυνᾶς· καὶ τοὺς πόδας χειμῶνος ὄντος ὠφέλει,   445
     ὥστε μὴ ῥιγῶν ἑκάστοτ'· ἀλλὰ τούτοις γ' οὐκ ἔνι
     οὐδ' ἐν ὀφθαλμοῖσιν αἰδὼς τῶν παλαιῶν ἐμβάδων.

LINE 441

δῆτα	"Really!?"; conveys surprise or, as here, indignation following εἶτα: *GP* 272 (cf. 24)
ἔν-ειμι	be in, be present, be in abundance
γῆρας, –ως, τό	old age
δηλαδή	(adv. < δῆλος, clear + δή) quite clearly
τούτω	"these two [slaves]" (dual subject may take pl. verb: S #955)
παλαιός (3)	old, old in years; former (cf. 317)
βία, ἡ	force; πρὸς βίαν = "by force"
χειρόω	overpower (cf. 439)
μιμνήσκω	remember (frequently with gen.: S #1356; cf. 354)
διφθέρα, ἡ	tanned skin, leather jacket worn by herdsmen {> *diphtheria*}
ἐξωμίς, –ίδος, ἡ	(< ὦμος, shoulder) tunic with one sleeve, leaving shoulder bare
αὐτοῖς	dat. of advantage: S #1481
ἐμ-πολάω	(> imperfect act. indic. 3 sing. ἠμπόλᾱ) purchase

LINE 445

κυνῆ, ἡ	"dog's skin"; leather cap
χειμών, –ῶνος, ὁ	winter (χειμῶνος ὄντος gen. abs.: S #2070) [< IE *ghei-*, winter; cogn. L. *hiems*; Sanskrit *Hima*laya]
ὠφελέω	help, do a service (cf. 121)
ῥῑγόω	(> pres. act. inf., spelled either ῥῑγοῦν or, as here, ῥῑγῶν: S #398, 655) be cold, shiver (ὥστε with inf. for natural result: S #2260)
ἑκάστοτε	(adv. < ἕκαστος, each + -τε, suffix indicating time: S #344) each time, regularly
ἀλλά	"further"; progressive: "I've spoken of that, but now let me speak of this . . .": *GP* 21–22
οὐ . . . οὐδέ	οὐδέ counts as a compound neg. or is an emphatic "not even": S #2761
αἰδώς, –ους, ἡ	sense of shame, respect
ἐμβάς, –άδος, ἡ	shoe (cf. 103). A joke: we expect δεσποτῶν but get ἐμβάδων.

Φι.   οὐκ ἀφήϲειϲ οὐδὲ νυνί μ’, ὦ κάκιϲτον θηρίον,
        οὐδ’ ἀναμνηϲθεὶϲ ὅθ’ εὑρὼν τοὺϲ βότρυϲ κλέπτοντά ϲε
        προϲαγαγὼν πρὸϲ τὴν ἐλάαν ἐξέδειρ’ εὖ κἀνδρικῶϲ,   450
        ὥϲτε ϲε ζηλωτὸν εἶναι; ϲὺ δ’ ἀχάριϲτοϲ ἦϲθ’ ἄρα.
        ἀλλ’ ἄνεϲ με καὶ ϲὺ καὶ ϲύ, πρὶν τὸν υἱὸν ἐκδραμεῖν.
Χο.   ἀλλὰ τούτων μὲν τάχ’ ἡμῖν δώϲετον καλὴν δίκην,
        οὐκέτ’ εἰϲ μακράν, ἵν’ εἰδῆθ’ οἷόϲ ἐϲτ’ ἀνδρῶν τρόποϲ
        ὀξυθύμων καὶ δικαίων καὶ βλεπόντων κάρδαμα.   455

LINE 448

θηρίον, τό	wild animal (cf. 23)
ἀνα-μιμνήϲκω	(ἀνά in composition often = "again") remind one of (cf. 443)
ὅθ’	= ὅτι
βότρυϲ, –υοϲ, ὁ	(> acc. pl. βότρυϲ) cluster of grapes
προϲ-άγω, aor.² -ήγαγον	
	bring to
ἐλάα, ἡ	olive tree (cf. 252)
ἐκ-δέρω, -έδειρα	skin, flay. Phil. comically undercuts the chorus leader's argument that the slaves should show appreciation for their former master!
κἀνδρικῶϲ	= καὶ ἀνδρικῶϲ (cf. 153)

LINE 451

ζηλωτόϲ (3)	(< ζηλόω, emulate; verbal adjs. in –τόϲ often express pass. meaning or possibility: S #472) worthy of emulation, deemed happy {> zeal, jealous}
ἀχάριϲτοϲ, –ον	(ἀ- priv. + χάριϲ, grace cf. 186) thankless, ungrateful
εἰμί	> imperfect 2 sing. ἦϲθα
ἄρα	"as I now realize"; with imperfect, marking a realization: GP 36–7 (cf. 3)
ἀν-ίημι, -ῆκα	(> aor. act. impv. 2 sing. ἄνεϲ) send forth, let loose
ἐκ-τρέχω, aor.² -έδραμον	
	run out (cf. 376)

LINE 453

τούτων	"for this" (gen. of crime: S #1375)
δίκην δίδωμι	(> fut. act. indic. dual δώϲετον) pay the price, suffer punishment
μακράν	(adv.) far; (time) long; εἰϲ μακράν = "for long"
οἶδα	(> subjv. 2 pl. εἰδῆθ’ = εἰδῆτε) know
ὀξύθῡμοϲ, –ον	quick to anger (cf. 406)
κάρδαμον, τό	cress, with a seed like mustard; a "mustard look" was a fierce expression

Βδ.	παῖε, παῖ', ὦ Ξανθία, τοὺς cφῆκας ἀπὸ τῆς οἰκίας.
Ξα.	ἀλλὰ δρῶ τοῦτ'.
Βδ.	ἀλλὰ καὶ cὺ τῦφε πολλῷ τῷ καπνῷ.
Ξα.	οὐχὶ coῦcθ'; οὐκ ἐς κόρακας; οὐκ ἄπιτε;
Βδ.	παῖε τῷ ξύλῳ·

καὶ cὺ προcθεὶς Αἰcχίνην ἔντυφε τὸν Cελλαρτίου.

ἆρ' ἐμέλλομέν ποθ' ὑμᾶc ἀποcοβήcειν τῷ χρόνῳ;   460

Φι.   ἀλλὰ μὰ Δί' οὐ ῥᾳδίως οὕτως ἂν αὐτοὺς διέφυγες,

LINE 456

456–87: A melee breaks out between the wasps and Bdel.'s slaves, who use smoke to shoo them away. The chorus back off, but they accuse Bdel. of being a would-be monarchist who deprives citizens of their legal rights.

παίω	strike (cf. 398)
ἀλλά	"But of course; I'm *doing* it . . ."; assentient, spoken by Xanthias: *GP* 16–17
ἀλλά	transition to impv.; spoken by Bdel. (cf. 240)
τύφω	smoke out

LINE 458

cεύω	hunt, drive away; here cοῦcθε = "shoo!" (cf. pass. impv. cοῦ, 209) Xanthias is addressing the mute slaves.
ἄπ-ειμι	(< εἶμι) go away
προc-τίθημι, -έθηκα	put to, add on, apply
Αἰcχίνης, –ου, ὁ	Aeschines, ridiculed as boaster and thus a source of hot air. Proper names ending in –ης may have an acc. in –ην or –η: S #264b; Αἰcχίνην is object of ptcp. προcθείς.
ἐν-τύφω	smoke, suffocate; "suffocate them with a billow of Aeschines": Hend.
Cελλάρτιος	Sellartius (cf. 325, another boasting son of Sellos, evidently)

LINE 460

μέλλω	to be about to (+ fut. inf.); in imperfect, "weren't we sure to . . . ?"
ἀπο-cοβέω, cοβήcω	scare away; make run away (*causative*)
χρόνος, ὁ	time; χρόνῳ = over time, eventually, at last {> *chrono*logy, *chron*icle}

LINE 461

ἀλλά	"Sorry, but that's not how this is going to work!"; invalidates previous statement, expresses opposition: *GP* 7
οὕτως	so (occasionally *follows* the adj. or noun it affects)
ἄν	with aor. indic. in past Contrary-to-Fact condit.: S #1302
αὐτούς	that is, the wasps
δια-φεύγω, aor.² -έφυγον	
	escape

Χο.

εἴπερ ἔτυχον τῶν μελῶν τῶν Φιλοκλέους βεβρωκότες.
ἆρα δῆτ᾽ οὐκ αὐτὰ δῆλα
τοῖς πένησιν, ἡ τυραννὶς ὡς λάθρᾳ γ᾽ ἐ-
λάμβαν᾽ ὑπιοῦσά με,   465
εἰ σύ γ᾽, ὦ πονωπόνηρε καὶ Κομηταμυνία,
τῶν νόμων ἡμᾶς ἀπείργεις ὧν ἔθηκεν ἡ πόλις,
οὔτε τιν᾽ ἔχων πρόφασιν
οὔτε λόγον εὐτράπελον,
αὐτὸς ἄρχων μόνος;   470

LINE 462

εἴπερ	"if" (but sometimes with a causal force, as the writer knows it to be true, and hence also "because": S #2246)
μέλος, –ους, τό	(> gen. pl. μελέων, contracted to μελῶν: S #171c) song; can also mean "limb" of a body (cf. 219)
Φιλοκλῆς, –έους, ὁ	Philocles, tragic poet, Aeschylus's nephew, known for his harsh style. The chorus are less effective because they have not kept a strict diet of Philocles's songs.
βιβρώσκω, βέβρωκα	(< βορά, food) eat (+ gen. with verb of eating: S #1355)

LINE 463

463–87: The chorus turn from physical to rhetorical attacks, accusing Bdel. of attempting to impose a tyranny or monarchy on Athens.

463–525: Meter: As in 403–62, mixed trochees and trochaic tetrameters (up to 477) are followed by trochaic tetrameters. The chorus may have withdrawn and returned to the orchestra.

δῆτα	"therefore," "so," "in that case"; conveys a logical, connective force: *GP* 271 (cf. 24)
αὐτά	"by themselves"
πένης, –ητος, ὁ	(< πένομαι, toil; cf. on πόνος, 192) one who must toil; poor person
ὡς	(conj.) "how" or "that"
λάθρα	(adv.) secretly
ἐλάμβανε	"was trying to take" (*conative* imperfect: S #1895)
ὕπ-ειμι	(< ὑπό, expressing something underhanded: S # 1698.4 + εἶμι) steal upon

LINE 466

εἰ ... γε	"if in fact you are doing this"; the speaker is not concerned with what may or may not be true apart from the qualification laid down in the subordinate clause: *GP* 141–42
πονωπόνηρος, –ον	troublesome troublemaker (not in LSJ; see Wilson, pp. 138–39)
Κομηταμυνίας, –ου, ὁ	(> voc. –ιᾶ < κομήτης, wearing long hair) "Long-Haired Amynias" (cf. 74); wearing hair long suggested a penchant for Spartan fashion and, seen through the lens of populist conspiracy-theory paranoia, reveals a desire for tyrannical, antidemocratic policies.
νόμος, ὁ	law [< IE *nem-, share, assign; cogn. L. *numerus*]
ἀπ-είργω	(< ἀπό + εἴργω, shut, bar way) keep away, debar acc. from gen. (cf. 334)
ὧν	(properly the rel. should be οὕς, acc. object of ἔθηκεν, but is gen. by attraction with its antecedent, νόμων: S #2522)

LINE 468

πρόφασις, –εως, ἡ	pretext, excuse, declared cause (cf. 174)
εὐτράπελος, –ον	(< εὖ + τρέπω, turn + –λος, adj. suffix: S #858.7) easily turning; dexterous, clever
μόνος (3)	alone; "autocratic" {> monastery, mono-}

Βδ.　ἔcθ' ὅπωc ἄνευ μάχηc καὶ τῆc κατοξείαc βοῆc
　　εἰc λόγουc ἔλθοιμεν ἀλλήλοιcι καὶ διαλλαγάc;

Χο.　coὺc λόγουc, ὦ μιcόδημε
　　καὶ μοναρχίαc ἐραcτὰ
　　καὶ ξυνὼν Βραcίδᾳ καὶ φορῶν κράcπεδα　　　　　475
　　cτεμμάτων τήν θ' ὑπήνην ἄκουρον τρέφων;　　476/7

Βδ.　νὴ Δί' ἤ μοι κρεῖττον ἐκcτῆναι τὸ παράπαν τοῦ πατρὸc
　　μᾶλλον ἢ κακοῖc τοcούτοιc ναυμαχεῖν ὁcημέραι.

Χο.　οὐδὲ μὴν οὐδ' ἐν cελίνῳ coὐcτὶν οὐδ' ἐν πηγάνῳ·　　480
　　τοῦτο γὰρ παρεμβαλοῦμεν τῶν τριχοινίκων ἐπῶν.

LINE 471

ἔcθ' ὅπωc	cf. 212 for the construction
ἄνευ	(prep. + gen.) without
κατοξύc, –εῖα, –υ	(κατά in composition intensifies: S #1690.3 + ὀξύc, sharp) piercing, shrill
βοή, ἡ	shout, scream
εἰc λόγουc ἐλθεῖν	converse, enter into discussion
ἀλλήλων	one another (exists only in gen., dat., acc.)
διαλλαγή, ἡ	(< διά, connoting reciprocity: S #1685.3 + ἀλλάττω, change, make other) exchange; (pl.) reconciliation (sc. εἰc with this acc.)

LINE 474

coύc	= coι εἰc (note also *ellipsis* for coὺc λόγουc <ἔλθωμεν>)
μῑcόδημοc, –ον	hating the common people
μοναρχία, ἡ	monarchy, rule by one person
ἐραcτήc, –οῦ, ὁ	lover (cf. 89)
Βρᾱcίδαc, –ου, ὁ	Brasidas, Spartan general
φορέω	bear habitually, carry; wear (cf. 116)
κράcπεδον, τό	edge, border; fringe
cτέμμα, –ατοc, τό	(< cτέφω, encircle, wreath) wreath, garland; wool {> *stemma*}
ὑπήνη, ἡ	beard
ἄκουροc, –ον	(< κουρά, haircut < κείρω cut) unshaven

LINE 477

ἤ μοι κρεῖττον	= ἤ μοι κρεῖττον ἂν ἦν (cf. 209)
ἐξ-ίcτημι, –έcτην	put out of place; stand apart from, abandon (+ gen.)
τὸ παράπαν	(adv. < παρά, beyond, beside + πᾶν, all) completely, altogether
τοcοῦτοc (3)	so great
ναυμαχέω	(< ναῦc, ship + μάχη, battle) engage in a sea battle; battle against (+ dat.)
ὁcημέραι	(adv. < ὅcαι + ἡμέραι) "as many days as are"; daily

LINE 480

μήν	a progressive use, adding fresh points: *GP* 336; after οὐδέ = "nor again": *GP* 340
cέλῑνον, τό	celery; being "in celery and rue" was proverbial for being "at the edge of" something
πήγανον, τό	rue. An herb native to the Balkans and Greece.
τοῦτο	refers to the previous sentence
παρ-εμ-βάλλω, –βαλῶ	(for παρά in composition, cf. 478) insert, put in beside
τριχοίνικοc, –ον	holding three *choinikes* (cf. 440)
ἔποc, –εοc, τό	word {> *epic*}

ἀλλὰ νῦν μὲν οὐδὲν ἀλγεῖς, ἀλλ' ὅταν ξυνήγορος
ταὐτὰ ταῦτά σου καταντλῇ καὶ ξυνωμότην καλῇ.

Βδ.   ἆρ' ἄν, ὦ πρὸς τῶν θεῶν, ὑμεῖς ἀπαλλαχθεῖτέ μου;
         ἦ δέδοκταί τοι δέρεσθαι καὶ δέρειν δι' ἡμέρας;   485

Χο.   οὐδέποτέ γ', οὔχ, ἕως ἄν τί μου λοιπὸν ᾖ—
         ὅστις ἡμῶν ἐπὶ τυραννίδ' ⟨ὧδ'⟩ ἐστάλης.

LINE 482

ἀλλὰ νῦν   "Well, anyway—where were we?"; the speaker breaks off reflections and describes future actions: *GP* 8; an *ellipsis* is assumed with the second ἀλλά: "but <you *will* feel pain> when"

ἀλγέω   be in pain

μέν . . . ἀλλά   "Aye, but . . ."; the ἀλλά clause answers the μέν clause, virtually invalidating it: *GP* 5

ξυνήγορος, ὁ   (> συν + ἀγορεύω, speak; cf. 35) prosecutor; a publicly appointed advocate to prosecute a case of significance such as treason or *euthynai*

ταὐτά   = τὰ αὐτά, "the same things" (cf. 22)

ταῦτα   "these things," that is, the charges of conspiracy

κατ-αντλέω   pour water over; pour a flood [of words/charges] over [you, in gen.]

καλέω   call (sc. σε as object, take ξυνωμότην as pred.)

LINE 484

ὤ   "Oh!" (exclam.; contrast ὦ, used with voc. for direct address)

πρός   "by [the gods]" (in oaths, + gen.)

ἀπ-αλλάττω, aor. pass. -ηλλάχθην
     release; (pass., + gen.) be free of, depart from, <u>leave me alone</u> (potential opt. with ἄν used in quests.: S #1831); cf. 473 on ἀλλάττω

δέρω   skin, flay (cf. 429)

διά   all through (+ gen., temporal), <u>all day long</u>

LINE 486

οὐδέποτέ γε   "Never!"; emphatic γε in neg. answer: *GP* 131

ἕως   so long as (with ἄν + subjv.: S #2423)

εἰμί   > pres. subjv. 3 sing. ᾖ

ὅστις   sc. antecedent σύ (= Bdel.)

ἡμῶν   "[tyranny] over us" (objective gen.: S #1331)

ἐπί   aiming at (+ dat.; with intention of: S #1689.3d)

ὧδε   (adv.) in this way

στέλλω, aor. pass. ἐστάλην
     make ready; send (cf. 424)

Βδ.
ὡς ἄπανθ' ὑμῖν τυραννίς ἐcτι καὶ ξυνωμόται,
ἤν τε μεῖζον ἤν τ' ἔλαττον πρᾶγμά τις κατηγορῇ.
ἧς ἐγὼ οὐκ ἤκουσα τοὔνομ' οὐδὲ πεντήκοντ' ἐτῶν·   490
νῦν δὲ πολλῷ τοῦ ταρίχους ἐcτὶν ἀξιωτέρα,
ὥστε καὶ δὴ τοὔνομ' αὐτῆς ἐν ἀγορᾷ κυλίνδεται.
ἢν μὲν ὠνῆταί τις ὀρφῶς, μεμβράδας δὲ μὴ 'θέλῃ,
εὐθέως εἴρηχ' ὁ πωλῶν πληcίον τὰς μεμβράδας·

LINE 488

488–511: Bdel. responds to their charges: the chorus are overreacting—there has not been a threat of tyranny for fifty years. Rather, Bdel.'s desire is for Phil. to live a more genteel life.

ὡς	(exclam.) "See how . . . !"
μείζων, –ον, –ονος	greater (cf. 258)
ἐλάττων, –ον, –ονος	(> ἐλαχύς, small; serves as comparative of μικρός) lesser [< IE *legʷh, light; cogn. L. *levis*; E. *light, lung*; Irish *leprechaun*]
ἤν	= ἐάν (Pres. Gen. condit.: S #2337)
ἧς	antecedent is τυραννίς
τοὔνομ'	= τὸ ὄνομα, name; word (cf. 133)
οὐδέ	(adv.) not even
πεντήκοντα	(indeclinable) fifty
ἔτος, –εος, τό	year (gen. of time within which: S #1444)
πολλῷ	dat. degree of difference: S #1513
τάριχος, –ους, τό	preserved fish (gen. of comparison: S #1431)
ἀξιώτερος (3)	(> comparative of ἄξιος, worthy) worthier; a better value, cheaper {> *axiomatic*}

LINE 492

καὶ δή	"See there!"; vividly signifies that something is actually taking place, sometimes signals entrance of a character: *GP* 250–51; introduces a climax: S #2847
αὐτῆς	that is, τυραννίς
κυλίνδω	roll, bandy about
ἢν ὠνῆται, . . . εἴρηκε	Pres. Gen. condit.: S #2337
ὀρφῶς, –ῶ, ὁ	(> acc. pl. –ῶς: S #238) perch. Perch was more expensive than sprats, so buying it would make someone seem an extravagant aristocrat.
μεμβράς, –άδας, ἡ	small sprats, anchovy
'θέλῃ	= ἐθέλω (by *aphaeresis*), comedy prefers ἐθέλω, tragedy θέλω
πωλέω	sell {> mono*poly*}
πληcίον	(adv.) nearby (cf. 42)

"οὗτος ὀψωνεῖν ἔοιχ' ἄνθρωπος ἐπὶ τυραννίδι."   495
ἢν δὲ γήτειον προσαιτῇ ταῖς ἀφύαις ἥδυσμά τι,
ἡ λαχανόπωλις παραβλέψασά φησι θατέρῳ·
"εἰπέ μοι· γήτειον αἰτεῖς· πότερον ἐπὶ τυραννίδι;
ἢ νομίζεις τὰς Ἀθήνας σοὶ φέρειν ἡδύσματα;"
Ξα.   κἀμέ γ' ἡ πόρνη χθὲς εἰσελθόντα τῆς μεσημβρίας,   500
ὅτι κελητίσαι 'κέλευον, ὀξυθυμηθεῖσά μοι
ἦρετ' εἰ τὴν Ἱππίου καθίσταμαι τυραννίδα.

LINE 495

ὀψωνέω   (< ὄψον, delicacies, cf. 301) buy fish and delicacies
ἔοιχ'   = ἔοικε, seems {> icon}
ἄνθρωπος   = ὁ ἄνθρωπος
ἐπί   (+ dat.) with an eye to, with the intention of
γήτειον, τό   leek, onion
προσ-αιτέω   (< αἰτέω, beg) ask in addition, ask for something free
ἀφύη, ἡ   sardine, small fry
ἥδυσμα, –ατος, τό   (< ἡδύς, sweet, cf. 272) a garnish, spice

LINE 497

λαχανόπωλις, –ιδος, ἡ   (< λάχανον, vegetable + πωλέω sell) green groceress [cf. λαχαίνω, dig]
παρα-βλέπω, –έβλεψα   take a side-long glance
θᾱτέρῳ   = τῷ ἑτέρῳ <ὀφθαλμῷ> (for the *ellipsis*, cf. LSJ s.v. ἕτερος IV.a) "with one eye," "looking
                        suspiciously, with side-long glance." It seems presumptuous to expect free spices—or
                        so the green groceress will claim!
πότερον . . . ἤ   whether . . . or (alternative quests.). MacD. suggests that the string of short syllables
                        at the end of 498 imply nagging or chattering.
Ἀθῆναι, –ων, αἱ   Athens (acc. subject of inf.)
φέρω   "pay" tax, bring as tribute: LSJ A.IV.5

LINE 500

κἀμέ   = καὶ ἐμέ
κἀμέ γε   "Yes (γε): that even (adv. καί) happened to *me* (ἐμέ)"
πόρνη, ἡ   (< πέρνημι, buy) prostitute, slut (often a bought slave); a ἑταίρα, by contrast, was a
                    higher-class courtesan who could be a free person.
χθές   (adv.) yesterday (cf. 242)
μεσημβρία, ἡ   (< μέσος, mid- + ἡμέρα, day) midday (gen. of time within which), cf. 179
κελητίζω   (< κέλης, riding horse) "ride horse (sc. ἵππος)"; sexual position with woman on
                    top: *MM* pp. 174–75
ὀξυθῡμέω, aor. pass. –θῡμήθην
                    be quick to provoke (cf. 406)
ἔρομαι, aor.² ἠρόμην   ask
Ἱππίας, –ου, ὁ   Hippias, Athenian tyrant of sixth century BC. A crude pun: a sexual position (riding a
                    ἵππος) brings to mind the name of the tyrant (Ἱππίας).
καθ-ίστημι   set down, establish (ind. quest. introduced by εἰ, "whether"; ἤρετο is secondary tense
                    yet the indic. καθίσταμαι is *retained* for vividness: S #2677a)

Βδ.　　　　ταῦτα γὰρ τούτοις ἀκούειν ἡδέ᾽, εἰ καὶ νῦν ἐγώ,
　　　　　τὸν πατέρ᾽ ὅτι βούλομαι τούτων ἀπαλλαχθέντα τῶν
　　　　　ὀρθροφοιτοσυκοφαντοδικοταλαιπώρων τρόπων　　　　　505
　　　　　ζῆν βίον γενναῖον ὥσπερ Μόρυχος, αἰτίαν ἔχω
　　　　　ταῦτα δρᾶν ξυνωμότης ὢν καὶ φρονῶν τυραννικά.
Φι.　　　νὴ Δί᾽ ἐν δίκῃ γ᾽· ἐγὼ γὰρ οὐδ᾽ ἂν ὀρνίθων γάλα
　　　　　ἀντὶ τοῦ βίου λάβοιμ᾽ ἂν οὗ με νῦν ἀποστερεῖς·

LINE 503

ταῦτα	"these [words]," that is, words such as "tyranny"
γάρ	"Let me elaborate"; introduces "a generalizing explanation of the preceding instances": MacD. Bdel. picks up from 499, ignoring Xanthias's interruption.
τούτοις	these people, that is, the chorus and Phil.
ἡδέ᾽	= ἡδέα (< ἡδύς)
εἰ	since (cf. MacD. and LSJ B.VI; = *siquidem*, if in fact, seeing that: *GP* 303). The εἰ . . . ἔχω clause is interrupted by the ὅτι βούλομαι clause.
ὅτι	because (note word order; the conj. is postponed)
ἀπ-αλλάττω, aor. pass. -ηλλάχθην	free from (cf. 484)
ὀρθροφοιτοσυκοφαντοδικοταλαίπωρος, –ον	(adj. > ὄρθρος, dawn + φοιτάω, wander, come and go + συκοφάντης, informers who took advantage of the legal system to file nuisance lawsuits + δίκη, lawsuit + ταλαίπωρος, –ον, miserable) early-prowling, base-informing, sad-litigious plaguey (or, Hend.: dawn-wandering, nuisance-suing, jury-serving, trouble-seeking). One of several of Ar.'s comically long compound words, this encapsulates the jurors' mode of life.
ζάω	live (πατέρα is acc. subject of inf. ζῆν) {> zoo-, zodiac}
γενναῖος (3)	(< γέννα, descent, birth) noble, genteel
Μόρυχος, ὁ	Morychus, famous as gourmand
αἰτία, ἡ	charge, accusation (ἔχω αἰτίαν + inf. = "I am charged with . . .") {> etiology}
φρονέω	be minded, have in mind (cf. 25)
τυραννικός (3)	tyrannical (for –ικός adjs. cf. 66)

LINE 508

γε	"Deservedly, by Zeus!"; γε follows word that it stresses; the word is sometimes preceded by an exclam. or oath; cf. 1474, *GP* 128
ὄρνις, ὄρνιθος, ὁ, ἡ	bird {> ornitho-}
γάλα, γάλακτος, τό	milk; bird's milk was a proverbial gourmand's delicacy. B-O report that even today bird's milk is "the slogan of the Alfa-Beta grocery store chain in Greece ('καὶ τοῦ πουλιοῦ τὸ γάλα!')" (< πουλί, "bird" in demotic). {> galaxy (milk spilled into the heavens from Hera's breast)}
ἄν	(with potential opt.; for repetition of ἄν: S #1765)
ἀπο-στερέω	(< στερέω, deprive) rob, defraud acc. of gen. (cf. 256)

οὐδὲ χαίρω βατίϲιν οὐδ' ἐγχέλεϲιν, ἀλλ' ἥδιον ἂν 510
δικίδιον ϲμικρὸν φάγοιμ' ἂν ἐν λοπάδι πεπνιγμένον.
Βδ.   νὴ Δί', εἰθίϲθηϲ γὰρ ἥδεϲθαι τοιούτοιϲ πράγμαϲιν·
ἀλλ' ἐὰν ϲιγῶν ἀνάϲχῃ καὶ μάθῃϲ ἁγὼ λέγω,
ἀναδιδάξειν οἴομαί ϲ' ὡϲ πάντα ταῦθ' ἁμαρτάνειϲ.
Φι.   ἐξαμαρτάνω δικάζων;
Βδ.   καταγελώμενοϲ μὲν οὖν 515
οὐκ ἐπαΐειϲ ὑπ' ἀνδρῶν, οὓϲ ϲὺ μόνον οὐ προϲκυνεῖϲ.

LINE 510

βατίϲ, –ίδοϲ, ἡ	a fish, perhaps skate
ἔγχελυϲ, –εωϲ, ἡ	eel. This and skate were delicacies that Phil. would renounce.
ἥδῑον	(adv. acc.) sweeter, with more pleasure (cf. 272)
δικίδιον, τό	(< δίκη + –ιδιον, dim. suffix: S #852.2) a little trial
λοπάϲ, –άδοϲ, ἡ	pot with a lid, for casserole (cf. 105)
πνίγω, πέπνῑγμαι	choke; bake in a covered pot

LINE 512

512–25: Bdel. now takes the quarrel in a new direction: he will make the case that serving on a jury is a mistake and that jurors are slaves, not masters.

ἐθίζω, εἰθίϲθην	(< ἔθοϲ, custom, habit + -ίζω of *denominative* vbs.) accustomed (cf. 94)
ἥδομαι	(< ἡδύϲ, cf. 272) enjoy (+ dat.)
ἀν-έχω, -έϲχον	(> aor. mid. 2 sing. ἀνάϲχῃ) hold up; (mid.) bear up, be patient
ἁγώ	= ἃ ἐγώ
ἀνα-διδάϲκω	(ἀνα- connotes "again": S #1682.3) teach; reteach, improve by instruction
οἴομαι	think, suppose (introduces indir. statement with inf.: S #2018; subject of inf. is omitted if it is the same as that of the governing verb: S #1973)
πάντα ταῦτα	acc. respect: S #1600
ἁμαρτάνω	err, miss the mark

LINE 515

ἐξ-αμαρτάνω	(< ἐξ- connoting thoroughness: S #1682.3 + ἁμαρτάνω, fail) blunder completely, fail utterly (used with suppl. ptcp.: S #2101)
κατα-γελάω	(< κατά, affecting someone adversely: S #1690.3) laugh at, laugh scornfully (cf. 57)
μὲν οὖν	"You don't know the half of it . . ." "And what's more . . . ," correcting the previous speaker; μέν is advers., emphasized by οὖν: GP 475
ἐπαΐω	(< ἐπ-, to, at + ἀΐω, hear) give ear to, perceive, understand (verb of perception + prtp. in ind. statement: S #2112b); "you don't understand that you're being laughed at"
ὑπό	by (gen. of agent: GP 475)
μόνον οὐ	all but
προϲκυνέω	(< κυνέω, kiss) worship, revere [< IE *kwas, kiss; cogn. E. *kiss*]

ἀλλὰ δουλεύων λέληθας.

Φι.   παῦε δουλείαν λέγων,
ὅστις ἄρχω τῶν ἁπάντων.

Βδ.   οὐ σύ γ', ἀλλ' ὑπηρετεῖς
οἰόμενος ἄρχειν· ἐπεὶ δίδαξον ἡμᾶς, ὦ πάτερ,
ἥτις ἡ τιμή 'στί σοι καρπουμένῳ τὴν Ἑλλάδα.   520

Φι.   πάνυ γε, καὶ τούτοισί γ' ἐπιτρέψαι 'θέλω.

Βδ.   καὶ μὴν ἐγώ.
ἄφετέ νυν ἅπαντες αὐτόν.

Φι.   καὶ ξίφος γέ μοι δότε.
ἢν γὰρ ἡττηθῶ λέγων σου, περιπεσοῦμαι τῷ ξίφει.

Βδ.   εἰπέ μοι, τί δ' ἤν, τὸ δεῖνα, τῇ διαίτῃ μὴ 'μμένῃς;

LINE 517

δουλεύω   (< δοῦλος, slave, cf. 59) serve as slave

παύω   stop (+ suppl. ptcp.: S #2098; cf. 37 for impv.)

ὅστις   no explicit antecedent; sc. μοι

οὐ σύ γ'   "No, you're *not*"; γε emphatic, following a pron. in neg. answer: GP 123, 131

ὑπ-ηρετέω   (< ὑπηρέτης, servant < ἐρέτης, rower) serve as under-rower; be a servant, attendant
                 {> *Russia* ("the land of rowing")}

LINE 519

ἐπεί   (conj.) since; "Since <you think I am wrong,> teach me" (with *ellipsis* of verb)

τῑμή, ἡ   honor; advantage, profit (cf. 106)

καρπόω   bear fruit; (mid.) reap fruit, exhaust the land; derive profit from

Ἑλλάς, –άδος, ἡ Greece

LINE 521

πάνυ γε   (adv. < πᾶν, all) "altogether," "very much so"; γε adds intensity: GP 135; S #2821

τούτοισι   the members of the chorus, or perhaps the audience

ἐπι-τρέπω, -έτρεψα (< τρέπω, turn) entrust (sc. the decision to arbitrators)

καὶ μήν   "So do I" or "That's right, and . . ."; expressing agreement with previous speaker:
                 GP 353–54

ἀφίημι, -ῆκα   (> aor. act. impv. 2 pl. ἄφετε) release (spoken to the slaves)

LINE 523

ἡττάομαι, ἡττήθην (< ἥττων, worse, weaker, compound of κακός) be inferior to, be defeated by (with σου,
                   comparative gen. with vbs. of inferiority: S #1402)

περι-πίπτω, -πεσοῦμαι fall on (+ dat., as with many compound vbs.: S #1544): cf. 120

ἤν   with subjv. in protasis + fut. indic. in apodosis = FMV: S #2323

τί δ' ἤν   "If that's the case, what if . . .?"; connective δέ, acknowledging logical sequence of
                thought: GP 174

δεῖνα, ὁ, ἡ, τό a certain one (distinguish δεινός, terrible, with acute on ultima)

τὸ δεῖνα   "That term—what is it?" "What do you call it?" A little aside made by the speaker to him-
                self as he gropes for the word δίαιτα; indeclinable in this exclam. usage, but cf. S #336.

δίαιτα, ἡ   mode of life; arbitration {> *diet*}

ἐμ-μένω   (< ἐν + μένω, wait) abide by (+ dat.)

Φι.	μηδέποτε πίοιμ' ἄκρατον μιϲθὸν ἀγαθοῦ δαίμονοϲ.	525
Χο.	νῦν δὴ τὸν ἐκ θἠμετέρου	[ϲτρ.
	γυμναϲίου δεῖ τι λέγειν	
	καινόν, ὅπωϲ φανήϲει—	
Βδ.	ἐνεγκάτω μοι δεῦρο τὴν κίϲτην τιϲ ὡϲ τάχιϲτα.	
	ἀτὰρ φανεῖ ποῖόϲ τιϲ ὤν, εἰ ταῦτα παρακελεύει;	530

LINE 525

μηδέποτε	never (μή: neg. for opt. of wish)
πίνω, aor.² ἔπιον	(> aor. opt. πίοιμι) drink (opt. of wish in a solemn vow: S #1814); cf. 21
ἄκρᾱτος, –ον	(< ἀ- priv. + κεράννῡμι, mix) unmixed. While the word was usually used of wine, here it is of jury pay! {> crasis, crater, idiosyncrasy}
δαίμων, –ονος, ὁ	spirit, divinity. The first libation of a symposium was dedicated to the ἀγαθὸς δαίμων, "Good Spirit" or "Good Fortune." (cf. 10)

526–48 Bdel. and Phil. will conduct a formal debate, and the chorus members will decide the winner. Bdel. even brings out a writing case so he can take notes on Phil.'s speech, and the chorus fear that if Phil. is defeated, the old men will cease to be respected.

This marks the beginning of the *agon*, the debate, which is structured into an opening *ode* or song (526–45), the *katakeleusmos* or "exhortation" (546–47), the *epirrhema*, the great speech by Phil. (548–619), a *pnigos* (620–30), *antode*, responding to the opening song (631–47), an *antikatakelusmos* (648–49), the *antepirrhema*, Bdel.'s rebuttal of Phil.'s speech (650–718), and an *antipnigos* (719–24).

526–48: Meter: A mixture of iambs and choriambs (– ◡ ◡ –), rounded off with two anapestic tetrameters (547–48).

LINE 526

δή	"Right now, to be exact…"; emphatic, following an adv.
θἠμετέρου	= τοῦ ἡμετέρου
τόν…	art. forms substantive with prep. phrase, "the man from our school"; cf. S #1153c
γυμνάϲιον, τό	(< γύμνος, naked + –ιον, suffix denoting place where: S #851) gymnasium, school
ὅπωϲ	"be sure that…": a] fut. indic. in exhortation: S #2213; or b] fut. indic. substituted for subjv. in purpose clause: S #2203
φαίνω, fut. pass. φανήϲομαι	
	(> fut. pass. 2 sing. φανήϲει) show; (pass.) appear. In referring to Phil., the chorus has shifted from 3 sing. (τὸν ἐκ…) to 2 sing. (φανήϲει). Construe φανήϲει with ptcp. λέγων, "you will plainly be speaking"; distinguish this ptcp. construction from that with inf.: φανήϲει εἶναι, "you will appear to be speaking (but may not be)": S #2106, 2143. Likewise in 530: φανεῖ … ὤν: "he will plainly be…."

LINE 529

κίϲτη, ἡ	basket, box (used here for writing materials)
ποῖος (3)	what kind of? (interrog.; logically it should precede φανεῖ)
παρα-κελεύομαι	recommend an action, give this advice (cf. 410)

Χο.   μὴ κατὰ τὸν νεανίαν
τονδὶ λέγων. ὁρᾷς γὰρ ὥς
coι μέγαc ἔcτ' ἀγὼν ⟨νῦν⟩
καὶ περὶ τῶν ἁπάντων.
εἰ γάρ, ὃ μὴ γένοιθ', οὗ-   535
τόc cε λέγων κρατήcει—

Βδ.   καὶ μὴν ὅc' ἂν λέξῃ γ' ἁπλῶc μνημόcυνα γράψομαι 'γώ.

Φι.   τί γάρ φαθ' ὑμεῖc, ἢν ὁδί με τῷ λόγῳ κρατήcῃ;

LINE 531

κατά   (+ acc.) like, similar to, in manner of; μὴ κατά = unlike (= "better than"?)

νεᾱνίᾱς, –ου, ὁ   youth (ref. to Bdel.); cf. 96

ὥς   that (verb of perception + ὥς: S #2110)

ἀγών, –ῶνος, ὁ   (< ἄγω, drive, gather; cf. 177) gathering (to see games); assembly; <u>contest</u>

LINE 535

εἰ γάρ   for if (distinguish from εἰ γάρ of wishes, "would that"; protasis: εἰ + fut. indic., a FMV or "Emotional Future" (S #2328) condit. expressing something feared; the apodosis usually conveys a threat, but when it comes, after the interruption by Bdel., it is the realization that they are impotent old men, 540–41)

γίγνομαι   become, happen (ὃ μὴ γένοιτο, "may it not happen," opt. of wish: S #1814; one of the few uses of the opt. to survive into Koine and Modern Greek)

κρατέω, –ήσω   (< κράτος, strength, cf. 58) overcome, defeat

LINE 537

καὶ μήν . . . γε   a] "Indeed, [I *will* defeat him] . . ."; in dialogue, expressing consent: *GP* 354–55 b] B-O suggest that καὶ μήν calls attention to something new, "Look here!"; *GP* 356–57

ὅσος, ὅση, ὅσον   (ὅσ' = neut. pl. ὅσα) as much as, everything that (+ subjv. with ἄν + fut. indic. = FMV rel. condit. clause: S #2565)

ἁπλῶς   (adv. < adj. ἁπλόος, plain) simply, <u>absolutely</u> everything

μνημόσυνον, τό   (< μνήμη, memory + –υνον, noun suffix: S #861.11) memorandum. That Bdel. thinks notes should be taken on Phil.'s speech is interesting evidence for the progress of literacy in classical Athens.

γράφω   write; (mid.) write for oneself, note down, have someone write down. The mid. *may* mean that a slave will do the actual writing. (cf. 97)

τί γάρ   "Now, *what* are you saying?"; in quests., requesting more information, *GP* 83. Phil. has ignored Bdel.'s interruption and responds to the chorus; he rephrases the protasis as FMV.

φαθ'   = φατέ

Χο.　οὐκέτι πρεσβυτῶν ὄχλος　　　　　　　　　　540
　　　χρήϲιμόϲ ἐϲτ᾽ οὐδ᾽ ἀκαρῆ·
　　　ϲκωπτόμενοι δ᾽ ἐν ταῖϲ ὁδοῖϲ
　　　θαλλοφόροι καλούμεθ᾽, ἀντ-
　　　ωμοϲιῶν κελύφη.
　　　ἀλλ᾽, ὦ περὶ τῆϲ πάϲηϲ μέλλων βαϲιλείαϲ ἀντιλογήϲειν　　　545
　　　τῆϲ ἡμετέραϲ, νυνὶ θαρρῶν πᾶϲαν γλῶτταν βαϲάνιζε.

LINE 540

πρεσβύτης, –ου, ὁ　old man {> *Presbyterian, priest*}

ὄχλος, ὁ　crowd {> *ochlocracy*}

ἐϲτ᾽　= ἔϲται

χρήϲιμος (3)　(< χράομαι LSJ C.II, use) useful (cf. 80)

ἀκαρής, –ές　(< ἀ- priv. + κείρω, cut hair; literally "hair too short to be cut") very short; (adv. acc.; ἀκαρῆ)
　　οὐδ᾽ ἀκαρῆ = not a bit (an unpretentious "expression of minimal quantity": *LA* 181)

LINE 542

σκώπτω　mock

ὁδός, ἡ　road, street (cf. 362)

θαλλοφόρος, –ον　(< θάλλος, young branch + φέρω, bear) carrying olive shoots. Old men were chosen to be olive-bearers, a ceremonial function at the Panathenaea.

καλέω, καλῶ　call (fut. mid. can be used in pass. sense: LSJ)

ἀντωμοσία, ἡ　(< ἀντί, opposite, in response + ὄμνυμι, swear) affidavit

κέλῦφος, –εος, τό　sheath, husk; <u>container</u>. The old men fear they will be worthless, discarded shells.

LINE 545

ὦ　instead of name in voc. the chorus uses μέλλων, "you who are about to . . ."

βασιλεῖᾱ, ἡ　(< βασιλεύς, king) kingdom, dominion {> *basilica, Basil*}

ἀντι-λογέω, –ήσω　deny; offer rebuttal, make the case against someone

θαρρέω　be of courage (cf. 387)

γλῶττα, ἡ　tongue; eloquence {> *gloss, glossary, polyglot*}

βασανίζω　(< βάσανος, touchstone, test) put to the test, prove; "<u>try</u> every type of . . . verbal strategy": B-O

Φι.   καὶ μὴν εὐθύς γ' ἀπὸ βαλβίδων περὶ τῆς ἀρχῆς ἀποδείξω
            τῆς ἡμετέρας ὡς οὐδεμιᾶς ἥττων ἐστὶν βασιλείας.
            τί γὰρ εὔδαιμον καὶ μακαριστὸν μᾶλλον νῦν ἐστι δικαστοῦ,   550
            ἢ τρυφερώτερον ἢ δεινότερον ζῷον, καὶ ταῦτα γέροντος;
            ὃν πρῶτα μὲν ἕρποντ' ἐξ εὐνῆς τηροῦσ' ἐπὶ τοῖσι δρυφάκτοις
            ἄνδρες μεγάλοι καὶ τετραπήχεις· κᾆπειτ' εὐθὺς προσιόντι
            ἐμβάλλει τις τὴν χεῖρ' ἁπαλὴν τῶν δημοσίων κεκλοφυῖαν·

LINE 548

548–604: Phil. gives an extended speech, though interrupted by Bdel., extolling the life of the juror.
Prominent men treat him with deference. Phil. describes the tactics that defendants use in court to win sympathy, and watching this spectacle further inflates his sense of importance. Politicians like Cleon do their best
to reinforce the jurors' feelings of superiority.

548–620: Anapestic tetrameters. MacD. notes that in *Clouds* and *Frogs* Ar. uses anapests for the side of an
argument with which Ar. sympathizes, possibly because anapests have a more dignified sound, and iambic
lines for the side he dislikes. Using anapests for both speeches in *Wasps* implies an even-handed approach.

καὶ μὴν . . . γε	"Very well . . ."; expressing consent (cf. 537)
βαλβίς, –ῖδος, ἡ	rope at starting and finishing lines of race-course; a <u>starting point</u>
ἀπο-δείκνῦμι, -δείξω	(< ἀπό + δείκνῦμι, show) point out, prove; show a person or thing as so or so {> para*digm*, *deic*tic}
ἡμετέρας	modifies ἀρχῆς
ὡς	that (conj.; generally, though, vbs. of showing take suppl. ptcp. for ind. disc.: S #2106, 2592c)
ἥττων, –ον, –ονος	worse (cf. 523)
οὐδεμίας . . . βασιλείας	gen. of comparison: S #1431

LINE 550

τί	anticipates ζῷον
εὐδαίμων, –ον, –ονος	blessed, happy (μᾶλλον + positive of adj., vs. adding a suffix –ότερος, creates an "analytic comparative," relatively rare in Ar.: *LA* 243, but used with compound adjs.: S #323a)
μακαριστός (3)	to be deemed happy, enviable (though in appearance a superl. of μάκαρ, actually a verbal adj. formed from verb μακαρίζω: S #472; cf. #323a on μᾶλλον with –τός adjs.)
δικαστής, –ου, ὁ	(< δίκη, justice + –της, suffix denoting agent: S #839a1) juror
τρυφερός (3)	(< θρύπτω, break into pieces, enfeeble) luxurious
καὶ ταῦτα	"and at that . . ." (cf. 253)
ζῷον, τό	animal, creature

LINE 552

ὅν	sc. "the juror" as antecedent
ἕρπω	creep; walk, stroll (cf. 272)
εὐνή, ἡ	bed
τηρέω	guard, watch for (cf. 210)
τετραπήχυς, –εια, –υ	(< πῆχυς, arm) four cubits (= six feet high) {> *tesserae*, *tetra*-}
κᾆπειτα	= καὶ ἔπειτα
πρόσ-ειμι	(< εἶμι) approach (sc. μοι with dat. ptcp. προσιόντι)
ἁπαλός (3)	tender, soft, uncalloused
δημόσιος (3)	public (τὰ δημόσια = public treasury; part. gen. with κλέπτω: S #1431)

ἱκετεύουcίν θ᾽ ὑποκύπτοντεc τὴν φωνὴν οἰκτροχοοῦντεc·   555
"οἴκτιρόν μ᾽, ὦ πάτερ, αἰτοῦμαί c᾽, εἰ καὐτὸc πώποθ᾽ ὑφείλου
ἀρχὴν ἄρξαc ἢ ᾽πὶ cτρατιᾶc τοῖc ξυccίτοιc ἀγοράζων."
ὃc ἔμ᾽ οὐδ᾽ ἂν ζῶντ᾽ ᾔδειν, εἰ μὴ διὰ τὴν προτέραν ἀπόφευξιν.

Βδ. τουτὶ περὶ τῶν ἀντιβολούντων ἔcτω τὸ μνημόcυνόν μοι.

Φι. εἶτ᾽ εἰcελθὼν ἀντιβοληθεὶc καὶ τὴν ὀργὴν ἀπομορχθεὶc   560
ἔνδον τούτων ὧν ἂν φάcκω πάντων οὐδὲν πεποίηκα,
ἀλλ᾽ ἀκροῶμαι πάcαc φωνὰc ἱέντων εἰc ἀπόφευξιν.

LINE 555

ἱκετεύω	(< ἱκέτηc, suppliant) approach as suppliant; plead
ὑπο-κύπτω	(< κύπτω, bend, bow) stoop, bow down (cf. 178)
οἰκτρο-χοέω	(< οἰκτρόc, pitiable + χέω, pour) pour forth piteously
οἰκτίρω	have pity on [< onomatopoeia from interjection οἴ]
καὐτόc	= καὶ αὐτόc
ὑφ-αιρέω, -εῖλον	(< ὑπό, suggesting furtiveness: S #1698.4 + αἱρέω, take) seize underneath; take underhandedly, filch
ἄρχω	begin; lead, hold office (with cogn. acc. ἀρχήν: S #1563)
ἐπί	in the time of (+ gen.)
cτρατιά, ἡ	military campaign (cf. 11)
ξύccιτοc, ὁ	(< ξύν + cῖτοc, grain, food) mess hall
ἀγοράζω	(< ἀγορά, marketplace + -αζω, denoting an action: S #866.6) purchase. The defendant imagines the addressee would embezzle some money for himself when buying supplies for the army.

LINE 558

ὅc	he (antecedent is the glad-handing politician of the previous sentence)
ζάω	live
οἶδα	(< imperfect indic. 3 sing. ᾔδειν, with ptcp. ζῶντα), "he didn't even know I was alive"
ἄν	+ imperfect: apodosis of Pres. Contrary-to-Fact condit., with διά ... ἀπόφευξιν serving as protasis
ἀπόφευξιc, -εωc, ἡ	(< ἀποφεύγω, be acquitted + –ιc, suffix denoting action from abstract idea: S #840a.2) acquittal
εἰμί	(> pres. impv. 3 sing. ἔcτω) let there be
μνημόcυνον, τό	note (cf. 538)

LINE 560

εἰc-έρχομαι, aor.² -ῆλθον	
	go inside (the courtroom)
ἀπο-μόργνῦμι, aor. pass. -εμόρχθην	
	wipe off, with ὀργήν, acc. respect = "my anger was wiped away"
τούτων ... πάντων	(part. gen. with οὐδέν)
ὧν	gen. by attraction to antecedent (S #2522) in a Pres. Gen. rel. condit.: ὧν ἂν φάcκω = whatever I promised
ἀκροάομαι	listen, hearken to (+ gen. of person, acc. of thing); cf. 391
ἵημι	(> pres. act. ptcp. gen. pl. ἱέντων) send; ἱέντες πάcαc φωνάc = "men making every sort of speech"
εἰc	+ acc. indicates purpose: S #1686

φέρ' ἴδω, τί γὰρ οὐκ ἔστιν ἀκοῦσαι θώπευμ' ἐνταῦθα δικαστῇ;
οἱ μέν γ' ἀποκλάονται πενίαν αὑτῶν, καὶ προστιθέασιν
κακὰ πρὸς τοῖς οὖσι ⟨κακοῖσιν⟩, ἕως ἂν ἰσωθῇ τοῖσιν ἐμοῖσιν·   565
οἱ δὲ λέγουσιν μύθους ἡμῖν, οἱ δ' Αἰσώπου τι γέλοιον·
οἱ δὲ σκώπτους', ἵν' ἐγὼ γελάσω καὶ τὸν θυμὸν καταθῶμαι.

LINE 563

φέρ' ἴδω	cf. 145
τί	anticipates θώπευμα
γάρ	for postponement in word order: *GP* 97; for τί γάρ, cf. 334, 538/39
ἔστιν	*orthotone*; cf. 212
θώπευμα, –ατος, τό	(< θώψ, flatterer, false friend + –μα, –ματος, suffix expressing the result of an action: S #841.2) flattery
μέν γε	"*Some* of them . . ."; μέν γε introduces an instance; γε concentrates attention on μέν and temporarily excludes the δέ clause: *GP* 159–60
ἀπο-κλάω	weep; bewails one's plight
πενία, ἡ	poverty (cf. 192 & 463)
αὑτῶν	= ἑαυτῶν
προσ-τίθημι	add, exaggerate

LINE 565

πρός	(+ dat.) in addition to
εἰμί	(> pres. dat. pl. nt. ptcp. οὖσι) being, existing
ἕως	until (with ἄν + subj.: S #2426)
ἰσόω, ἰσώθην	(< ἴσος, equal + –οω, suffix, usually *factitive*: S #866.3) make equal
ἐμοῖσιν	sc. κακοῖς
μῦθος, ὁ	word; story, tale. The word μῦθος comes to mean "myth" in our sense of the word only in Plato: LSJ I.2 and II.3.
Αἴσωπος, ὁ	Aesop, the teller of fables
γέλοιος (3)	humorous (cf. 57)

LINE 567

σκώπτω	mock; crack jokes
γελάω, ἐγέλασα	laugh (cf. 57)
κατα-τίθημι, -έθηκα	place down; (mid.) put aside

κἂν μὴ τούτοις ἀναπειθώμεσθα, τὰ παιδάρι᾽ εὐθὺς ἀνέλκει
τὰς θηλείας καὶ τοὺς υἱεῖς τῆς χειρός, ἐγὼ δ᾽ ἀκροῶμαι,
τὰ δὲ cυγκύψανθ᾽ ἅμα βληχᾶται· κἄπειθ᾽ ὁ πατὴρ ὑπὲρ αὐτῶν   570
ὥσπερ θεὸν ἀντιβολεῖ με τρέμων τῆς εὐθύνης ἀπολῦσαι·
"εἰ μὲν χαίρεις ἀρνὸς φωνῇ, παιδὸς φωνὴν ἐλεήcαιc·"
εἰ δ᾽ αὖ τοῖς χοιριδίοις χαίρω, θυγατρὸς φωνῇ με πιθέcθαι.
χἠμεῖς αὐτῷ τότε τῆς ὀργῆς ὀλίγον τὸν κόλλοπ᾽ ἀνεῖμεν.
ἆρ᾽ οὐ μεγάλη τοῦτ᾽ ἔcτ᾽ ἀρχὴ καὶ τοῦ πλούτου καταχήνη;   575

LINE 568

κἂν	= καὶ ἐάν
παιδάριον, τό	(< παῖς, child + –αριον, dim. suffix: S #852.3) young child
ἀν-έλκω	drag up
θῆλυς, –εια, –υ	female; <u>daughters</u> [< IE *dhe(i)-, suck; cogn. L. *femina, fetus, fecundus, felix* (fertile)]
υἱός, –οῦ, ὁ	(nom./acc. pl. υἱεῖς) son (cf. 134)
χείρ, χειρός, ἡ	hand (part. gen. with verb of touching, "by the hand" LSJ II.3; S #1346) {> *chiro-*}
συγ-κύπτω, -έκυψα	(< κύπτω, bend) stoop and lay heads together, cower together
βληχάομαι	(< βληχή, bleating) bleat, wail. The final -α of ἅμα scans short before βλ-. [< *onomatopoeia*]
τρέμω	tremble
εὔθυνα, ἡ	(< εὐθύς, straight, cf. 102) setting straight; audit. These εὔθυναι were financial audits conducted at the end of a term of public office to ensure nothing had been embezzled.
ἀπο-λύω, -έλυσα	release from, acquit of charge (+ gen.: S #1392) {> *dialysis, paralysis*}

LINE 572

ἀρνός, τοῦ, τῆς	lamb (gen.; nom. ἀρήν only occurs in inscriptions)
ἐλεέω, ἠλέησα	have pity on (opt. wish: S #1814, as apodosis in Pres. Gen. condit.: S #2300d; 2 sing. -αις is more common in Plato and Xen., -ειας in drama: S #668D) cf. 393
χοιρίδιον, τό	(dim. of χοῖρος, pig) piglet (with double entendre: female genitalia: *MM* p. 131)
πείθω, aor.² ἔπιθον	persuade; (mid.) listen to, comply with, obey (+ dat.; sc. ἀντιβολεῖ); ἔπιθον is a poetic alternative to ἔπεισα (cf. 101)
χἠμεῖς	= καὶ ἡμεῖς
ὀλίγον	(adv. acc.) a little (cf. 214)
κόλλοψ, –οπος, ὁ	peg of lyre by which strings were tightened; "lower the pitch of our anger"
ἀν-ίημι, -ῆκα	(> aor. indic. ἀνεῖμεν) slacken, let loose (*gnomic aorist*, apodosis of condit., cf. 99)

LINE 575

πλοῦτος, ὁ	wealth {> *plutocracy*} [< IE *pleu-, flow (wealth is "overflowing"); cogn. L. *pluo*; E. *flood*]
καταχήνη, ἡ	(< κατά, against, adversely + χάσκω, aor.² ἔχανον, gape, cf. 342) derision, mockery

Βδ.   δεύτερον αὖ cου τουτὶ γράφομαι, τὴν τοῦ πλούτου καταχήνην·

       καὶ τἀγαθά μοι μέμνηc᾽ ἄχειc φάcκων τῆc Ἑλλάδοc ἄρχειν.

Φι.   παίδων τοίνυν δοκιμαζομένων αἰδοῖα πάρεcτι θεάcθαι.

       κἂν Οἴαγροc εἰcέλθη φεύγων, οὐκ ἀποφεύγει πρὶν ἂν ἡμῖν

       ἐκ τῆc Νιόβηc εἴπη ῥῆcιν τὴν καλλίcτην ἀπολέξαc.   580

       κἂν αὐλητήc γε δίκην νικᾷ, ταύτηc ἡμῖν ἐπίχειρα

       ἐν φορβειᾷ τοῖcι δικαcταῖc ἔξοδον ηὔληc᾽ ἀπιοῦcι.

LINE 576

δεύτεροc (3) | next, second {> *Deuteronomy, deuteragonist*} [δεύτεροc = "missing, be second" < IE **deu(s)-*, lack]

τἀγαθά | = τὰ ἀγαθά

μιμνήcκω | (> perf. impv. 2 sing. μέμνηcο) remind; (mid.) <u>mention</u> (perf. as pres., cf. 354); cf. 443

ἄχειc | = ἅ ἔχειc

φάcκω | (< φημί, say + -cκω: S #526e) assert, allege (+ inf. in ind. statement), "alleging that you rule Greece" (cf. 36)

Ἑλλάc, –άδοc, ἡ | Greece

LINE 578

τοίνυν | "Furthermore," "Again,"; logical, introducing new example: *GP* 575

δοκιμάζω | (< δοκιμαcία, the procedure for registering boys into their *deme* at age 18) test; examine

αἰδοῖον, τό | (< αἰδώc, awe, shame, cf. 447) private parts; (pl.) genitals: *MM* p. 113

LINE 579

κἂν | cf. 568

Οἴαγροc, ὁ | Oeagrus, evidently an actor who had a part in a *Niobe*

ἀπο-φεύγω | go free; be acquitted

Νιόβη, ἡ | Niobe, mythological figure and subject of plays by Aeschylus and Sophocles

ῥῆcιc, ἡ | (< εἴρω, speak) speech, esp. rehearsed {> *rhetoric*}

κάλλιcτοc (3) | (superl. of καλόc) beautiful {> *kaleidoscope, calligraphy*}

ἀπο-λέγω, -έλεξα | pick out; choose, select

LINE 581

αὐλητήc, –οῦ, ὁ | *aulos* player. The αὐλόc, though often rendered as "flute," was a reed instrument used for musical accompaniment in the theater. {> hydr*aulic*}

νῑκάω | win (with cogn. acc. δίκην, lawsuit, common in legal language: S #1576)

ἐπίχειρα, τά | (pl.) (< χείρ, hand, cf. 569) wages of manual labor, <u>reward</u> (ταύτηc refers to the δίκη)

φορβειά, ἡ | (< φέρβω, feed) halter for a horse; <u>mouthband</u> worn by αὐλητήc when performing

ἔξοδοc, ἡ | way out, departure; music played at end of drama, finale (cf. 361)

αὐλέω, ηὔληcα | play the *aulos* (*gnomic aorist* in condit.; cf. 99 on Pres. Gen.)

ἄπ-ειμι | go out, exit; ἡμῖν ἀπιοῦcι, "for us as we were leaving"

κἂν ἀποθνήσκων ὁ πατήρ τῳ δῷ καταλείπων παῖδ' ἐπίκληρον,
κλάιειν ἡμεῖς μακρὰ τὴν κεφαλήν εἰπόντες τῇ διαθήκῃ
καὶ τῇ κόγχῃ τῇ πάνυ σεμνῶς τοῖς σημείοισιν ἐπούσῃ,   585
ἔδομεν ταύτην ὅστις ἂν ἡμᾶς ἀντιβολήσας ἀναπείσῃ.
καὶ ταῦτ' ἀνυπεύθυνοι δρῶμεν· τῶν δ' ἄλλων οὐδεμί' ἀρχή.

Βδ.   τουτὶ γάρ τοι σεμνόν· τούτων ὧν εἴρηκας μακαρίζω·
τῆς δ' ἐπικλήρου τὴν διαθήκην ἀδικεῖς ἀνακογχυλιάζων.

LINE 583

ἀπο-θνήσκω	die (Ar. uses only the compounded form in the pres.)
τῳ	= τινι, someone (note enclitic; distinguish from art. τῷ)
δίδωμι	(> aor. act. subjv. 3 sing. δῷ) give
κατα-λείπω	leave behind, bequeath {> eclipse, ellipse}
ἐπίκληρος, ἡ	(< κλῆρος, lot, inheritance) heiress, a daughter who accompanied an inheritance {> cleromancy, clerk}
κλάιω	cry, suffer (intrans. here); "Too bad!" The jurors will ignore the provisions of the will; they tell the will and the case protecting the seals (which are virtually personified) to go weep.
μακρά	(adv. acc.) long (cf. 106)
κεφαλή, ἡ	head (acc. object of κλάιειν); cf. 43
διαθήκη, ἡ	(< διατίθημι, arrange) testament, covenant; will
κόγχη, ἡ	seashell; case to protect document seals
σεμνῶς	(adv. < σεμνός (3) stately; pompous, cf. 135) pompously
σημεῖον, τό	sign; seal {> semantic, semaphore}
ἔπ-ειμι	(< εἰμί) be upon

LINE 586

ταύτην	the girl
ὅστις	antecedent omitted: "we give the girl to <the man> who persuaded . . ."
ταῦτ'	= ταῦτα
ἀνυπεύθῦνος, –ον	not subject to εὔθῦναι (cf. 571); <u>unaccountable</u>
τῶν δ' ἄλλων οὐδεμί' ἀρχή	
	= τῶν δ' ἄλλων [ἀρχῶν], οὐδεμία [ἄλλη] ἀρχή [ἀνυπεύθῦνός ἐστίν], "of the other [offices], no [other] office [is unaccountable]": jurors did not submit to εὔθῦναι.

LINE 588

τουτὶ γάρ τοι	"Yes, you know, *this* at least is grand . . ."; τουτὶ with *deictic* iota is limitative: "this and nothing else"; γάρ is assentient, "Yes," following a demonstrative pron.: *GP* 89, S #2806; τοι, "you know," "I tell you," implies an audience; a homely particle "unsuited to serious drama": *GP* 538
σεμνός (3)	revered, impressive (cf. 135)
τούτων	gen. of cause with verb of praise: S #1405
ὧν	gen. by attraction; should be ἅ εἴρηκας
μακαρίζω	(< μάκαρ, blessed, cf. 639) deem someone happy; congratulate (sc. σε); cf. 428
ἀνα-κογχυλιάζω	(< ἀνά, with reversing force: S #1682.3 + κόγχη, seashell) remove the seal case. A double entendre: "unseal her virginity," *MM* p. 142, though B-O see a reference to the way shellfish spout water.

Φι. ἔτι δ' ἡ βουλὴ χὠ δῆμος, ὅταν κρῖναι μέγα πρᾶγμ' ἀπορήσῃ,   590
ἐψήφισται τοὺς ἀδικοῦντας τοῖσι δικασταῖς παραδοῦναι·
εἶτ' Εὔαθλος χὠ μέγας οὗτος Κολακώνυμος ἀσπιδαποβλὴς
οὐχὶ προδώσειν ἡμᾶς φασιν, περὶ τοῦ πλήθους δὲ μαχεῖσθαι.
κἂν τῷ δήμῳ γνώμην οὐδεὶς πώποτ' ἐνίκησεν, ἐὰν μὴ
εἴπῃ τὰ δικαστήρι' ἀφεῖναι πρώτιστα μίαν δικάσαντας·   595
αὐτὸς δὲ Κλέων ὁ κεκραξιδάμας μόνον ἡμᾶς οὐ περιτρώγει,
ἀλλὰ φυλάττει διὰ χειρὸς ἔχων καὶ τὰς μυίας ἀπαμύνει.

LINE 590

βουλή, ἡ	Council of 500. Athenian legislation was routinely recorded as "decreed by the Council and the People": ἔδοξε τῇ βουλῇ καὶ τῷ δήμῳ; cf. Meiggs & Lewis #46, 52. (cf. 169)
χὠ	= καὶ ὁ
κρίνω, ἔκρῑνα	judge, decide (cf. 53)
ἀπορέω, ἠπόρησα	(< πόρος, passage; cf. 308) be at a loss
ψηφίζω, ἐψήφισμαι	(< ψῆφος, pebble for voting; cf. 94) count; (mid.) vote
παρα-δίδωμι, -έδωκα	hand over

LINE 592

Εὔαθλος, ὁ	(< εὐ, good, well + ἆθλον, contest) Evathlus, known for conducting prosecutions
Κολακώνυμος, ὁ	(< κόλαξ, "flatterer" + Cleonymus, who was accused of throwing away his shield in battle; cf. 16) Kolakonymus
ἀσπιδαποβλής, –ῆτος, ὁ	
	(< ἀσπίς, shield + ἀποβάλλω, throw) one who throws away his shield; a coward (ὁ + ἀσπιδ- = ἀσπιδ- by *crasis*)
προ-δίδωμι, -δώσω	betray (inf. in ind. statement after verb of saying: S #2016)

LINE 594

κἂν	= καὶ ἐν
γνώμη, ἡ	a motion in assembly (γνώμην, cogn. acc. with νῑκάω, cf. 581); cf. 368
πρώτιστος (3)	superl. of πρῶτος, though πρῶτος is itself strictly speaking a superl. formed from πρό: LSJ s.v. πρότερος B.
εἷς, μία, ἕν	one (δικαστὰς μίαν [δίκην] δικάσαντας). After hearing one case, perhaps a morning's work, jurors could call it a day and go home.

LINE 596

κεκραξιδάμας, –αντος, ὁ	
	(< κράζω, κέκρᾱγα, cf . 1103 shout + δαμάω, subdue; Ar.'s coinage) he who conquers in bawling, "scream-champion" (Hend.) {> *adamant, diamond*}
μόνον ἡμᾶς	"us, alone, he does not bite," that is, he bites everyone else
περι-τρώγω	nibble around, take bites out of (cf. 164)
διὰ χειρός	holds "in the hand"; LSJ s.v. χείρ II.6.c
μυῖα, ἡ	fly [< IE *mu-, fly; cogn. L. *musca* (> *mosquito*); E. *midge*]
ἀπ-αμύνω	ward off, keep away (cf. 197)

cὺ δὲ τὸν πατέρ' οὐδ' ὁτιοῦν τούτων τὸν cαυτοῦ πώποτ' ἔδραcαc.
ἀλλὰ Θέωροc—καίτούcτὶν ἀνὴρ Εὐφημίδου οὐδὲν ἐλάττων—
τὸν cπόγγον ἔχων ἐκ τῆc λεκάνηc τἀμβάδι' ἡμῶν περικωνεῖ.   600
cκέψαι μ' ἀπὸ τῶν ἀγαθῶν οἵων ἀποκλήειc καὶ κατερύκειc,
ἣν δουλείαν οὖcαν ἔφαcκεc καὶ ὑπηρεcίαν ἀποδείξειν.

LINE 598

598–605: Phil. now directly addresses his father, claiming that Bdel. has not treated him as well as Cleon has, and that Bdel. is depriving him of the benefits of the life of the juror.

ὁτιοῦν	(< ὅστις + οὖν; LSJ s.v. ὅστις IV.2.b; often with neg.) "anything whatsoever"
τούτων	actions like the protective ones just described
Θέωροc, ὁ	Theorus (cf. 42)
καίτούcτὶν	= καίτοι ἐστίν
Εὐφημίδηc, –ου, ὁ	(< εὔφεμος, utter sounds of good omen + –ιδης, *patronymic* suffix: S #845.4) Euphemides, unknown (gen. of comparison)
οὐδέν	in no way (adv. acc.)
cπόγγοc, ὁ	sponge
λεκάνη, ἡ	bowl, pail {> *lecano*mancy}
ἐμβάδιον, τό	small shoe (cf. 103)
περι-κωνέω	smear with pitch, blacken. He uses a sponge to apply the pitch from a bowl and blacken or seal up shoes.

LINE 601

σκέπτομαι, ἐσκεψάμην

	(> aor. mid. impv. 2 sing. σκέψαι) look about, consider, examine (used almost exclusively in aor. in Attic)
οἵων	displaced word order: οἵων should follow σκέψαι, precede τῶν ἀγαθῶν
ἀπο-κλήω	(< κλής, bar, key; cf. 113) shut off, exclude acc. from gen.
κατ-ερύκω	(< ἐρύκω, keep in) hold back, detain
ἥν	antecedent is τὰ ἀγαθά; rel. should be ἅ but is attracted into fem. sing. of δουλείαν
οὖσαν	suppl. ptcp. in ind. statement after ἀποδείξειν, verb of showing: S #2106
ὑπηρεσία, ἡ	ship's crew; service (cf. 518)
ἀπο-δείκνῡμι, -δείξω	show, demonstrate (inf. in ind. statement after ἔφασκες, verb of saying: S #2016); cf. 548

Βδ. ἔμπληϲο λέγων· πάντωϲ γάρ τοι παύϲει ποτὲ κἀναφανήϲει
    πρωκτὸϲ λουτροῦ περιγιγνόμενοϲ τῆϲ ἀρχῆϲ τῆϲ περιϲέμνου.

Φι. ὃ δέ γ' ἥδιϲτον τούτων ἐϲτὶν πάντων, οὗ 'γὼ 'πελελήϲμην,   605
    ὅταν οἴκαδ' ἴω τὸν μιϲθὸν ἔχων, κἄπειθ' ἥκονθ' ἅμα πάντεϲ

LINE 603

ἐμ-πίμπλημι	(> aor. mid. impv. 2 sing. ἔμπληϲο) fill up; (mid.) have one's fill (cf. 380, 424)
λέγων	suppl. ptcp. with verb of ceasing, enduring: S #2098
πάντωϲ	(adv.) completely
γάρ τοι	the two particles retain their separate force: "For, you know, you will …": *GP* 549, but see MacD.
παύω	(> fut. mid. 2 sing. indic. παύϲει) stop, leave off doing (with suppl. ptcp.: S #2098)
ἀνα-φαίνω, fut. pass. φανήϲομαι	
	(> fut. pass. 2 sing. indic. ἀναφανήϲει) display, reveal; (pass.) appear plainly as, "you will be revealed as": S #528. Bdel. is saying that Phil. will be shown to be an arsehole so filthy that not even the grand power of Phil.'s position as a juror could wash it out. Father-son relations are at their lowest here!
πρωκτόϲ, ὁ	arsehole (here, pred. to the 2 sing. subject of ἀναφανήϲει) {> *proct*ology}
λουτρόν, τό	(< λούω, wash) bath, washing
περι-γίγνομαι	prevail, overcome (+ gen.); Phil. is cast as a πρωκτόϲ too filthy to wash.
ἀρχῆϲ	in apposition to λουτροῦ; the authority of serving on a jury would be like the cleansing action of a bath, but is not up to it
περιϲέμνοϲ (2)	(< περί in composition, "exceedingly": S #1693.4 + ϲέμνοϲ) very august, pompous

605–30: Bdel. describes the best part: the welcome he gets when he returns home and is supplied with food and drink. He feels as powerful as Zeus!

LINE 605

ὅ	= his thought before he was interrupted
δέ γε	"as I was saying"; picks up thread of thought after interruption, *GP* 154
ἥδιϲτοϲ (3)	superl. of ἡδύϲ, sweet
ἐπι-λήθω	(> plup. mid. 1 sing. ἐπελελήϲμην < λήθη, forgetfulness; cf. 212) cause to forget; (mid.) forget (+ gen.)
ὅταν	whenever (introduces eight subjv. vbs, with Phil.'s fantasy of returning home)
οἴκαδε	(adv.) homeward
εἶμι	(> pres. subjv. 1 sing. ἴω) go
ἥκω	arrive (sc. με with ἥκοντα)

ἀσπάζωνται διὰ τἀργύριον, καὶ πρῶτα μὲν ἡ θυγάτηρ με
ἀπονίζῃ καὶ τὼ πόδ᾽ ἀλείφῃ καὶ προσκύψασα φιλήσῃ
καὶ παππίζους᾽ ἅμα τῇ γλώττῃ τὸ τριώβολον ἐκκαλαμᾶται,
καὶ τὸ γύναιόν μ᾽ ὑποθωπεῦσαν φυστὴν μᾶζαν προσενέγκῃ,
κἄπειτα καθεζομένη παρ᾽ ἐμοὶ προσαναγκάζῃ, "φάγε τουτί,
ἔντραγε τουτί." τούτοισιν ἐγὼ γάνυμαι, κοὐ μή με δεήσῃ

610

LINE 607

ἀσπάζομαι	welcome, greet
ἀργύριον, τό	(dim. of ἄργυρος, silver < ἀργός, shining; cf. 50) money, small coin
μέν	answered not by δέ but by καί: *GP* 374
ἀπο-νίζω	wash
πούς, ποδός, ὁ	(> nom./acc. dual πόδε) foot
ἀλείφω	(< "euphonic" alpha: LSJ + λίπος, fat, oil) anoint
προσ-κύπτω, -έκυψα	bend down, stoop over
φιλέω	love; kiss: *MM* pp.181–82

LINE 609

παππίζω	call someone "daddy"
ἅμα	(adv.) at same time
γλῶττα, -ης, ἡ	tongue (cf. 547)
τριώβολον, τό	three-obol coin, the payment for jury duty (cf. 52)
ἐκ-καλαμάομαι	pull out with fishing rod, "fish out" (cf. 381)
γύναιον, τό	(< γυνή, woman, wife + -ιον, dim. suffix: S #852.1) little woman, wifey (though neut., governs fem. ptcp. καθεζομένη) {> gynecology} [< IE *g^{w}en, woman; cogn. E. queen]
ὑπο-θωπεύω	(> neut. aor. ptcp. -εῦσαν < ὑπό, suggesting furtiveness: S #1698.4 + θώψ, false friend; cf. 563) flatter, win by flattery
φυστή, ἡ	(< φυσάω, blow, puff) a light pastry or puff
μᾶζα, ἡ	(< μάσσω, knead) cake, made of barley, milk, wine and oil {> magma, mass} [< IE *mag-/menk—, knead; cogn. E. make, mingle]
προσ-φέρω, -ήνεγκα	bring forward, present

LINE 611

καθ-έζομαι	take a seat, sit down
προσ-αναγκάζω	(< πρός, "in addition" + ἀνάγκη, necessity) constrain besides, also force
ἐν-έτραγον	gobble up, eat dessert (aor. only in compound forms); cf. 164
τούτοισι	"all these things that people do for me"
γάνυμαι	be glad at (+ dat.)
οὐ μή	not at all (cf. 394)
δεῖ	(> aor. act. subjv. 3 sing. impers. δεήσῃ) it is necessary

εἰς cὲ βλέψαι καὶ τὸν ταμίαν, ὁπότ' ἄριστον παραθήσει
καταρασάμενος καὶ τονθορύcας· ἀλλ' ἢν μή μοι ταχὺ μάξῃ,
τάδε κέκτημαι πρόβλημα κακῶν, cκευὴν βελέων ἀλεωρήν.
κἂν οἶνόν μοι μὴ 'γχῇc cὺ πιεῖν, τὸν ὄνον τόνδ' εἰcκεκόμιcμαι
οἴνου μεcτόν, κᾆτ' ἐγχέομαι κλίναc· οὗτοc δὲ κεχηνὼc
βρωμηcάμενοc τοῦ cοῦ δίνου μέγα καὶ cτράτιον κατέπαρδεν.

615

LINE 613

cὲ βλέψαι	the short vowel of cὲ is here scanned long before βλ-; contrast 570.
ταμίας, –ου, ὁ	(< τέμνω, ταμεῖν, cut) one who carves and distributes; <u>steward</u>
ὅποτε	when; interrog. conj. after βλέψαι, "to look at you [and wonder] when"
ἄριστον, τό	morning meal (cf. 306)
παρα-τίθημι, -θησω	offer, serve
κατ-αράομαι, -ηρᾱσάμην	
	(< κατά, adversely: S #1690.3 + ἀρά, prayer, curse) curse
τονθορύζω, ἐτονθόρυσα	
	grumble
μάσσω, ἔμαξα	knead
τάδε	that is, his jury pay
κτάομαι, κέκτημαι	acquire; (perf.) possess [< IE *tke-, gain control; cogn. Persian *Xerxes*, "ruling over men"]
πρόβλημα, –ατος, τό	(< προβάλλω, throw forward) something projecting; hurdle; a defense, "a <u>shield</u> from troubles" (pred. to τάδε; obj. gen. with κακῶν: S #1331)
cκευή, ἡ	(< cκεῦος, vessel, device; [pl.] weapon) attire; <u>equipment</u>
βέλος, –εος, τό	(< βάλλω, throw) weapon, missile
ἀλεωρή, ἡ	(< ἀλέομαι, avoid) defense, shelter from (with cκευή; in hexameter, a mock-epic quotation)

LINE 616

ἐγ-χέω, -έχεα	pour (at 617 Bdel. shifts to mid. and pours for himself; for the uncontracted aor.: S #543a)
πίνω, aor.² ἔπιον	(> aor. act. inf. πιεῖν) drink (inf. of purpose: S # 2008)
ὄνος, ὁ, ἡ	ass, donkey; **a**] a kind of wine vessel which, like a donkey, will open its mouth, bray, and fart at the goblet that Phil. offers; **b**] a colloquial expression for some kind of large jar, offstage, that can carry a "donkey-load" of wine: B-O
εἰc-κομίζω, -κεκόμιcμαι	
	bring in, transport
μεcτός (3)	full of (+ gen.)
κᾆτ'	= καὶ εἶτα
κλίνω, ἔκλῑνα	tip, tilt (distinguish aor. ptcp. κλῑνᾱc from acc. pl. noun κλίνᾱc "couch"); cf. 123
οὗτος	the wine vessel
χάσκω, κέχηνα	yawn, gape open (cf. 342)
βρωμάομαι, ἐβρωμηcάμην	
	(< βρέμω, roar) bray, bellow
δίνος, ὁ	(< δίνη, eddy) whirling; goblet
cτράτιος (3)	warlike (adv. acc. cτράτιον)
κατα-πέρδομαι, -έπαρδον	
	fart at (+ gen.; uncompounded πέρδομαι is intrans.); cf. 394

ἆρ' οὐ μεγάλην ἀρχὴν ἄρχω καὶ τοῦ Διὸς οὐδὲν ἐλάττω,

ὅςτις ἀκούω ταῦθ' ἅπερ ὁ Ζεύς;   620

ἢν γοῦν ἡμεῖς θορυβήςωμεν,

πᾶς τίς φηςιν τῶν παριόντων,

"οἷον βροντᾷ τὸ δικαςτήριον,

ὦ Ζεῦ βαςιλεῦ."

κἂν ἀςτράψω, ποππύζουςιν   625

κἀγκεχόδαςίν μ' οἱ πλουτοῦντες

καὶ πάνυ ςεμνοί.

LINE 619

ἀρχὴν ἄρχω	cogn. acc.; cf. 557 and S #1563
ἐλάττων	(> ἐλάττω is a contracted acc. sing. of ἐλάττονα: S #293) less (cf. 489)
Ζεύς, Διός, ὁ	gen. of comparison: S #1431 (cf. 97)
ἀκούω	hear; be spoken of, have things said of, have a reputation (used as pass. of λέγειν: S #1752); cf. 436
ταῦθ'	= τὰ αὐτά

Meter: 621–30: Phil. concludes his speech with a rapidly spoken *pnigos*, delivered in a ten-line run of anapestic dimeters.

LINE 621

γοῦν	for instance (cf. 262)
θορυβέω, ἐθορύβησα	roar, create an uproar (subjv. in Pres. Gen. protasis)
πάρ-ειμι	go by, pass by; οἱ πάριοντες = the passersby
οἷον	how (exclam.)
βροντάω	thunder (cf. 323)
δικαστήριον, τό	courtroom
βασιλεύς, –εως, ὁ	king

LINE 625

κἄν	= καὶ ἄν
ἀστράπτω, ἤστραψα	(< ἀστεροπή, lightning < possible compound of ἀστήρ, star + ὄψ, eye/face) hurl lightning
ποππύζω	cluck; an *onomatopoeic* sound, perhaps a clucking or snapping sound, serving as apotropaic when lightning was heard; also used of calling a horse or man
ἐγ-χέζω, -κέχοδα	(< χέζω, shit) shit in pants; be afraid of (*frequentative* perf.: MacD.); *MM* p. 189
πλουτέω	be rich (cf. 575)

καὶ σὺ δέδοικάς με μάλιστ' αὐτός·

νὴ τὴν Δήμητρα δέδοικας. ἐγὼ δ'

ἀπολοίμην εἰ σὲ δέδοικα.   630

Χο.   οὐπώποθ' οὕτω καθαρῶς   [ἀντ.

 οὐδενὸς ἠκούσαμεν οὐ-

δὲ ξυνετῶς λέγοντος.

Φι.   οὔκ, ἀλλ' ἐρήμας ᾤεθ' οὕτω ῥᾳδίως τρυγήσειν.

καλῶς γὰρ ᾔδειν ὡς ἐγὼ ταύτῃ κράτιστός εἰμι.   635

LINE 628

Δημήτηρ, –τρος, ἡ   (> acc.: -τρα) Demeter

ἀπ-όλλῡμι   destroy; (mid.) perish (ἀπολοίμην, opt. of wish: S #2300d)

631–49: The chorus congratulate Phil. on his persuasive speech; they cannot imagine what Bdel. will say to refute it.

631–49: Meter: The exchange between the chorus and Bdel. mixes iambs and choriambs, rounded off with two anapestic tetrameters (648–49).

LINE 631

καθαρῶς   (adv.) purely, clearly

ξυνετῶς   (adv. < συνίημι, understand) intelligently

LINE 634

οὔκ, ἀλλ'   "<You're right, you have> not <heard anyone speak so clearly,> but . . ."; *ellipses*

ἐρῆμος (3)   alone, isolated; unwatched. To this sc. ἀμπέλους, fem., grape vines, but the reference is to an ἐρήμη δίκη, a lawsuit that is undefended and goes by default. {> *eremite, hermit*}

οἴομαι   (> imperfect 3 sing. indic. ᾤεθ' = ᾤετο) think; Bdel. is subject (cf. 514)

ῥᾳδίως   (adv. < a fuller form of ῥᾷ, easily) easily

τρυγάω, -ήσω   (perhaps < τρύξ, unfermented wine) gather, harvest (inf. in indir. statement after οἴομαι, verb of thinking: S #2018)

οἶδα   (> ᾔδειν; cf. 558) know; Bdel. is subject (cf. 4)

ὡς   introduces indir. statement in *retained indicative*: S #2615

ταύτῃ   in this way

κράτιστος (3)   most powerful (cf. 209)

Χο.　　　ὡς δ᾽ ἐπὶ πάντ᾽ ἐλήλυθεν
　　　　κοὐδὲν παρῆλθεν, ὥστ᾽ ἔγωγ᾽
　　　　ηὐξανόμην ἀκούων,
　　　　κἂν μακάρων δικάζειν
　　　　αὐτὸς ἔδοξα νήσοις,　　　　　　　　　　640
　　　　ἡδόμενος λέγοντι.

Φι.　　　ὥσθ᾽ οὗτος ἤδη σκορδινᾶται κἄστιν οὐκ ἐν αὑτοῦ.
　　　　ἦ μὴν ἐγώ σε τήμερον σκύτη βλέπειν ποιήσω.

LINE 636

ὡς	how (exclam.)
ἐπ-έρχομαι, -ελήλυθα	go over, explain. a] ἐπὶ πάντ᾽ ἐλήλυθεν, "explain everything" assumes *tmesis*; b] but normally in Ar. only insignificant words intervene between the prefix and verb (S #1651), so other editors take ἐπὶ as a separate prep.: "try everything."
παρ-έρχομαι, -ῆλθον	pass by, disregard
αὐξάνω	grow, swell with pride [< IE *aug-, increase; cogn. L. *augeo*; E. *wax* (grow)]
κἂν	= καὶ ἐν (take ἐν with νήσοις)
μάκαρ, –αρος	(adj.) blessed, used of gods and the departed (μακάριος was used of human beings, 1292, 1512)
δοκέω, ἔδοξα	seem to do, think (+ inf.)
νῆσος, ἡ	island. The Islands of the Blessed were a legendarily happy place for the souls of those favored by the gods.
ἥδομαι	(< ἡδύς, sweet) enjoy (+ dat.: S #1595b); cf. 272

LINE 642

σκορδινάομαι	gape, stretch limbs, fidget
οὐκ ἐν αὑτοῦ	"not in his own [usual condition/house]" (note shift from 3 sing. οὗτος in 642 to 2 sing. σε in 643)
ἦ μήν	introduces a confident statement, often in oaths and pledges; examples in Ar. are mostly with the fut. indic. and threatening in tone: *GP* 350 (cf. 258)
τήμερον	(adv.) today (cf. 179)
σκῦτος, –ους, τό	hide; σκύτη βλέπειν = look whipped (i.e., when he sees the lash he fears flogging)

Χο.   δεῖ δέ σε παντοίας πλέκειν
       εἰς ἀπόφευξιν παλάμας·   645
       τὴν γὰρ ἐμὴν ὀργὴν πεπᾶ-
       ναι χαλεπὸν ⟨νεανίᾳ⟩
       μὴ πρὸς ἐμοῦ λέγοντι.
       πρὸς ταῦτα μύλην ἀγαθὴν ὥρα ζητεῖν σοι καὶ νεόκοπτον,
       ἢν μή τι λέγῃς, ἥτις δυνατὴ τὸν ἐμὸν θυμὸν κατερεῖξαι.

LINE 644

παντοῖος (3)	(< πᾶν, all + –ιος, adj. suffix: S #858.2) of all sorts
πλέκω	weave; devise
ἀπόφευξις, –εως, ἡ	acquittal. The chorus here see Phil. as accuser and Bdel. as defendant. (cf. 558)
παλάμη, ἡ	palm of hand; wiles, cunning
πεπαίνω, ἐπέπᾱνα	(< πέπων, ripe + –αινω, *denominative* verb suffix: S #866.7) become ripe, soften {> dys*pepsia*} [< IE *pekʷ,*- cook, ripen; cogn. L. *coquo*; E. *pumpkin*]
χαλεπός (3)	difficult (sc. ἐστίν)
μή	(+ ptcp. = condit.: S # 2728)
πρός	(+ gen.) fitting to, from the point of view of; "It's hard for a youth to soften my anger if he is not speaking in my favor."

LINE 649

πρός	(+ acc.) with a view to
μύλη, ἡ	millstone
ὥρα, ἡ	season; time (for omission of ἐστίν: S #1985, 2004); cf. 346
νεόκοπτος, –ον	(< νέος, new + κόπτω, cut: cf. 275) fresh-chiseled
δυνατός (3)	capable
κατ-ερείκω, -έρειξα	(< κατά completely, adversely + ἐρείκω, rend, pound) grind down, crush. The chorus's anger is like a substance that can only be ground by a millstone.

Βδ.   χαλεπὸν μὲν καὶ δεινῆc γνώμηc καὶ μείζονοc ἢ ʼπὶ τρυγῳδοῖc   650
          ἰάcαcθαι νόcον ἀρχαίαν ἐν τῇ πόλει ἐντετακυῖαν.
          ἀτάρ, ὦ πάτερ ἡμέτερε Κρονίδη—
Φι.   παῦcαι καὶ μὴ πατέριζε.
          εἰ μὴ γὰρ ὅπωc δουλεύω ʼγώ, τουτὶ ταχέωc με διδάξειc,
          οὐκ ἔcτιν ὅπωc οὐχὶ τεθνήξειc, κἂν χρῇ cπλάγχνων μʼ ἀπέχεcθαι.

650–724: Bdel.'s speech, although interrupted with interjections from Phil., presents a starkly different view. Jurors are being exploited: the three-obol wage they receive is only a fraction of state income, while the politicians are pocketing obscene amounts for themselves. The sense of juror entitlement is only an illusion.

650–724: Meter: Following the pattern established in Phil.'s speech (though without exact correspondence), Bdel.'s speech will be delivered in anapestic tetrameters (648–718), with an anapestic *pnigos* (719–24).

LINE 650

χαλεπὸν μέν	A formal, rhetorical opening; take ἰάcαθαι as subject with preds. χαλεπόν and γνώμης, a gen. of quality: S #1320; γνώμης in turn is modified by δεινῆς and μείζονος.
μείζων, -ον, -ονος	greater (cf. 258)
ἐπί	in the power of (+ dat.)
τρυγῳδός	(< τρυγῳδία, a parody of τραγῳδία, < τρύξ, τρυγός, new wine with lees in it; comedy is a genre connected with wine) = κωμῳδός, "comic"; "an intellect greater than that in the power of comedians"
ἰάομαι, ἰᾱσάμην	heal, cure [cogn. ἰᾱτρός, doctor]
ἐν-τήκω, -τέτηκα	(< τήκω, melt) sink in, be absorbed in (Mss. read ἐντετοκυῖαν, inborn)
ἀτάρ	but (transitional, introducing a prayer: LA 16)
Κρονίδης, -ου, ὁ	(< Κρόνος + -ιδης, *patronymic* suffix: S #845.1) son of Kronos, Zeus
παῦσαι	stop (cf. 37 on pres. vs. aor. impvs.)
πατερίζω	(< πατήρ + -ίζω) call "father"; Bdel. was invoking Zeus, but Phil., with typical self-importance, thinks Bdel. was addressing *him*.

LINE 653

ὅπως	in what way, how (rel. or ind. interrog. clause: S #2668d)
δουλεύω	be a slave (cf. 59)
τουτί	refers to ὅπως clause
οὐκ ἔστιν ὅπως	the apodosis of a FMV condit.: S #2328 (cf. 211)
θνῄσκω, τεθνήξω	(> fut. perf. τεθνήξεις, inflected like a fut. act.: S #659a) die; you will have died = you will be dead (cf. 583)
κἂν	cf. 568
σπλάγχνον, τό	sacrificial meat (mostly used in pl.) {> spleen}
ἀπ-έχω	keep from; (mid.) abstain from. Those accused of murder were prohibited from joining religious rituals.

Βδ.   ἀκρόασαί νυν, ὦ παππίδιον, χαλάσας ὀλίγον τὸ μέτωπον·   655
        καὶ πρῶτον μὲν λόγισαι φαύλως, μὴ ψήφοις ἀλλ' ἀπὸ χειρός,
        τὸν φόρον ἡμῖν ἀπὸ τῶν πόλεων ϲυλλήβδην τὸν προσιόντα·
        κἄξω τούτου τὰ τέλη χωρὶς καὶ τὰς πολλὰς ἑκατοστάς,
        πρυτανεῖα, μέταλλ', ἀγοράς, λιμένας, μιϲθώϲεις, δημιόπρατα.
        τούτων πλήρωμα τάλαντ' ἐγγὺς διϲχίλια γίγνεται ἡμῖν.   660

LINE 655

ἀκροάομαι, ἠκροασάμην
    hearken, listen to (aor. impv. 2 sing. ἀκρόασαι; distinguish from aor. act. inf. ἀκροάσαι)
παππίδιον, τό   (dim. of πατήρ) dear father
χαλάω, ἐχάλασα   relax
μέτωπον, τό   (< μετά, among + ὤψ, face) forehead; frown {> my*opia*, tricerat*ops*}
λογίζομαι, ἐλογισάμην
    (aor. act. impv. 2 sing. λόγισαι) calculate (aor. inf. would be λογίσαι)
φαύλως   (adv.) roughly, simply
φόρος, ὁ   (< φέρω) tribute; revenue, income from the Delian League to Athens
ϲυλλήβδην   (adv. < συν + λαμβάνω, take + adv. ending -ην; S #344) all together, in total, in short
πρόσ-ειμι   (< εἶμι) go toward; come in (of revenue)

LINE 658

κἄξω   = καὶ ἔξω; ἔξω (+ gen.) outside of (i.e., in addition to the tribute)
τέλος, –εος, τό   offering, <u>tax</u>. For this and the following seven accs. sc. λόγισαι; Bdel. tallies up the sources of income for Athens, including taxes and fees. {> *toll*, phila*tely*}
χωρίς   (adv.) separately (used in stylistically marked passages: *LA* 256)
ἑκατοστή, ἡ   (< ἑκατόν, hundred, cf. 663 + –στος, suffix for ordinals: S #347) 1 percent tax
πρυτανεῖα, τά   (< πρυτανεῖον, town hall, < πρύτανις, lord, ruler) sum of money deposited to the city for a lawsuit
μέταλλον, τό   mine; (pl.) silver mines
ἀγορά, –ᾶς, ἡ   fees were derived from the Agora
λιμήν, –ένος, ὁ   (< λείμων, moist meadow) harbor
μίσθωσις, –εως, ἡ   (< μισθός, pay; cf. 300 + –σις, suffix denoting action expressing abstract ideas) rental of property owned by state
δημιόπρᾱτα, τά   (< δήμιος, public + πρᾱτός, for sale) confiscated goods

LINE 660

πλήρωμα, –ατος, τό   (< πληρόω, make full) full measure, sum total (cf. 380)
τάλαντον, τό   balance; anything weighed; a <u>talent</u>, monetary unit worth six thousand drachmas, perhaps = one million dollars
ἐγγύς   (adv.) nearby; nearly, almost
διϲχίλιοι, –αι, –α   (< δίς twice + χίλιοι, one thousand [rarely in sing.]) two thousand {> *kilo*}
γίγνομαι   come to, add up to (in reckoning numbers)

ἀπὸ τούτου νυν κατάθες μιςθὸν τοῖςι δικαςταῖς ἐνιαυτοῦ
ἓξ χιλιάςιν—κοὔπω πλείους ἐν τῇ χώρᾳ κατέναςθεν—,
γίγνεται ἡμῖν ἑκατὸν δήπου καὶ πεντήκοντα τάλαντα.

Φι.   οὐδ' ἡ δεκάτη τῶν προσιόντων ἡμῖν ἄρ' ἐγίγνεθ' ὁ μιςθός.
Βδ.   μὰ Δί' οὐ μέντοι.
Φι.   καὶ ποῖ τρέπεται δὴ 'πειτα τὰ χρήματα τἄλλα;   665
Βδ.   εἰς τούτους τοὺς "οὐχὶ προδώςω τὸν Ἀθηναίων κολοςυρτόν,
       ἀλλὰ μαχοῦμαι περὶ τοῦ πλήθους ἀεί." ςὺ γάρ, ὦ πάτερ, αὐτοὺς
       ἄρχειν αἱρεῖ σαυτοῦ τούτοις τοῖς ῥηματίοις περιπεφθείς.

LINE 661

κατα-τίθημι, -έθηκα	set down; set aside as paid
ἐνιαυτός, ὁ	year; a] gen. of measure with μιςθόν: S #1325 or b] gen. of time, period within which: S #1444
ἕξ	six (indeclinable)
οὔπω	(adv.), not yet; κοὔπω = καὶ οὔπω
πλείων, πλεῖον, -ονος	(> nom. pl. m./f. πλείονες contracts to πλείους < comparison of πολύς, much) more (cf. 260)
χώρα, ἡ	place; land, countryside (cf. 230)
κατα-ναίω, aor. pass. -ενάσθην	(poetic aor. pass. 3 pl. κατέναςθεν) make to dwell. The verse appears to be quotation from poetry.
ἑκατον	one hundred [< IE *dekm, ten + suffix -tom; cogn. L. centum; E. hundred] (aspiration from ἕν, one)
δήπου	(particle < δή, indeed + που, I suppose) presumably, I suppose; "The certainty of δή is toned down by the doubtfulness of που": GP 267. δήπου is rarely found in tragedy, only once in Thucydides, frequently in comedy and prose. It adds touch of irony or doubt in stating a case that would seem to be certain: S #2850.
πεντήκοντα	fifty (cf. 490)

LINE 664

δεκάτη, ἡ	(< δέκα, ten) one tenth {< dean, decade}
ἄρα	"I now see"; with imperfect, of something just realized (cf. 3)
μέντοι	"Indeed! It isn't"; concurring and echoing words of prior speaker: GP 401
τρέπω	turn; (mid.) turn in a direction; go (cf. 135)
δή	"exactly where?"; emphatic after. ποῖ (interrog. adv., "to where?"); with surprise: GP 211 (cf. 21)
τἄλλα	= τὰ ἄλλα, the rest of

LINE 666

τούς	an example of the ability of the art. to create a substantive, referring to "men who say, 'οὐχὶ ... αἰεί'": S #1153g
προ-δίδωμι, -δώσω	give away in advance; betray
Ἀθηναῖος (3)	Athenian
κολοσυρτός, ὁ	(< κολο- [etymology unexplained] + σύρω, sweep [cf. 673] = "swept down a river"?) noisy rabble
αἱρέω	(> pres. mid. 2 sing. indic. αἱρεῖ) take; (mid.) choose {> heresy}
ῥημάτιον, τό	(dim. of ῥῆμα, word) little word, pet phrase (cf. ῥῆσις, 580)
περι-πέττω, aor. pass. -επέφθην	(< πέττω, cook) bake around the crust; dress up; cajole {> peptic}

κᾆθ᾽ οὗτοι μὲν δωροδοκοῦϲιν κατὰ πεντήκοντα τάλαντα
ἀπὸ τῶν πόλεων ἐπαπειλοῦντεϲ τοιαυτὶ κἀναφοβοῦντεϲ,   670
"δώϲετε τὸν φόρον, ἢ βροντήϲαϲ τὴν πόλιν ὑμῶν ἀνατρέψω."
ϲὺ δὲ τῆϲ ἀρχῆϲ ἀγαπᾷϲ τῆϲ ϲῆϲ τοὺϲ ἀργελόφουϲ περιτρώγων.
οἱ δὲ ξύμμαχοι, ὡϲ ᾔϲθηνται τὸν μὲν ϲύρφακα τὸν ἄλλον
ἐκ κηθαρίου λαγαριζόμενον καὶ τραγαλίζοντα τὸ μηδέν,
ϲὲ μὲν ἡγοῦνται Κόννου ψῆφον, τούτοιϲι δὲ δωροφοροῦϲιν   675

LINE 669

κᾆθ᾽	cf. 239
δωροδοκέω	(< δῶρον, gift + δέχομαι, δεδοκημένος, irregular mid./pass. perf. ptcp., receive) take bribe {> Thermi*dor*; Pan*dora*}
κατά	(+ acc.) according to; at a time
πεντήκοντα	fifty (cf. 490)
ἐπ-απειλέω	(< ἀπειλαί, threats, in pl.) threaten
τοιαυτί	= τοιαυτά, such, "[threats] like these" (-α is dropped before deictic iota -ί: S #333g)
ἀνα-φοβέω	(< φόβος, fear) frighten away, terrify {> -*phobe*}
φόρος, ὁ	tribute, income (cf. 657)
βροντάω, ἐβρόντησα	thunder (cf. 323)
ἀνα-τρέπω, -τρέψω	overturn

LINE 672

ἄρχη, ἡ	empire
ἀγαπάω	love; be contented with (+ suppl. ptcp. with verb of emotion: S #2100)
ἀργέλοφοι, οἱ	feet of sheepskin; rinds, scraps
περι-τρώγω	nibble around, gnaw (cf. 164)
ξύμμαχος, ὁ	ally
ὡς	because (causal conj.)
αἰσθάνομαι	(> perf. mid. 3 pl. ᾔσθηνται) perceive (verb of perception + ptcp.: S #2100)
σύρφαξ, –ᾱκος, ὁ	(< σύρω, drag, sweep?) the crowd, rabble
ἄλλος (3)	other; rest of (cf. 85)

LINE 674

κηθάριον, τό	(dim. of κηθίς, ballot box) voting urn, ballot box
λαγαρίζομαι	(< λαγαρός, hollow, thin) earning a poor living (from the ballot box); get thin, scrape by
τραγαλίζω	(< variant of τρώγω, aor.[2] τραγεῖν, gnaw) feast on
τὸ μηδέν	μή used with ptcp. in condit. clause: S #2728, 2731
μέν	after the first μέν, with σύρφακα, a fresh μέν is added for clarity: "you, yes, *you*": GP 384–85
ἡγέομαι	consider, believe (cf. 269)
Κόννος	Connus. Identity uncertain; a "Simple Simon"?
δωροφορέω	bring present, give as a bribe. Examples of twelve bribes follow in a list, with *asyndeton*, capped off with πλουθυγίεια.

ὕρχας, οἶνον, δάπιδας, τυρόν, μέλι, σήσαμα, προσκεφάλαια,
φιάλας, χλανίδας, στεφάνους, ὅρμους, ἐκπώματα, πλουθυγίειαν·
σοὶ δ' ὦν ἄρχεις, πολλὰ μὲν ἐν γῇ, πολλὰ δ' ἐφ' ὑγρᾷ πιτυλεύσας,
οὐδεὶς οὐδὲ σκορόδου κεφαλὴν τοῖς ἑψητοῖσι δίδωσιν.

Φι. μὰ Δί', ἀλλὰ παρ' Εὐχαρίδου καὐτὸς τρεῖς γ' ἄγλιθας μετέπεμψα.   680
ἀλλ' αὐτήν μοι τὴν δουλείαν οὐκ ἀποφαίνων ἀποκναίεις.

LINE 676

ὕρχη, ἡ	jar for preserved fish
δάπις, –ιδος, ἡ	(< var. of τάπης, carpet) carpet, richly woven coverlet
τῡρός, ὁ	cheese
μέλι, –ιτος, τό	honey (cf. 107)
σήσαμον, τό	seed of sesame plant
προσκεφάλαιον, τό	(< κεφαλή, head) pillow, cushion
φιάλη, ἡ	broad bowl or pan used for pouring libations in ritual
χλανίς, –ίδος, ἡ	(< χλαῖνα, cloak, cf. 678 + –ις, –ιδος, dim. suffix: S #853) light cloak or blanket, of a lighter weave than the χλαῖνα (cf. 738)
στέφανος, ὁ	wreath, crown (cf. 476)
ὅρμος, ὁ	(< εἴρω, string + –μος, suffix used of tangible items: S #861) necklace
ἔκπωμα, –ατος, τό	(< πῶμα, drink) drinking cup (cf. 616)
πλουθυγίεια, ἡ	(< πλοῦτος, wealth + ὑγίεια, health; Ar.'s coinage) weath and health {> hygiene}

LINE 678

ὧν	part. gen. with οὐδείς; also gen. object of ἄρχω
ὑγρά, ἡ	(< ὑγρός, wet) the sea
πιτυλεύω, ἐπιτύλευσα	
	(< πίτυλος, splash of oar) ply with the oar
οὐδεὶς οὐδέ	"No one even gives . . ." (compounded neg. οὐδέ reinforces οὐδείς)
σκόροδον, τό	garlic
ἑψητός (3)	(< ἕψω, boil) boiled; (pl.) esp. boiled fish

LINE 680

μὰ Δία	"No, they don't" or "You're right! They don't!" (cf. 169)
Εὐχαρίδης, –ου, ὁ	Eucharides, evidently a grocer who sold garlic
καὐτός	= καὶ αὐτός
ἄγλῑς, –ῖθος, ἡ	cloves of garlic (used only in pl.)
μετα-πέμπω, -έπεμψα	send for
ἀπο-φαίνω	show, point out
ἀπο-κναίω	(< κναίω, scrape) rub, worry, get on my nerves

Βδ.
οὐ γὰρ μεγάλη δουλεία 'cτὶν τούτους μὲν ἅπαντας ἐν ἀρχαῖς
αὑτούς τ' εἶναι καὶ τοὺς κόλακας τοὺς τούτων μιcθοφοροῦντας;
cοὶ δ' ἤν τις δῷ τοὺς τρεῖς ὀβολούς, ἀγαπᾷς· οὓς αὐτὸς ἐλαύνων
καὶ πεζομαχῶν καὶ πολιορκῶν ἐκτήcω πολλὰ πονήcας.   685
καὶ πρὸς τούτοις ἐπιταττόμενος φοιτᾷς, ὃ μάλιστά μ' ἀπάγχει,
ὅταν εἰcελθὸν μειράκιόν cοι κατάπυγον, Χαιρέου υἱός,
ὡδὶ διαβάς, διακινηθεὶς τῷ cώματι καὶ τρυφερανθείς,
ἥκειν εἴπῃ πρῲ κἀν ὥρᾳ δικάcονθ', "ὡς ὅcτις ἂν ὑμῶν
ὕcτερος ἔλθῃ τοῦ cημείου, τὸ τριώβολον οὐ κομιεῖται·"   690

LINE 682

γάρ	"[I say this] because is it not . . . ?"
τούτους	that is, the highly paid politicians
μισθοφορέω	earn salary
δίδωμι, ἔδωκα	(> aor. indic. subjv. 3 sing. δῷ) give
ἀγαπάω	treat with affection, be fond of
ἐλαύνω	drive; row
πεζομαχέω	(< πεζός, foot soldier < πούς, foot) fight on foot
πολιορκέω	(< πόλις, city + ἕρκος, enclosure) besiege a city
κτάομαι, ἐκτησάμην	(> aor. indic. mid. 2 sing. ἐκτήσω) possess; earn (cf. 615)
πονέω, ἐπόνησα	(< πόνος, toil) labor

LINE 686

πρός	(+ dat.) in addition to
ἐπι-τάττω	order, command; (pass.) submit to orders (cf. 69)
φοιτάω	move about, go to and fro (*frequentatives* often end in -αω: S #867)
ὅ	which; that is, the fact that you put up with being ordered around
ἀπ-άγχω	choke; irk, infuriate {> *angina*}

LINE 687

μειράκιον, τό	(dim. of μεῖραξ, young girl) youth
καταπύγων, -ον, -ονος	
	accustomed to anal intercourse (cf. 83)
Χαίρεας, -ου, ὁ	Chaireas; unknown, aside from being father of this unnamed effeminate youth
ὡδί	in this way (Attic strengthened form of ὧδε; demonstrative adv. of ὅδε)
δια-βαίνω, -έβην	stand with legs apart
δια-κῑνέω, -εκῑνήθην	move slightly, waggle, with mincing movements (cf. 403)
σῶμα, -ατος, τό	body
τρυφεραίνομαι, aor. pass. ἐτρυφεράνθην	
	(< τρυφή, delicacy, cf. 551 + -αινω, suffix: S #866.7) be fastidious, dandied up (B-O see a *factitive* sense for the suffix, suggesting a self-consciously sought charm)

LINE 689

ἥκειν	(sc. σε as acc. subject) "he tells you to <u>arrive</u> on time"
πρῴ	(adv.) early in the morning
ἐν ὥρᾳ	on time
δικάσοντα	fut. ptcp. to denote purpose: S #2065
σημεῖον, τό	signal (gen. of comparison: S #1402); cf. 585
κομίζω, κομιῶ	carry away, (mid.) acquire for self (fut. apodosis in FMV rel. clause); cf. 616

119

αὐτὸς δὲ φέρει τὸ συνηγορικόν, δραχμήν, κἂν ὕστερος ἔλθῃ·
καὶ κοινωνῶν τῶν ἀρχόντων ἑτέρῳ τινὶ τῶν μεθ’ ἑαυτοῦ,
ἤν τίς τι διδῷ τῶν φευγόντων, ξυνθέντε τὸ πρᾶγμα δύ’ ὄντε
ἐσπουδάκατον, κᾆθ’ ὡς πρίονθ’ ὁ μὲν ἕλκει ὁ δ’ ἀντενέδωκε·
σὺ δὲ χασκάζεις τὸν κωλακρέτην, τὸ δὲ πραττόμενόν σε λέληθεν.   695

Φι.   ταυτί με ποιοῦς; οἴμοι, τί λέγεις; ὥς μου τὸν θῖνα ταράττεις,
           καὶ τὸν νοῦν μου προσάγει μᾶλλον, κοὐκ οἶδ’ ὅ τι χρῆμά με ποιεῖς.

Βδ.   σκέψαι τοίνυν ὡς, ἐξόν σοι πλουτεῖν καὶ τοῖσιν ἅπασιν,

LINE 691

φέρω	receive pay (LSJ IV.5)
συνηγορικόν, τό	advocate's fee (cf. 482 on the ξυνήγορος)
δραχμή, ἡ	drachma; six obols and evidently the daily pay for an advocate—and twice the rate of a juror
κἂν	= καὶ ἐάν
κοινωνέω	(< κοινός, common) share {> *coeno-*, epicene}
οἱ ἄρχοντες οἱ μεθ’ ἑαυτοῦ	
	the fellow officials with him (i.e., the ξυνήγοροι)

LINE 693

τι	"something"; that is, a bribe
ξυν-τίθημι, -έθηκα	(> dual aor. ptcp. ξυνθέντε) put together, construct, arrange. Chaereas's son and the fellow ξυνήγορος team up as a pair.
πρᾶγμα, –ατος, τό	thing, matter; the business of lawyering and taking bribes (cf. 30)
σπουδάζω, perf. ἐσπούδακα	
	(< σπουδή, zeal) be eager, zealous; be serious
κᾆθ’	= καὶ εἶτα with *crasis, elision* preceding aspiration: S #62, 70, 124
πρίω	(> πρίονθ’ = dual pres. act. ptcp. πρίοντε) saw (i.e., with the cutting tool)
ἕλκω	draw, <u>pull</u> (cf. 268)
ἀντ-εν-δίδωμι, -έδωκα	give way in turn; <u>push</u>

LINE 695

χασκάζω	(< *frequentative* of χάσκω) keep gaping at, "gape after in eager expectation"
κωλακρέτης, ὁ	(< κῶλον, member, body part, flesh + ἀγείρειν, gather) "ham-collector"; treasurer, paymaster
πράττω	do; τὸ πραττόμενον = "what's being done" (cf. 30)
ταυτί	strengthened Attic form of neut. pl. ταῦτα, adv. acc.
ποιέω	do something to someone (with double acc.; LSJ B.I.2); cf. 261
ὡς	how (exclam.)
θίς, θῖνός, ὁ, ἡ	a heap; mud, sand; "the depths of my feelings"
ταράττω	stir up
προσ-άγω	draw near; (mid.) bring over to one's side
ὅστις	(> neut. sing. ὅ τι) what (indef. rel. pron. in indir. quest.; distinguish from conj. ὅτι)

ὑπὸ τῶν ἀεὶ δημιζόντων οὐκ οἶδ' ὅπῃ ἐγκεκύκλησαι,

ὅςτις πόλεων ἄρχων πλείςτων ἀπὸ τοῦ Πόντου μέχρι Cαρδοῦς   700

οὐκ ἀπολαύεις πλὴν τοῦθ' ὃ φέρεις ἀκαρῆ· καὶ τοῦτ' ἐρίω cοι

ἐνcτάζουcιν κατὰ μικρὸν ἀεὶ τοῦ ζῆν ἕνεχ' ὥςπερ ἔλαιον.

βούλονται γάρ cε πένητ' εἶναι· καὶ τοῦθ' ὧν οὕνεκ' ἐρῶ cοι·

ἵνα γιγνώcκῃς τὸν τιθαcευτήν, κᾆθ' ὅταν οὗτός c' ἐπιcίζῃ

ἐπὶ τῶν ἐχθρῶν τιν' ἐπιρρύξας, ἀγρίως αὐτοῖς ἐπιπηδᾷς.   705

LINE 699

cκέπτομαι, ἐcκεψάμην	consider (cf. 601)
τοίνυν	"Furthermore," "Again"; introducing a fresh argument: *GP* 575 (cf. 578)
ὡς	(conj.) that, how
ἔξεcτι	(> neut. acc. ptcp. ἔξον) it is possible (impers. verb in acc. absolute: S #2059, 2076A)
πλουτέω	be rich (cf. 575)
δημίζω	claim to support the δῆμος; be a populist (cf. 34)
ὅπῃ	in what way; οὐκ οἶδ' ὅπῃ = "I don't know in what way," "somehow or other"
ἐγ-κυκλόω	(> perf. mid./pass. 2 sing. ἐγκεκύκλησαι) encircle (cf. 132)
πλεῖcτος (3)	greatest number (cf. 260)
Πόντος, ὁ	Pontus; the Black Sea
μέχρι	(+ gen.) as far as
Cαρδώ, –οῦς, ἡ	Sardinia. Although some cities in the Black Sea paid tribute to Athens, it is preposterous to claim that the Athenians had any control over Sardinia—or almost anywhere else in the west.

LINE 701

ἀπο-λαύω	enjoy
τοῦθ'	= jury pay (which is likened to oil)
ἀκαρής, –ές	too short; (adv. acc.) οὐκ . . . ἀκαρῆ = "not a bit" (cf. 541)
ἔριον, τό	wool; "they drip it into you . . ." a] "as into wool" or b] "with a glob of wool")
ἐν-cτάζω	(< cτάζω, drip) drop into, drip (subject of verb is "corrupt populist politicians")
κατὰ μικρόν	a little at a time
ἕνεκα	(prep. + gen.) because of, for the sake of (with τοῦ ζῆν, artic. inf.: S #2025)
ἔλαιον, ὁ	olive, olive oil (cf. 252)

LINE 703

πένης, –ητος, ὁ	poor person (cf. 464)
οὕνεκα	(< οὗ ἕνεκα, but is used as prep. in its own right, = simple ἕνεκα, with gen.)
ὧν οὕνεκα	= ἐκείνων οὕνεκα ἅ, "for these reasons, which I will tell . . ."

LINE 704

τιθαcευτής, ὁ	(< τιθαcός, tamed, domestic + –της, suffix denoting agency: S #839a1) tamer, trainer
ἐπι-cίζω	(< cίζω, hiss) hiss to make a dog sic, whistle ("trainer" is subject) [< *onomatopoeia*]
ἐπί	at (+ acc., expressing hostility: S #1689.3.d)
ἐχθρός (3)	enemy (cf. 418)
ἐπι-ρρύζω, –έρρυξα	(< ρύζω, snarl; double -ρρ- after vowel in composition: S #80) set a dog on someone [< *onomatopoeia*]
ἀγρίως	(adv.) fiercely
ἐπι-πηδάω	leap upon, assault (cf. 227)

εἰ γὰρ ἐβούλοντο βίον πορίσαι τῷ δήμῳ, ῥᾴδιον ἦν ἄν.
εἰσίν γε πόλεις χίλιαι αἳ νῦν τὸν φόρον ἡμῖν ἀπάγουσι·
τούτων εἴκοσιν ἄνδρας βόσκειν εἴ τις προσέταξεν ἑκάστῃ,
δύο μυριάδ' ἂν τῶν δημοτικῶν ἔζων ἐν πᾶσι λαγῴοις
καὶ στεφάνοισιν παντοδαποῖσιν καὶ πυῷ καὶ πυριάτῃ,   710
ἄξια τῆς γῆς ἀπολαύοντες καὶ τοῦ 'ν Μαραθῶνι τροπαίου.
νῦν δ' ὥσπερ ἐλαολόγοι χωρεῖθ' ἅμα τῷ τὸν μισθὸν ἔχοντι.

Φι.   οἴμοι, τί πέπονθ'; ὡς νάρκη μου κατὰ τῆς χειρὸς καταχεῖται,
        καὶ τὸ ξίφος οὐ δύναμαι κατέχειν, ἀλλ' ἤδη μαλθακός εἰμι.

LINE 706

εἰ ... ἄν	Pres. Contrary-to-Fact condit.: S #2304
πορίζω	provide (cf. 365)
γε	"There *are* a thousand cities . . ."; emphatic and quasi-connective; usually γάρ introduces an explanation: *GP* 145
χίλιοι, –αι, –α	thousand (cf. 660); in fact, only some 370 cities were paying tribute.
ἀπ-άγω	return; pay
εἴκοσι	twenty (indeclinable; modifies ἄνδρας)
βόσκω	feed, support (cf. 313)
προσ-τάττω, –έταξα	assign, command; "assigned to each [city] to support twenty men"
ἕκαστος (3)	(< ἑκάς + τις, "everyone for himself") each

LINE 709

μυριάς, –άδος, ἡ	(> dual μυριάδε) the number 10,000. There may have been 30,000 male citizens at this date; the idea that 20,000 could benefit from public support is plausible.
δημοτικός (3)	of the common people (cf. 35)
ζάω	live (aor. in protasis of Contrary-to-Fact condit. + imperfect ἔζων apodosis), cf. 506
λαγῷος (3)	(< λαγώς, hare) of the hare; sc. κρέα = hare meat; delicacies
παντοδαπός (3)	of every kind
πυός, –οῦ, ὁ	beestings, first milk after birth (milk that is richer than usual)
πυριάτη, ἡ	beesting pudding
ἄξιος (3)	worthy of, in a manner befitting (+ gen.) (cf. 491)
ἀπο-λαύω	enjoy (cf. 701)
Μαραθών, –ῶνος, ὁ	Marathon, site of the Athenian victory over Persia in 490 BC
τρόπαιον, τό	(< τροπή, turning, rout of enemy) trophy

LINE 712

ἐλαολόγος, ὁ	(< ἐλάα, olive + λέγω, choose) olive picker; seasonal laborers, paid a pittance
χωρέω	move on (cf. 230)

LINE 713

νάρκη, ἡ	numbness
κατα-χέω	pour over (cf. 7)
κατ-έχω	hold fast, possess
μαλθακός (3)	soft, effeminate; weak (poetic; prose equivalent is μαλακός, 738)

Βδ.   ἀλλ' ὁπόταν μὲν δείcωc' αὐτοί, τὴν Εὔβοιαν διδόαcιν   715

            ὑμῖν, καὶ cῖτον ὑφίcτανται κατὰ πεντήκοντα μεδίμνουc

            πορεῖν· ἔδοcαν δ' οὐπώποτέ cοι· πλὴν πρῴην πέντε μεδίμνουc,

            καὶ ταῦτα μόλιc ξενίαc φεύγων, ἔλαβεc κατὰ χοίνικα κριθῶν.

            ὧν οὕνεκ' ἐγώ c' ἀπέκλειον ἀεὶ

            βόcκειν ἐθέλων καὶ μὴ τούτουc   720

            ἐγχάcκειν cοι cτομφάζονταc.

LINE 715

ὁπόταν	(= ὅποτε + ἄν) whenever
δείδω, ἔδεισα	fear ("populist politicians" continues to be the subject); Graves suggests that the aor. implies sudden fright (cf. 109)
Εὔβοια, ἡ	(< εὐ + βοῦς, "Well-Cattled") Euboea, island to the east of Attica; a source of grain
cῖτος, ὁ	grain, either wheat or barley
ὑφίστημι	place under; (pass.) place oneself under an engagement, <u>promise</u>
κατά	(+ acc., used in counting) by, to the tune of
μέδιμνος, ὁ	a measure of grain, about a bushel; 1 *medimnos* was composed of 48 *choinikes* (a *choinix* was ca. one quart; cf. 440). Fifty *medimnoi* are an absurdly large amount of grain, but the implied generosity fails to materialize: not only does a typical Athenian receive a mere five *medimnoi*, which are doled out in stingy *choinix* measures, but he even has to prove his citizenship.

LINE 717

πορίζω, πορίω	provide, supply (fut. inf. reflects fut. indic. of orig. statement: S #1867c); cf. 365
πρῴην	the day before yesterday; lately
καὶ ταῦτα	and at that (with ptcp., as in 252, 1184, 1189)
μόλις	(adv.) with difficulty
ξενία, ἡ	(< ξένος, guest, host; cf. 82) hospitality; <u>a charge of not being a legal citizen</u> (gen. of charge: S #1375)
χοῖνιξ, –ικος, ἡ	*choinix*, about a quart of grain (cf. 440)
κρῑθή, ἡ	barley; a less desirable choice if wheat was possible

LINE 719

ὧν οὕνεκα	cf. 703
ἀπο-κλείω	lock up; shut up, as if in prison (cf. 113)
βόcκω	feed (both βόcκειν and ἐγχάcκειν depend on ἐθέλων; τούτουc cτομφίζονταc is acc. subject of ἐγχάcκειν); cf. 313
ἐγ-χάcκω	gape, scoff at, with dat. (cf. 342)
cτομφάζω	(< cτόμφος, bombastic < cτέμβω, shake, abuse) rant, vaunt

καὶ νῦν ἀτεχνῶς ἐθέλω παρέχειν
ὅ τι βούλει coι,
πλὴν κωλακρέτου γάλα πίνειν.

Χο. ἦ που coφὸς ἦν ὅcτιc ἔφαcκεν, "πρὶν ἂν ἀμφοῖν μῦθον ἀκούcηc,   725
οὐκ ἂν δικάcαιc." cὺ γὰρ οὖν νῦν μοι νικᾶν πολλῷ δεδόκηcαι·
ὥcτ᾿ ἤδη τὴν ὀργὴν χαλάcαc τοὺc cκίπωναc καταβάλλω.
ἀλλ᾿, ὦ τῆc ἡλικίαc ἡμῖν τῆc αὐτῆc cυνθιαcῶτα,
πιθοῦ πιθοῦ λόγοιcι, μηδ᾿ ἄφρων γένῃ   [cτρ.
μηδ᾿ ἀτενὴc ἄγαν ἀτεράμων τ᾿ ἀνήρ.   730

LINE 722

ἀτεχνῶς   (< ἄτεχνος, without skill) simply, absolutely
ὅ τι   whatever (cf. 697)
γάλα, –ακτος, τό milk (cf. 508); the joke is that "bird's milk" was a proverbial delicacy (cf. 508), but for
                 a juror the "milk" of the κωλακρέτης, the treasurer, is jury pay (cf. 695)

725–59: The chorus announce, perhaps to our surprise, that they have been persuaded by Bdel. and they urge
Phil. to accept his son's help. Bdel. promises to provide every creature comfort to his father, but Phil. cannot
imagine life without jury duty.

725–35: Meter: After a short *sphragis* in anapestic tetrameters (725–28), probably delivered by the chorus
leader, the chorus as a whole join in (in midsentence) with a lyrical mixture of iambics and dochmiacs (729–
35). Dochmiacs were used in agitated passages in tragedy; possibly they help convey a sense of urgency in the
chorus's message to Phil. Note *responsion*: 729–35 *strophe* = 743–49 *antistrophe*.

LINE 725

ἦ που   affirmative ἦ, but που suggests a hesitation: *GP* 286
ἄμφω, τώ   (> dual, gen. ἀμφοῖν) both. B-O note that, until this point, the chorus have shown
                 little interest in the ideal of impartiality.
πρίν ἄν   + subjv.; πρίν = "until" when the principal clause is neg.: S #2432
μῦθος, ὁ   speech (cf. 566)
γὰρ οὖν   "For the fact is . . ."; "οὖν adds to γάρ the idea of importance or essentiality": *GP* 446
νικάω   be victorious
πολλῷ   by far (dat. of degree of difference: S #1513)
δοκέω, δεδόκημαι   seem (δεδόκημαι is a poetic alternative to mid./pass. perf. δέδογμαι)
χαλάω, ἐχάλαcα   slacken
cκίπων, –ωνος, ὁ   staff, crutch
κατα-βάλλω   throw down

LINE 728

ἡλικία, ἡ   age, time of life, generation (cf. 245)
cυνθιαcώτης, ὁ   comrade; fellow in a *thiasos*, a group of Bacchic revelers
ἄφρων, –ον, –ονος (< α- priv. + φρήν, mind, cf. 8) without sense, foolish
γίγνομαι   (> aor. subjv. 2 sing. γένῃ) be, become (prohib. subjv., with μή: S #1800)
ἀτενής, –ές   (< α- intensive, a variant on α- copulative: S #885.4 + τείνω, stretch, cf. 337) earnest,
                 stubborn
ἄγαν   (< old acc. of adj. μέγας) excessively
ἀτεράμων, –ον   unsoftened, merciless (used of Marathon veterans at *Ach.* 181; this and ἀτενής seem
                 drawn from tragic diction)

εἴθ' ὤφελέν μοι κηδεμὼν ἢ ξυγγενὴς
εἶναί τις ὅςτις τοιαῦτ' ἐνουθέτει.
coì δὲ νῦν τις θεῶν παρὼν ἐμφανὴς
ξυλλαμβάνει τοῦ πράγματος, καὶ δῆλός ἐcτιν εὖ ποιῶν·
cὺ δὲ παρὼν δέχου.   735

Βδ.   καὶ μὴν θρέψω γ' αὐτὸν παρέχων
ὅcα πρεσβύτῃ ξύμφορα, χόνδρον
λείχειν, χλαῖναν μαλακήν, cιcύραν,
πόρνην, ἥτις τὸ πέος τρίψει
καὶ τὴν ὀcφῦν.   740
ἀλλ' ὅτι cιγᾷ κοὐδὲν γρύζει,
τοῦτ' οὐ δύναταί με προcέcθαι.

LINE 731

ὀφείλω, aor.² ὤφελον	help; <u>would that</u> (εἴθε or εἰ γάρ with aor. ὤφελον + pres. or aor. inf. express an unattainable wish: S #1780–81)
κηδεμών, –ονος, ὁ	protector, guardian (cf. 242)
ξυγγενής, –ες	kinsman
ἐμφανής, –ές	visible, appearing in person
ξυλ-λαμβάνω	collect; lay hold of (+ gen); <u>assist</u> dat. with gen.
δῆλος (3)	clear; "he is <u>clearly</u> helping …" (with ptcp.: S #2107)
εὖ ποιέω	help

Meter: 736–42: Anapestic dimeters; these are less lyrical, and more insistent, because Bdel. wants it to be quite clear that he will support Phil.

LINE 736

καὶ μήν … γε	καὶ μήν expresses agreement with previous speaker, "And indeed I will!": GP 353; γε defines new idea sharply, "this and nothing else": GP 119–20
πρεσβύτης, ὁ	old man (cf. 540)
ξύμφορος (3)	(< συμφέρω, bring together, contribute) advantageous, useful (contrast ξυμφορά, ἡ, event, mishap)
χόνδρος, ὁ	porridge, soup
λείχω	lick {> *lichen*}
χλαῖνα, ἡ	large cloak made of wool, worn over the χίτων, the "tunic" which was worn next to the skin [> borrowed into L. *laena*, a coat]
μαλακός (3)	soft [< IE *mel-*, soft; cogn. L. *blandus*; E. *melt*; a root different from that of μαλθακός, 714]
σισύρα, ἡ	thick cloak of goatskin or sheepskin, coarser than a χλαῖνα
πόρνη, ἡ	(< πέρνημι, sell, cf. 179) prostitute
πέος, πέους, τό	penis, cock; a blunt vulgarity, with no euphemistic force: *MM* p. 108 {> pencil} [< IE *pes*, rub; cogn. L. *penis* (tail, penis)]
τρίβω, τρίψω	rub, massage; in a rel. clause of purpose, "so that she can …": S #2554). No one in Ar. is embarrassed to acknowledge sexual desire; a son even assumes it of his father! (cf. 33)
ὀσφῦς, –ύος, ἡ	loins
ὅτι	"<u>the fact that</u> he is silent …" (S #2577, on dependent statements; the clause is in apposition to τοῦτ' of 742)
γρύζω	grunt (cf. 374)
τοῦτο	antecedent for ὅτι, subject of δύναται
προσ-ίημι, -ῆκα	admit, allow, approve; (with acc. of person) attract, please

Χο.   νενουθέτηκεν αὐτὸν εἰς τὰ πράγμαθ’, οἷς   [ἀντ.
        τότ’ ἐπεμαίνετ’· ἔγνωκε γὰρ ἀρτίως,
        λογίζεταί τ’ ἐκεῖνα πάνθ’ ἁμαρτίας   745
        ἃ σοῦ κελεύοντος οὐκ ἐπείθετο.
        νῦν δ’ ἴσως τοῖσι σοῖς λόγοις πείθεται,
        καὶ σωφρονεῖ μέντοι μεθιστὰς εἰς τὸ λοιπὸν τὸν τρόπον
        πειθόμενός τέ σοι.
Φι.   ἰώ μοί μοι.
Βδ.   οὗτος, τί βοᾷς;   750
Φι.   μή μοι τούτων μηδὲν ὑπισχνοῦ.
        κείνων ἔραμαι, κεῖθι γενοίμαν,
        ἵν’ ὁ κῆρύξ φησι, "τίς ἀψήφιστος; ἀνιστάσθω."

LINE 743

Meter: 743–49: The *antistrophe* to 729–35; a lyrical mixture of iambics and dochmiacs.

ἐπι-μαίνομαι	make someone madly in love with; (mid.) be mad about (+ dat.) {> *manic, mania*}
γιγνώσκω	know, come to recognize, know by observation (cf. 72)
ἀρτίως	just now (cf. 11)
λογίζομαι	calculate, reckon (cf. 656)
ἁμαρτία, ἡ	error (pred. acc.); cf. 515
κελεύω	order, urge (σοῦ κελεύοντος, gen. abs.: S #2070, perhaps with concessive sense, "even though")
πείθομαι	(mid./pass.) be persuaded, obey (with neut. acc. of respect ἅ, "in which things he wouldn't be persuaded even though you were urging")

LINE 747

σωφρονέω	(< σῶς, sound + φρήν, mind) be prudent
καί . . . μέντοι	"Here is my next thought"; introducing a new argument: GP 414
μεθ-ίστημι	(< μετά implying alteration: S #1691.4) change 750–59: Meter: anapestic dimeters.

LINE 750

ἰώ μοί μοι	"Alas! Woe is me!" Exclam. of grief, frequently in tragedy; loss of juror status is a crushing loss for Phil. and in these lines he casts himself as a tragic victim.
μή . . . μηδέν	simple + compound neg., cf. 679; S #2761
τούτων	that is, the features of the comfortable life described above
ὑπισχνέομαι	(> pres. impv. 2 sing. ὑπισχνοῦ < ὑπό, under + ἔχω, take) promise
κείνων	that is, those things over there in the courtroom (poetic/paratragic for ἐκείνων)
ἔραμαι	(cf. ἔρως, love) love, lust after (+ gen.)
κεῖθι	(adv. < ἐκεῖ + -θι, suffix denoting place: S #342) there (poetic/paratragic for ἐκεῖθι)
γίγνομαι	(> γενοίμαν: Doric –μαν for Attic –μην: S #462D, importing tragic style) be, become (opt. wish: S #1814)
ἵνα	(+ indic.) where (only instance of this use of ἵνα in *W*.)
κῆρυξ, –υκος, ὁ	herald
ἀψήφιστος, –ον	(ἀ- priv. + ψῆφος, vote; cf. 94) not having voted

κἀπισταίην ἐπὶ τοῖς κημοῖς
ψηφιζομένων ὁ τελευταῖος.   755
σπεῦδ', ὦ ψυχή.—ποῦ μοι ψυχή;—
πάρες, ὦ σκιερά—.μὰ τὸν Ἡρακλέα
μὴ νυν ἔτ' ἐγὼ 'ν τοῖσι δικασταῖς
κλέπτοντα Κλέωνα λάβοιμι.

Βδ.   ἴθ', ὦ πάτερ, πρὸς τῶν θεῶν ἐμοὶ πιθοῦ.   760
Φι.   τί σοι πίθωμαι; λέγ' ὅ τι βούλει πλὴν ἑνός.
Βδ.   ποίου; φέρ' ἴδω.
Φι.   τοῦ μὴ δικάζειν. τοῦτο δὲ
        Ἅιδης διακρινεῖ πρότερον ἢ 'γὼ πείσομαι.

LINE 754

ἀν-ίστημι	(> pres. mid. impv. 3 sing. ἀνιστάσθω) raise, make to stand up; (mid.) <u>stand up</u>
ἐφ-ίστημι	(> aor. act. opt. 1 sing. ἐπισταίην) stand by
κημός, ὁ	voting urn (cf. 99)
τελευταῖος (3)	last, final

LINE 756

σπεύδω	hasten
παρ-ίημι	(> πάρες aor. act. impv. 2 sing.) let drop; relax; make way, let me pass
σκιερός (3)	(< σκιά, shadow; cf. 191) shady; Phil. quotes verses from Euripides's *Bellerophon*, "Let me pass, you shadowy foliage, let me cross the watery dells, I am eager to see the heaven above . . ."
νυν	"in that case," "if you're telling the truth"; Phil. now finds it plausible that Cleon could be guilty of embezzlement.

760–834: Bdel. explains his plan: Phil. can stay at home and judge cases involving household transgressions. Even Phil. can now see the advantages: he will have easy access to food and a toilet.

760–862: Meter: Iambic trimeters. Dialogue between Phil. and Bdel.; the chorus fall silent.

LINE 760

εἶμι	(> pres. impv. 2 sing. ἴθι) go; here = "please" (cf. 162)
τί πίθωμαι	"In what matter am I to follow you?" (delib. subjv.: S #1805; τί is not "why?" but "in respect to what thing?")
ποῖος (3)	(interrog. pron.) of what sort? or, here, simply "what?" (= τίνος)
φέρ' ἴδω	"Well, let's see." (cf. 145)
μή	the regular neg. with articular inf.: S #2712
Ἅιδης, -ου, ὁ	Hades (note that the iota is adscript; alphabetize as if Ἁδη-)
δια-κρίνω, -κρίνῶ	distinguish, decide; "Hades will decide" = "one or the other of us will die" (cf. 53)
πείθω, πείσω	(> fut. mid./pass. πείσομαι) obey, comply (πείσομαι is prob. not < πάσχω, though it would indeed be a hardship)

Βδ.   cὺ δ' οὖν, ἐπειδὴ τοῦτο κεχάρηκαc ποιῶν,

          ἐκεῖcε μὲν μηκέτι βάδιζ', ἀλλ' ἐνθάδε   765

          αὐτοῦ μένων δίκαζε τοῖcιν οἰκέταιc.

Φι.   περὶ τοῦ; τί ληρεῖc;

Βδ.   ταῦθ' ἅπερ ἐκεῖ πράττεται·

          ὅτι τὴν θύραν ἀνέῳξεν ἡ cηκὶc λάθρᾳ,

          ταύτηc ἐπιβολὴν ψηφιεῖ μίαν μόνην.

          πάντωc δὲ κἀκεῖ ταῦτ' ἔδραc ἑκάcτοτε.   770

          καὶ ταῦτα μὲν νῦν εὐλόγωc· ἢν (δ') ἐξέχῃ

LINE 764

δ' οὖν	"As for *you* . . ." The combination often follows σύ; δέ contrasts rather than joins and οὖν marks out the opposed idea as essential: *GP* 460. "All right, then, if that's what *you* want . . ."; cf. 6, "defiant assent": *GP* 466
χαίρω, κεχάρηκα	enjoy (+ suppl. ptcp.: S #2100); cf. 186
ἐκεῖcε	(adv. < ἐκεῖ, there + –cε, suffix like –δε and –ζε denoting place whither: S #342) to there (that is, to court)
μέν . . . ἀλλά	the μέν is answered by ἀλλά; the suggested concession in the ἀλλά clause is a bargain, not a surrender: *GP* 6
ἐνθάδε	"here [at home]"
αὐτοῦ	(adv.) right here, on the spot
οἰκέτηc, –ου, ὁ	(< οἶκοc, house + –τηc, suffix indicating agency: S #839.1) household slave

LINE 767

τοῦ	= τίνοc (S #334)
ληρέω	(< λῆροc, nonsense) be foolish (cf. 1370)
ταῦθ'	= τὰ αὐτά
ἀν-οίγνῡμι, -έῳξα	open; "opening the door" may refer to sexual intercourse: *MM* p. 137. The double augment in ἀνέῳξεν, receiving both syllabic (-ε-) and temporal (-ῳ-) augments, derives from the fact that the verb formerly began with a digamma (ϝοίγνῡμι) and thus received a *syllabic augment* (ἐϝοίγ-); a temporal augment (-οι- > -ῳ-) was added in an apparent transference of quantity: S #434.
cηκίc, -ιδοc, ἡ	(< cηκόc, enclosure) servant girl born in household
λάθρᾳ	(adv.) secretly, by stealth
ἐπιβολή, ἡ	(< ἐπιβάλλω, throw upon) fine, penalty; sexual imposition: *MM* p. 121 (take ταύτηc as an obj. gen.)
ψηφίζω, -ιῶ	(> fut. mid. indic. 2 sing. ψηφιεῖ; cf. 591) a] "vote a penalty of one <drachma> only" with ἐπιβολήν in apposition to understood δραχμήν; b] "vote her a single stiff penalty" (Hend., pun intended!)

LINE 770

πάντωc	in all ways; in any case, assuredly
κἀκεῖ	= καὶ ἐκεῖ, that is, in the courts
ἑκάcτοτε	each time, always, regularly (at end of verse, as at 446, 1283)
εὐλόγωc	(adv.) with good reason
ἐξ-έχω	stand out, appear (first of four subjv. protases in FMV condits.)

εἴλη, κατ᾽ ὀρθὸν ἡλιάσει πρὸς ἥλιον·
ἐὰν δὲ νείφη, πρὸς τὸ πῦρ καθήμενος·
ὕοντος εἴσει· κἂν ἔγρη μεσημβρινός,
οὐδείς σ᾽ ἀποκλήσει θεσμοθέτης τῇ κιγκλίδι.   775

Φι.   τουτί μ᾽ ἀρέσκει.
Βδ.   πρὸς δὲ τούτοις γ᾽, ἢν δίκην
        λέγη μακράν τις, οὐχὶ πεινῶν ἀναμενεῖς
        δάκνων σεαυτὸν καὶ τὸν ἀπολογούμενον.
Φι.   πῶς οὖν διαγιγνώσκειν καλῶς δυνήσομαι
        ὥσπερ πρότερον τὰ πράγματ᾽ ἔτι μασώμενος;   780

LINE 772

εἴλη, ἡ   sun's heat
ὀρθός   (3) straight; κατ᾽ ὀρθόν = in a straight line, <u>correctly</u> (calling attention to the pun on
                       εἴλη, ἡλιάζομαι and ἥλιος—all in a single line); cf. 216
ἡλιάζομαι, ἡλιάσομαι (> mid. fut. indic. 2 sing. ἡλιάσει) sit in the Eliaea court
ἥλιος, ὁ   sun {> *helio-*}

LINE 773

νείφω   snow [< IE *sneig^wh*, snow; cogn. L. *nix, nivis*; E. *snow*]
πῦρ, πυρός, ὁ   fire (cf. 284)
ὕω   rain (ὕοντος: gen. abs. without noun or pron.: S # 2072, though we can sc. τοῦ θεοῦ as
                       the subject; gen. abs. can function as protasis in condit.: S #2070.d), cf. 263
εἴσειμι   (> indic. 2 sing. εἴσει) go inside (< εἶμι; indic. functions in Attic as fut. of ἔρχομαι)
ἐγείρω, aor.² mid. ἠγρόμην
                       (> aor. mid. subjv. 2 sing. ἔγρη) awaken; (mid.) wake self up (cf. 101)
μεσημβρινός (3)   (< μέσος, middle + ἡμέρα, day + –ινος, adj. suffix denoting time: S #858.12) at noon,
                       at midday.
ἀπο-κλήω, -κλήσω   shut out (cf. 198). Would-be jurors arriving after the σημεῖον, cf. 690, would not be
                       admitted to the courts.
θεσμοθέτης, –ου, ὁ   (θεσμός, law + τίθημι, establish + –της, suffix denoting agent: S #839a.1) the name of
                       six of the nine Archons, with supervisory powers over courtrooms and jurors
κιγκλίς, –ίδος, ἡ   gate of court; the bar (cf. 124)

LINE 776

μ᾽   = μοι
ἀρέσκω   please, satisfy (3 sing. impers. often with dat., but sometimes with acc., and μ᾽ would more
                       likely be an *elision* for με than μοι) [< perhaps related to ἀραρίσκω, fit < IE *ar-*, fit together]
δέ ... γε   "Yes, and what's more . . ."; picks up thread of his interrupted speech: *GP* 154
δίκη, ἡ   lawsuit; <u>speech in lawsuit</u>
πεινάω   (< πεῖνα, hunger) be hungry
ἀνα-μένω, -μενῶ   wait for (cf. 524)
δάκνω   bite, gnaw (cf. 253)

LINE 779

δια-γιγνώσκω   know one from the other; distinguish; decide, "judge the cases" (πράγματα)
μασάομαι   chew

Βδ.   πολλῷ γ᾽ ἄμεινον· καὶ λέγεται γὰρ τουτογί,
       ὡς οἱ δικασταὶ ψευδομένων τῶν μαρτύρων
       μόλις τὸ πρᾶγμ᾽ ἔγνωσαν ἀναμασώμενοι.

Φι.   ἀνά τοί με πείθεις. ἀλλ᾽ ἐκεῖν᾽ οὔπω λέγεις,
       τὸν μισθὸν ὁπόθεν λήψομαι.

Βδ.   παρ᾽ ἐμοῦ.

Φι.   καλῶς,   785
       ὁτιὴ κατ᾽ ἐμαυτὸν κοὐ μεθ᾽ ἑτέρου λήψομαι.

LINE 781

γε	"Actually, it *will* be much better"; affirmative contradicting a denial: *GP* 132
ἀμείνων	(> adv. acc. ἄμεινον) better (cf. 173)
καὶ . . . γάρ	"For in fact they say this": *GP* 109–11 (cf. 269)
τουτογί	τοῦτο with a γε infix and *deictic* suffix characteristic of comedy
ψεύδομαι	lie (in gen. abs.: S #2070)
μόλις	(adv.) with difficulty
γιγνώσκω, aor.² ἔγνων	recognize, know; <u>decide</u>
ἀνα-μασάομαι	(< ἀνά, again: S #1882–83) chew over again, ruminate

LINE 784

ἀνὰ . . . πείθω	persuade; *tmesis*: S #1650–51. In Ar. the prefix is normally separated from the verb by only minor words such as particles, so this may be a parody of high tragic language (Starkie), though its use in dialogue may be "colloquial intensification": *LA* 250.
τοι	"You know"; a "homely" particle, "revealing the speaker's emotional or intellectual state": *GP* 541. Phil. is softening his resistance.
ὁπόθεν	from where? (cf. 311)
καλῶς	(adv. < καλός) "Good!" "Well said!" (in answers; LSJ C.II.6)
ὁτιή	Attic comic. colloquial form of causal ὅτι; the -η adds reinforcement: *LA* 245 (cf. 1155).
κατ᾽ ἐμαυτόν	by myself, on my own, individually
κοὐ	= καὶ οὐ

αἴϲχιϲτα γάρ τοί μ' ἠργάϲατο Λυϲίϲτρατος
ὁ ϲκωπτόλης. δραχμὴν μετ' ἐμοῦ πρῴην λαβὼν
ἐλθὼν διεκερμάτιζετ' ἐν τοῖϲ ἰχθύϲιν,
κἄπειτ' ἐνέθηκε τρεῖϲ λοπίδαϲ μοι κεϲτρέων·   790
κἀγὼ 'νέκαψ'· ὀβολοὺϲ γὰρ ᾠόμην λαβεῖν·
κᾆτα βδελυχθεὶϲ ὀϲφρόμενοϲ ἐξέπτυϲα·

LINE 787

Λυϲίϲτρατος, –ου, ὁ   (< λύω, release + ϲτράτος, army, like the protagonist of Ar.'s famous comedy) Lysistratus; known for practical jokes and socially prominent, to judge from 1302, where he also is named. The name is a "dependent determinative compound" in which the substantive (ϲτράτος) stands in the sense of an oblique case (here, acc.) to the other part, the verb λύω: S #897.2.

αἴϲχιϲτος (3)   (superl. of αἰϲχρός, shameful) absolutely disgraceful

γάρ τοι   "For, you know, . . ."; "each article retains its proper force": *GP* 549

ἐργάζομαι, ἠργαϲάμην

    (< ἔργον, work) work, perform; (with double acc.) do acc. to acc. {> *erg, energy, liturgy*}

μ'   = με

ϲκωπτόλης, –ου, ὁ   (< ϲκώπτω, mock) mocker, jester

δραχμή, ἡ   Jury pay was three obols (half a drachma), but pay would be distributed in one-drachma coins and thus two jurors had to make change (cf. 52, 691)

πρῴην   lately, the other day (cf. 717)

δια-κερματίζω   (< διά + κέρμα, fragment, coin < κείρω cut; cf. 477) change into small coins

ἰχθύς, –ύος, ὁ   fish; οἱ ἰχθύες = "the fish market" {> *ichthyology*}

ἐν-τίθημι, –έθηκα   insert, put into hand

λοπίς, –ίδος, ἡ   (< λέπω, peel) fish scale

κεϲτρεύς, –έως, ὁ   a type of fish, grey mullet, with silvery scales that could be mistaken for small change such as one-obol coins

---

LINE 791

κἀγώ   = καὶ ἐγώ

ἐγ-κάπτω, –έκαψα   (< κάπτω, gulp) gulp down

βδελύττομαι, aor. pass. ἐβδελύχθην

    (< βδελυρός, disgusting) be sick, nauseous (cf. 134)

ὀϲφραίνομαι, aor.[2] ὠϲφρόμην

    (< ὀϲμή, smell) catch scent of, smell

ἐκ-πτύω, -έπτυσα   (< πτύω, spit) spit out

κᾆθ᾽ εἷλκον αὐτόν.

Βδ.   ὁ δὲ τί πρὸς ταῦτ᾽ εἶφ᾽;

Φι.   ὅ τι;

ἀλεκτρυόνος μ᾽ ἔφασκε κοιλίαν ἔχειν·

"ταχὺ γοῦν καθέψεις τἀργύριον," ἦ δ᾽ ὃς λέγων.   795

Βδ.   ὁρᾷς ὅσον καὶ τοῦτο δῆτα κερδανεῖς.

Φι.   οὐ πάνυ τι μικρόν, ἀλλ᾽ ὅπερ μέλλεις ποίει.

Βδ.   ἀνάμενέ νυν· ἐγὼ δὲ ταῦθ᾽ ἥξω φέρων.

LINE 793

ἕλκω	draw, drag, collar; drag into court (LSJ II.3); perhaps "I tried to drag him," a *conative* imperfect: S #1895
εἶφ᾽	= εἶπε (note the *elision* even with change of speaker following this word)
τί … ὅ τι	direct and indir. interrog. prons.; cf. 48 on ὅπως
ἀλεκτρυών, –ονος, ὁ	cock; thought to be able to digest anything
κοιλία, ἡ	belly, intestines {> *celiac, coela*canth}
γοῦν	at any rate (cf. 262)
καθ-έψω	(< κατά + ἕψω, boil) boil down; digest. Part of the joke is that Lysistratus claims that Phil. *did* swallow the coins and they they were boiled down into fish scales by Phil.'s digestive process.
τἀργύριον	= τὸ ἀργύριον, money (cf. 607)
ἠμί	(imperfect indic. 3 sing. ἦ) say (for the *pleonasm* of λέγων: S #2147b)
ὅς ἥ ὅ	this one; he (demonstrative pron., LSJ A.II.3)

LINE 796

τοῦτο	that is, the advantage of being paid individually, by his son; acc. of respect; ὅσον is the dir. object of κερδανεῖς
δῆτα	"You're *really* going to benefit"; emphatic: GP 277
κερδαίνω, -ανῶ	(< κέρδος, gain + -αινω, suffix for *denominative* verb: S #866.7) derive profit, gain
οὐ πάνυ τι μικρόν	οὐ πάνυ, with *litotes* = "quite big": S #3032
ὅπερ	on –περ cf. 146
ποιέω	(> pres. act. impv. 2 sing. ποίει) do
ἀνα-μένω	wait (cf. 777)
ταῦθ᾽	we shortly find out that "these things" will be convenient paraphernalia such as a chamber pot, brazier, soup bowl, and rooster

Φι.   ὅρα τὸ χρῆμα, τὰ λόγι’ ὡς περαίνεται.

ἠκηκόη γὰρ ὡς Ἀθηναῖοί ποτε   800

δικάσοιεν ἐπὶ ταῖς οἰκίαισι τὰς δίκας,

κἂν τοῖς προθύροις ἐνοικοδομήσει πᾶς ἀνὴρ

αὑτῷ δικαστηρίδιον μικρὸν πάνυ,

ὥσπερ Ἑκατεῖον πανταχοῦ πρὸ τῶν θυρῶν.

Βδ.   ἰδού. τί ἔτ’ ἐρεῖς; ὡς ἅπαντ’ ἐγὼ φέρω,   805

ὅσαπέρ γ’ ἔφασκον κἄτι πολλῷ πλείονα.

ἁμὶς μέν, ἢν οὐρητιάσῃς, αὑτηὶ

παρά σοι κρεμήσετ’ ἐγγὺς ἐπὶ τοῦ παττάλου.

LINE 799

ὅρα τὸ χρῆμα	"see the thing," but virtually = "see" (a redundant usage of χρῆμα "frequently expressed where it might be omitted," LSJ II.2); cf. 266
λόγιον, τό	oracle, prophecy
ὡς	how
περαίνω	(< πέρας, end, limit) fulfill
ἀκούω, ἀκήκοα	(> 2nd pluperfect act. indic. 1st sing. ἠκηκόη: LSJ) hear
ὡς	verb of perception takes ptcp. when denoting physical perception; it may take ὡς when denoting intellectual perception: S #2110; opt. after secondary sequence: S #2615
Ἀθηναῖοι	names of peoples are given without definite art.: S #1138
πρόθυρον, τό	area outside courtyard door
δικάσοιεν δίκας	judge cases. The cogn. acc. is esp. common in legal terminology: S #1377, 1576; δικάσοιεν is an example of the rare fut. opt., used almost exclusively in ind. statement.
ἐν-οικοδομέω, -ησω	(< ἐν + οἶκος, house + δέμω, build) build (fut. indic., despite the fut. opt. of δικάσοιεν in the same clause: S #2615a,b)
δικαστηρίδιον, τό	(< δικαστήριον + –ιδιον, dim. suffix: S #852.2) small courtroom
Ἑκατεῖον, –ου, τό	shrine of Hekate, a goddess who protected crossroads; shrines to her were set up in front of houses
πανταχοῦ	(adv.) everywhere

LINE 805

ἰδού	"There!" may be the best tr. of this aor. impv. of ὁράω; the act of looking is almost irrelevant.
ὡς	since; with *ellipsis* of introductory clause: "<You won't have anything to say,> since …"
ὅσοσπερ	as many as, exactly as great as: LSJ s.v. ὅσος III.4
γε	"Precisely as many"; emphatic with adjs. or advs. expressing size and intensity: *GP* 120; and, as here, with rel. prons.: *GP* 123
κἄτι	= καὶ ἔτι
ἀμίς, –ίδος, ἡ	ἀμίς = ἡ ἀμίς; chamber pot
οὐρητιάω, ἐουρητίασα	
	(οὖρον, urine; cf. 394 + –ιαω, suffix; cf. 277) want to urinate (aor. subjv. in FMV condit.)
κρέμαμαι, fut. pass. κρεμήσομαι	
	hang (cf. 298)
ἐγγύς	(adv.) near, at hand
πάτταλος, ὁ	peg. The word could also refer to a phallus, making this perhaps "a sarcastic joke about his old father's manifestly limp member": *MM* p. 123, though B-O suggest that πάτταλος ought to mean "erection."

133

Φι.	ϲοφόν γε τουτὶ καὶ γέροντι πρόϲφορον
	ἐξηῦρεϲ ἀτεχνῶϲ φάρμακον ϲτραγγουρίαϲ. 810
Βδ.	καὶ πῦρ γε τουτί· καὶ προϲέϲτηκεν φακῆ
	ῥοφεῖν, ἐὰν δέῃ τι.
Φι.	τοῦτ' αὖ δεξιόν·
	κἂν γὰρ πυρέττω, τόν γε μιϲθὸν λήψομαι.
	αὐτοῦ μένων γὰρ τὴν φακῆν ῥοφήϲομαι. 815
	ἀτὰρ τί τὸν ὄρνιν ὡϲ ἔμ' ἐξηνέγκατε;
Βδ.	ἵνα γ', ἢν καθεύδῃϲ ἀπολογουμένου τινόϲ,
	ᾄδων ἄνωθεν ἐξεγείρῃ ϲ' οὑτοϲί.

LINE 809

πρόϲφοροϲ, –ον   (< προϲφέρω, apply to) suitable (to a dat.)
ἐξ-ευρίϲκω, aor.² -ηῦρον
          find out (cf. 85)
ἀτεχνῶϲ   absolutely (cf. 722)
φάρμακον, τό   drug; remedy
ϲτραγγουρία, ἡ   (< ϲτράγξ, trickle + οὖρον, urine; cf. 394) strangury, weak urine flow

LINE 811

πῦρ, πυρόϲ, τό   fire (Bdel. would bring a brazier) (cf. 284)
προϲ-ίϲτημι, –έϲτηκα
          place near; stand nearby (The perf. act. is one of the tenses of ἵϲτημι that is intrans.: S #819; the perf. has a pres. meaning: S #1946, and if προϲέϲτηκεν stands in for a pres., we have a Pres. Gen. condit.: S #2337.)
φακῆ, ἡ   (< φακόϲ, lentil soup) lentil soup
ῥοφέω, deponent fut. ῥοφήϲομαι
          slurp down (inf. of purpose: S #2008)
δέομαι   need (cf. 109) a] (> 2 sing. subjv. δέῃ) "if <u>you need</u> something" or b] (> 3 sing. subjv. δέῃ < impers. δεῖ) "if something <u>is necessary</u>"

LINE 813

κἄν   = καὶ ἐάν; even if: GP 301–2
πυρέττω   be ill of a fever (cf. 284)
αὐτοῦ   (adv.) right here
ἀτάρ   but, with a sudden change of topic: GP 52 (cf. 15)
ὄρνιϲ, –ιθοϲ, ὁ   bird (in Attic, usually a rooster)
ὡϲ   to, toward (prep. + acc. of person with verb of motion: S #1702)
ἐκ-φέρω, –ήνεγκα   bring out

LINE 816

γε   "<u>Why</u>, it's so that . . ."; used in response to a quest.: GP 133
ἄνωθεν   from above (cf. 204)
ἐξ-εγείρω   awaken, rouse (subjv. after ἵνα: S #2193). Because a purpose clause refers to fut. time, this serves as the apodosis of a FMV condit. whose protasis is ἢν καθεύδῃϲ: S #2326 (cf. 101).

Φι.	ἓν ἔτι ποθῶ, τὰ δ' ἄλλ' ἀρέσκει μοι.	
Βδ.	τὸ τί;	
Φι.	θήρῷον εἴ πως ἐκκομίcαιc τὸ τοῦ Λύκου.	
Βδ.	πάρεcτι τουτί, καὐτὸc ἄναξ οὑτοcί.	820
Φι.	ὦ δέcποθ' ἥρωc, ὡc χαλεπὸc ἄρ' ἦcθ' ἰδεῖν.	
Βδ.	οἷόcπερ ἡμῖν φαίνεται Κλεώνυμοc.	
Φι.	οὔκουν ἔχει γ' οὐδ' αὐτὸc ἥρωc ὢν ὅπλα.	
Βδ.	εἰ θᾶττον ἐκαθίζου cύ, θᾶττον ἂν δίκην ἐκάλουν.	
Φι.	κάλει νυν, ὡc κάθημ' ἐγὼ πάλαι.	825

LINE 818

ποθέω	desire, yearn for
ἀρέσκω	be pleasing to (+ dat.); cf. 776
τὸ τί;	"What is it?"; the questioner supplies the art. of an expected answer, "The . . . what?": MacD.
θήρῷον	= τὸ ἡρῶον, shrine of a hero (cf. 389)
εἴ πως	if somehow (cf. 399)
ἐκ-κομίζω, -εκόμισα	bring out (the opt. as protasis of Future Less Vivid condit. without an apodosis: S #2329; but εἰ + opt. can also express a wish: S #1815); cf. 616
Λύκος, ὁ	Lykos (cf. 389); his shrine abutted the courts. Apparently a slave, οὑτοcί, fat and without a phallus, comes out to stand in as "Lykos," positioning himself next to "this" (τουτί) altar already on the stage.

LINE 820

ὡς	how (exclam.)
ἄρα	"I now see," "It's just hit me"; with imperfect, of something just realized (cf. 3)
εἰμί	(> imperfect indic. 2 sing. ἦσθα) be
ἰδεῖν	see (expexegetical inf., with χαλεπός: S #2002)

LINE 822

οἷόσπερ	(on -περ cf. 146) "which is precisely what Cleonymus seems like" = "just as hard to see as Cleonymus" (on Cleonymus, cf. 19)
οὔκουν . . . γε	"Admittedly, he doesn't have any equipment" (in dialogue, in neg. answers: *GP* 423; with qualified acquiescence in preceding statement: S #2953e)
εἰμί	(> pres. ptcp. masc. sing. nom. ὤν) be
ὅπλον, τό	weapon; tool, equipment; genitals. Cleonymus was ridiculed in comedy for dropping his shield and running from battle; he would be lacking "equipment" in more than one way: *MM* p. 123. (cf. 27)

LINE 824

θᾶττων, –ον, –ονος	(nt. acc. as adv.) sooner (cf. 180)
καθ-ίζω	seat, set; (mid.) sit, take seat (cf. 90)
καλεῖν δίκην	call on a case, bring a case to court (legalese, if not esp. technical: *LA* 77–78; here in pres. Contrary-to-Fact condit.: S #2304). Bdel. plays the part of the presiding magistrate.
νυν	(enclitic adv.) now (cf. 30)
πάλαι	(adv.) for a long time (with pres. tense : "I have been . . .": S #1885)

Βδ.   φέρε νυν, τίν' αὐτῷ πρῶτον εἰσαγάγω δίκην;
       τί τις κακὸν δέδρακε τῶν ἐν τῴκίᾳ;
       ἡ Θρᾷττα προσκαύσασα πρῴην τὴν χύτραν—
Φι.   ἐπίσχες, οὗτος· ὡς ὀλίγου μ' ἀπώλεσας.
       ἄνευ δρυφάκτου τὴν δίκην μέλλεις καλεῖν,   830
       ὃ πρῶτον ἡμῖν τῶν ἱερῶν ἐφαίνετο;
Βδ.   μὰ τὸν Δί' οὐ πάρεστιν.
Φι.   ἀλλ' ἐγὼ δραμὼν
       αὐτὸς κομιοῦμαι τό γε παραυτίκ' ἔνδοθεν.
Βδ.   τί ποτε τὸ χρῆμ'; ὡς δεινὸν ἡ φιλοχωρία.

LINE 826

εἰσ-άγω, aor.² -ήγαγον

    introduce (delib. subjv.: S #1805)

δράω   make, do (cf. 247)

τῴκίᾳ   = τῇ οἰκίᾳ; οἱ ἐν τῇ οἰκίᾳ = "members of the household"

Θρᾷττα, ἡ   Thratta; a common name for slave girls from Thrace

προσ-κάω, -έκαυσα   set on fire, burn besides (Attic spelling of -καίω) {> *calm* (via L. *cauma* (heat of the day), *caustic*, holo*caust*, *cautery*}

πρῴην   (adv.) lately, the other day (cf. 717)

χύτρα, ἡ   (< χέω, pour, cf. 7) an earthenware pot used for cooking

LINE 829

ἐπ-έχω, aor.² -έσχον   (aor. impv. 2 sing. ἐπίσχες: S #466.1b on this impv. ending) hold back

οὗτος   "Hey, you" (cf. 1)

ὀλίγου   (< ὀλίγου [sc. δεῖ], lack a little) almost, all but (gen. of separation with δεῖ: S #1399)

ἄνευ   (+ gen.) without

ὅ   which, that is, the fact that railings were the first entry-point into court

ἱερός (3)   divine, holy; τὰ ἱερά, offerings, holy objects. Rituals of mystery religions entailed a revelation of holy objects; the fence is the lawcourt equivalent. (cf. 308)

LINE 832

τρέχω, aor.² ἔδραμον   run (cf. 376)

κομίζω, -ιῶ   carry away; (mid.) get for oneself

παραυτίκα   (adv. < αὐτίκα, immediately) at the present moment, right now. Although in Hdt. τὸ π. can be adverbial, here τό perhaps creates a substantive: S #1153e: "the first thing at hand"

γε   "right *now*"; emphatic: *GP* 117

ἔνδοθεν   from within (cf. 350)

φιλοχωρία, ἡ   fondness for a place, local attachment; perhaps a hint of medical pathology: "place addiction"

835–62: A slave, probably Xanthias, emerges to report that the dog Labes has stolen Sicilian cheese; this crime will provide Phil. with a case to hear in the home court. Although the play has exhibited a remarkable unity of time (all in one day, from dawn to evening) and place (in front of the house), the action can be thought to move "inside" the house or at least into a courtyard.

Ξα.	βάλλ' ἐc κόρακαc. τοιουτονὶ τρέφειν κύνα.	835
Βδ.	τί δ' ἐcτὶν ἐτεόν;	
Ξα.	οὐ γὰρ ὁ Λάβηc ἀρτίωc,	
	ὁ κύων, παράξαc εἰc τὸν ἰπνὸν ἀναρπάcac	
	τροφαλίδα τυροῦ Cικελικὴν κατεδήδοκεν;	
Βδ.	τοῦτ' ἄρα πρῶτον τἀδίκημα τῷ πατρὶ	
	εἰcακτέον μοι· cὺ δὲ κατηγόρει παρών.	840
Ξα.	μὰ Δί' οὐκ ἔγωγ', ἀλλ' ἅτερόc φηcιν κύων	
	κατηγορήcειν, ἤν τιc εἰcάγῃ γραφήν.	
Βδ.	ἴθι νυν, ἄγ' αὐτὼ δεῦρο.	
Ξα.	ταῦτα χρὴ ποιεῖν.	
Βδ.	τουτὶ τί ἐcτι;	
Φι.	χοιροκομεῖον Ἑcτίαc.	
Βδ.	εἶθ' ἱεροcυλήcαc φέρειc;	

LINE 835

βάλλω	throw; (intrans.) go away
τρέφω	nourish, help (inf. of exclam.: S #2015); "Just imagine! Keeping a dog like that!"

LINE 836

τί δ' ἐcτίν	the δέ can convey surprise: *GP* 175
ἐτεόν	(adv.) really (cf. 8)
οὐ γάρ	"[I am angry,] because didn't Labes just now . . . ?"; indignant quest. answering a quest.: S #2805b, *GP* 79
Λάβηc, –ητοc, ὁ	(< λαβεῖν, "grab"; tr. as "Grabes," "Grip," "Grab' em") Labes, the household dog; he is a stand-in for Laches, the politician and general who was active in the 420s and perhaps accused of embezzlement in Sicily when he was there in 427–425. Laches was going to be prosecuted in court today anyway, said the chorus (240).
παρ-ἀττω, –ῆξα	(< παρά, alongside + ἄττω, dart) dart past
ἰπνόc, ὁ	oven, furnace; place of the oven, that is, <u>kitchen</u> (cf. 139).
ἀν-αρπάζω, –ήρπαca	snatch up (cf. 17)
τροφαλίc, –ίδοc, ἡ	(< τρέφειν, curdle, cf. 110, and note *ablaut*) a fresh piece of cheese
τῦρόc, ὁ	cheese (cf. 676)
Cικελικόc (3)	(< Cικελία + –ικοc, adj. suffix: S #858.6) Sicilian
κατ-ἐcθίω, -εδήδοκα	(< κατά, completely + ἐcθίω, eat) eat it all up, devour

LINE 839

ἄρα	"in that case"; like ἄρα, marks the realization of a truth: *GP* 45
ἀδίκημα, –ατοc, τό	wrong, crime
εἰc-άγω	(> verbal εἰcακτέον) lead in; bring into court (with μοι dat. of agent in personal construction of verbal adj.: S#1488, 2151; πατρί is indirect obj.)

LINE 841

ἅτεροc	= ὁ ἕτεροc (it will emerge that this second dog is a stand-in for Cleon; cf. 895)
τιc	The "someone" is the magistrate introducing the charge into court; cf. 824–25
εἶμι	(> pres. impv. 2 sing. ἴθι) come
αὐτώ	dual = the two dogs
χοιροκομεῖον, τό	(< χοῖροc, pig + κομεῖν, care for) pigsty. Sacrificial pigs were kept in a household pen.
Ἑcτία, ἡ	Hestia, goddess of household; a sacrifice would begin with a prayer to Hestia.

Φι.   οὔκ, ἀλλ' ἵνα   845
          ἀφ' Ἑστίας ἀρχόμενος ἐπιτρίψω τινά.
          ἀλλ' εἴσαγ' ἀνύσας, ὡς ἐγὼ τιμᾶν βλέπω.
Βδ.   φέρε νυν, ἐνέγκω τὰς σανίδας καὶ τὰς γραφάς.
Φι.   οἴμοι, διατρίβεις κἀπολεῖς τριψημερῶν·
          ἐγὼ δ' ἀλοκίζειν ἐδεόμην τὸ χωρίον.   850
Βδ.   ἰδού.
Φι.   κάλει νυν.
Βδ.   ταῦτα δή.
Φι.   τίς οὑτοςὶ
          ὁ πρῶτός ἐστιν; ἐς κόρακας. ὡς ἄχθομαι
          ὅτιὴ 'πελαθόμην τοὺς καδίσκους ἐκφέρειν.
Βδ.   οὗτος σύ, ποῖ θεῖς;
Φι.   ἐπὶ καδίσκους.
Βδ.   μηδαμῶς.
          ἐγὼ γὰρ εἶχον τούσδε τοὺς ἀρυστίχους.   855

LINE 845

ἱεροσῦλέω, ἱεροσῦλησα

         (< ἱερόν, temple + σῦλάω, strip) commit sacrilege; here, by stealing a pigpen from a temple of Hestia

ἐπι-τρίβω, -έτρῖψα   crush, destroy

τῑμάω   honor; <u>assess punishment</u> (cf. 106)

βλέπω   look; "have an eye to . . ." + inf.: LSJ II

LINE 848

σανίς, –ίδος, ἡ   wooden tablet for announcing trials (cf. 349)

γραφή, ἡ   document for indictment

δια-τρίβω   rub; waste time

τρῑψημερέω   (< τρίβω, rub + ἡμέρα, day) waste the day.

ἀλοκίζω   (< αὖλαξ, furrow from plowing) plow; trace lines in wax tablets; write

χωρίον, τό   plot of land; <u>space</u> (on wax tablet). Bdel. seems to refer to drawing a line in a wax tablet (cf. 106)

LINE 851

ἰδού   "Look!" (cf. 805)

ταῦτα δή   = "All right!" "Very well"; assentient use of δή, like γε: *GP* 227 (cf. 142)

ἄχθομαι   be burdened; (of mental oppression) be vexed

ὅτιή   because (cf. 786)

ἐπι-λανθάνω, aor.² -έλαθον

         cause to forget; (mid.) forget

καδίσκος, ὁ   voting urn (cf. 321)

ποῖ   (interrog. adv.) to where? (for locative iota, cf. 317)

θέω   run, move quickly

ἀρύστιχος, ὁ   (< ἀρύω, draw, ladle + –ιχος, dim. suffix: S # 853) small jug or cup for drawing liquid; <u>ladle</u>

Φι.   κάλλιϲτα τοίνυν. πάντα γὰρ πάρεϲτι νῷν
              ὅϲων δεόμεθα, πλήν γε δὴ τῆϲ κλεψύδραϲ.

Βδ.   ἡδὶ δὲ δὴ τίϲ ἐϲτιν; οὐχὶ κλεψύδρα;

Φι.   εὖ γ' ἐκπορίζειϲ αὐτὰ κἀπιχωρίωϲ.

Βδ.   ἀλλ' ὡϲ τάχιϲτα πῦρ τιϲ ἐξενεγκάτω   860
              καὶ μυρρίναϲ καὶ τὸν λιβανωτὸν ἔνδοθεν,
              ὅπωϲ ἂν εὐξώμεϲθα πρῶτα τοῖϲ θεοῖϲ.

LINE 856

κάλλιϲτοϲ (3)	excellent (cf. 580)
τοίνυν	"That's fine, then"; affirmative, responding to previous speaker: *GP* 573
νῷν	(> gen./dat. dual pron.) us two
γε δή	"with one *really big* exception"; the combination is rare in verse; both are emphatic pcls.: *GP* 244–45
δὲ δή	"Well, exactly what is this here?"; in surprised or crucial quests.: *GP* 259; ἡδί suggests that Bdel. is pointing at the chamberpot, which can serve as a water clock.
εὖ γε	well, rightly [> *euge* in Latin comedy]
ἐκ-πορίζω	provide (cf. 365)
ἐπιχωρίωϲ	(adv. < ἐπί, at + χώρα, country) according to local custom. Only in Athens would one expect a water clock to be ready at hand!

LINE 860

ἀλλά	"Never mind that—will someone . . . ?"; transition to impv. in 2 sing.: *GP* 15
πῦρ, πυρόϲ, τό	fire, for burning incense on the altar. Formal religious language is used in these lines.
μυρρίνη, ἡ	myrtle garlands, which worshippers would wear on their heads [< Semitic loan word]
λιβανωτόϲ, ὁ	frankincense (cf. 96)
ὅπωϲ ἄν	that (ὅπωϲ ἄν has a solemn tone when used for a purpose clause; cf. 178)
εὔχομαι, ἠυξάμην	pray (cf. 388)

Χο.	καὶ μὴν ἡμεῖς ἐπὶ ταῖς σπονδαῖς	
	καὶ ταῖς εὐχαῖς	
	φήμην ἀγαθὴν λέξομεν ὑμῖν,	865
	ὅτι γενναίως ἐκ τοῦ πολέμου	
	καὶ τοῦ νείκους ξυνέβητον.	
Βδ.	εὐφημία μὲν πρῶτα νῦν ὑπαρχέτω.	[στρ.
Χο.	ὦ Φοῖβ᾽ Ἄπολλον Πύθι᾽, ἐπ᾽ ἀγαθῇ τύχῃ	
	τὸ πρᾶγμ᾽, ὃ μηχανᾶται	870
	ἔμπροσθεν οὗτος τῶν θυρῶν,	

863–90: The trial begins with the customary prayers to the gods; the chorus sing to Apollo, as does Bdel., though Bdel. asks in particular that Phil.'s harsh disposition be softened.

863–74: Meter: Anapests, mostly dimeters (863–67), iambic trimeters (868–69), iambs ending with a dodrans [– ⏑ ⏑ – ⏑ –] (870–73), and a cultic cry (874). These lines leading up to the dog trial constitute "a piece of dramatic punctuation, providing rhythmic and musical variety."

LINE 863

καὶ μήν	"Yes, indeed . . ."; in dialogue, expresses consent: GP 353
ἐπί	(+ dat.) for reason of, on the occasion of; "to celebrate"
σπονδή, ἡ	libation; (pl.) truce, reconciliation. Bdel. and Phil. are seen to have reconciled.
εὐχή, ἡ	prayer (cf. 387)
φήμη, ἡ	(> φημί, say; cf. 74) oracle; good report, utterance
λέγω, λέξω	speak, talk (fut. λέξω, not ἐρῶ, is used of oracles)
ὅτι	causal conj.
γενναίως	(adv.) nobly, in high-born manner, gentlemanly manner (cf. 504)
πόλεμος, ὁ	war
νεῖκος, –ους, τό	strife, quarrel
ξυμ-βαίνω, aor.² -έβην	(> aor. indic. 2 dual ξυνέβητον) stand together; come to agreement

LINE 868

εὐφημία, ἡ	(< εὐ + φημί, speak, cf. 74) use of words of good omen only (= avoidance of words of bad omen, sometimes = religious silence). A proclamation of εὐφημία was a standard opening of a prayer ceremony; ill-omened speech was to be avoided: LA 42–45.
ὑπ-άρχω	(> pres. impv. 3 sing. ὑπαρχέτω) exist in the beginning, begin; be. ὑπάρχω, always used by Ar. in solemn, formal contexts, became a synonym for εἰμί by the end of the fifth century: LA 192.
Φοῖβος, ὁ	Phoebus, an epithet of Apollo; "pure," "radiant"
Ἀπόλλων, –ωνος, ὁ	(> voc. Ἄπολλον) Apollo
Πύθιος (3)	(< Πυθώ, Pytho, an older name for Delphi) Pythian, epithet of Apollo as god of oracles
ἐπί	(+ dat.) for purpose of, with
τύχη, ἡ	fortune, luck (cf. 62)
μηχανάομαι	(< μηχανή, contrivance, cf. 149) contrive, engineer
ἔμπροσθεν	(+ gen.) in front of
οὗτος	= Bdel.

ἄπαcιν ἡμῖν ἁρμόcαι

παυcαμένοιc πλάνων.

ἰήιε Παιάν.

Βδ.   ὦ δέcποτ' ἄναξ γεῖτον Ἀγυιεῦ, τοὐμοῦ προθύρου προπύλαιε,   875

δέξαι τελετὴν καινήν, ὦναξ, ἣν τῷ πατρὶ καινοτομοῦμεν,

παῦcόν τ' αὐτοῦ τοῦτο τὸ λίαν cτρυφνὸν καὶ πρίνινον ἦθοc,

ἀντὶ cιραίου μέλιτοc cμικρὸν τῷ θυμιδίῳ παραμείξαc·

ἤδη δ' εἶναι τοῖc ἀνθρώποιc

LINE 872

ἁρμόζω, ἥρμοσα	fit together, <u>guide</u> (ἁρμόcαι: iussive inf.: S #2013, frequently in prayers) a] transitive: Apollo as subject and πρᾶγμα as dir. obj. of ἁρμόcαι; b] intrans., πρᾶγμα as subject: "May the scheme turn out well." [< IE *ar-, fit together; cf. ἄρτιος, 11]
πλάνη, ἡ	wandering, roaming (the daily trip to the lawcourt) {> *planet* (a "wandering" star)}
ἰήιος (3)	invoked with cry ἰή (an exclam. of joy); epithet of Apollo
Παιάν, –ᾶνος, ὁ	Paean, the physician of the gods in Homer; a title of Apollo as god of healing. ἰήιε Παιάν was a cultic cry at the end of a prayer: LA 45–47.

875–90: Meter: Anapestic tetrameters (875–78), anapests (879–84), iambic trimeters (885–86), and iambs ending with a dodrans (887–90), the *antistrophe* in *responsion* to the *strophe* (868–73).

LINE 875

γείτων, –ονος, ὁ	neighbor
Ἀγυιεύς, –έως, ὁ	epithet of Apollo, guardian of the streets, "Sidewalk Apollo" (Hend.). An altar and perhaps a stone pillar dedicated to Apollo were on stage.
πρόθυρον, τό	area outside courtyard door
προπύλαιος (3)	(< πύλη, gate) before the gate
τελετή, ἡ	rite at cultic initiation (cf. 121). Prayer and sacrifice may not be new, but the purpose of inaugurating a household courtroom is.
ὦναξ	= ὦ ἄναξ
καινοτομέω	(< καινός, new + τομέω, cut) cut fresh into (the metaphor is from mining); begin something new {> -*tomy*, a*tom*, dicho*tomy*, epi*tome*}
λίᾱν	too (cf. 56)
στρυφνός (3)	sour, astringent; harsh
πρίνινος (3)	(< πρῖνος, oak + –ινος, suffix of *denominative* adj. of material: S #858.12) made from oak (cf. 383)
ἦθος, –εος, τό	character, disposition
ἀντί	(+ gen.) instead of; just like
σίραιον, τό	new wine boiled down, syrup. cίραιον seems to have been sweet, but see B-O.
μέλι, –ιτος, τό	honey (take μέλιτος with cμικρόν)
θυμίδιον, τό	(< θῡμός, spirit + -ιδιον, dim. suffix: S #852.2) little heart
παρα-μείγνῡμι, -έμειξα	
	infuse, intermix (acc. with dat.)

ἤπιον αὐτόν, τοὺς φεύγοντάς τ’
ἐλεεῖν μᾶλλον τῶν γραψαμένων,   880
κἀπιδακρύειν ἀντιβολούντων,
καὶ παυσάμενον τῆς δυσκολίας
ἀπὸ τῆς ὀργῆς
τὴν ἀκαλήφην ἀφελέσθαι.   884

Χο.   ξυνευχόμεσθα ⟨ταὐτά⟩ σοι κἀπᾴδομεν   [ἀντ.
νέαισιν ἀρχαῖς ἕνεκα τῶν προλελεγμένων.
εὔνοι γάρ ἐσμεν ἐξ οὗ
τὸν δῆμον ᾐσθόμεσθά σου
φιλοῦντος ὡς οὐδεὶς ἀνὴρ
τῶν γε νεωτέρων.   890

LINE 879

εἶναι	infs. εἶναι, ἐλεεῖν, with acc. subject αὐτόν, are iussive; or, suppose *ellipsis* of a main verb such as δός, "grant that he . . .": S #2013c
ἤπιος (3)	gentle (here, pred.)
ἐλεέω	pity, show mercy on (cf. 393)
ἐπι-δακρύω	(< δάκρυον, tear) weep over, shed tears for; (intrans.) burst into tears (cf. 390)
ἀντι-βολέω	(< βάλλω) meet; supplicate (ἀντιβολούντων: gen. abs. with ptcp. alone: S #2072)
δυσκολία, ἡ	peevishness, bad temper (cf. 106)
ἀκαλήφη, ἡ	nettle, sting; prickliness
ἀφ-αιρέω, aor.² -εῖλον	remove

LINE 885

ξυν-εύχομαι	join in prayer (cf. 388)
ταὐτά	= τὰ αὐτά
σοι	that is, Bdel.; dat. with ὁ αὐτός, "the same as you," S #1500
ἐπ-ᾴδω	sing in accompaniment
ἀρχή, ἡ	magistracy; authority, government; institution
ἕνεκα	(prep. + gen.) on account of, on the strength of, because of
προ-λέγω, -λέλεγμαι	foretell, proclaim; προλελεγμένα = "what has already been said," "pronouncements" (a prosaic word in an otherwise solemn passage)
ἐσμέν	"I have long been and still am . . ."; present of past and present combined: S #1885; expresses an action begun in the past and continued into the pres.
εὔνους, –ουν	well-disposed, kindly (cf. 335)
ἐξ οὗ	ever since
γε	"<u>at least</u> among younger men"; limitative γε, *GP* 140. Younger men, like Bdel., were seen as conservative, less sympathetic to the old democrats of the jury.

⟨ἰήιε Παιάν.⟩

Βδ. εἴ τις θύρασιν ἡλιαστής, εἰσίτω·
ὡς ἡνίκ' ἂν λέγωσιν, οὐκ εἰσφρήσομεν.

Φι. τίς ἄρ' ὁ φεύγων οὗτος; ὅσον ἁλώσεται.

Βδ. ἀκούετ' ἤδη τῆς γραφῆς. "ἐγράψατο
Κύων Κυδαθηναιεὺς Λάβητ' Αἰξωνέα   895
τὸν τυρὸν ἀδικεῖν ὅτι μόνος κατήσθιεν
τὸν Σικελικόν. τίμημα κλῳὸς σύκινος."

Φι. θάνατος μὲν οὖν κύνειος, ἢν ἅπαξ ἁλῷ.

891–906. The trial of Labes commences. Bdel. plays the magistrate as formalities get underway and charges are read. The language shifts from religious to legal and oratorical registers.

891–1008: Meter: Iambic trimeters.

LINE 891

θύρᾱσι	at the door, outside
εἴσειμι	(> pres. impv. 3 sing. εἰσίτω) enter
ἡλιαστής, –οῦ, ὁ	juror (cf. 206)
ὡς	causal conj.
εἰσ-φρέω, -φρήσω	admit, allow inside (cf. 125)
ἡνίκ' ἂν λέγωσιν	"Once the speeches begin . . ." (ἡνίκ' ἂν + subjv. = temporal clause of the FMV type, with the fut. indic. εἰσφρήσομεν as main verb: S #2401)
ἄρα	"Just *who* . . . ?"; like ἄρα, enlivening the interrog. τίς: B-O
ὅσον	(adv. acc., exclam.) how greatly, how thoroughly

LINE 894

γραφή, ἡ	indictment (gen. after ἀκούω: S #1361)
Κυδαθηναιεύς, –έως, ὁ	(declension like βασιλεύς: S #275) of Cydathenaeum, a *deme* of Attica, of which Cleon was a member. This corroborates identification of the Κύων as Cleon.
Λάβης, –ητος, ὁ	Labes (cf. 836)
Αἰξωνεύς, –έως, ὁ	of Aixone, a *deme* of Attica, of which Laches was a member (cf. 836)
κατ-εσθίω, aor.² -ήσθιον	eat up, devour
τίμημα, –ατος, τό	penalty (cf. τῑμάω, 106)
κλῳός, ὁ	dog collar [perhaps cogn. with κλῇς, key; cf. 154]
σύκινος (3)	of fig-wood (cf. 145)

LINE 898

θάνατος, ὁ	death (cf. 583)
μὲν οὖν	"No, on the contrary . . ."; corrects previous speaker (cf. 515)
κύνειος (3)	fitting for a dog. A "dog's death" was proverbially horrible.
ἅπαξ	once, a single time (adv. used after condit. and temporal conjs.) [ἁ- copulative, denoting collectivity or accumulation: S #885.4 (cf. ἅμα, ἅπας) + IE *pag-*, fix; cf. πήγνυμι, fasten)
ἁλίσκομαι, aor.² ἑάλων	(> aor. act. subjv. 3 sing. ἁλῷ) be caught; be convicted (cf. 355)

Βδ.   καὶ μὴν ὁ φεύγων οὑτοcὶ Λάβηc πάρα.

Φι.   ὦ μιαρὸc οὗτοc· ὡc δὲ καὶ κλέπτον βλέπει,   900

οἷον cεcηρὼc ἐξαπατήcειν μ' οἴεται.

ποῦ δ' ⟨ἔcθ'⟩ ὁ διώκων, ὁ Κυδαθηναιεὺc κύων;

ΚΥΩΝ

αὖ αὖ.

Βδ.   πάρεcτιν.

Ξα.   ἕτεροc οὗτοc αὖ Λάβηc,

ἀγαθόc γ' ὑλακτεῖν καὶ διαλείχειν τὰc χύτραc.

Βδ.   cίγα, κάθιζε. cὺ δ' ἀναβὰc κατηγόρει.   905

Φι.   φέρε νυν ἅμα τήνδ' ἐγχεάμενοc κἀγὼ ῥοφῶ.

LINE 899

καὶ μήν   "Lo and behold . . ." A new topic is introduced or a new character comes on stage: *GP* 351, 356 (cf. 537); yet Labes will have a nonspeaking part.

πάρα   = πάρεcτι (contrast prep. παρά, accented on ultima)

ὤ   (exclam., not a voc.) "Oh!"

ὡς   how (exclam.)

καί   emphasizes following word: *GP* 316

κλέπτω   (> neut. acc. pres. act. ptcp. κλέπτον) thievishly (adv. acc. with βλέπω; LSJ I.2)

οἷον   (adv. acc.) how

σαίρω, σέσηρα   grin, malicious smirk

αὖ αὖ   "Bow-wow"; this is one Greek rendering of a dog bark; elsewhere one finds βαῦ βαύ. B-O point out that "Arf-arf" is a better phonetical match for αὖ αὖ.

ἕτερος (3)   another. Xanthias cynically believes the prosecutor to be as larcenous as the defendant.

LINE 904

ὑλάκτω   bark (intrans.; *epexegetical* inf. after adj.: S #2002)

γε   "He's 'good' at barking . . ."; with sarcasm: *GP* 128

δια-λείχω   (< διά "denotes intensity, continuance or fulfillment": S #1685.3 + λείχω, lick) lick clean (cf. 738)

χύτρα, ἡ   pot (cf. 828)

cῖγᾶ   "Be quiet!" (on the aspect of impvs., cf. 37, *LA* 258) The impvs. are addressed to Xanthias; with σύ he turns to the Dog.

τήνδ'   sc. φακῆν, soup

ἐγ-χέω   pour in (cf. 616)

κἀγώ   = καὶ ἐγώ. The καί and ἅμα correlate, "At the same time <he is making the prosecution>, *I* will slurp this <soup> . . ."

ῥοφέω   slurp down (cf. 812)

907–41: The Dog of Kydathenaion states the case for the prosecution: "Labes stole cheese and didn't share any of it with me!" Kitchen utensils are called to testify.

Κυ.　τῆς μὲν γραφῆς ἠκούσαθ’ ἣν ἐγραψάμην,
　　ἄνδρες δικασταί, τουτονί. δεινότατα γὰρ
　　ἔργων δέδρακε κἀμὲ καὶ τὸ ῥυππαπαῖ.
　　ἀποδρὰς γὰρ εἰς τὴν γωνίαν τυρὸν πολὺν　　　　　　910
　　κατεσικέλιζε κἀνέπλητ’ ἐν τῷ σκότῳ—
Φι.　νὴ τὸν Δί’ ἀλλὰ δῆλός ἐστ’· ἔμοιγέ τοι
　　τυροῦ κάκιστον ἀρτίως ἐνήρυγεν
　　ὁ βδελυρὸς οὗτος.
Κυ.　　　　　　κοὐ μετέδωκ’ αἰτοῦντί μοι.
　　καίτοι τίς ὑμᾶς εὖ ποιεῖν δυνήσεται,　　　　　　915
　　ἢν μή τι κἀμοί τις προβάλλῃ, τῷ Κυνί;

LINE 907

μέν | μέν *solitarium*, with no antithesis; opening a speech with μέν was common in fifth-century orators like Antiphon and Andocides, and Ar.'s mock speeches are modeled on them: *GP* 383, *LA* 261.
τουτονί | one indicts an acc. defendant + gen. of charge
ἔργον, τό | deed (ἔργων is part. gen. with superl.: S #1315)
δράω, δέδρᾱκα | do. Like ἐγραψάμην in previous line, δράω takes two types of accs., internal, δεινότατα, and external, κἀμὲ καὶ τό ῥ.: S #1622. The perf. tense is a feature of lawcourt oratory: *LA* 133.
ῥυππαπαῖ | "Yo ho ho," cry of Athenian sailors; τὸ ῥυππαπαῖ = "shipmates"
ἀπο-διδρᾱ́σκω, aor.² -έδρᾱν | run away; escape by stealth (used of runaway slaves), cf. 126, 376
γωνία, ἡ | corner { > diag*onal*, poly*gon*}
κατα-σικελίζω | "Sicilize"; consume (Starkie notes other vbs. compounded with κατά imply "waste" or "destruction.") Sicily was known for its gourmands.
ἐμ-πίμπλημι, mid. aor.² ἐνεπλήμην | (> aor. mid. indic. 3 sing. ἐνέπλητο) fill up; (mid.) have one's fill, stuff self (cf. 380, 424)
σκότος, ὁ | darkness (cf. 256)

LINE 912

ἀλλά | "Why it's as plain as can be"; expressing assent with a statement just made: *GP* 18
γέ τοι | "And I have a good reason for saying this . . ."; "τοι usually strengthens, and coheres with, the (limitative) γε, so that γέ τοι is practically a livelier form of the much commoner γοῦν, 'at any rate' "; here it gives a reason for accepting a proposition: *GP* 550.
ἐν-ερεύγομαι, aor.² -ήρυγον | belch (with intern. acc.: S #1554a, and descriptive gen.: S #1323; cf. ὄζω, 38)
βδελυρός (3) | repulsive, disgusting (cf. 134)
μετα-δίδωμι, aor.² -έδωκα | (< μετά, among + δίδωμι, give) share
αἰτέω | request; ask (for a bribe); (circumstantial ptcp. αἰτοῦντι could be temporal, "when I was asking," or perhaps concessive, "although . . .": S #2061, 2066)

LINE 915

εὖ ποιεῖν | help, benefit
καί | also, too
προ-βάλλω | throw to, put forward (object of the verb is τι, suggesting a scrap of food; προβάλλῃ is subj. in protasis of a FMV condit.: S #2323)

Φι.   οὐδὲν μετέδωκεν οὐδὲ τῷ κοινῷ γ᾽, ἐμοί.

            θερμὸς γὰρ ἀνὴρ οὐδὲν ἧττον τῆς φακῆς.

Βδ.   πρὸς τῶν θεῶν, μὴ προκαταγίγνωσκ᾽, ὦ πάτερ,

            πρὶν ἄν γ᾽ ἀκούσῃς ἀμφοτέρων.

Φι.   ἀλλ᾽, ὦγαθέ,   920

            τὸ πρᾶγμα φανερόν ἐστιν· αὐτὸ γὰρ βοᾷ.

Κυ.   μή νυν ἀφῆτέ γ᾽ αὐτόν, ὡς ὄντ᾽ αὖ πολὺ

            κυνῶν ἁπάντων ἄνδρα μονοφαγίστατον,

            ὅστις περιπλεύσας τὴν θυείαν ἐν κύκλῳ

            ἐκ τῶν πόλεων τὸ σκῖρον ἐξεδήδοκεν.   925

LINE 917

κοινός (3)	common; τὸ κοινόν = "the public"
οὐδέ . . . γε	"not even"; γε in a retort: *GP* 156; normally placed after the art., here it follows the noun: *GP* 149.
ἐμοί	in apposition to κοινῷ, as if Phil. represents the Athenian *demos*!
θερμός (3)	hot, hot-headed (cf. 331)
ἥττων, –ον, –ονος	worse, less (cf. 523); adv. acc. οὐδὲν ἧττον "no less" = "just as much as"
φακῆς	soup (cf. 811; here gen. of comparison)

LINE 919

προ-κατα-γιγνώσκω	vote against beforehand, prejudge. The word is also found in the orators.
πρίν	(conj.; cf. 579) until (takes subjv. + ἄν after a neg. clause in pres. expressing a general truth: S #2445)
ἀμφότερος (3)	both (almost never sing.)
γε	"until and unless"; limitative, with conj. πρίν: *GP* 141–42
φανερός (3)	clear, open-and-shut
αὐτὸ γὰρ βοᾷ	"for the case itself cries out"; "the facts bark for themselves": Hend.

LINE 922

γε	"*Don't* let him off . . ."; sharpens tone of an impv.: *GP* 125–26
ὡς	on the grounds that (ὡς + ptcp. "states the ground of belief on which the agent acts . . . without implicating the speaker or writer": S #2086)
αὖ	moreover, secondly. MacD. sees satire of "speakers who produce the same argument over again as if it were a new one"; B-O suggest the possibility of an interjected "Arf!"
κυνῶν	for gen. with superl.: S #1434. Note the comic juxtaposition of κυνῶν and ἄνδρα, Labes and Laches being muddled.
μονοφαγίστατος, –ον	(< μόνος, alone + φαγεῖν, eat) eating alone, most piggish. The superl. is probably Ar.'s own coinage; superls. formed from –ίστατος often carry a pejorative connotation: *LA* 243.
περι-πλέω, –έπλευσα	sail around (cf. 122)
θυεία, ἡ	bowl, for mixing food
σκῖρον, τό	hard rind of cheese. Nibbling around the edge is like sailing around Sicily, embezzling money.
ἐξ-εσθίω, perf. –εδήδοκα	eat up

Φι.   ἐμοὶ δέ γ' οὐκ ἔστ' οὐδὲ τὴν ὑδρίαν πλάσαι.

Κυ.   πρὸς ταῦτα τοῦτον κολάσατ'—οὐ γὰρ ἄν ποτε
          τρέφειν δύναιτ' ἂν μία λόχμη κλέπτα δύο—
          ἵνα μὴ κεκλάγγω διὰ κενῆς ἄλλως ἐγώ·
          ἐὰν δὲ μή, τὸ λοιπὸν οὐ κεκλάγξομαι.   930

Φι.   ἰοὺ ἰού.
          ὅσας κατηγόρησε τὰς πανουργίας.
          κλέπτον τὸ χρῆμα τἀνδρός. οὐ καὶ σοὶ δοκεῖ,
          ὦλεκτρυών; νὴ τὸν Δί'· ἐπιμύει γέ τοι.
          ὁ θεσμοθέτης· ποῦ 'σθ' οὗτος; ἀμίδα μοι δότω.   935

LINE 926

δέ γε   "And *me* not being able to mend . . . !"; a lively retort: *GP* 152–54

οὐκ ἔστ'   It isn't possible (orthotone ἔστι: cf. 212)

ὑδρία, ἡ   water jar

πλάττω, aor. –ἔπλασα   mold, shape; mend. Phil. is too poor to mend what he has, and πλάσαι also means "cement" accd. to a scholion (but see B-O); Ph's poverty contrasts with Labes's extravagant appetite. (cf. 108)

πρός   (+ acc.) with a view to, in consideration of

LINE 928

ἄν   repetition of ἄν with potential opt.: S #1765

λόχμη, ἡ   copse, thicket

κλέπτης, –ου, ὁ   (> nom. and acc. dual, κλέπτα) thief. Κύων tacitly admits that he, too, is a thief.

κλάζω, perf. κέκλαγγα

      scream, shout, bark (κεκλάγγω: an example of a rare non-*periphrastic* perf. act. subjv., usually formed from ptcp. + ὦ, ῇς, ῇ, etc.: S #692; perf. with pres. meaning: S #1946; κεκλάγξομαι in following line is fut. perf. used as fut.: S #581). Cleon poses as a watchdog who vigilantly guards the city and whose barks could alert it to threats and conspiracies—as long as he is rewarded.

κενός (3)   empty, vain; διὰ κενῆς = "in vain"; pleonastic with ἄλλως, "without purpose" {> *ceno*taph}

LINE 931

ἰού   "Wow!" (cry of surprise or distress, here probably joy; outside the meter)

πανουργία, ἡ   knavery; (pl.) crimes, acts of villainy (cf. 1227)

χρῆμα, –ατος, τό   thing (for this redundant usage, cf. 799)

ὦλεκτρυών   = ὦ ἀλεκτρυών, cock, rooster

ἐπι-μύω   (< ἐπί, implying reciprocity: S #1689 + μύω, close eyes or mouth; shut eyes) wink at (cf. 92)

γέ τοι   "*At any rate,* he <the cock> is winking in agreement" (cf. 912)

θεσμοθέτης, –ου, ὁ   magistrate (cf. 775; nom. for voc.). Phil. regards Bdel. as standing in this official capacity.

ἀμίς, –ίδος, ἡ   chamber pot (cf. 807). Perhaps Phil. will now fill the ἀμίς so it can serve as a water clock, suggest B-O.

Βδ.   αὐτὸς καθελοῦ· τοὺς μάρτυρας γὰρ εἰςκαλῶ.
       Λάβητι μάρτυρας παρεῖναι τρύβλιον,
       δοίδυκα, τυρόκνηςτιν, ἐςχάραν, χύτραν,
       καὶ πάντα τὰ ςκεύη τὰ προςκεκαυμένα.
       ἀλλ᾽ ἔτι ςύ γ᾽ οὐρεῖς καὶ καθίζεις οὐδέπω;   940
Φι.   τοῦτον δέ γ᾽ οἶμ᾽ ἐγὼ χεςεῖςθαι τήμερον.
Βδ.   οὐκ αὖ ςὺ παύςει χαλεπὸς ὢν καὶ δύςκολος,
       καὶ ταῦτα τοῖς φεύγουςιν, ὧν ὀδὰξ ἔχει;
       ἀνάβαιν᾽, ἀπολογοῦ. τί ςεςιώπηκας; λέγε.

LINE 936

καθ-αιρέω, aor.² -εῖλον

    (aor. mid. impv. 2 sing. καθελοῦ) take down, get (sc. ἀμίδα as object)

παρεῖναι   "Be present!" (iussive inf. with seven acc. subjects; for an inf. in proclamation, cf. 386)

τρύβλιον, τό   bowl

δοῖδῦξ, –ῦκος, ὁ   pestle

τῡρόκνηςτις, –ιδος, ἡ

    (< τῡρός, cheese + κνάω, scrape) cheese grater

ἐςχάρα, ἡ   fireplace; brazier

χύτρα, ἡ   pot (cf. 828)

LINE 939

ςκεῦος, τό   tool, weapon; utensil, pot (cf. 615)

προς-κάω, perf. mid./pass. -κέκαυμαι

    burn besides, burnt at the fire (προςκεκαυμένα, a pun on προςκεκλημένα, "summoned" to court), cf. 828

γε   "Are *you* still pissing?"; emphatic with pron. ςυ: *GP* 123

οὐρέω   urinate, piss; *MM* p. 194 (cf. 394)

οὐδέπω   (adv.) and not yet

τοῦτον   = Labes, subject of inf. χεςεῖςθαι

χέζω, χεςοῦμαι   shit. It is assumed that fear causes men to soil themselves: *MM* p. 189–90. (cf. 626)

τήμερον   today (cf. 179)

942–79: Bdel. asks Labes to take the stand and defend himself, but Labes is struck dumb, so Bdel. speaks in his defense, bringing Labes's children up to make Phil. feel more sympathy.

LINE 942

δύςκολος, –ον   peevish, grouchy (cf. 106)

καὶ ταῦτα   (adv.) and at that (cf. 252)

φεύγουςιν   against the defendants (dat. of disadvantage: S #1481)

ὀδάξ   (adv.) by biting with the teeth (cf. 164)

ἔχομαι   (> 2 sing. mid. ἔχει) hold on to, cling to (+ gen.)

ςιωπάω, perf. ςεςιώπηκα

    be silent. Bdel. here addresses Labes, who is unable to speak. {> apo*siopesis*}

Φι.	ἀλλ' οὐκ ἔχειν οὗτός γ' ἔοικεν ὅ τι λέγῃ.	945
Βδ.	οὔκ, ἀλλ' ἐκεῖνό μοι δοκεῖ πεπονθέναι,	
	ὅπερ ποτὲ φεύγων ἔπαθε καὶ Θουκυδίδης·	
	ἀπόπληκτος ἐξαίφνης ἐγένετο τὰς γνάθους.	
	πάρεχ' ἐκποδών· ἐγὼ γὰρ ἀπολογήσομαι.	
	χαλεπὸν μέν, ὦνδρές, ἐστι διαβεβλημένου	950
	ὑπεραποκρίνεσθαι κυνός, λέξω δ' ὅμως.	
	ἀγαθὸς γάρ ἐστι καὶ διώκει τοὺς λύκους.	
Φι.	κλέπτης μὲν οὖν οὗτός γε καὶ ξυνωμότης.	
Βδ.	μὰ Δί', ἀλλ' ἄριστός ἐστι τῶν νυνὶ κυνῶν,	

LINE 945

ὅ τι λέγῃ   "which he might say" (indir. delib. subjv.; the rel. has no expressed antecedent, therefore sc. "something," "anything.") Sometimes a respondent repeats the quest., using the indef. rel., before his reply: S #2670, but this respondent is silent and Phil. answers for him.

Θουκυδίδης, -ου, ὁ   Thucydides son of Melesias, a political opponent of Pericles (not to be confused with the historian). He was ostracized in 443, evidently put on trial at some point after his return in 433, but became tongue-tied in court or failed to defend himself.

ἀπόπληκτος, -ον   (< ἀποπλήττω, disable) paralyzed (a verbal adj. formed from the aor. pass. principal part by adding the suffix to the stem: S #471; when compounded with a prep., such adjs. are accented on the ultima and denote possibility—ἀποπληκτός would mean "paralyzable"—while accents on the antepenult have the force of a perf. pass. ptcp.—thus ἀπόπληκτος means "having been paralyzed": S #425c.N.; cf. 399 for πλήττω)

ἐξαίφνης   (adv.) suddenly (cf. 49)

γνάθος, -ου, ἡ   jaw (acc. respect, of body part: S #1601a) paralyzed in jaw = "struck dumb" (cf. 370)

LINE 949

παρ-έχω   hold beside; allow; move, make way

ἐκποδών   (adv. < ἐκ, out, away + πούς, ποδός foot) away from the feet, out of the way; πάρεχε ἐκποδών = "make yourself scarce." Labes now steps down and Bdel. begins a defense speech.

δια-βάλλω, perf. mid./pass. διαβέβλημαι   slander {> *diabolical, devil*}

μέν   "preparatory" anticipating δέ, introducing first limb of an antithesis: GP 369

ὑπερ-απο-κρίνομαι   (< ὑπέρ, on behalf of + ἀπό, separation + κρίνω, distinguish) reply for someone else, make a defense on someone's behalf (a compound found only in Ar.). Bdel. shifts roles; no longer playing the presiding magistrate, he will become a defense attorney.

LINE 952

λύκος, ὁ   wolf {> *lycanthrope*}[< IE *wlkʷo-, wolf; cogn. L. *lupus*; E. *wolf*]

μὲν οὖν   "On the contrary" (cf. 515)

οἷός τε πολλοῖς προβατίοις ἐφεστάναι. 955

Φι. τί οὖν ὄφελος, τὸν τυρὸν εἰ κατεσθίει;

Βδ. ὅ τι; σοῦ προμάχεται καὶ φυλάττει τὴν θύραν,

καὶ τἄλλ᾽ ἄριστός ἐστιν· εἰ δ᾽ ὑφείλετο,

σύγγνωθι. κιθαρίζειν γὰρ οὐκ ἐπίσταται.

Φι. ἐγὼ δ᾽ ἐβουλόμην ἂν οὐδὲ γράμματα, 960

ἵνα μὴ κακουργῶν ἐνέγραφ᾽ ἡμῖν τὸν λόγον.

LINE 955

οἷός τε   able to (+ inf.). (Some editors think that the τε is a needed conj., and that we cannot take it as οἷός τε, with a suppressed ἐστί, + inf. = "be able to"; disposition, not ability, is indicated.)

προβάτιον, τό   (dim. of πρόβατον) sheep. The sheep stand in for the Athenian people (cf. 32)

ἐφ-ίστημι, perf. -έστηκα

    (> perf. act. inf. ἐφεστάναι) set over, attend to (+ dat.; intrans.: S #819); tr. as a pass., "be set over"

ὄφελος, -ους, τό   help, use (sc. ἐστί); cf. 121

LINE 957

ὅ τι   "'What?' <you ask>"; ind. interrog., repeating the quest.: S #2670

προ-μάχομαι   fight on behalf of (+ gen.)

τἄλλ᾽   = τὰ ἄλλα, "for the rest," "in other respects" (adv. acc.)

ὑφ-αιρέω   (> aor. mid. 3 sing. ὑφείλετο) steal (in a simple past condit., "with no implication as to its reality"; S #2298)

συγ-γιγνώσκω, aor.² -έγνων

    (> aor. impv. 2 sing. σύγγνωθι: S #684) think with, agree with; make allowance for, <u>forgive</u>, <u>pardon</u>

κιθαρίζω   play the *kithara*. A *kithara* was the standard type of lyre in the sixth and fifth centuries. Being able to play was a sign of an elite education; an inability to do so marked a man as uneducated—a flimsy plea for extenuating circumstances in court, though evidently Labes was able to write well enough to get into trouble.

ἐπίσταμαι   know how to (distinguish from ἐφίστημι above, though prob. derived from it)

LINE 960

ἐβουλόμην ἄν   "I should have liked" (sc. αὐτὸν ἐπίστασθαι; an unobtainable wish: S # 1789)

γράμμα, -ατος, τό   (< γράφω + -μα, -ματος, suffix expressing result of action: S #841.2) letter; (pl.) writing (cf. 97)

ἵνα   + indic. in past tense "for a final clause that cannot now be fulfilled, because the action or event on which it depends has not been fulfilled": MacD.

κακουργέω   (< κακός, evil + ἔργον, deed) do evil, falsify (tr. ptcp. κακουργῶν as adv.: "dishonestly," "thievishly"); Laches was apparently charged with falsification of financial accounts.

ἐγ-γράφω   inscribe, write out; enter in the public register. The verb was used of official documents and accounts, λόγοι.

Βδ.　　　ἄκουσον, ὦ δαιμόνιέ, μου τῶν μαρτύρων.
　　　　ἀνάβηθι, τυρόκνηστι, καὶ λέξον μέγα·
　　　　cὺ γὰρ ταμιεύους' ἔτυχες. ἀπόκριναι cαφῶς,
　　　　εἰ μὴ κατέκνηcαc τοῖc cτρατιώταιc ἄλαβεc.　　　　　965
　　　　φηcὶ κατακνῆcαι.
Φι.　　　　　　　　　νὴ Δί', ἀλλὰ ψεύδεται.
Βδ.　　　ὦ δαιμόνι', αἰδοῦ τοὺc ταλαιπωρουμένουc.
　　　　οὗτοc γὰρ ὁ Λάβηc καὶ τραχήλι' ἐcθίει
　　　　καὶ τὰc ἀκάνθαc, κοὐδέποτ' ἐν ταὐτῷ μένει.
　　　　ὁ δ' ἕτεροc οἷόc ἐcτιν. οἰκουρὸc μόνον·　　　　　　970
　　　　αὐτοῦ μένων γάρ, ἅττ' ἂν εἴcω τιc φέρῃ,
　　　　τούτων μεταιτεῖ τὸ μέροc· εἰ δὲ μή, δάκνει.

LINE 962

τυρόκνηστις, –ιδος, ἡ　　cheese grater (cf. 938). We can only guess as to how the Cheese Grater was costumed (note, at least, the fem. gender of the noun); we soon find that it was essentially a nonspeaking role.

ταμιεύω　　serve as steward, treasurer, paymaster. A general would have a ταμίας supervise the distribution of money to the troops (cf. 613).

ἀπο-κρίνομαι, -έκρῑνα
　　answer, reply to

cαφῶς　　(adv.) clearly

κατα-κνάω, -έκνηcα　　scrape away, grate. Grating cheese is like paying soldiers with the money that he received (ἄλαβεc = ἃ ἔλαβεc) from the Sicilian cities. The Cheese Grater, either by nodding or whispering inaudibly to the audience, affirms that she did grate it out.

cτρατιώτης, -ου, ὁ　　(< cτρατόc, army + -της, suffix for agent: S #839a.1) soldier

νή Δί'　　"Yes, she *says* so, but . . ."; expressing concurrence: S #1596b.

ψεύδομαι　　lie

LINE 967

αἰδέομαι　　(< αἰδώc, sense of shame, cf. 447) be ashamed; show respect for

ταλαιπωρέω　　(< τάλα-, suffering; πωρόc is uncertain) endure, suffer hardship; (pass.) be worn out

τραχήλια, τά　　(< τράχηλοc, neck) scraps of meat from the neck

ἄκανθα, ἡ　　thorn, thistle; fishbones

οὐδέποτε　　(adv.) and not ever, never; "He never stays in the same place (ἐν ταὐτῷ)"; Labes must constantly move around to find food.

LINE 970

οἷος　　(exclam.)

οἰκουρός, –ον　　(< οἶκοc, house + οὖροc, guardian) watching the house. As a stay-at-home watchdog, Cleon/Κύων is unimpressive; and in truth Cleon spent relatively little time abroad on military campaigns. {> Arcturus}

αὐτοῦ　　right there

μετ-αιτέω　　(< μετά, after, in quest of + αἰτέω, ask) ask for, demand share of

μέρος, τό　　part; share {> poly*mer*}

δάκνω　　bite (cf. 253)

Φι.	αἰβοῖ. τί τόδε ποτ' ἔcθ' ὅτῳ μαλάττομαι;
	κακόν τι περιβαίνει με κἀναπείθομαι.
Βδ.	ἴθ', ἀντιβολῶ c', οἰκτίρατ' αὐτόν, ὦ πάτερ, 975
	καὶ μὴ διαφθείρητε. ποῦ τὰ παιδία;
	ἀναβαίνετ', ὦ πόνηρα, καὶ κνυζούμενα
	αἰτεῖτε κἀντιβολεῖτε καὶ δακρύετε.
Φι.	κατάβα, κατάβα, κατάβα, κατάβα.
Βδ.	καταβήcομαι.
	καίτοι τὸ "κατάβα" τοῦτο πολλοὺς δὴ πάνυ 980
	ἐξηπάτηκεν. ἀτὰρ ὅμωc καταβήcομαι.
Φι.	ἐc κόρακαc. ὡc οὐκ ἀγαθόν ἐcτι τὸ ῥοφεῖν.
	ἐγὼ γὰρ ἐπεδάκρυcα νῦν, γνώμην ἐμήν,
	οὐδέν ποτέ γ' ἀλλ' ἢ τῆc φακῆc ἐμπλήμενοc.
Βδ.	οὔκουν ἀποφεύγει δῆτα;

LINE 973

αἰβοῖ	cf. 37
μαλάττω	(< μαλακός, soft) soften (cf. 738)
περι-βαίνω	walk around, encircle, close in on
οἰκτίρω, ᾤκτῖρα	pity (the verb is pl., as if there were a courtroom full of jurors), cf. 328
δια-φθείρω	destroy; "Don't keep ruining him" (prohib. subjv., unusually in pres. : S #1800c)
παιδίον, τό	small boy (cf. 293)
κνυζέομαι	whimper, whine (of dogs and children). At this point, mute actors, boys dressed as puppies, enter the stage, though B-O point out that if the kitchen utensils were also played by mute actors, the stage would be getting crowded.
κατα-βαίνω, -βήσομαι, aor.² -έβην	
	(> aor. impv. 2 sing. κατάβα) step down from the witness stand. Line 979 is the only iambic trimeter in *W.* containing five trisyllabic feet: MacD.

980–1008: Bdel. finishes the defense and steps down. Phil. is now ready to vote and convict, but Bdel., by switching the urns for acquittal and conviction, tricks him into acquitting Labes.

LINE 980

δή	"*Many* people"; emphatic, with adjs. expressing indef. quantity: *GP* 205
ἐξ-απατάω, perf. -ηπάτηκα	
	cheat, deceive. Evidently there were speakers who cut their speeches short when told to step down under the impression that they had persuaded the jury, only to discover otherwise.

LINE 982

ὡς	(exclam., modifying οὐκ ἀγαθόν) "How bad it is . . ."
ἐπι-δακρύω, -εδάκρυσα	
	weep over, (intrans.) burst into tears (apparently hot soup makes him tear up)
νῦν	now, present time (note that an aor. need not be past time)
γνώμη, ἡ	judgment, resolution (the acc. γνώμην ἐμήν can mean "in my opinion"; other editors take it as the direct object of ἐπεδάκρυσα, or emend to ἀπεδάκρυσα, "I wept away my better judgment")
οὐδὲν ἀλλ' ἤ	= nothing but = "only"; ἀλλά used after negs., followed by an exception: *GP* 25, S #2778

Φι.	χαλεπὸν εἰδέναι.	985
Βδ.	ἴθ᾽, ὦ πατρίδιον, ἐπὶ τὰ βελτίω τρέπου.	
	τηνδὶ λαβὼν τὴν ψῆφον ἐπὶ τὸν ὕστερον	
	μύσας παρᾷξον κἀπόλυσον, ὦ πάτερ.	
Φι.	οὐ δῆτα· κιθαρίζειν γὰρ οὐκ ἐπίσταμαι.	
Βδ.	φέρε νύν σε τηδὶ τὴν ταχίστην περιάγω.	990
Φι.	ὅδ᾽ ἔσθ᾽ ὁ πρότερος;	
Βδ.	οὗτος.	
Φι.	αὕτη ᾽νταῦθ᾽ ἔνι.	
Βδ.	ἐξηπάτηται κἀπολέλυκεν οὐχ ἑκών.	
	φέρ᾽ ἐξεράσω.	
Φι.	πῶς ἄρ᾽ ἠγωνίσμεθα;	
Βδ.	δείξειν ἔοικεν. ἐκπέφευγας, ὦ Λάβης.	
	πάτερ πάτερ, τί πέπονθας; οἴμοι. ποῦ ᾽σθ᾽ ὕδωρ;	995

LINE 985

οὔκουν ... δῆτα	"So, he's not getting off, then?"; connective in quests.: *GP* 272
ἀπο-φεύγω	be acquitted (cf. 579)
πατρίδιον, τό	(dim. of πατήρ) daddy
βελτίων, –ον, –ονος	(> βελτίω is a contraction of neut. acc. pl. βελτίονα: S #293) better; used as a comparative of ἀγαθός [cogn. βέλτιστος, cf. 233]
τρέπω	(> pres. mid. impv. 2 sing. τρέπου) turn; (mid.) turn oneself, change <one's attitude>
ὕστερος	(3) latter, next (sc. καδίσκος, voting urn). A first urn, πρότερος καδίσκος, is for conviction; the second is for acquittal (cf. 214)
μύω, ἔμυσα	shut eyes, wink (cf. 934)
παρ-ᾴττω, -ῇξα	dart past (cf. 837)
ἀπο-λύω, –έλυσα	acquit (cf. 571)

LINE 989

δῆτα	"Absolutely *not*!"; emphatic in neg. statements, rejecting a suggestion: *GP* 275. Phil.'s claim that he does not know how to play the lyre (κιθαρίζειν) echoes the feeble line of defense that Bdel. used at 959; he is claiming that he has no other way to earn a living.
φέρε νυν	come now (cf. 54)
τηδί	(adv.) in this way
τάχιστην	the fastest (sc. ὁδόν, way, fem. acc. sing.)
περι-άγω	lead around
αὕτη	sc. ψῆφος
ἔνι	= ἔνεστι, "In she goes."
ἑκών, ἑκοῦσα, ἑκόν	willing, readily, voluntarily

LINE 993

ἐξ-εράω, -ήρασα	(< ἐξ + ἐράω, pour) disgorge, pour out. The urn of voting tokens is emptied.
ἄρα	"Tell me! How did we do?"; lively, even impatient, interest in quests.: *GP* 39
ἀγωνίζομαι, perf. ἠγώνισμαι	
	(< ἀγών, contest, trial: cf. 534) contend for prize, fare in a trial
δείκνῡμι, δείξω	show; "it will be clear" (an occasional intrans., impers. usage; LSJ 4)

ἔπαιρε cαυτόν.

Φι.   εἰπέ νυν ἐκεῖνό μοι,
ὄντωc ἀπέφυγε;

Βδ.   νὴ Δί᾽.

Φι.   οὐδέν εἰμ᾽ ἄρα.

Βδ.   μὴ φροντίcῃc, ὦ δαιμόνι᾽, ἀλλ᾽ ἀνίcταcο.

Φι.   πῶc οὖν ἐμαυτῷ τοῦτ᾽ ἐγὼ ξυνείcομαι,
φεύγοντ᾽ ἀπολύcαc ἄνδρα; τί ποτε πείcομαι;   1000
ἀλλ᾽, ὦ πολυτίμητοι θεοί, ξύγγνωτέ μοι·
ἄκων γὰρ αὔτ᾽ ἔδραcα κοὐ τοὐμοῦ τρόπου.

Βδ.   καὶ μηδὲν ἀγανάκτει γ᾽. ἐγὼ γάρ c᾽, ὦ πάτερ,
θρέψω καλῶc, ἄγων μετ᾽ ἐμαυτοῦ πανταχοῖ,
ἐπὶ δεῖπνον, εἰc ξυμπόcιον, ἐπὶ θεωρίαν,   1005

LINE 996

ἐπ-αίρω	raise; rouse, stir up; "buck up"
ὄντως	(adv.) really (formed from ptcs. ὤν, οὖσα, ὄν < εἰμί, describing what actually *exists*; perhaps coined by sophists in the 420s)
ἄρα	"Ugh. I see . . . "; expresses "surprise attendant upon disillusionment": *GP* 35. The anguish is paratragic.
φροντίζω, ἐφρόντιϲα	consider, heed; worry about it (cf. 25)
ἀνίστημι	(> pres. mid. impv. 2 sing., ἀνίστασο) stand up
ξύν-οιδα, -είσομαι	(+ ἐμαυτῷ and acc.) be conscious of; "How will I live with this on my conscience, that I acquitted . . . ?"

LINE 1001

πολυτίμητος –ον	(< πολύ + verbal adj. of τῑμάω, honor, cf. 106) highly honored (a prayer-like epithet: *LA* 20)
ξυγ-γιγνώσκω	forgive (cf. 959)
ἄκων, ἄκουσα, ἆκον	(< Attic contraction for ἀ- + ἕκων, willing, cf. 992) unwilling, involuntarily
αὔτ᾽	= αὐτό (after *elision* the accent is thrown back to what was the penult, but remains acute: S #174)
τρόπος, ὁ	character; οὐ τοὐμοῦ τρόπου = "it was unlike me" (gen. of quality: S #1320, usually used as pred.)

LINE 1003

ἀγανακτέω	be annoyed, vexed
γε	"<u>Yes, yes</u>, and don't take it so hard"; gives assent to his excuse: *GP* 133–34, S #2825
ἄγω	lead, bring (distinguish ptcp. ἄγων from noun ἀγών, –ῶνος, ὁ, contest, struggle)
πανταχοῖ	in every direction (for locative suffix –οι: S #342)
ξυμπόσιον, τό	(< ξύν + πόσις, drinking) symposium, drinking party (cf. συμπότης, 21)
θεωρία, ἡ	(< θεάομαι, behold, view as spectator; cf. 59) spectacle, show (cf. 54 on θεατής)
δι-άγω	carry through; (of time) spend, pass

ὥcθ' ἡδέως διάγειν cε τὸν λοιπὸν χρόνον·
κοὐκ ἐγχανεῖταί c' ἐξαπατῶν Ὑπέρβολοc.
ἀλλ' εἰcίωμεν.

Φι.   ταῦτά νυν, εἴπερ δοκεῖ.

Χο.   ἀλλ' ἴτε χαίροντεc ὅποι βούλεcθ'.
        ὑμεῖc δὲ τέωc,   1010
        ὦ μυριάδεc ἀναρίθμητοι,
        νῦν τὰ μέλλοντ' εὖ λέγεcθαι
        μὴ πέcῃ φαύλωc χαμᾶζ'
        εὐλαβεῖcθε.
        τοῦτο γὰρ cκαιῶν θεατῶν
        ἐcτι πάcχειν, κοὐ πρὸc ὑμῶν.

LINE 1006

ἐγ-χάcκω, -χανοῦμαι	scoff at (+ dat.); cf. 721
Ὑπέρβολοc, -ου, ὁ	Hyperbolus, democratic politician, known for initiating prosecutions; a leading demagogue after the death of Cleon in 422, though ostracized in 416 and assassinated in 411
ἀλλά	a break in thought, transitioning to hort. subv.: *GP* 15 (cf. 240)
ταῦτα	"Yes," "Very well" (cf. 142)

1009–59: The *Parabasis*. The actors withdraw, leaving the chorus and chorus leader alone on stage. After the *kommation* (κομμάτιον < κόπτω, cut = an introductory "snippet," 1009–14), the chorus leader gives his speech explaining and defending the poet's career, and finishes with a *pnigos* (1051–59).

1009–14: Anapests (1009–11) and trochees (1112–14).

LINE 1009

ὅποι	to where (indef. rel. adv., correlative with ποῖ "to where?": S #346)
ἴτε, βούλεcθε	to Phil. and Bdel.; ὑμεῖc to the audience
τέωc	(adv. correlative with conj. ἕωc, while) for a while, in the meantime
μῦριάc, –άδοc, ἡ	the number 10,000; a countless amount. The chorus move into a poetic register, perhaps quoting a traditional phrase (cf. 709).
ἀναρίθμητοc, –ον	(ἀ- priv. + verbal adj. of ἀριθμέω denoting possibility, accent on antepenult: S #425c) countless, immeasurable (cf. 333)

LINE 1011

τὰ μέλλοντα εὖ λέγεcθαι

	things about to be spoken well, "the wise words to follow" (neut. pl. subject of sing. verb πέcῃ)
φαύλωc	(adv.) slightly, easily, carelessly
χαμᾶζε	(adv.) to the ground (with χαμαί, 43, and χαμᾶθεν, 249, W. illustrates all adverbial endings to denote space: S #342)
εὐλαβέομαι	take care (+ μή + subjv.; object clause after verb of effort: S #2210)
cκαιόc (3)	left; unlucky; clumsy (cκαιῶν θεατῶν, gen. of quality: S #1320)
πρόc	characteristic of (+ gen.)

1015–24: Ar. is upset at his audience. In the first three years of his career (427–425 BC), Ar.'s comedies were produced "covertly," under the names of other people; this is described as a kind of ventriloquism in which Ar. served as a controlling spirit who made another poet speak his words. Ar. is thus like the legendary spirit Eurycles, who uttered prophecies through the bellies of other people. (An alternative view: the "secret" phase was even before 427 BC; see Somm. and B-O.)

1015–50: Meter: Anapestic tetrameters.

νῦν αὖτε, λεώ, προσέχετε τὸν νοῦν, εἴπερ καθαρόν τι φιλεῖτε.　　1015
μέμψασθαι γὰρ τοῖσι θεαταῖς ὁ ποιητὴς νῦν ἐπιθυμεῖ.
ἀδικεῖσθαι γάρ φησιν πρότερος πόλλ’ αὐτοὺς εὖ πεποιηκώς·
τὰ μὲν οὐ φανερῶς ἀλλ’ ἐπικουρῶν κρύβδην ἑτέροισι ποιηταῖς,
μιμησάμενος τὴν Εὐρυκλέους μαντείαν καὶ διάνοιαν,
εἰς ἀλλοτρίας γαστέρας ἐνδὺς κωμῳδικὰ πολλὰ χέασθαι·　　1020
μετὰ τοῦτο δὲ καὶ φανερῶς ἤδη κινδυνεύων καθ’ ἑαυτόν,

LINE 1015

αὖτε	(adv.) again; an old-fashioned word more at home in epic. This is not the first time that Ar. has addressed the audience and asked for their favor.
λεώς, –ῶ, ὁ	(> voc. sing.: λεώ) people
προσ-έχω	hold to, apply
καθαρός (3)	clear, plain; genuine, frank
μέμφομαι, ἐμεμψάμην	blame, chastise (+ dat.). Ar. is still sore at the audience about the third-place finish of *Clouds* in the previous year.

LINE 1018

φησίν	The chorus speak of the poet in 3rd sing.; subject of φημί is also subject of inf.
πρότερος (3)	before, sooner; "undeservedly," "without provocation"
εὖ ποιεῖν	benefit (with πολλά, adv. acc.)
τὰ μέν	(adv. acc.) "partly": MacD.
φανερῶς	(adv.) openly
ἐπι-κουρέω	(< ἐπίκουρος, ally) assist (+ dat.)
κρύβδην	(adv. < κρύπτω, hide + –δην, adv. suffix: S #344) secretly
μιμέομαι, ἐμιμησάμην	imitate {> *mime, mimetic*}
Εὐρυκλῆς, –έους, ὁ	Eurycles, the prophetic spirit
μαντεία, ἡ	(< μάντις, seer) prophetic power (cf. 159)
διάνοια, ἡ	thought, purpose; device
ἀλλότριος (3)	(< ἄλλος, another) belonging to someone else
γαστήρ, –στρός, ἡ	stomach (cf. 195)
ἐν-δύω, aor.² –έδυν	go into, slip into
κωμῳδικός (3)	comic, of comedy
χέω, aor. mid. ἐχεάμην	
	pour; (mid.) make acc. pour out

LINE 1021

κινδῡνεύω	(< κίνδῡνος, danger + –ευω, verbal suffix denoting a condition: S #866.4) be daring, take a risk
καθ’ ἑαυτόν	by himself, on his own responsibility
οἰκεῖος (3)	of the house; belonging to oneself, one's own
Μοῦσα, ἡ	Muse. The notion seems to be that each poet has his own Muse; the Muses are likened to a team of horses pulling a chariot.
στόμα, –ατος, τό	mouth {> *stomach*}
ἡνιοχέω, ἡνιόχησα	(ἡνία, bridle, reins + ἔχω) hold the reins; drive, guide

οὐκ ἀλλοτρίων ἀλλ' οἰκείων Μουςῶν ςτόμαθ' ἡνιοχήςας.
ἀρθεὶς δὲ μέγας καὶ τιμηθεὶς ὡς οὐδεὶς πώποτ' ἐν ὑμῖν,
οὐκ ἐκχαλάςαι φηςὶν ἐπαρθεὶς οὐδ' ὀγκῶςαι τὸ φρόνημα,
οὐδὲ παλαίςτρας περικωμάζειν πειρῶν· οὐδ' εἴ τις ἐραςτὴς   1025
κωμῳδεῖςθαι παιδίχ' ἑαυτοῦ μιςῶν ἔςπευςε πρὸς αὐτόν,
οὐδενὶ πώποτέ φηςι πιθέςθαι, γνώμην τιν' ἔχων ἐπιεικῆ,
ἵνα τὰς Μούςας αἷςιν χρῆται μὴ προαγωγοὺς ἀποφήνῃ.

LINE 1023

αἴρω, aor. pass. ἤρθην	
	raise (cf. 51)
τῑμάω, aor. pass. ἐτῑμήθην	
	honor (cf. 106)
ἐκ-χαλάω, ἐξεχάλαςα	(< ἐκ + χαλάω, slacken) let go from; slack off
οὐκ φηςίν	"he denies that he . . ." (οὐκ and οὐδέ are *adherescent* with φηςίν: S #2692)
ἐπ-αίρω, aor. pass. ἐπήρθην	
	raise up; ἐπαρθείς = "being over-confident"
ὀγκόω, ὤγκωσα	(< ὄγκος, bulk) swell, puff up {> oncology}
φρόνημα, –ατος, τό	thought; pride, conceit. It is possible that Ar. is mocking Eupolis, his rival comic poet, for having exalted himself.

1025–28: Ar. claims that he has acted with integrity, never allowing his comedies to become vehicles for people settling private scores.

LINE 1025

παλαίςτρα, ἡ	(< παλαίω, wrestle + –τρα, suffix for place: S #851.6) palaestra; wrestling school
περι-κωμάζω	(< κῶμος, revel) carouse around
πειράω	try (sometimes used of erotic forays); "cruising the wrestling schools looking for a pick-up" (Hend.) {> pirate, empirical}
ἐράςτης, –ου, ὁ	(< ἔρως, love) lover, usually of a man in love with a younger beloved
κωμῳδέω	satirize, ridicule
παιδικά, τά	(< παῖς, boy + –ικος, adj. suffix) boyish; (pl., but of a single person) boyfriend
μιςέω	hate
ςπεύδω, ἔςπευςα	urge, plead with him to (+ πρός + acc. = pressure someone: LSJ II.6). Most take this to mean "the lover, hating his boyfriend, urged the poet (αὐτόν) that he [the boyfriend] be ridiculed."
οὐδενί . . . φηςι πιθέςθαι	
	Ar. "refused to comply with anyone" (οὐδενί is a compound neg. that confirms the first neg., οὐδέ: S #2761)
γνώμη, ἡ	purpose
ἐπιεικής, –ές	(< ἐπί + εἰκός, reasonable) suitable, respectable
χράομαι	use (indic., stating a fact within subordinate clause: S #2545)
προαγωγός, ὁ	(< προ-άγω, bring forward, lead on) pimp, procurer
ἀπο-φαίνω, aor. –έφηνα	
	show; make acc. into acc. (subjv. after ἵνα)

οὐδ᾽ ὅτε πρῶτόν γ᾽ ἦρξε διδάσκειν, ἀνθρώποις φής᾽ ἐπιθέσθαι,
ἀλλ᾽ Ἡρακλέους ὀργήν τιν᾽ ἔχων τοῖσι μεγίστοις ἐπεχείρει,
θρασέως ξυστὰς εὐθὺς ἀπ᾽ ἀρχῆς αὐτῷ τῷ καρχαρόδοντι,
οὗ δεινόταται μὲν ἀπ᾽ ὀφθαλμῶν Κύννης ἀκτῖνες ἔλαμπον,
ἑκατὸν δὲ κύκλῳ κεφαλαὶ κολάκων οἰμωξομένων ἐλιχμῶντο

1030

1029–50: When Ar. produced comedies under his own name, he attacked a great monster in public life (Cleon) and thereby proved himself to be a bulwark against evil—yet the audience did not sufficiently appreciate his poetry. (Note: lines 1029–37 are recycled in Ar., *Peace* 751–60.)

LINE 1029

οὐδέ ... γε	"nor yet"; connective, in continuous speech: *GP* 156
ὅτε πρῶτον	when at first; as soon as
διδάσκω	teach; <u>serve as</u> <u>didaskalos</u> ("producer" or "director") of a drama. In 424 Ar. for the first time served as producer of his own play, *Knights*; in that comedy, he attacked Cleon, a task that required a Herculean effort because it was like taking on a jagged-tooth monster.
ἄνθρωπος, ὁ	person; ordinary people (cf. 168)
ἐπι-τίθημι, aor.² -έθηκα	
	attack (+ dat.; intro. by οὐδὲ ... φησί, "he denies that he attacked ...")
Ἡρακλῆς, ὁ	Heracles; though a low-brow, appetite-driven character in drama (cf. 60), in my-thology he heroically confronted monsters.
μέγιστος (3)	(superl. of μέγας) greatest
ἐπι-χειρέω	put hand to work; make attempt on; attack; "kept on attacking" (imperfect of re-peated action: S #1893) (cf. 581)
θράσεως	(< θάρσος, courage, with *metathesis*, exchange of vowel and consonant: -αρ- > -ρα-) boldly (cf. 387)
ξυν-ίστημι, aor.² -έστην	
	stand together; stand up against, be engaged with (+ dat.)
καρχαρόδους, –οντος, ὁ	
	(< καρχαρέος, rough + ὀδούς, tooth) the one with sharp, jagged teeth. Cerberus, the watchdog of Hades, was called "jagged tooth"; the epithet here refers to Cleon.

LINE 1032

ὀφθαλμός, ὁ	eye (cf. 430)
Κύννη, ἡ	name of a prostitute. The spectators might be expecting to hear the gen. κυνός, since the "rays of the Dog-Star" attacked him in the hottest part of the summer, suggests Somm.
ἀκτίς, –ῖνος, ἡ	ray, beam of light
λάμπω	light, shine (cf. 62)
ἑκατόν	hundred (indeclinable). The description recalls Hesiod's Typhoeus, which also has one hundred heads. (cf. 663)
οἰμώζω, οἰμώξομαι	cry οἴμοι; lament, wail, be accursed, damned; (with suggestion of purpose in fut. ptcp.) "destined for damnation" (cf. 24)
λιχμάω	lick, play with the tongue; (mid.) play like serpents

περὶ τὴν κεφαλήν, φωνὴν δ᾽ εἶχεν χαράδρας ὄλεθρον τετοκυίας,
φώκης δ᾽ ὀσμήν, Λαμίας δ᾽ ὄρχεις ἀπλύτους, πρωκτὸν δὲ καμήλου.   1035
τοιοῦτον ἰδὼν τέρας οὔ φησιν δείσας καταδωροδοκῆσαι,
ἀλλ᾽ ὑπὲρ ὑμῶν ἔτι καὶ νυνὶ πολεμεῖ· φησίν τε μετ᾽ αὐτὸν
τοῖς ἠπιάλοις ἐπιχειρῆσαι πέρυσιν καὶ τοῖς πυρετοῖσιν,

LINE 1034

φωνή, ἡ	voice (cf. 36)
χαράδρα, ἡ	mountain torrent (which cuts, χαράττει, a ravine down a mountainside). Cleon was known for his demagogic rhetoric, compared here to a torrent.
ὄλεθρος, ὁ	(< ὄλλῡμι, cf. 412) destruction, death (here, object of τετοκυίας)
τίκτω, perf. τέτοκα	give birth to, engender; produce
φώκη, ἡ	seal
ὀσμή, ἡ	(< ὄζω, smell, cf. 38) smell, odor
Λαμία, ἡ	Lamia, an ogress; said to have eaten other women's children. This may suggest that, if Lamia was a woman, someone with "Lamia's balls" was no man at all; or it may mean Lamia was a hermaphrodite; or that she could transform herself.
ὄρχις, –εως, ὁ	(> acc. pl. ὄρχεις) testicle, ball: *MM* pp. 124–25 {> orchid, orchiectomy}
ἄπλυτος, –ον	(< πλύνω, wash) unwashed
κάμηλος, –ου, ὁ, ἡ	camel. If Cleon's arsehole was like a camel's, which was large and loose, then Cleon would be εὐρύπρωκτος: *MM* p. 214 #20. [< Semitic loan word, cf. Hebrew *gamal*]

LINE 1036

τέρας, –ατος, τό	sign, portent; marvel, monstrosity. The monster is the vision of Cleon described here.
οὐ + φημί	deny (οὐ adherescent; cf. 1023)
κατα-δωροδοκέω	(< κατά, against, adversely + δωροδοκέω, cf. 669) take bribes, betray someone by taking bribes
πολεμέω	fight
μετ᾽ αὐτόν	μετά + acc. = "after," that is, after attacking Cleon in 424. And in the year after that, "last year" (423), Ar. attacked "chills and fevers," evidently meaning that he attacked people who assaulted fathers and grandfathers and who acted as *sycophants* by filing nuisance lawsuits against innocent people. None of these actions squares with the surviving, revised *Clouds*, so Ar. may be referring to the first version of *Clouds*, performed at the Dionysia of 423, or perhaps to a comedy performed at the Lenaea of 423.
ἠπίαλος, ὁ	shiver, chill; nightmare demon
ἐπι-χειρέω	attack (cf. 1038)
πέρυσιν	(adv.) last year
πυρετός, ὁ	fever (cf. 813)

οἳ τοὺς πατέρας τ' ἦγχον νύκτωρ καὶ τοὺς πάππους ἀπέπνιγον
κατακλινομένους ἐν ταῖς κοίταις, ἐπὶ τοῖσί τ' ἀπράγμοσιν ὑμῶν   1040
ἀντωμοσίας καὶ προσκλήσεις καὶ μαρτυρίας συνεκόλλων,
ὥστ' ἀναπηδᾶν δειμαίνοντας πολλοὺς ὡς τὸν πολέμαρχον.

LINE 1039

ἄγχω	strangle, throttle
νύκτωρ	at night (cf. 123)
πάππος, ὁ	grandfather
ἀπο-πνῑ́γω	choke (cf. 511)
κοίτη, ἡ	(< κεῖμαι, lie down) marriage bed, bed (cf. 213 on κοιμάω)
ἐπί	(+ dat.) into, among (hostility)
ἀπράγμων, –ον, –ονος	
	(ἀ- priv. + πρᾶγμα, action) free from business; keeping clear of politics, peaceable. Ar. admired the ἀπράγμονες, who did not meddle in political affairs; by contrast, the πολυπράγμονες were officious busy-bodies.
ἀντωμοσία, ἡ	(< ἀντόμνῡμι, swear in turn) affidavits made by plaintiff and defendant against one another
πρόσκλησις, ἡ	(< προσκαλέω, summon into court + –σις, suffix denoting action: S #840a.2) a legal summons
μαρτυρία, ἡ	(< μάρτυς, witness) witness testimony, statement of evidence
συγ-κολλάω	(< κόλλα, glue) glue together; assemble, put together (used of documents); (for subjects of this verb sc. ἠπίαλοι καὶ πυρετοί)

LINE 1042

ἀνα-πηδάω	(< ἀνά, up + πηδάω, leap) jump up and hurry to
δειμαίνω	(< δεῖμα, fear, cf. 715 + –αινω, suffix for *denominative* vbs.: S #866.7) fear, be afraid
ὡς	(+ acc. of person) toward, to
πολέμαρχος, ὁ	(< πόλεμος, war + ἄρχων, leader) "war-lord," but in classical Athens, the Polemarch was one of the judicial magistrates to whom Athenians would register a legal complaint, esp. concerning noncitizens. Evidently the *sycophants* attacked in this passage of *W.* were noncitizens.

τοιόνδ' εὑρόντες ἀλεξίκακον τῆς χώρας τῆσδε καθαρτήν,
πέρυσιν καταπροΰδοτε καινοτάτας σπείραντ' αὐτὸν διανοίας,
ἃς ὑπὸ τοῦ μὴ γνῶναι καθαρῶς ὑμεῖς ἐποιήσατ' ἀναλδεῖς·
καίτοι σπένδων πόλλ' ἐπὶ πολλοῖς ὄμνυσιν τὸν Διόνυσον
μὴ πώποτ' ἀμείνον' ἔπη τούτων κωμῳδικὰ μηδέν' ἀκοῦσαι.

1045

LINE 1043

τοιόσδε, –άδε, –όνδε	(< τοῖος, such + -δε) such as this
ἀλεξίκακος, –ον	(< ἀλέξω, ward off) keeping off evil (an epithet of Heracles). The poet is compared to Hercules, who purged the earth of monsters; the poet sowed novel ideas but the spectators, out of ignorance, rejected them by allowing his comedy *Clouds* to lose. It was some of the best comic poetry ever composed! {< Ale*x*ander}
χώρα, ἡ	place, country (cf. 230)
καθαρτής, –οῦ, ὁ	(< καθαρός, clean + –της, suffix denoting agency: S #839a.1) purifier; used of Heracles
πέρυσιν	(adv.) last year (specifically, the failure of *Clouds* at the Dionysia of 423)
κατα-προ-δίδωμι, aor.² -έδωκα	
	betray utterly. (Were it uncontracted, καταπροΰδοτε would be spelled καταπροέδοτε, but ο + ε contract into ου: S #59; on the *coronis* cf. 3)
σπείρω, ἔσπειρα	sow {> sperm, dia*spora*}
διάνοια, ἡ	thought, idea (διανοίας is direct object of ptcp. σπείραντα; αὐτόν, referring to the poet, Ar., is acc. subject of σπείραντα.)
ὑπὸ τοῦ μὴ γνῶναι	"because of your ignorance" (ὑπό often with gen. of agent, also used with other causes; μή is neg. in art. inf.: S #2712)
καθαρῶς	(adv.) purely, clearly
ἀναλδής, –ές	(< ἀν-, ἀ- priv.: S #885.1 + ἀλδαίνω, nourish) feeble, fruitless, barren

LINE 1046

σπένδω	pour libations. An oath was more serious if accompanied by libations.
ἐπί	in addition to (+ dat.)
ὄμνῡμι	swear by (+ acc.)
Διόνῡσος, –ου, ὁ	Dionysus, as god of drama
ἀμείνων, –ον, –ονος	stronger, better (cf. 173)
ἔπος, –εος, τό	word; verses, poetry (cf. 481)
τούτων	gen. of comparison
ἀκούω, ἤκουσα	hear (μή is used with inf. ἀκοῦσαι after ὄμνῡμι: S #2726; μηδένα is acc. subject of the inf.; ἔπη is object)

τοῦτο μὲν οὖν ἐcθ' ὑμῖν αἰcχρὸν τοῖc μὴ γνοῦcιν παραχρῆμα,
ὁ δὲ ποιητὴc οὐδὲν χείρων παρὰ τοῖcι cοφοῖc νενόμιcται,
εἰ παρελαύνων τοὺc ἀντιπάλουc τὴν ἐπίνοιαν ξυνέτριψεν.   1450
ἀλλὰ τὸ λοιπὸν τῶν ποιητῶν,
ὦ δαιμόνιοι, τοὺc ζητοῦνταc
καινόν τι λέγειν κἀξευρίcκειν
cτέργετε μᾶλλον καὶ θεραπεύετε,
καὶ τὰ νοήματα cῴζεcθ' αὐτῶν,   1055
εἰcβάλλετέ τ' εἰc τὰc κιβωτοὺc
μετὰ τῶν μήλων. κἂν ταῦτα ποιῆθ',

LINE 1048

μὲν οὖν	Probably not the corrective μὲν οὖν, common in dialogue (cf. 515), but simply transitional οὖν and μέν anticipating δέ: *GP* 470
αἰcχρός (3)	shameful, disgraceful
τοῖς μὴ γνοῦσιν	"for anyone who doesn't know" (μή with ptcp. when referent is indef.)
παραχρῆμα	(adv., < παρά + χρῆμα, need) right away, immediately
χείρων, –ον, –ονος	worse (cf. 439)
παρά	(+ dat.) in the eyes of
παρ-ελαύνω	drive past, overtake. The metaphor is from chariot racing
ἀντίπαλος, –ον	(< ἀντί + πάλη, wrestling, a backformation from παλαίω; cf. 1025) wrestling rival, rival, adversary
ἐπίνοια, ἡ	afterthought, second thought; novel conception (cf. 346)
ξυν-τρίβω, -έτρῖψα	(< ξύν, together + τρίβω, rub) shatter, crash. Ar. likens himself to a charioteer who had an accident when he was just about to overtake his competitors.

1051–59: Meter: The *pnigos*, composed of anapests (primarily dimeters), urging the audience to cherish poets and save their ideas.

LINE 1051

ζητέω	seek (ζητοῦνταc is object of cτέργετε καὶ θεραπεύετε; take part. gen. ποιητῶν with τοὺc ζητοῦνταc; ἐξευρίcκειν and λέγειν are obj. infs. with ζητοῦνταc)
ἐξ-ευρίcκω	find out (ἐξ- implies completion or thoroughness: S #1688.2)
cτέργω	love, cherish, show affection for
θεραπεύω	(< θεράπων, attendant) serve, attend to
νόημα, –ατος, τό	(< νοέω, think + –μα, –ματος, suffix denoting result of an action: S #841.2) thought
cῴζω	save, preserve
εἰc-βάλλω	throw in, put in (object of this verb is τὰ νοήματα)
κῑβωτός, ἡ	wooden chest, box
μῆλον, τό	apples; citrons. These μῆλα, like mothballs or cedar chips, were packed with clothes to keep away moths; thus the thoughts of the poets will be preserved.
ἔτος, –ους, τό	year (cf. 490)
διά	(+ gen.) throughout the year (S #1685.b)
ἱμάτιον, τό	cloak, (pl.) clothes (cf. 408)
ὄζω, ὀζήσω	smell, smell of; (impers., contrast 39) there is a smell of (+ descriptive gen.: S #1354, arising from a gen. of source: S #1410; ὀζήσει is a fut. indic. apodosis of FMV condit. of which ἐὰν . . . ποιῆτε is the protasis.)
δεξιότης, –ητος, ἡ	(< δέξιος, on right hand, skillful + –οτης, suffix expressing a quality: S #840b4) dexterity, cleverness. Fem. abstract nouns ending in –ότης are rare in Ar. and can be associated with the intellectualized language of the sophists; similar are –μα nouns like νόημα above: *LA* 137–39.

ὑμῖν δι' ἔτους τῶν ἱματίων

ὀζήσει δεξιότητος.   1059

ὦ πάλαι ποτ' ὄντες ἡμεῖς ἄλκιμοι μὲν ἐν χοροῖς,   [στρ.

ἄλκιμοι δ' ἐν μάχαις,   1061

καὶ κατ' αὐτὸ τοῦτο μόνον

ἄνδρες ἀλκιμώτατοι.

πρίν ποτ' ἦν, πρὶν ταῦτα· νῦν δ'

οἴχεται, κύκνου τε πολι-

ώτεραι δὴ αἵδ' ἐπανθοῦσιν τρίχες.   1065

LINE 1060

1060–21: The *epirrhematic syzygy*, which includes an ode (1060–70), speech (*epirrhema*, 1071–90), antode (1091–1101), and speech (*antepirrhema*, 1102–21). In the ode, members of the chorus describe themselves: once fearsome in choruses, battle, and (apparently) bed, age has diminished their powers, but they have little regard for the frivolous behavior of today's youth.

1060–70: Meter: Trochees.

ἄλκιμος (3)	(< ἀλκή, strength + –ιμος, adj. suffix denoting ability: S #858.9) strong, valiant
χορός, ὁ	dance, chorus (cf. 230)
κατ' αὐτὸ τοῦτο	as far as this very thing is concerned (possibly pointing at their *phalli*)
πρίν	(adv.) earlier, once (distinguish from conj.; note *anaphora*, repetition of πρίν)
κύκνος, ὁ	swan {> *cygnus*}
πολιώτερος (3)	(comparative adj. < πολιός, grey/white) whiter (than a κύκνου, gen. of comparison)
δή	"actually whiter," "whiter indeed"; Ar. generally avoids δή after an adj., but here he may be quoting a poem by Timocreon of Rhodes.
ἐπ-ανθέω	(< ἄνθος, flower) bloom, be in flower {> *antho-*}
θρίξ, τριχός, ἡ	hair (on the loss of aspiration, from θρ. to τρ., Sihler #138). It is standard, at least in prose, for demonstrative prons. like ὅδε to be accompanied by the art. (e.g., τῶν λειψάνων τῶνδε), but the art. is frequently omitted in poetry and, perhaps relevant for αἵδε τρίχες, when contempt is being expressed: S #1178.

ἀλλὰ κἀκ τῶν λειψάνων δεῖ τῶνδε ῥώμην
νεανικὴν cχεῖν· ὡc ἐγὼ τοὐμὸν νομίζω
γῆραc εἶναι κρεῖττον ἢ πολλῶν κικίννουc
νεανιῶν καὶ cχῆμα κεὐρυπρωκτίαν.   1070
εἴ τιc ὑμῶν, ὦ θεαταί, τὴν ἐμὴν ἰδὼν φύcιν
εἶτα θαυμάζει μ' ὁρῶν μέcον διεcφηκωμένον,
ἥτιc ἡμῶν ἐcτιν ἡ 'πίνοια τῆc ἐγκεντρίδοc,
ῥᾳδίωc ἐγὼ διδάξω, "κἂν ἄμουcοc ᾖ τὸ πρίν".

LINE 1066

λείψανον, τό	(< λείπω, leave) remnant, (pl.) remains
ῥώμη, ἡ	strength
ἔχω, aor.² ἔcχον	get, have; summon up
ὡc	causal conj.
γῆραc, –ωc, τό	old age (cf. 277)
κίκιννοc, ὁ	ringlets
cχῆμα, –ατοc, τό	(< cχεῖν, hold) shape, posture; style, dress
εὐρυπρωκτία, ἡ	(< εὐρύc, wide + πρῶκτοc, anus) "lewdness"; having an anus that has been widened from penetration: *MM* p. 210 (cf. *W.* 604)

1071–90: The chorus leader speaks: their wasp nature made them good young warriors when they fought the Persians at Marathon in 490 and at Thermopylae and Salamis in 480. The events recounted constitute a free rendition of those battles: the infantry charge was at Marathon, the stinging pursuit sounds like Marathon, the darkening of the skies by arrows was at Thermopylae, Athens was burned after Thermopylae in 480, and the owl was at Salamis.

1071–90: Trochaic tetrameters

LINE 1071

ἰδών . . . ὁρῶν	Not quite redundant: a glimpse (aor. ptcp. ἰδών) at the general appearance, but with continued viewing (pres. ptcp. ὁρῶν) a specific feature is visible.
φύcιc, –εωc, ἡ	nature, natural appearance, form {> *physics, hypothesis*} [< IE *bheuǝ-*, exist, grow; cogn. L. *fieri*; E. *be*]
θαυμάζω	wonder, marvel (cf. 13)
μέcοc (3)	middle, in the middle
δια-cφηκόομαι	(< cφήξ, wasp, cf. 224 + –οω, suffix for *factitive* vbs., denoting "to cause" or "to make": S #866.3) be made like a wasp, be wasp-waisted (pass.)
ἥτιc	indir. interrog.
ἐπίνοια, ἡ	thought; purpose, <u>significance</u>
ἐγκεντρίc, –ίδοc, ἡ	stinger (cf. 427)
ῥᾳδίωc	(adv.) easily
ἄμουcοc, –ον	(< ἀ- priv. + Μοῦcα) without a Muse; unschooled, inelegant. The quoted words are from the *Stheneboia*, a lost tragedy by Euripides
τὸ πρίν	art. with adv. usage

ἐϲμὲν ἡμεῖϲ, οἷϲ πρόϲεϲτι τοῦτο τοὐρροπύγιον,   1075
Ἀττικοὶ μόνοι δικαίωϲ ἐγγενεῖϲ αὐτόχθονεϲ,
ἀνδρικώτατον γένοϲ καὶ πλεῖϲτα τήνδε τὴν πόλιν
ὠφελῆϲαν ἐν μάχαιϲιν, ἡνίκ᾽ ἦλθ᾽ ὁ βάρβαροϲ,
τῷ καπνῷ τύφων ἅπαϲαν τὴν πόλιν καὶ πυρπολῶν,
ἐξελεῖν ἡμῶν μενοινῶν πρὸϲ βίαν τἀνθρήνια.   1080
εὐθέωϲ γὰρ ἐκδραμόντεϲ "ξὺν δορὶ ξὺν ἀϲπίδι"
ἐμαχόμεϲθ᾽ αὐτοῖϲι, θυμὸν ὀξίνην πεπωκότεϲ,
ϲτὰϲ ἀνὴρ παρ᾽ ἄνδρ᾽, ὑπ᾽ ὀργῆϲ τὴν χελύνην ἐϲθίων·

LINE 1075

πρόϲ-ειμι   be added, be attached to

ὀρροπύγιον, τό   (< ὄρροϲ, coccyx + πῡγή, buttocks + ιον, dim. suffix) rump, tail. By now we have a few clues about the wasps' costume. There may have been padding for the body segments and a tight waist, and a stinger was attached to the rump. Unless the stinger could swing through the legs, there would also have been a phallus.

Ἀττικόϲ   (3) Attic

ἐγγενήϲ, –έϲ   native, inborn

αὐτόχθων, –ον, –ονοϲ

     (< αὐτόϲ, itself + χθών, earth) born of the earth, indigenous. Athenians proudly claimed to be the original inhabitants of Attica. {> chthonic, auto*chthon*} [< IE *dhghem-*, earth; cogn. L. *humus, homo, humanus*; E. bride*groom*]

ἀνδρικώτατοϲ (3)   most manly, courageous

γένοϲ, –ουϲ, τό   kind, race

πλεῖϲτοϲ (3)   most (here, adv. acc.; cf. 700)

ὠφελέω, aor. ὠφέληϲα

     help (ὠφελῆϲαν is aor. act. neut. ptcp., accent fixed on penult; by contrast indic. 3 pl. ὠφέληϲαν has recessive accent: S #425.) The help they provided was, above all, to repel the Persians in 490 and 480.

τύφω   fill with smoke, spew (cf. 457)

πυρ-πολέω   light a fire, burn down

ἐξ-αιρέω, aor.² -εῖλον   remove, do away with, eradicate

μενοινάω   desire to

πρὸϲ βίαν   forcefully

ἀνθρήνιον, τό   (< ἀνθρήνη, hornet or wasp) wasp's nest

LINE 1081

ἐκ-τρέχω, aor.² -έδραμον

     run out (cf. 376)

δόρυ, –ατοϲ, τό   plank; spear-shaft (Attic dat. sing. δορί; the phrase ξὺν δορὶ ξὺν ἀϲπίδι (note *asyndeton*) is quoted from a tragedy; this, and ξὺν θεοῖϲ below, may be fossilized phrases that preserve the use of the older ξύν.) [< IE *deru*, tree, wood, be firm; cogn. E. *tree, true*; Celtic *druid* (cf. 4 for –*id* of *druid*)]

ἀϲπίϲ, –ίδοϲ, ἡ   shield (cf. 17)

ὀξίνηϲ, –εϲ   (< ὀξύϲ, sharp) tart, bitter

πίνω, perf. πέπωκα   drink

χελύνη, ἡ   lip

ὑπὸ δὲ τῶν τοξευμάτων οὐκ ἦν ἰδεῖν τὸν οὐρανόν.

ἀλλ' ὅμως ἐωσάμεσθα ξὺν θεοῖς πρὸς ἑσπέραν.   1085

γλαῦξ γὰρ ἡμῶν πρὶν μάχεσθαι τὸν στρατὸν διέπτατο.

εἶτα δ' εἱπόμεσθα θυννάζοντες εἰς τοὺς θυλάκους,

οἱ δ' ἔφευγον τὰς γνάθους καὶ τὰς ὀφρῦς κεντούμενοι·

ὥστε παρὰ τοῖς βαρβάροις πανταχοῦ καὶ νῦν ἔτι

μηδὲν Ἀττικοῦ καλεῖσθαι σφηκὸς ἀνδρικώτερον.   1090

LINE 1084

τόξευμα, –ατος, τό   (< τοξεύω, shoot with arrow + –μα, –ματος, suffix denoting result of action: S #841.2) arrow

οὐκ ἦν   it was not possible

ἑσπέρα, ἡ   evening (cf. 100)

γλαῦξ, γλαῦκος, ἡ   owl. The symbol of Athena and a good omen for Athenians.

στρατός, ὁ   army

δια-πέτομαι, -επτάμην

     fly through (cf. 16)

LINE 1087

ἕπομαι   follow (imperfect εἱπόμεσθα: the augment εἱ is actually syllabic: the verb was once σέπομαι; augmented it would be ἐσέπομαι, but initial /s/ became /h/; contraction of the *syllabic augment* ἐ and stem formed εἱ: S #431)

θυννάζω   (< θύννος, tuna, tunny-fish) spear tunny-fish; harpoon

θύλακος, ὁ   pouch, bag; Persian trousers

γνάθος, ἡ   jaw; acc. respect = "in the face" (cf. 948)

ὀφρῦς, –ύος, ἡ   brow, eyebrows

LINE 1089

μηδέν   When ὥστε introduces a clause of natural result with inf., the neg. is μή.

πανταχοῦ   (adv.) everywhere

ἀνδρικώτερος (3)   more manly; more courageous (cf. 153)

ἆρα δεινὸς ἦ τόθ᾽, ὥϲτε ταῦτα μὴ δεδοικέναι,   [ἀντ.
καὶ κατεϲτρεψάμην
τοὺϲ ἐναντίουϲ, πλέων ἐ-
κεῖϲε ταῖϲ τριήρεϲιν;
οὐ γὰρ ἦν ἡμῖν ὅπωϲ
ῥῆϲιν εὖ λέξειν ἐμέλλο-   1095
μεν τότ᾽ οὐδὲ ϲυκοφαντήϲειν τινὰ
φροντίϲ, ἀλλ᾽ ὅϲτιϲ ἐρέτηϲ ἔϲοιτ᾽ ἄριϲτοϲ.

1091–01: The chorus reflect on the military qualities that were valued when they were young, contrasting that with the young people today who simply indulge in nuisance lawsuits and steal tribute.

1091–1101: Meter: Trochees; the *antistrophe* responding to the *strophe* in lines 1060–70.

LINE 1091

ἆρα	cf. 4
ἦ	= ἦν (the "I" subject of ἦ serves also as subject of inf. δεδοικέναι)
κατα-ϲτρέφω	(< κατά, down + ϲτρέφω, turn) overturn; (mid.) subdue
ἐναντίοϲ (3)	(ἐν + ἄντιος, facing) opposite; adversaries
πλέω	sail (cf. 122)
ἐκεῖϲε	to that place (cf. 104). After the Greek victory over the Persian infantry at Plataea in summer 479, the Athenians sailed to Asia Minor and defeated the Persians at Mycale, which appears to be the place in question.
τριήρης, –ους, ἡ	(< τρί + ἐρε-, row cf. 518) sc. ναῦς; trireme, warship with three banks of rowers

LINE 1094

ὅπως	+ past indic. ἐμέλλομεν in a purpose clause expressing unfulfilled purpose (cf. 961)
ῥῆσις, –εως, ἡ	(< ἐρῶ, say) speech (perhaps rehearsed; cf. 580)
ϲυκοφαντέω	(< σῦκον, fig, cf. 145 + -φάντης < φαίνω show = fig-revealer) slander, conduct nuisance prosecution (τινα is dir. object of ϲυκφαντήϲειν, which is fut. inf. after μέλλω). The word derives perhaps from a time when exporting figs was illegal and subject to prosecution; the term came to apply to anyone who used the court system for opportunistic purposes (on *sycophants*, cf. 1038).
φροντίς, –ίδος, ἡ	(< φρονέω, think; cf. 25 + -ις, –ιδος suffix: S #863b12) thought, care (nom. subject of ἦν in 1094)
ἐρέτης, –ου, ὁ	rower (cf. 518)
ἔσοιτο	a rare instance of a fut. opt. of εἰμί used in indir. quest., cf. 801, S #2677

τοιγαροῦν πολλὰς πόλεις Μήδων ἑλόντες
αἰτιώτατοι φέρεσθαι τὸν φόρον δεῦρ᾽   1100
ἐσμέν, ὃν κλέπτουσιν οἱ νεώτεροι.
πολλαχῇ σκοποῦντες ἡμᾶς εἰς ἅπανθ᾽ εὑρήσετε
τοὺς τρόπους καὶ τὴν δίαιταν cφηξὶν ἐμφερεστάτους.
πρῶτα μὲν γὰρ οὐδὲν ἡμῶν ζῷον ἠρεθιcμένον
μᾶλλον ὀξύθυμόν ἐcτιν οὐδὲ δυcκολώτερον·   1105
εἶτα τἄλλ᾽ ὅμοια πάντα cφηξὶ μηχανώμεθα.

LINE 1098

τοιγαροῦν   "It is for that reason…" The particle is strongly emphatic, conveying the effect that
                 "the logical connection is regarded as more important than the ideas connected": *GP*
                 566–67 (only instance in Aristophanes; more common in prose)

αἰτιώτατος (3)   responsible for (something + inf.)

φέρω   bring; pay tax or tribute (cf. 499). Inf. φέρεcθαι here is pass. and φόρον the acc. sub-
                 ject; tribute was paid by cities recaptured from the Persians and then forced into the
                 Delian League.

1102–21: How is a wasp like a juror? The chorus leader describes different courts that were in session in
Athens. Precisely which court the Archon supervised is not known. The Eleven presided over the "Inserted
Court," evidently called that because it was built in a confined space. The Odeon was also used as a courtroom.

1102–21: Meter: Trochaic tetrameters.

LINE 1102

πολλαχῇ   (< πολλαχ- + –ι suffix denoting place where: S #342) in many places; in many ways

σκοπέω   behold; examine, inspect (cf. 246)

εἰς ἅπαντα   in every respect, in all things

δίαιτα, ἡ   way of living (cf. 524)

ἐμφερέστατος (3) (superl. of ἐμφερής < ἐμ-φέρω, bring in) answering to, resembling (+ dat., with accs. of
                 respect τρόπους and δίαιταν)

LINE 1104

ζῷον, τό   animal (cf. 551)

ἐρεθίζω, perf. mid./pass. ἠρέθιcμαι
                 provoke

ὀξύθυμος, –ον   sharp-tempered (cf. 406, 550)

δύcκολος, –ον   grouchy (cf. 106)

ὅμοιος (3)   similar; (adv. acc. ὅμοια) "in a way similar to wasps": LSJ C.I.1 and MacD.

μηχανάομαι   (< μηχανή, contrivance, cf. 149) contrive, engineer

ξυλλεγέντες γὰρ καθ' ἑσμοὺς ὥσπερ εἰς ἀνθρήνια,
οἱ μὲν ἡμῶν οὗπερ ἄρχων, οἱ δὲ παρὰ τοὺς ἕνδεκα,
οἱ δ' ἐν ᾠδείῳ δικάζους', ὧδε πρὸς τοῖς τειχίοις
ξυμβεβυσμένοι πυκνόν, νεύοντες εἰς τὴν γῆν, μόλις   1110
ὥσπερ οἱ σκώληκες ἐν τοῖς κυττάροις κινούμενοι.
εἴς τε τὴν ἄλλην δίαιτάν ἐσμεν εὐπορώτατοι.
πάντα γὰρ κεντοῦμεν ἄνδρα κἀκπορίζομεν βίον.
ἀλλὰ γὰρ κηφῆνες ἡμῖν εἰσιν ἐγκαθήμενοι
οὐκ ἔχοντες κέντρον, οἳ μένοντες ἡμῶν τοῦ φόρου   1115
τὸν γόνον κατεσθίουσιν οὐ ταλαιπωρούμενοι.

LINE 1107

συλ-λέγω, aor.² pass. -ἐλέγην
    gather

ἑσμός, ὁ
    swarm of bees [LSJ and B-O derive this word from ἕζομαι, sit; R. Beekes derives it from ἵημι on the grounds that swarms are characterized not by sitting but by moving]

ἀνθρήνιον, τό
    wasps' nest (cf. 1080)

οὗπερ ἄρχων
    "where the Archon [presided]" (for -περ suffix, cf. 146)

οἱ ἕνδεκα
    The Eleven, judicial officials who presided over the "Inserted Court," τὸ Παράβυστον

Ὠιδεῖον, τό
    (< ᾠδή, song + -ειον, suffix denoting place: S #851.1) The Odeon, a public building for performances and law courts

τειχίον, τό
    (dim. of τεῖχος, city wall; cf. 130) wall of a building

ξυμ-βύω, perf. mid./pass. –βέβυσμαι
    cram in

πυκνός (3)
    (< πύκα, strong, Sihler #290.b) close, compact, crowded (adv. acc. here)

νεύω
    nod, bend forward

μόλις
    (adv.) with difficulty, scarcely (cf. 718)

σκώληξ, –ηκος, ὁ
    worm, larva {> *scoliosis*}

κύτταρος, ὁ
    cell of honey comb

κῑνέω
    move, stir up (cf. 403)

LINE 1112

δίαιτα, ἡ
    way of living (cf. 524)

εὔπορος (3)
    (< εὖ + πόρος, passage, cf. 308) easy to travel through; (of persons) full of resources, ingenious

ἐκ-πορίζω
    provide (cf. 365)

LINE 1114

ἀλλὰ γάρ
    "But <our efforts are wasted> for . . ." (MacD.); "But the thing is . . ." (Somm.). A sudden transition: the particles mark "a contrast between what is irrelevant or subsidiary, and what is vital, primary or decisive": *GP* 101–2.

κηφήν, –ῆνος, ὁ
    drone, a male who has no stinger and stays at home, doing no work

ἐγ-κάθημαι
    sit among

γόνος, ὁ, ἡ
    child; <u>product</u>, that is, what jurors receive from the tribute

ταλαιπωρέω
    labor, work for something (cf. 967)

τοῦτο δ' ἔστ' ἄλγιστον ἡμῖν, ἤν τις ἀστράτευτος ὢν
ἐκροφῇ τὸν μισθὸν ἡμῶν, τῆσδε τῆς χώρας ὕπερ
μήτε κώπην μήτε λόγχην μήτε φλύκταιναν λαβών.
ἀλλά μοι δοκεῖ τὸ λοιπὸν τῶν πολιτῶν ἔμβραχυ   1120
ὅστις ἂν μὴ 'χῃ τὸ κέντρον μὴ φέρειν τριώβολον.

Φι.   οὔτοι ποτὲ ζῶν τοῦτον ἀποδυθήσομαι,
          ἐπεὶ μόνος μ' ἔσωσε παρατεταγμένον,
          ὅθ' ὁ βορέας ὁ μέγας ἐπεστρατεύσατο.

Βδ.   ἀγαθὸν ἔοικας οὐδὲν ἐπιθυμεῖν παθεῖν.   1125

LINE 1117

ἄλγιστος (3)	(superl. of ἀλγεινός < ἄλγος, pain) most painful
ἀστράτευτος, –ον	(< ἀ- priv. + στρατός, army) never having served in army, draft dodger
ἐκ-ροφέω	gulp down (ἐκροφῇ is subjv. in protasis of Pres. Gen. condit.)
χώρα, ἡ	place, country
κώπη, ἡ	handle; handle of oar; oar
λόγχη, ἡ	spear head; spear, lance
φλύκταινα, ἡ	(< φλύω, bubble) blister (from rowing or marching)

LINE 1120

πολίτης, –ου, ὁ	free member of a πόλις; citizen
ἔμβραχυ	(< ἐμ + βραχύς, short) in brief, shortly; often with ὅστις = "whosoever" {> brachy-}
'χῃ	= ἔχῃ (by aphaeresis: S #76)

1122–73: The *parabasis* over, the chorus fall silent. Phil. and Bdel. return to the stage. Bdel. will try to re-educate Phil. in the niceties of elite society, starting with apparel. Phil. resists the idea of discarding his threadbare cloak.

1122–1264: Meter: Iambic trimeters, though interrupted with snatches of lyric poems in various meters (see on 1226–27, 1232–35, 1238–39, 1241–42, 1245–48).

LINE 1122

οὔτοι	indeed not. Frequently used before protestations and asseverations: *GP* 544
ἀπο-δύω, fut. pass. –δυθήσομαι	
	strip a person of clothes (ἀποδύομαι pass., takes acc. of article of clothing)
τοῦτον	"this [old cloak]"; Bdel. is trying to do a favor, something "good," by offering a nice new cloak (χλαῖνα, 1132) to replace the old, worn-out one (τρίβων).
παρα-τάττω, perf. mid./pass. -τέταγμαι	
	place side by side; be drawn up in battle; παρατεταγμένος = "when I was in the ranks"
Βορέας, –ου, ὁ	North Wind. The audience perhaps expected to hear ὁ βασιλεὺς ὁ μέγας, a reference to the Persian invasion (cf. 265).
ἐπι-στρατεύω, aor. mid. -εστρατευσάμην	
	march against, invade (cf. 11)

Φι.   μὰ τὸν Δί’, οὐ γὰρ οὐδαμῶς μοι ξύμφορον.
                  καὶ γὰρ πρότερον ἐπανθρακίδων ἐμπλήμενος
                  ἀπέδωκ’ ὀφείλων τῷ κναφεῖ τριώβολον.

Βδ.   ἀλλ’ οὖν πεπειράcθω γ’, ἐπειδήπερ γ’ ἅπαξ
                  ἐμοὶ cεαυτὸν παραδέδωκας εὖ ποιεῖν.   1130

Φι.   τί οὖν κελεύεις δρᾶν με;

Βδ.   τὸν τρίβων’ ἄφες,
                  τηνδὶ δὲ χλαῖναν ἀναβαλοῦ τριβωνικῶς.

Φι.   ἔπειτα παῖδας χρὴ φυτεύειν καὶ τρέφειν,
                  ὅθ’ οὑτοcί με νῦν ἀποπνῖξαι βούλεται;

Βδ.   ἔχ’, ἀναβαλοῦ τηνδὶ λαβών, καὶ μὴ λάλει.   1135

Φι.   τουτὶ τὸ κακὸν τί ἐcτι, πρὸς πάντων θεῶν;

Βδ.   οἱ μὲν καλοῦcι Περcίδ’, οἱ δὲ καυνάκην.

LINE 1126

οὐδαμῶς	in no way at all (cf. 79)
καὶ γάρ	for in fact (cf. 269)
ἐπανθρακίδες, –ων, αἱ	(< ἀνθρακίδες, fried fish < ἄνθραξ, charcoal) small fish for frying, sprats (in gen. with verb of filling; cf. 424)
ὀφείλω	owe, be in debt (cf. 3)
κνάφευς, –έως, ὁ	fuller, clothes-cleaner (also spelled γν-). Evidently Phil. soiled his clothes after eating sprats—but it was worth it to him to pay for the old τρίβων to be cleaned.

LINE 1129

ἀλλ’ οὖν	"Have a try anyhow!"; in answers, introducing a protest: *GP* 442
πειράω, perf. mid./pass. πεπείραμαι	try (< perf. impv. 3 sing. πεπειράθω) = "let it have been tried"
ἐπειδήπερ γε	especially since, once and for all
ἅπαξ	(adv.) once, a single time, already (cf. 898)
εὖ ποιεῖν	benefit (inf. of purpose, often after verb of giving or entrusting, παραδίδωμι: S #2008, 2009); cf. 1018
τρίβων, –ωνος, ὁ	threadbare cloak (cf. 33)
ἀφ-ίημι, aor.² -ῆκα	(> aor. act. impv. 2 sing. ἄφες) release, get rid of, take off
χλαῖνα, ἡ	woolen cloak (cf. 738)
ἀνα-βάλλω	toss up; throw cloak over shoulder, put on
τριβωνικῶς	in a practiced manner, deftly. A pun on τρίβων, which means either "cloak" or "practiced"; cf. 1429. In the next few scenes adjs. formed from –ικός are used repeatedly, mimicking a trend among sophisticates in the 420s: *LA* 140. [The suffix –ικός has an IE root, *-(i)ko-, cogn. E. –*ing*, -*ish*]

LINE 1133

φυτεύω	beget
ἀπο-πνί γω, –έπνῖξα	choke, suffocate, stifle
ἔχ’	= ἔχε, hold, grab, "Here" (used when handing something to another; often followed by impv.)
λαλέω	babble, chatter [< *onomatopoeia*]
Περcίς, –ίδος	(adj.) Persian (sc. χλαῖνα)
καυνάκης, –ου, ὁ	thick Persian cloak with tufts of fur [loan word < Babylonian *gaunaka*, hairy]

Φι.   ἐγὼ δὲ cιcύραν ᾠόμην Θυμαιτίδα.

Βδ.   κοὐ θαῦμά γ'· εἰc Cάρδειc γὰρ οὐκ ἐλήλυθαc.

        ἔγνωc γὰρ ἄν· νῦν δ' οὐχὶ γιγνώcκειc.

Φι.   ἐγώ;   1140

        μὰ τὸν Δί' οὗτοι νῦν γ'· ἀτὰρ δοκεῖ γέ μοι

        ἐοικέναι μάλιcτα Μορύχου cάγματι.

Βδ.   οὔκ, ἀλλ' ἐν Ἐκβατάνοιcι ταῦθ' ὑφαίνεται.

Φι.   ἐν Ἐκβατάνοιcι γίγνεται κρόκηc χόλιξ;

LINE 1138

cιcύρα, ἡ   goat- or sheepskin cloak (cf. 738)

Θυμαιτίc, –ίδοc   (adj.) from Thumaetidae, a coastal *deme* of Attica. B-O point out this is also the adj.
                       form of the name of the phratry Thumaitis; both names derive from Thumaitis, the
                       last king descended from Theseus. Bdel. cannot tell a simple, locally manufactured
                       cloak from an exotic, imported one.

θαῦμα, –ατοc, τό   something to marvel at, a wonder (cf. 13)

Cάρδειc, –εων, αἱ   Sardis, capital of Lydia, where Persian luxury goods were available. A note of conde-
                       scension can be detected in "You've never gone to Sardis."

ἔγνωc ἄν   "You would've known . . ." (ἄν with past potential indic., often with 2nd person:
                       S #1784a)

νῦν δέ   but as it is

οὗτοι . . . γε   "indeed, *now* I do not"; the particle οὗτοι "does little more than add force to the
                       negation": *GP* 543.

Μόρυχοc, ὁ   Morychus, who perhaps had a bag packed with good food (cf. 506)

cάγμα, –ατοc, τό   (< cάττω, pack + –μα, –ματοc, suffix denoting result of action: S #841.2) covering; cov-
                       ering of a shield; a large cloak; pack, bag

LINE 1143

Ἐκβάτανα, τά   Ecbatana, capital of Media (cf. 12)

ὑφαίνω   (< ὑφή, web + –αινω, suffix for *denominative* verb: S #866.7) weave; (mid.) weave one-
                       self (a cloak)

κρόκη, ἡ   woolen thread

χόλιξ, –ικοc, ἡ   guts of oxen; sausage. Apparently the tassels hanging from the cloak, or the amount of
                       wool stuffed into it, remind him of sausages.

Βδ. πόθεν, ὦγάθ'; ἀλλὰ τοῦτο τοῖσι βαρβάροις   1145
      ὑφαίνεται πολλαῖς δαπάναις. αὕτη γέ τοι
      ἐρίων τάλαντον καταπέπωκε ῥᾳδίως.
Φι. οὔκουν ἐριώλην δῆτ' ἐχρῆν αὐτὴν καλεῖν
      δικαιότερον ἢ καυνάκην;
Βδ.   ἔχ', ὦγαθέ,
      καὶ στῆθ' ἀναμπισχόμενος.
Φι.   οἴμοι δείλαιος·   1150
      ὡς θερμὸν ἡ μιαρά τί μου κατήρυγεν.

LINE 1145

πόθεν	Whence? = How can it be? = "Nonsense"
βάρβαρος, ὁ	βαρβάροις could be a] dat. of advantage, woven "for" the barbarians or b] (less likely but possible) dat. of personal agent; though normally only used with perf. and pluperf., in other tenses dat. can be used as agent when "the person is treated as a thing in order to express scorn": S #1492.
δαπάνη, ἡ	(< δάπτω, devour) expense, cost (dat. of circumstance: S #1527)
αὕτη	that is, the χλαῖνα
γέ τοι	"I tell you this because . . ."; giving a reason for accepting a proposition: *GP* 550; a livelier form of γοῦν, cf. 912
ἔριον, τό	wool (often in pl., ἔρια); cf. 701
κατα-πίνω, -πέπωκα	drink down; consume (the subject αὕτη = the χλαῖνα)

LINE 1148

οὔκουν . . . ἐχρῆν	"Wouldn't it have been more accurate . . .?" (οὔκουν in excited quests.; cf. 47)
ἐριώλη, ἡ	whirlwind, hurricane (Ar. sees a pun on ἔριον, wool, and ὀλλύναι, consume, ruin)
δῆτα	"to call it a *wool-ruiner* instead of . . .?"; emphatic, in quests.: *GP* 272
ἔχε	"keep still"; "hold still"
ἵστημι, aor.² ἔστην	(> aor. impv. 2 sing. στῆθι) stand; stand still (aor.² is intrans.)
ἀν-αμπ-ισχόμενος	"while being dressed up," "being redressed"; a verb not otherwise attested, but it could be a ptcp. from a] ἀμπ-έχω, aor.² ἤμπισχον, surround; (mid.) put around oneself, wear; or b] ἀμπ-ίσχω, the redupl. pres. of ἔχω.
ὡς (3)	exclam.
θερμός	hot, warm (cf. 331)
κατ-ερεύγω, aor.² -ήρυγον	belch, internal acc. θέρμον onto gen. μου (cf. 913)

Βδ.	οὐκ ἀναβαλεῖ;	
Φι.	μὰ Δί’ οὐκ ἔγωγ’.	
Βδ.	ἀλλ’, ὦγαθέ—	
	Φι. εἴπερ γ’ ἀνάγκη, κρίβανόν μ’ ἀμπίσχετε.	
Βδ.	φέρ’, ἀλλ’ ἐγώ σε περιβάλω·	
Φι.	σὺ δ’ οὖν ἴθι.	
	παράθου γε μέντοι καὶ κρεάγραν.	
Βδ.	τιὴ τί δή;	1155
Φι.	ἵν’ ἐξέλῃς με πρὶν διερρυηκέναι.	
Βδ.	ἄγε νυν ὑπολύου τὰς καταράτους ἐμβάδας,	
	τασδὶ δ’ ἀνύσας ὑποδοῦ σὺ τὰς Λακωνικάς.	

LINE 1152

ἀνάγκη, ἡ	necessity (sc. ἐστί) + inf.
κρίβανος, ὁ	oven, baking pot. The clothes make Phil. as hot as if he were being baked.
φέρε	"Well, come on . . ."; introduces an aor. subjv. (cf. 54)
ἀλλά	"Well, let *me* put it on . . ."; speaker offers alternative suggestion: *GP* 9.
περι-βάλλω, aor.² -έβαλον	
	put around (distinguish aor. subjv. περιβάλω from fut. indic. περιβαλῶ)
σύ	spoken to the slave, who takes away the τρίβων
δ’ οὖν	"You can go . . ."; permissive, with ἴθι (cf. 6, 764)

LINE 1155

παρα-τίθημι, aor.² -έθηκα	
	put nearby
γε μέντοι	"But <u>all the same</u>, if you must, at least . . ."; adversative: *GP* 413
κρεάγρα, ἡ	(< κρέας, meat + ἀγρέω, seize) meat hook. If Phil. is going to be baked like meat, there should at least be a utensil on hand to pull him out of the oven. {> pan*creas*, *creatine*}
τιή "	Why!?" (cf. 786), redundant with τί δή
ἐξ-αιρέω aor.² -εῖλον	take out, remove
δια-ρρέω, perf. -ρρύηκα	
	flow through; waste away, cook away {> *diarrhea*, *rhythm*, *hemorrhoid*}
ὑπο-λύω	loose; (mid.) untie
κατάρᾶτος, -ον	(< καταράομαι, call curses down upon, cf. 614) accursed
Λακωνική, ἡ	Spartan shoe; evidently a type of shoe superior to the ἐμβάδες he was wearing; note another –ικός adj.

Φι.   ἐγὼ γὰρ ἂν τλαίην ὑποδήϲαϲθαί ποτε
        ἐχθρῶν παρ' ἀνδρῶν δυϲμενῆ καττύματα;   1160

Βδ.   ἔνθεϲ ποτ', ὦ τᾶν, κἀπόβαιν' ἐρρωμένωϲ
        εἰϲ τὴν Λακωνικὴν ἀνύϲαϲ.

Φι.   ἀδικεῖϲ γέ με
        εἰϲ τὴν πολεμίαν ἀποβιβάζων τὸν πόδα.

Βδ.   φέρε, καὶ τὸν ἕτερον.

Φι.   μηδαμῶϲ τοῦτόν γ', ἐπεὶ
        πάνυ μιϲολάκων αὐτοῦ 'ϲτιν εἷϲ τῶν δακτύλων.   1165

Βδ.   οὐκ ἔϲτι παρὰ ταῦτ' ἄλλα.

Φι.   κακοδαίμων ἐγώ,
        ὅϲτιϲ ἐπὶ γήρᾳ χίμετλον οὐδὲν λήψομαι.

LINE 1159

γάρ   "What!? Could I bear to . . .?"; an answer in the form of a quest., with dissentient
               tone: *GP* 77–78

τλάω, aor.² ἔτλην   dare; endure, bear (+ ἄν, potential opt.)

ὑπο-δέω, -έδησα   bind under; (mid.) fasten under feet

δυσμενής, –ές   (adj. < δυσ-, bad, cf. 106 + μένος, force) full of ill will, hostile

κάττῠμα, –ατος, τό (< καττύω, stitch) anything stitched of leather; shoe sole. This may be a parody of
                    a tragic line; only in high style does Ar. place a prep. between adj. and noun, notes
                    Starkie.

ἐν-τίθημι   (> aor. act. impv. 2 sing. ἔνθες) put in, insert

ὦ τᾶν   my good friend (cf. 373)

ἀπο-βαίνω   step off; push foot down

ἐρρωμένως   forcefully, firmly (cf. 230)

LINE 1162

πολέμιος (3)   of the enemy

ἀπο-βιβάζω   (< βιβα- < βαίνω + -αζω, *causative* verb suffix: S #866.6) make to get off, disembark;
               <u>cause to step</u>. Phil. fears that being made to step into an "enemy" shoe is like making
               him set foot into enemy territory (*ellipsis* of γῆν); translators pun on "sole" and
               "soil."

LINE 1164

μηδαμῶς   μή often goes with prohib. subjv., though here with *ellipsis* of verb, e.g., "Don't <put
               on> this one!"

μῑσολάκων, –ωνος, ὁ
               (< μῑσέω, hate + Λάκων, Laconian) Spartan-hater, anti-Spartan

οὐκ ἔστι παρὰ ταῦτ' ἄλλα
               "there is no other way but this" (παρά + acc. = compared with)

γῆρας, γήρως, τό   old age, + ἐπί, in addition to (cf. 277)

χίμετλον, τό   (< χεῖμα, winter; cf. 445) chilblain, corn. Phil. comically regrets the comfort that the
               new shoes will bring, preferring to suffer with his Athenian ἐμβάδες.

Βδ.	ἄνυςόν ποθ' ὑποδηςάμενοc· εἶτα πλουςίωc
	ὡδὶ προβὰc τρυφερόν τι διαcαλακώνιcον.
Φι.	ἰδού. θεῶ τὸ cχῆμα, καὶ cκέψαι μ' ὅτῳ	1170
	μάλιcτ' ἔοικα τὴν βάδιcιν τῶν πλουςίων.
Βδ.	ὅτῳ; δοθιῆνι cκόροδον ἠμφιεcμένῳ.
Φι.	καὶ μὴν προθυμοῦμαί γε cαυλοπρωκτιᾶν.

LINE 1168

ἀνύω, ἤνυσα	accomplish, make haste; (+ ptcp.) "hurry up and . . ." (elsewhere in *W.*, e.g., 1158 above, Ar. uses the ptcp. ἀνύσας; cf. 30)
ὑποδέομαι	put on (cf. 1159)
ὡδί	in this way (cf. 688)
προ-βαίνω, aor.² προὔβην	
	step forward
τρυφερός (3)	delicate; (adv. acc.) effeminately, voluptuously (cf. 551)
δια-σαλακωνίζω	(> 2 sing. aor. impv. διασαλακώνισον < σαλάκων, pretentious < σάλος, turbulent motion of sea) swagger (with pun on Λάκων)
ἰδοῦ	"There!" (cf. 805)
θεάομαι	(> pres. impv. 2 sing. θεῶ) watch (cf. 59)
σκέψαι	consider (cf. 610)
σχῆμα, –ατος, τό	bearing, gait (cf. 1070)
ὅτῳ	"To whom am I similar?" (ὅστις introduces ind. quest., though here ὅτῳ = τίνι of dir. quest.; cf. on ὅπως, 48)
βάδισις, –εως, ἡ	(< βαδίζω, walk; cf. 180) walking gait (acc. respect)
πλούσιος (3)	wealthy (part. gen. with ὅτῳ; cf. 575 and adv. πλουσίως in 1168)

LINE 1172

δοθιήν, –ῆνος, ὁ	small abscess, boil
σκόροδον, τό	garlic, thought to have therapeutic qualities
ἀμφι-έννῡμι, perf. mid./pass. ἠμφίεσμαι	
	clothe, dress dat. with acc.; put acc. on dat. (dat. ἠμφιεσμένῳ evidently agrees with ὅτῳ, not with δοθιῆνι). Some compound vbs. form their perf. redupl. at beginning of the prep., thus ἠμφ-, where initial ἀ- is lengthened: S #442a. Bdel. seems to be saying that Phil. walks like someone whose foot has an abscess, although it has been treated (cf. 408).
καὶ μήν	"Actually, what I really want to do is . . ."; *adversative: GP 357*
προ-θῡμέομαι	be eager to
σαυλοπρωκτιάω	(< σαῦλος, of swaggering gait + πρωκτός, rump) waggle the bottom

Βδ.	ἄγε νυν, ἐπιστήcει λόγουc cεμνοὺc λέγειν	
	ἀνδρῶν παρόντων πολυμαθῶν καὶ δεξιῶν;	1175
Φι.	ἔγωγε.	
Βδ.	τίνα δῆτ' ἂν λέγοιc;	
Φι.	πολλοὺc πάνυ.	
	πρῶτον μὲν ὡc ἡ Λάμι' ἁλοῦc' ἐπέρδετο,	
	ἔπειτα δ' ὡc ὁ Καρδοπίων τὴν μητέρα—	
Βδ.	μὴ 'μοιγε μύθουc, ἀλλὰ τῶν ἀνθρωπίνων,	
	οἵουc λέγομεν μάλιcτα, τοὺc κατ' οἰκίαν.	1180
Φι.	ἐγῷδα τοίνυν τῶν γε πάνυ κατ' οἰκίαν	
	ἐκεῖνον ὡc "οὕτω ποτ' ἦν μῦc καὶ γαλῆ—"	
Βδ.	ὦ cκαιὲ κἀπαίδευτε—Θεογένηc ἔφη	
	τῷ κοπρολόγῳ, καὶ ταῦτα λοιδορούμενοc—	
	μῦc καὶ γαλᾶc μέλλειc λέγειν ἐν ἀνδράcιν;	1185

1174–1207: With Phil.'s apparel set, Bdel. now tries to teach him how to converse with upper-class dinner companions. Unfortunately, many topics of conversation presuppose experiences that Phil. has never had, such as participation in Olympic games or embassies.

LINE 1174

πολυμαθής, -ές	knowing much, cultivated {> *polymath*}
τίνα	sc. λόγον
Λαμία, ἡ	cf. 1035
Καρδοπίων, ὁ	Kardopion. An unknown character of folkore or fable, the name perhaps < κάρδοποc, kneading trough. The verb is lost when Phil. is interrupted.
μήτηρ, μητρός, ἡ	mother

LINE 1179

μή	sc. λέγε or εἴπῃς
μῦθος, ὁ	tale, fable (cf. 566)
ἀνθρώπινος (3)	(< ἄνθρωπος + -ινος, suffix forming *denominative* adj. of material: S #858.12) human, of human beings. Stories about real people are contrasted with μῦθοι about gods and heroes.
ἐγῷδα	= ἐγὼ + οἶδα. Bdel. is thinking of stories we *tell* at home, κατ' οἰκίαν, but Phil. takes it to mean stories about things that *happen* at home.
τοίνυν	"All right, then . . .'"; responding, repeating previous speaker: *GP* 571
γε	"Yes—*at home*"; in assent, echoes words of previous speaker (κατ' οἰκίαν): *GP* 136
οὕτω ποτ' ἦν	traditional way of introducing fables, "Once upon a time . . ."
μῦς, μυός, ὁ	(> acc. pl. μῦς) mouse (cf. 140)
γαλῆ, ἡ	ferret (cf. 363)
σκαιός (3)	clumsy, "lout," "oaf" (cf. 1013)
ἀπαίδευτος, -ον	(< ἀ- priv. + παιδεύω, teach) uneducated (two-ending verbal adj. has accent on antepenult: S #425c)
Θεογένης, -ους, ὁ	Theogenes, "God-born"; a politician; a boorish boaster who had no business criticizing anyone else
κοπρολόγος, ὁ	(< κόπρος, excrement + λέγω, gather, LSJ B.I) dung-collector [> Eng. *coprolite*, fossilized dung]
καὶ ταῦτα	"and at that" (cf. 252)
λοιδορέω	abuse, revile; (mid.) rail at, be rude to (+ dat.)

Φι.   ποίουϲ τινὰϲ δὲ χρὴ λέγειν;

Βδ.   μεγαλοπρεπεῖϲ,

ὡϲ ξυνεθεώρειϲ Ἀνδροκλεῖ καὶ Κλειϲθένει.

Φι.   ἐγὼ δὲ τεθεώρηκα πώποτ' οὐδαμοῖ,

πλὴν εἰϲ Πάρον, καὶ ταῦτα δύ' ὀβολὼ φέρων.

Βδ.   ἀλλ' οὖν λέγειν χρή ϲ' ὡϲ ἐμάχετό γ' αὐτίκα   1190

Ἐφουδίων παγκράτιον Ἀϲκώνδᾳ καλῶϲ,

ἤδη γέρων ὢν καὶ πολιόϲ, ἔχων δέ τοι

πλευρὰν βαθυτάτην χἠρακλείαν λαγόνα καὶ

θώρακ' ἄριϲτον.

Φι.   παῦε παῦ', οὐδὲν λέγειϲ.

πῶϲ ἂν μαχέϲαιτο παγκράτιον θώρακ' ἔχων;   1195

LINE 1186

μεγαλοπρεπής, -ές (< μέγας, big + πρέπει, be fitting) befitting a great man; impressive

ξυν-θεωρέω, perf. τεθεώρηκα

 (< ξυν + θέα, sight) go on an embassy together (+ dat.). A θεωρός is an envoy who travels to see something; often this referred to an ambassador sent on a mission to consult an oracle (cf. 1005).

Ἀνδροκλῆς, -ους, ὁ Androcles, democratic politician, assassinated by oligarchs in 411

Κλειϲθένης, -ους, ὁ Cleisthenes, ridiculed in comedy as effeminate

οὐδαμοῖ to nowhere (suffix –οι is strictly speaking locative, "*in* no place": S #342, but advs. of rest are found with vbs. of motion, notes Graves)

Πάρος, ἡ Paros, Aegean island (islands are fem.: S# 199b)

φέρω earn (LSJ A.IV.5). Two obols were probably the wage for a rower in a trireme; the closest Phil. ever came to an ambassador was to row his ship.

LINE 1190

ἀλλ' οὖν ... γε "Well, in that case, at least, you should . . ."; rejecting a suggestion and introducing a second-best suggestion: MacD., *GP* 442

αὐτίκα right away; <u>for example</u>

παγκράτιον, τό (< πᾶν + κράτος, power) pancration, a violent wrestling match in which punching, kicking, and choking, but not biting or eye-gouging, were allowed

Ἐφουδίων, ὁ Ephudion, said to be an athlete who won the pancration at the Olympics in 464 BC

Ἀϲκώνδας, -ου, ὁ Askondas, evidently Ephudion's younger competitor

βαθύτατος (3) (superl. of βαθύς; cf. 216) deepest; massive

Ἡράκλειος (3) Heraclean

λαγών, -όνος, ἡ (< λαγαρός, hollow; cf. 674) the hollow below the ribs, flank

θώραξ, -ᾱκος, ὁ torso, abdomen; breastplate. Bdel. means "chest," but Phil., thinking he means "breastplate," is confused: how could anyone wrestle wearing armor?

Βδ. οὕτω διηγεῖϲθαι νομίζουϲ' οἱ ϲοφοί.
     ἀλλ' ἕτερον εἰπέ μοι· παρ' ἀνδράϲι ξένοιϲ
     πίνων ϲεαυτοῦ ποῖον ἂν λέξαι δοκεῖϲ
     ἐπὶ νεότητοϲ ἔργον ἀνδρικώτατον;
Φι. ἐκεῖν' ἐκεῖν' ἀνδρειότατόν γε τῶν ἐμῶν,   1200
     ὅτ' Ἐργαϲίωνοϲ τὰϲ χάρακαϲ ὑφειλόμην.
Βδ. ἀπολεῖϲ με. ποίαϲ χάρακαϲ; ἀλλ' ὡϲ ἢ κάπρον
     ἐδιώκαθέϲ ποτ' ἢ λαγών, ἢ λαμπάδα
     ἔδραμεϲ, ἀνευρὼν ὅ τι νεανικώτατον.
Φι. ἐγᾦδα τοίνυν τό γε νεανικώτατον·   1205
     ὅτε τὸν δρομέα Φάϋλλον ὢν βούπαιϲ ἔτι
     εἷλον διώκων λοιδορίαϲ ψήφοιν δυοῖν.

LINE 1196

διηγέομαι	(διά, through + ἡγέομαι, lead, cf. 269) set out in detail; <u>recount, tell stories</u>
νεότηϲ, –ητοϲ, ὁ	youth (+ ἐπί = "in the time of [your] youth")
ἀνδρικώτατοϲ	(3) most manly, courageous (cf. 153, 1077). Bdel. uses this superl. of a trendy, recently formed –ικόϲ adj. and is "corrected" in the subsequent line by Phil., who uses the less fashionable synonym ἀνδρειότατοϲ: *LA* 140–41.
Ἐργαϲίων, –ωνοϲ, ὁ	(< ἐργάζω, work: "Workman") Ergasion; prob. a fictional name
χάραξ, –ακοϲ, ὁ, ἡ	(< χαράϲϲω, make pointed) vine-prop

LINE 1202

ποῖοϲ (3)	used in repeating the words of a previous speaker, to express scornful surprise (LSJ I.2): "Vine-props indeed!"
ὥϲ	sc. λέγε or εἰπέ
κάπροϲ, ὁ	boar
διώκω, aor.² ἐδιώκαθον	chase (this aor. is formed by adding -θ- to the pres. stem, though whether this is aor.² or imperfect is unclear: S #490A). Hunting was at least more respectable than stealing vine-props.
λαγῶϲ, –ώ, ὁ	hare
λαμπάϲ, –άδοϲ, ἡ	torch; torch-race (λαμπάδα is internal acc. with ἔδραμεϲ: S #1576)
ἀν-ευρίϲκω, aor.² -ηῦρον	find out; <u>think up</u>
τοίνυν	responding, repeating words of previous speaker: *GP* 571 (cf. 1181)

LINE 1206

δρομεύϲ, –εωϲ, ὁ	(< δρόμοϲ, race course + –ευϲ, suffix denoting agency: S #839a5) runner
Φάϋλλοϲ	Phaullus, a well-known athlete of the earlier fifth century. Phil. slips from the athletic, εἷλον διώκων, "Pursuing, I caught up with him," to the legal, "Prosecuting, I convicted him."
βούπαιϲ, –αιδοϲ, ὁ	(< βοῦϲ, bull + παῖϲ) youth, lad; "boy as strong as an ox"
λοιδορία, ἡ	abuse; slander, defamation (gen. of charge: S #1375)
ψήφοιν δυοῖν	two votes (dat. of degree of difference: S #1513)

Βδ.   παῦ'· ἀλλὰ δευρὶ κατακλινεὶς προςμάνθανε
                ξυμποτικὸς εἶναι καὶ ξυνουςιαςτικός.

Φι.   πῶς οὖν κατακλινῶ; φράζ' ἀνύςας.

Βδ.   εὐςχημόνως.   1210

Φι.   ὡδὶ κελεύεις κατακλινῆναι;

Βδ.   μηδαμῶς.

Φι.   πῶς δαί;

Βδ.   τὰ γόνατ' ἔκτεινε, καὶ γυμναςτικῶς
                ὑγρὸν χύτλαςον ςεαυτὸν ἐν τοῖς ςτρώμαςιν.

1208–64: Bdel. now tries to teach Phil. how to recline and dine at a symposium. They talk about songs to sing at dinner; Bdel. recommends the telling of Aesopic fables.

LINE 1208

κατα-κλίνω, aor.² κατεκλίνην
    (aor. act. ptcp. κατακλῖνείς; note accent on ultima: S #425) lay; (pass.) lie, recline. Symposiasts would recline on couches (κλίναι). κατακλῖνῶ at 1210 is surely aor. pass. subjv. though in form is identical to fut. act. indic.; κατακλινῆναι at 1211 is aor. pass. inf.

προσ-μανθάνω   learn besides, learn something new

ξυμποτικός (3)   symposiastic, suited to a ξυμπόσιον. More –ικός adjs.

ξυνουσιαστικός (3)   (< ξυν + ουσία, being together, socializing) sociable, convivial

εὐσχημόνως   (adv. < εὐ + σχῆμα, appearance) gracefully, elegantly

LINE 1212

δαί   "If not that, *how*, then?"; colloquial δή, after interrog.: *GP* 263; after rejection of a suggestion: MacD.

γόνυ, –ατος, τό   knee (cf. 910)

ἐκ-τείνω   (< τείνω, stretch, cf. 337) stretch out

γυμναστικώς   (adv. < γύμνος, naked + –ικος) athletically, with control and poise

ὑγρός (3)   wet; (adv. acc.) in a fluid way, lithely, flexibly (cf. 678)

χυτλάζω, ἐχύτλασα   (< χύτλον, liquid < χέω, pour) pour out; throw down

στρῶμα, –ατος, τό   (< στόρνῡμι, spread + –μα, –ματος, suffix denoting result of action: S #841.2) anything spread out, coverlets, rugs to be spread over the κλῖναι

ἔπειτ' ἐπαίνεσόν τι τῶν χαλκωμάτων,
ὀροφὴν θέασαι, κρεκάδι' αὐλῆς θαύμασον·   1215
ὕδωρ κατὰ χειρός· τὰς τραπέζας εἰσφέρειν·
δειπνοῦμεν· ἀπονενίμμεθ'· ἤδη σπένδομεν.

Φι.   πρὸς τῶν θεῶν, ἐνύπνιον ἐστιώμεθα;
Βδ.   αὐλητρὶς ἐνεφύσησεν· οἱ δὲ συμπόται
εἰσὶν Θέωρος, Αἰσχίνης, Φᾶνος, Κλέων,   1220
ξένος τις ἕτερος πρὸς κεφαλῆς, Ἀκέστορος.
τούτοις ξυνὼν τὰ σκόλι' ὅπως δέξει καλῶς.

LINE 1214

ἐπ-αινέω, -ῄνεσα	approve, praise. The prefix ἐπί perhaps intensifies αἰνέω, "speak," "approve," though in truth uncompounded αἰνέω was not used in Attic, and the force of the prefix was probably not felt.
χάλκωμα, –ατος, τό	(< χαλκός, copper or bronze + the –μα suffix) something made of bronze, e.g., goblets, jugs
ὀροφή, ἡ	(< ἐρέφω, roof over) ceiling
θεάομαι, ἐθεᾱσάμην	(> aor. act. impv. 2 sing. θέᾱσαι; cf. 54) view, gaze at
θαυμάζω, ἐθαύμασα	marvel at (cf. 13)
κρεκάδια, –ων, τά	(< κρέκω, weave) tapestry, curtain. A *hapax* in Greek, and earliest evidence for tapestries.
αὐλή, ἡ	hall, court (cf. 131)
τράπεζα, ἡ	(< τετρα- , four, cf. 553 + πέζος, on foot) table. Yet Sihler #389.3b suggests that the word "table" was formed before four-legged tables were invented, and tripods are attested earliest in IE.
δειπνέω	make a meal, dine. Short phrases describe the course of this imaginary rehearsal banquet.
ἀπονίζω, perf. mid./pass. ἀπονένιμμαι	
	wash off (after dinner, cf. 608); the "water for the hands" at 1216 was for washing before dinner.
σπένδω	pour libations (cf. 1046)

LINE 1218

ἐνύπνιον, τό	dream; prob. adv. acc., "as if in a dream" (cf. 25)
ἑστιάω	(< ἑστία, hearth of house) receive at hearth; entertain, dine on
αὐλητρίς, –ίδος, ἡ	(< αὐλός, flute + –τρις, suffix denoting fem. agent: S #839b1) girl who plays the *aulos* (for which cf. 1477)
ἐμ-φῡσάω, -έφῡσα	blow in, play
Θέωρος, ὁ	Theorus (cf. 42). The men named here were members of high society; all seem to have been historical individuals.
Αἰσχίνης, ὁ	Aeschines (cf. 459)
Φᾶνος, ὁ	Phanus, an associate of Cleon
Κλέων, ὁ	Cleon (cf. 62)
ἐπὶ κεφαλῆς	at the head (of the table)
Ἀκέστωρ, –ορος, ὁ	Ἀκέστορος = ὁ Ἀκέστορος, the son of the foreign-born Athenian dramatist Akestor
σκόλιον, τό	drinking song. A *skolion* was a short song that would be sung at symposia. One symposiast would sing a verse or two and pass it along to the man seated next to him. {> *scoliosis*} [< σκέλος, leg < IE *skel, bend, crooked (were songs presented in irregular order?)]
ὅπως	+ fut. indic. (cf. 289)
δέχομαι, δέξομαι	receive, take up (a song)

Φι.   ἄληθες; ὡς οὐδείς γε Διακρίων ἐγώ.
Βδ.   τάχ᾽ εἴσομαι· καὶ δὴ γάρ εἰμ᾽ ἐγὼ Κλέων,
        ᾄδω δὲ πρῶτος Ἁρμοδίου, δέξει δὲ σύ.   1225
        "οὐδεὶς πώποτ᾽ ἀνὴρ ἔγεντ᾽ Ἀθήναις—"
Φι.   —οὐχ οὕτω γε πανοῦργος ⟨οὐδὲ⟩ κλέπτης.
Βδ.   τουτὶ σὺ δράσεις; παραπολεῖ βοώμενος·
        φήσει γὰρ ἐξολεῖν σε καὶ διαφθερεῖν
        κἀκ τῆσδε τῆς γῆς ἐξελᾶν.
Φι.   ἐγὼ δέ γε,   1230
        ἐὰν ἀπειλῇ, νὴ Δί᾽ ἑτέραν ᾄσομαι·

LINE 1223

ἀλήθης, -ες	true; ἄληθες (ironical, with accent on antepenult: S #292a): "Oh, *really*."
ὡς οὐδείς γε	"Like no one"; "I'll take it up better than any of the Diacrians."
Διάκριος (3)	someone from Diacria, the foothill district northeast of Athens
καὶ δή	"Suppose so-and-so happens"; of an imaginary realization: *GP* 253 (cf. 492). Bdel. pretends to be Cleon for a moment.
Ἁρμόδιος, ὁ	In 514 BC Harmodius helped assassinate Hipparchus, the brother of the tyrant Hippias, and became a hero of the early democracy. (sc. μέλος as object of verb ᾄδω, though some edd. see a part. gen., "sing something from Harmodius")

1226–27: Meter: These two lines are in "phalaecians" ($\times \times - \cup \cup - \cup - \cup - -$), a meter used by Sappho, Alcaeus, and other skolia.

LINE 1226

ἔγεντ᾽	= ἐγένετο, poetic *syncope*
Ἀθήναις	at Athens (dat. of place: S #1531; the spelling -αις was replacing Ἀθήνησι: *LA* 241 n. 50; Starkie, however, sees not locative but dat. of interest, "born to Athens")
γε	a second speaker interrupts and finishes the speech of a first: *GP* 137.
πανοῦργος, -ον (3)	(< πᾶν, all + ἔργον, deed) "someone who will do anything," a scoundrel
κλέπτης, -ου, ὁ	thief. Phil. is now ready to attack Cleon.

LINE 1228

παρ-απόλλῡμι, -απολῶ	
	(παρά suggests "amiss," "wrongly": S #1692.4 + ἀπόλλῡμι, perish) destroy, waste; (mid.) perish to no purpose
βοάω	shout at; (pass.) be shouted at. Shouting was a feature of Cleon's oratory. Some editors suggest mid., "as you shout out."
ἐξ-όλλῡμι, -ολῶ	destroy utterly
ἐξ-ελαύνω, -ελῶ	drive out, expel
ἀπειλέω	threaten (here a subjv. in FMV condit.: S #2323; not a compound verb, cf. 670)
ᾄδω, ᾄσομαι	sing (with its object ἑτέραν sc. ᾠδήν)

1232–35: Meter: A glyconic ($\times \times - \cup \cup - \cup -$) that has been expanded to $\times \times - \smile\smile - \smile\smile - \smile\smile - \cup -$, a fourteen-syllable meter found in Alcaeus.

        "ὤνθρωφ᾽, οὗτος ὁ μαιόμενος τὸ μέγα κράτος,

        ἀντρέψεις ἔτι τὰν πόλιν· ἁ δ᾽ ἔχεται ῥοπᾶς."   1235

Βδ.   τί δ᾽ ὅταν Θέωρος πρὸς ποδῶν κατακείμενος

        ᾄδῃ Κλέωνος λαβόμενος τῆς δεξιᾶς·

        "Ἀδμήτου λόγον, ὦταῖρε, μαθὼν τοὺς ἀγαθοὺς φίλει."

        τούτῳ τί λέξεις σκόλιον;

Φι.   ᾠδί πως ἐγώ.   1240

        "οὐκ ἔστιν ἀλωπεκίζειν,

        οὐδ᾽ ἀμφοτέροισι γίγνεσθαι φίλον."

Βδ.   μετὰ τοῦτον Αἰσχίνης ὁ Σέλλου δέξεται,

        ἀνὴρ σοφὸς καὶ μουσικός, κᾆτ᾽ ᾄσεται·

LINE 1234

ὤνθρωφ᾽	= ὦ ἄνθρωπε (*crasis* of ὦ + ἀνθ-; *elision* of final -ε before aspirated οὗτος). This line is adapted from Alcaeus (fr. 141 LP), likely an attack on the tyrant Pittacus; originally written in Aeolic, Ar. has largely converted it into Attic.
μαίομαι	strive for, pursue
κράτος, –ους, τό	power, authority (cf. 58)
ἀν-τρέπω, -τρέψω	overturn (ἀν- for ἀνά by *syncope*, the loss of vowel between consonants: S #44b)
τάν	= τήν (Aeolic alpha for Attic/Ionic eta); similarly ἁ = ἡ
ῥοπή, ἡ	(< ῥέπω, turn the scale, sink) the sinking of the scale, <u>the critical moment</u> (part. gen. with ἔχομαι, "cling to," "be close to," a verb of touching: S #1345)

LINE 1236

Θέωρος, ὁ	cf. 42
κατά-κειμαι	recline. Theorus is imagined as being seated at either Cleon's or Phil.'s feet. (cf. 213)

LINE 1238

1238–39: Meter: Greater Aesclepiad ($- - - \smile\smile - - \smile\smile - - \smile\smile - \smile -$), the meter of Sappho's second book. Parker notes that Bdel.'s taste in lyric poetry is highly conservative.

δεξιά, ἡ	right hand (another gen. with verb of touching), cf. 65
Ἄδμητος, ὁ	Admetus, king of Thessaly and husband of Alcestis. This *skolion* was said to have been composed by Praxilla. As the story (λόγος) goes, Alcestis was saved from death by Heracles, Admetus's noble (ἀγαθός) friend; the story is told in Euripides's *Alcestis*.
ἑταῖρος, ὁ	comrade, friend
ᾠδί πως	"in some such way as this"; though other editors read ᾠδικῶς, "lyrically"

LINE 1241

1241–42: Meter: An Aeolic meter ($- - \smile\smile - \smile - -$, a "hagesichorean") with an added $- \smile -$ in 1242, verses found in lyric or tragedy rather than skolia.

ἀλωπεκίζω	(< ἀλώπηξ, fox + -ιζω suffix: S #866.6) play the fox. These two lines apparently quote a lyric poem {> *alopecia* (loss of hair, like mange on a fox)}
ἀμφότερος (3)	both (cf. 920)
Σέλλος, ὁ	Sellus, here father of Aischines (but cf. 325 and 459)
μουσικός (3)	(Μοῦσα + -ικος suffix) skilled in music; cultured.

"χρήματα καὶ βίον 1245
Κλειταγόρᾳ τε κἀμοὶ μετὰ Θετταλῶν—"
Φι.   —πολλὰ δὴ διεκόμπασας σὺ κἀγώ.
Βδ.   τουτὶ μὲν ἐπιεικῶς σύ γ' ἐξεπίστασαι·
ὅπως δ' ἐπὶ δεῖπνον εἰς Φιλοκτήμονος ἵμεν— 1250
παῖ παῖ, τὸ δεῖπνον, Χρῦσε, συσκεύαζε νῷν,
—ἵνα καὶ μεθυσθῶμεν διὰ χρόνου.
Φι.   μηδαμῶς.
κακὸν τὸ πίνειν· ἀπὸ γὰρ οἴνου γίγνεται
καὶ θυροκοπῆσαι καὶ πατάξαι καὶ βαλεῖν,
κἄπειτ' ἀποτίνειν ἀργύριον ἐκ κραιπάλης. 1255

1245–48: Meter: Dodrans: – ◡ ◡ – ◡ (1245–47), phalaecian (cf. 1226 above).

LINE 1245

Κλειταγόρα, ἡ	(< κλειτός, famous + ἀγορά, assembly) *Kleitagora* was the title of a well-known *skolion*; Kl. herself may have been a poetess, priestess, or prostitute.
μετά	(+ gen.) with, among, amid
Θετταλοί, οἱ	Thessalians
δή	emphatic after adjs. of indef. quantity: GP 205
δια-κομπάζω, -εκόμπασα	(< διά, "often of rivalry": S #1685.3 + κόμπος, clash, boast) boast against one another

LINE 1249

ἐπιεικῶς	(adv.) fairly, reasonably well, respectably (cf. 1027)
ἐξ-επίσταμαι	know thoroughly
ὅπως	+ fut. indic. (cf. 289)
Φιλοκτήμων, –μονος, ὁ	(< φίλος + κτάομαι, acquire = "Lover of Possessions") Philoctemon, a (possibly) fictional rich man
Χρῦσος, ὁ	(< χρῦσός, gold) Chrysos, "Goldie"? (slave's name, perhaps given for blond hair)
συ-σκευάζω	(< σύν + σκεῦος, utensil) make ready, pack up (σύν before σ and a consonant becomes συ-: S #101a)
νῷν	(> 1 dual dat. pron.: S #325) we two
μεθύσκω, aor. pass. ἐμεθύσθην	(< μέθυ, wine) intoxicate, inebriate; (pass.) be drunk {> amethyst (protects owner from drunkenness), *methylene*}
διὰ χρόνου	after an interval, at last (used with intervals of time: S #1685c)

LINE 1254

θυροκοπέω	(< θύρα, door + κόπτω, strike) break down a door
πατάσσω, ἐπάταξα	beat, strike (the infs. πατάξαι καὶ βαλεῖν also at 1422; evidently a stock phrase)
ἀπο-τίνω, ἀπο-τείσω	pay (for 1263 below, mss. spell fut. ἀποτίσω, but fifth-century inscriptions have ἀποτείσω)
κραιπάλη, ἡ	hangover, drinking party. All of this will come to pass when Phil. drunkenly assaults passersby on the way home from the symposium and they demand recompense.

Βδ.   οὔκ, ἢν ξυνῇς γ᾽ ἀνδράσι καλοῖς τε κἀγαθοῖς.

ἢ γὰρ παρῃτήσαντο τὸν πεπονθότα,

ἢ λόγον ἔλεξας αὐτὸς ἀστεῖόν τινα,

Αἰσωπικὸν γέλοιον ἢ Συβαριτικόν,

ὧν ἔμαθες ἐν τῷ συμποσίῳ· κᾆτ᾽ εἰς γέλων   1260

τὸ πρᾶγμ᾽ ἔτρεψας, ὥστ᾽ ἀφείς σ᾽ ἀποίχεται.

Φι.   μαθητέον τἄρ᾽ ἐστὶ πολλοὺς τῶν λόγων,

εἴπερ ἀποτείσω μηδέν, ἤν τι δρῶ κακόν.

ἄγε νυν, ἴωμεν· μηδὲν ἡμᾶς ἰσχέτω.   1264

LINE 1256

ξυνῇς	(> pres. subjv. 2 sing. of ξύνειμι) be in company of
οἱ καλοί τε κἀγαθοί	the beautiful and well-born; (in a social sense) gentlemen, aristocrats
παρ-αιτέομαι	plead with; beg off, intercede with (akin to the *gnomic aorist*, used "in imaginary scenes and in descriptions of manners and customs"; it may be tr. as pres.: S #1932)
πάσχω, πέπονθα	suffer; ὁ πεπονθώς = the victim
ἀστεῖος (3)	(< ἄστυ, town + –ιος, adj. suffix: S #858) town-bred; urbane, witty {> L. *astutus* (practiced in town = clever) > E. *astute*}
Αἰσωπικός (3)	(< Αἴσωπος + –ικος suffix) Aesopic (cf. 566)
γέλοιος (3)	humorous, funny (cf. 57)
Συβαριτικός (3)	Sybaritic. Sybaris was a Greek colony in Southern Italy, destroyed in 510 BC. A type of fable was named after it.
γέλως, –ωτος, ὁ	(> acc. sing. γέλων, poetic alternative to γέλωτα; cf. 57) laughter
τρέπω	turn, direct toward; change
ἀφίημι	(> masc. sing. aor. act. ptcp. ἀφείς) release; acquit
ἀπ-οίχομαι	depart, be gone (subject is ὁ πεπονθώς)

LINE 1262

μαθητέον	verbal of μανθάνω: S #2149
τἄρ᾽	= τοι + ἄρα, "So, in that case, I'll have you know..." (cf. 299)
ἄγε νυν	"come now" (cf. 211)
ἴσχω	hold back, stop (redupl. form of ἔχω)

Χο. πολλάκις δὴ 'δοξ' ἐμαυτῷ
δεξιὸς πεφυκέναι καὶ σκαιὸς οὐδεπώποτε·
ἀλλ' Ἀμυνίας ὁ Σέλλου μᾶλλον, οὐκ τῶν Κρωβύλου,
οὗτος ὅν γ' ἐγώ ποτ' εἶδον
ἀντὶ μήλου καὶ ῥοᾶς δει-   1269
πνοῦντα μετὰ Λεωγόρου· πεινῇ γὰρ ἧπερ Ἀντιφῶν·
ἀλλά πρεσβεύων γὰρ εἰς Φάρσαλον ᾤχετ'·
εἶτ' ἐκεῖ μόνος μόνοις
τοῖς Πενέσταισι ξυνῆν τοῖς
Θετταλῶν, αὐτὸς πενέστης ὢν ἐλάττων οὐδενός.   1274

1265–91: The actors leave the stage and the chorus perform the "Second Parabasis"; they throw satirical barbs at Amynias, Autonomes's three sons (Arignotus, an unnamed actor, and Ariphrades), and Cleon.

1265–74: Meter: Trochees.

LINE 1265

πολλάκις	(adv. < πολλά + -ακις, suffix of time: S #344) often
'δοξ'	= ἔδοξα
φύω, πέφῦκα	be born, be by nature {> physics, physio-, neophyte}
σκαιός (3)	awkward, stupid (cf. 1013)
Ἀμῦνίας, ὁ	(cf. 74) It is unclear whether the chorus is saying that Amynias is more clever or more stupid, though a joke can work either way.
κρώβυλος, ὁ	a roll or curl of hair worn on crown of head. Presumably Amynias wore his hair like this (cf. κομηταμυνίας, 466); thus οἱ ἐκ τῶν Κρωβύλου are those "descended from the sons of Krobulos."
ὅς γε	"<u>because</u> he . . ."; γε has causal force following a rel. pron.: S #2826 (cf. 146)
μῆλον, τό	apple (cf. 1057). Evidently Leogoros offers richer fare than simple apples and pomegranates.
ῥόα, ἡ	(perhaps < ῥεῖν, flow, for the richness of its juice) pomegranate
δειπνέω	dine, with luxurious fare, instead of eating simple apples and pomegranates
Λεώγορος, ὁ	Leogoros, a wealthy Athenian, known for wealth and fine food
πεινάω	(> πεινῇ instead of the expected -ᾷ; -αε- can contract into η instead of ᾱ: S #641) be hungry
ἧπερ	in the same way (replacing the more common ὥσπερ, only here in W.: LA 264 n. 168)
Ἀντιφῶν, –φῶντος, ὁ	Antiphon; either the wealthy oligarch or a man ridiculed in Cratinus's Wine Flask of 423 BC. If the oligarch was meant, then "being hungry like Antiphon" means not being hungry at all.

LINE 1271

ἀλλὰ . . . γάρ	"But, more than that . . ."; contrasts what is irrelevant with what is vital: GP 101 (cf. 1114)
πρεσβεύω	be the eldest; serve as an ambassador (cf. 540)
Φάρσαλος, ὁ	Pharsalus, a chief city in Thessaly
οἴχομαι	(> imperfect 3 sing. ᾤχετο) went
πενέστης, –ου, ὁ	(< πένομαι, toil, cf. 192 + –της, suffix denoting agency: S #839.1) laborer, poor man. "Penestai" were a class of serfs in Thessaly. If Amynias was poor himself (πενέστης ὢν ἐλάττων οὐδενός), then he was a good choice as ambassador to the Penestai of Thessaly; μόνος μόνοις suggests they met privately.
ξύνειμι	(> imperfect 3 sing. ξυνῆν) be with

ὦ μακάρι' Αὐτόμενες, ὥς ϲε μακαρίζομεν.　　　　　　　　　[ϲτρ.
παῖδαϲ ἐφύτευϲαϲ ὅτι χειροτεχνικωτάτουϲ·
πρῶτα μὲν ἅπαϲι φίλον ἄνδρα τε ϲοφώτατον,
τὸν κιθαραοιδότατον, ᾧ χάριϲ ἐφέϲπετο·
τὸν δ' ὑποκριτὴν ἕτερον ἀργαλέον ὡϲ ϲοφόν·
εἶτ' Ἀριφράδη πολύ τι θυμοϲοφικώτατον,　　　　　　　　1280
ὅντινά ποτ' ὤμοϲε μαθόντα παρὰ μηδενόϲ
{ἀλλ' ἀπὸ ϲοφῆϲ φύϲεωϲ αὐτόματον ἐκμαθεῖν}
γλωττοποιεῖν εἰϲ τὰ πορνεῖ' εἰϲιόνθ' ἑκάϲτοτε.
< . . . >　　　　　　　　　　　　　　　　　　　　　[ἀντ.

LINE 1275

1275–91: Meter: Paeonic tetrameters ($- \smile\smile\smile - \smile\smile\smile - \smile\smile\smile - \smile -$) in the *epirrhema* (1275–82) and *antepirrhema* (1284–90) with trochaic tetrameters at 1283 and 1291.

Αὐτομένηϲ, –ου, ὁ	Automenes; unknown
ὡϲ	exclam.
μακαρίζω	deem blessed (cf. 428)
φυτεύω	beget (cf. 1133)
ὅτι	as ____ as possible (to strengthen a superl.: S #1086)
χειροτεχνικώτατοϲ (3)	
	(< χείρ, hand + τέχνη, skill + superl. suffix) most handicraft-able, "consummate artist"

LINE 1278

κιθαραοιδότατοϲ (3)	(< κίθαρα + ἀοίδοϲ, singer) singing to *kithara* (cf. 959). The musically talented son seems to be Arignotus.
ἐφ-έπω, aor.² -έϲπον	wield, apply; (mid.) attend, follow (+ dat.) (cf. 1087)
ὑποκριτήϲ, –οῦ, ὁ	(< ὑποκρίνομαι, answer) one who answers; <u>actor</u> (cf. 53)
ἀργαλέοϲ (3)	(< ἄλγοϲ, pain) troublesome, difficult; (sc. ἔϲτι) "[it's] difficult [to say] how . . ." By *dissimilation* λ becomes ρ when λ appears in the same word: S #129a.

LINE 1280

Ἀριφράδηϲ, –ουϲ, ὁ	(ἀρι-, intensifying prefix suggesting excellence + φραδήϲ, wise = "Very Wise") Ariphrades, ridiculed elsewhere for cunnilingus
θυμοϲοφικόϲ (3)	(< θυμόϲ, soul + ϲοφόϲ, wise + –ικοϲ) intrinsically talented, naturally inspired. Ariphrades was said to have been a student of the philosopher Anaxagoras.
ὄμνῡμι, ὤμοϲα	swear (sc. Αὐτομένηϲ as subject; ὤμοϲε governs acc. ὅντινα + inf. in ind. statement: S #2017; μαθόντα and εἰϲιόντα are circumstantial ptcps. in acc. agreeing with ὅντινα)
παρὰ μηδενόϲ	μή is the neg. after vbs. of swearing: S #2725
αὐτόματοϲ (3)	self-moving, on one's own (though many editors delete line 1282)
ἐκ-μανθάνω	(< ἐκ implying thoroughness: S #1688.2) learn by heart
γλωττοποιέω	(< γλῶττα + ποιέω) do it with the tongue; perform cunnilingus: *MM* p. 185
πορνεῖον, τό	(< πόρνη, prostitute + –ειον, suffix denoting place: S #851.1) brothel
εἰϲιόνθ'	= εἰϲιόντα (< εἴϲ-ειμι, enter)
ἑκάϲτοτε	(adv.) every time; regularly (cf. 446)
	Note that after line 1283, ten lines that would correspond to the *strophe* 1265–74 appear to be missing.

εἰσί τινες οἵ μ' ἔλεγον ὡς καταδιηλλάγην,
ἡνίκα Κλέων μ' ὑπετάραττεν ἐπικείμενος   1285
καί με κακίσας ἔκνισε· κᾆθ', ὅτ' ἀπεδειρόμην,
οὔκτος ἐγέλων μέγα κεκραγότα θεώμενοι,
οὐδὲν ἄρ' ἐμοῦ μέλον, ὅσον δὲ μόνον εἰδέναι
σκωμμάτιον εἴποτέ τι θλιβόμενος ἐκβαλῶ.

LINE 1284

οἵ μ' ἔλεγον ὡς	"who said about me that I . . ."; a slightly illogical shift in construction, but clarity is preserved; cf. S #2634.
κατα-δι-αλλάττω, aor.² pass. -διηλλάγην	
	reconcile again; but κατά can mean "adversely," and Starkie understands it as "I betrayed my cause by reconciling." In 1291, however, it becomes clear that Cleon's belief that Ar. had reconciled with him was mistaken (cf. 473).
ὑπο-ταράττω	(< ὑπό, below, into submission + ταράττω, stir up) disturb into submission, undermine. This evidently refers to a quarrel with Cleon subsequent to *Knights* of 424 BC, though Ar. refrained from attacking Cleon in the *Clouds* of 423—the "reconciliation" imagined in the previous line. (cf. 696)
ἐπί-κειμαι	press upon, attack
κακίζω, ἐκάκισα	(< κακός + -ιζω suffix) reproach, heap abuse on
κνίζω, ἔκνισα	scratch, sting; irritate
ἀπο-δείρω	flay (cf. 429)
οὔκτος	= οἱ ἐκτός, "those outside," those who are not involved, the general public, who enjoyed watching him being flayed alive
γελάω	laugh at (cf. 57)
κράζω, perf. κέκρᾱγα	scream, shout (sc. Κλέωνα with κεκρᾱγότα), cf. 103

LINE 1288

ἄρα	"as it seems," "after all"; a realization (cf. 3)
μέλει	(> acc. neut. ptcp. μέλον) it is a care (impers.; with object of care in gen.; sc. dat. of person αὐτοῖς: S #1467). Here acc. absolute (S #2076), governing εἰδέναι "they weren't concerned about me—except only to know whether . . ."
ὅσον δὲ μόνον	except only
σκωμμάτιον, τό	(dim. of σκῶμμα < σκώπτω, mock) a little joke
εἴποτε	if ever, whether
θλίβω	squeeze, press
ἐκ-βάλλω, -βαλῶ	toss out (ἐκβαλῶ is in an ind. quest. governed by εἰδέναι; because the main verb is the imperfect ἐγέλων, one might expect an opt. ἐκβαλοῖ, but the fut. indic. is *retained*: S #2619a.)

ταῦτα κατιδὼν ὑπό τι μικρὸν ἐπιθήκιϲα· 1290
εἶτα νῦν ἐξηπάτηϲεν ἡ χάραξ τὴν ἄμπελον.
Ξα. ἰὼ χελῶναι μακάριαι τοῦ δέρματοϲ,
{καὶ τριϲμακάριαι τοῦ 'πὶ ταῖϲ πλευραῖϲ}
ὡϲ εὖ κατηρέψαϲθε καὶ νουβυϲτικῶϲ
κεράμῳ τὸ νῶτον, ὥϲτε τὰϲ πλευρὰϲ ϲτέγειν. 1295
ἐγὼ δ' ἀπόλωλα ϲτιζόμενοϲ βακτηρίᾳ.

LINE 1290

καθ-οράω, aor.² κατ-εῖδον

	(<κατά, with intensive force + ὁράω, look) look carefully, perceive
ὑπό τι	just a bit, to some degree (LSJ s.v. ὑπό F.II, *LA* 250 n. 93)
πιθηκίζω	(< πίθηκος, ape + -ίζω) play the ape
χάραξ, –ακος, ὁ, ἡ	vine prop, stake (cf. 1201)
ἄμπελος, ἡ	grapevine. Grapevines needed stakes for support; that a stake should deceive a grapevine means that the stake has unexpectedly pulled away and let the grapevine collapse. Cleon, similarly, was surprised that Ar. would return to the attack.

1292–1325: The Second Parabasis over, Xanthias arrives to describe the symposium: Phil. has disgraced himself by insulting other guests, esp. Lysistratus and Thouphrastus, and hitting bystanders as he drunkenly staggered home.

1292–1325: Meter: Iambic trimeter.

LINE 1292

ἰώ	(interj.) "Ah!"; used to convey suffering and summon aid
χελώνη, ἡ	tortoise (cf. 428)
δέρμα, –ατος, τό	skin, shell (gen. of cause is used in exclams. and preceded by interjections: S #1405); cf. 429
τριϲμακάριος (3)	thrice-blessed
τοῦ 'πὶ ταῖς πλευραῖς	"[your shell], the one covering your sides." This line, which is metrically incomplete, may have been introduced from an explanatory marginal gloss.
κατ-ερέφω, –ήρεψα	(< κατά + ἐρέφω, cover with a roof) roof over; (mid.) roof over what is one's own (cf. 206)
νουβυϲτικῶς	(< νοῦς, mind + βύω, stuff full) full of sense, cleverly
κέραμος, ὁ	pot, jar; tile
ϲτέγω	cover, protect (cf. 67)
νῶτον, τό	back
ϲτίζω	tattoo, mark, brand; beat black and blue {> *stigma*}
βακτηρία, ἡ	walking staff (cf. 33)

189

Χο.   τί δ' ἐστίν, ὦ παῖ; παῖδα γάρ, κἂν ᾖ γέρων,
      καλεῖν δίκαιον ὅστις ἂν πληγὰς λάβῃ.

Ξα.   οὐ γὰρ ὁ γέρων ἀτηρότατον ἄρ' ἦν κακὸν
      καὶ τῶν ξυνόντων πολὺ παροινικώτατος;   1300
      καίτοι παρῆν Ἵππυλλος, Ἀντιφῶν, Λύκων,
      Λυσίστρατος, Θούφραστος, οἱ περὶ Φρύνιχον.
      τούτων ἁπάντων ἦν ὑβριστότατος μακρῷ.

LINE 1297

παῖς, παιδός, ὁ   (> voc. παῖ) boy, slave. παῖ would be a normal way of addressing a slave. The joke here is that Xanthias, the slave, is an old man. Of course one expects children to be beaten; why not this slave too? Ar. may also be parodying a tragedy in which a character said τί δ' ἐστίν, ὦ παῖ;

κἄν   = καὶ ἐάν in Pres. Gen. condit.: S #2337

δίκαιον   sc. ἐστί

πληγή, ἡ   (< πλήττω, strike, cf. 399) a hit, blow

LINE 1299

οὐ γάρ   "[Why, let me explain why I'm cursing;] it's because . . ."; an indignant quest. answering a quest. (cf. 836)

ἄρα   "as I now see" (cf. 3)

ἀτηρός   (< ἄτη, blindness, recklessness + –ρος, adj. suffix: S #858.13) baneful

ξύνειμι   be with; οἱ ξύνοντες = those present, those in the company (gen. with superl.: S #1315)

παροινικός (3)   (< παρά, amiss + οἶνος, wine + –ικος) misbehaving from too much wine

καίτοι   and yet (adversative: GP 556)

Ἵππυλλος, ὁ   Hippyllos; unknown

Ἀντιφῶν, –ῶντος, ὁ   Antiphon (cf. 1270)

Λύκων, –ωνος, ὁ   Lycon, a socially and politically prominent Athenian

Λυσίστρατος, ὁ   Lysistratus (cf. 787)

Θούφραστος, ὁ   Thouphrastus; unknown

Φρύνιχος, ὁ   Phrynichus, a prominent politician who was one of the leaders of the oligarchic regime of the 400 and was assassinated in 411 BC. The phrase οἱ περί suggests there was a coterie. B-O point out that we do not have enough information about these men to draw conclusions about the social significance of this gathering, but we can assume that they are wealthy if boorish.

ὕβριστος (3)   (< ὕβρις, violence) insolent

μακρῷ   dat. of degree of difference: S #1513

εὐθὺς γὰρ ὡς ἐνέπλητο πολλῶν κἀγαθῶν,
ἀνήλατ᾽, ἐσκίρτα, ᾽πεπόρδει, κατεγέλα,   1305
ὥσπερ καχρύων ὀνίδιον εὐωχημένον,
κᾆτυπτε δή με νεανικῶς "παῖ παῖ" καλῶν.
εἶτ᾽ αὐτόν, ὡς εἶδ᾽, ἤκασεν Λυσίστρατος·
"ἔοικας, ὦ πρεσβῦτα, νεοπλούτῳ Φρυγὶ
κλητῆρί τ᾽ εἰς ἀχυρὸν ἀποδεδρακότι."   1310

LINE 1304

ἐμ-πίμπλημι, aor.² pass. ἐν-επλήμην
    be filled (+ gen.; cf. 380, 424)

ἀν-άλλομαι, aor. -ηλάμην
    (< ἀνά + ἅλλομαι, leap) leap up

σκιρτάω   (*frequentative* of σκαίρω, skip: S #867) leap around

πέρδομαι, πέπορδα   fart (plup. ἐπεπόρδει is used as an imperfect); on farting as an expression of glee or friskiness: *MM* p. 196

κατα-γελάω   laugh at, laugh scornfully (cf. 515)

κάχρυς, –υος, ἡ   parched barley

ὀνίδιον, τό   little donkey (dim. of ὄνος, donkey, though Starkie suggests it is not a true dim.—there is no little donkey—but rather a *hypocoristic*, a pet name)

εὐωχέω, perf. mid./pass. εὐώχημαι
    feast; (mid.) enjoy (+ gen. with vbs. of eating: S #1355)

τύπτω   beat {> *type*}

δή   "He was *beating* me!"; emphasizes ἔτυπτε

LINE 1308

εἰκάζω, ἤκασα   (< ἔοικα, seem like + -αζω) portray; make a comparison. The initial εἰ-of this verb augments as ἠ-: S #437.

πρεσβύτης, –ου, ὁ   old man (cf. 540)

νεόπλουτος, –ον   (< νέος, new + πλοῦτος, wealth) nouveau riche

Φρύξ, –υγός   (adj.) Phrygian; this Phrygian would be a barbarian or ex-slave (cf. 433)

ἀχῦρός, ὁ   bran

ἀπο-διδράσκω, -δέδρᾱκα
    run away (cf. 126, 910)

ὁ δ’ ἀνακραγὼν ἀντήκαϲ’ αὐτὸν πάρνοπι
τὰ θρῖα τοῦ τρίβωνοϲ ἀποβεβληκότι,
Ϲθενέλῳ τε τὰ ϲκευάρια διακεκαρμένῳ.
οἱ δ’ ἀνεκρότηϲαν, πλήν γε Θουφράϲτου μόνου·
οὗτοϲ δὲ διεμύλλαινεν, ὡϲ δὴ δεξιόϲ.   1315
ὁ γέρων δὲ τὸν Θούφραϲτον ἤρετ’· "εἰπέ μοι,
ἐπὶ τῷ κομᾷϲ καὶ κομψὸϲ εἶναι προϲποιεῖ,
κωμῳδολοιχῶν περὶ τὸν εὖ πράττοντ’ ἀεί;"

LINE 1311

ἀνα-κράζω, aor.² -έκραγον	
	cry out
ἀντ-εικάζω	(< ἀντί, in return + εἰκάζω, liken) compare in answer
πάρνοψ, –οποϲ,ὁ	locust; a locust has a "dry and hungry look": Phil. insults Lysistratus for his impoverished appearance.
θρῖον, τό	fig-leaf; the "wings" of a locust
τρίβων, –ωνοϲ, ὁ	threadbare cloak (cf. 33); evidently a gen. of explanation: S #1322, "leaves which are its cloak": MacD.
ἀπο-βάλλω, perf. –βέβληκα	
	throw off, lose
Ϲθένελοϲ, ὁ	Sthenelus, a tragic poet. It appears that Sthenelus, impoverished, had to sell off his props and costumes.
ϲκευάριον, τό	(dim. of ϲκεῦοϲ, τό, implement, cf. 615) small utensils; <u>stage props</u>
δια-κείρω, perf. mid./pass. -κέκαρμαι	
	cut off; (pass.) shorn of

LINE 1314

ἀνα-κροτέω	(< κρότοϲ, beating noise) lift up and strike; applaud
πλήν	except (prep. + gen.)
δια-μυλλαίνω	(perhaps < διά, in different directions + μύλλον, lip) purse lips, make a sour face
ὡϲ δή	"As he fancies himself being"; ironical use of emphatic δή: GP 231

LINE 1316

ἔρομαι, aor.² ἠρόμην	ask (cf. 502)
τῷ	= τίνι; ἐπὶ τῷ = for what reason? Why?
κομάω	(< κόμη, hair) let hair grow; be haughty {> comet (a "long-haired" star)}
κομψόϲ (3)	elegant, refined, chic (used of people who give themselves airs)
προϲ-ποιέω	make over to; (mid.) pretend
κωμῳδολοιχέω	(< κωμῳδόϲ, comedian + λείχω, lick) "clown-lick"; play the parasite; suck up to someone
ὁ εὖ πράττων	someone doing well

τοιαῦτα περιύβριζεν αὐτοὺϲ ἐν μέρει,
ϲκώπτων ἀγροίκωϲ καὶ προϲέτι λόγουϲ λέγων   1320
ἀμαθέϲτατ' οὐδὲν εἰκότας τῷ πράγματι.
ἔπειτ', ἐπειδὴ 'μέθυεν, οἴκαδ' ἔρχεται
τύπτων ἅπαντας, ἤν τις αὐτῷ ξυντύχῃ.
ὁδὶ δὲ καὶ δὴ ϲφαλλόμενοϲ προϲέρχεται.
ἀλλ' ἐκποδὼν ἄπειμι πρὶν πληγὰϲ λαβεῖν.   1325

Φι.   ἄνεχε, πάρεχε.
        κλαύϲεταί τιϲ τῶν ὄπιϲθεν ἐπακολουθούντων ἐμοί·

LINE 1319

περι-υβρίζω	(< περί, beyond, exceedingly: S #1693.4 + ὑβρίζω, insult) insult wantonly
αὐτούς	= the other guests at the party
μέρος, -ους, τό	share, part; ἐν μέρει: in turn, "one after another" (cf. 972)
ϲκώπτω	mock
ἀγροίκως	like a rustic; stupidly {> *agronomy*}
προϲέτι	(< πρός, in addition + ἔτι, yet) over and over, besides
ἀμαθής, –ές	(ἀ- priv. + μάθος, learning) ignorant
ἔοικα	(> nom. sing. masc. ptcp. εἰκώς) seem like; be fitting to (+ dat.); λόγους . . . οὐδὲν εἰκότας = "completely inappropriate language"
τῷ πράγματι	= the "situation"; the party he was at

LINE 1322

μεθύω	be drunk (only used in pres. and imperfect; for fut. and aor. Greek uses μεθύσκω; cf. 1252)
οἴκαδε	(adv.) homeward (cf. 255)
τύπτω	beat (cf. 1323)
ξυν-τυγχάνω, aor.² -έτυχον	meet up with
καὶ δή	"Look!"; signifies that something is actually taking place (cf. 492)
ϲφάλλω	make fall; (pass.) be tripped, stagger
ἐκποδών	out of the way (cf. 949)
πληγή, ἡ	blow, beating (πληγὰς λαμβάνειν serves as pass. of τύπτω), cf. 399

1326–63: Phil., belligerently drunk, returns from the party, followed by people he has attacked and accompanied by Dardanis, a flute-girl with whom he has absconded from the party.

1326–40: Meter: Trochaic for the "drunken and irascible song" (Parker) in 1326–31 and 1335–40, with iambic dimeters at 1335–38. The aggrieved man interrupts at 1332–34 with iambic trimeters.

LINE 1326

ἀν-έχω	hold up; stand up (cf. 513)
κλάω, κλαύσομαι	cry, "be sorry"
ὄπισθεν	(adv.) behind
ἐπ-ακολουθέω	(ἐπί + ἀκολουθέω, follow, < α- copulative + κέλευθος, path) follow close upon, pursue (+ dat.) {> *acolyte*, an*acoluthon*}

οἷον, εἰ μὴ 'ρρήϲεθ', ὑμᾶϲ,

ὦ πόνηροι, ταυτηὶ τῇ δᾳδὶ φρυκτοὺϲ ϲκευάϲω.   1330

ANHP   ἦ μὴν ϲὺ δώϲειϲ αὔριον τούτων δίκην

ἡμῖν ἅπαϲιν, κεἰ ϲφόδρ' εἶ νεανίαϲ.

ἀθρόοι γὰρ ἥξομέν ϲε προϲκαλούμενοι.

Φι.   ἰηῦ ἰηῦ, "καλούμενοι".   1335

ἀρχαῖά γ' ὑμῶν. ἀρά γ' ἴϲθ' ὡϲ οὐδ' ἀκούων ἀνέχομαι

δικῶν; ἰαιβοῖ αἰβοῖ.

LINE 1329

οἷον	how (exclam.)
ἔρρω, ἐρρήϲω	begone, get lost (mostly in impv.)
δᾴϲ, δᾳδόϲ, ἡ	torch
φρυκτόϲ (3)	(< φρύγω, roast) small fish for frying
ϲκευάζω, ϲκευάϲω	(< ϲκεῦοϲ, utensil) prepare, make ready; esp. to prepare food

LINE 1332

ἦ μήν	"I swear"; "I warn you" (cf. 258)
δίκην δίδωμι	pay the price, suffer punishment (cf. 453)
αὔριον	(adv.) tomorrow [< IE *aus-, dawn; cf. ἕωϲ, 366]

LINE 1334

ἀθρόοϲ (3)	(ἀ- copulative, cf. 898 + θρόοϲ, murmur of a crowd) taken together, in crowds, in a body
προϲ-καλέω	call upon; (mid.) summon into court (fut. ptcp. to indicate purpose after a verb of coming: S #2065)

LINE 1335

ἰηῦ	Hah! (derisive). In a role reversal, Phil. will have nothing to do with the court system and speaks as if he is the son of the family.
γε	"How old-fashioned!"; contemptuous, with repetition of previous speaker's words, here καλούμενοι: GP 129
ἀρά γ'	adds liveliness to the quest.: GP 50 (cf. 4)
οἶδα	(> impv. 2 sing. ἴϲθι) know
ἀν-έχομαι	put up with (here with suppl. ptcp. ἀκούων: S #2098; note also δικῶν, gen. of thing heard: S #1361); cf. 513
ἰαιβοῖ αἰβοῖ	Yech! Ugh! Agh! (cf. 37)

τάδε μ' ἀρέσκει· βάλλε κημούς.

οὐκ ἄπει; ποῦ 'cτ' ἡλιαcτής; ἐκποδών.   1340

ἀνάβαινε δεῦρο, χρυcομηλολόνθιον,

τῇ χειρὶ τουδὶ λαβομένη τοῦ cχοινίου.

ἔχου· φυλάττου δ', ὡc cαπρὸν τὸ cχοινίον·

ὅμωc γε μέντοι τριβόμενον οὐκ ἄχθεται.

ὁρᾷc ἐγώ c' ὡc δεξιῶc ὑφειλόμην   1345

μέλλουcαν ἤδη λεcβιεῖν τοὺc ξυμπόταc·

ὧν οὕνεκ' ἀπόδοc τῷ πέει τῳδὶ χάριν.

ἀλλ' οὐκ ἀποδώcειc οὐδ' ἐφιαλεῖc, οἶδ' ὅτι,

ἀλλ' ἐξαπατήcειc κἀγχανεῖ τούτῳ μέγα·

LINE 1339

τάδε	that is, anything to do with lawsuits and jurors, now that he is a defendant
ἀρέσκω	please (cf. 776)
κημός, ὁ	funnel-shaped top of voting urn (cf. 99)

LINE 1341

Meter: 1341–1449: Phil. continues, now in iambic trimeter.

ἄπειμι	(> pres. indic. 2 sing. ἄπει) go away
ἡλιαστής, –οῦ, ὁ	juror (cf. 206)
ἐκποδών	(adv.) out of the way (cf. 949)
χρυσομηλολόνθιον, τό	(< χρῡσός, golden + μηλολόνθη, cockchafer, a type of beetle [< μῆλον, sheep + ὄλυνθος, fig (beetles are parasitic on figs)] + –ιον, dim. suffix) golden little beetle. Phil. addresses Dardanis, the slave girl and flute player.
σχοίνιον, τό	rope. Actually, she seems to be grabbing his limp phallus: *MM* p. 130.
ἔχομαι	hold fast to (cf. 1235)
σαπρός (3)	rotten; worn out (cf. 38)
τρίβω	rub, with sexual connotation: *MM* p. 176
ἄχθομαι	be irritated, mind (with suppl. ptcp.: S #2100)

LINE 1346

λεσβίζω, –ιῶ	act like the Lesbian women; perform fellatio: *MM* p. 183
ὧν οὕνεκα	why, for this reason (cf. 703)
πέος, πέους, τό	penis (cf. 739)
ἐφ-ιάλλω, -ιαλῶ	(< ἐπί + ἰάλλω, send forth) undertake, carry out; apply [hand] to [the penis] (perhaps a *factitive* of ἅλλομαι, cf. 130)
ἐγ-χάσκω, -χανοῦμαι	scoff at (cf. 721)

πολλοῖς γὰρ ἤδη χἀτέροις αὔτ' ἠργάσω.   1350
ἐὰν γένῃ δὲ μὴ κακὴ νυνὶ γυνή,
ἐγώ c' ἐπειδὰν οὑμὸς υἱὸς ἀποθάνῃ,
λυσάμενος ἔξω παλλακήν, ὦ χοιρίον.
νῦν δ' οὐ κρατῶ 'γὼ τῶν ἐμαυτοῦ χρημάτων·
νέος γάρ εἰμι. καὶ φυλάττομαι cφόδρα·   1355
τὸ γὰρ υἵδιον τηρεῖ με, κἄcτι δύcκολον
κἄλλως κυμινοπριcτοκαρδαμογλύφον.
ταῦτ' οὖν περί μου δέδοικε μὴ διαφθαρῶ·
πατὴρ γὰρ οὐδείc ἐcτιν αὐτῷ πλὴν ἐμοῦ.

LINE 1350

ἐργάζομαι, aor. ἠργασάμην

    work, do (do acc. to dat.). What she "does" is to cheat other men. (cf. 787)

ἀπο-θνήσκω   die. A logical consequence of the comic reversal that is central to the *W*.: Phil. acts like a son fantasizing about what he will be free to do when his father is dead. A young man falling in love with a prostitute would be the engine of many a later comedy. (cf. 583)

λύω   unbind; (mid.) get someone freed; buy

παλλακή, ἡ   concubine; kept woman

χοιρίον, τό   (dim. of χοῖρος, pig) piglet; slang for "pussy": *MM* p. 131

νῦν δ'   but as it is

κρατέω   be master over (+ gen.)

φυλάττομαι   "I am guarded" (pass., not mid.)

LINE 1356

υἵδιον, τό   (dim. of υἱός, son) little son. He reverts to being a father, with a son.

τηρέω   watch over (cf. 210)

δύσκολος, –ον   grouchy (cf. 106)

καὶ ἄλλως   and on top of that

κυμῖνοπριστοκαρδαμογλύφος, –ον

    (< see following entries) "cumin-splitting-cress-scraper"; a skinflint; someone who tries to split a small cumin seed into something smaller

κύμῖνον, τό   cumin seed, "a tiny object of minuscule value": B-O

πριστός (3)   (< πρίω, cut, split) sawn

κάρδαμον, τό   a kind of cress

γλύφω   carve, cut; scrape {> hiero*glyph*ic}

LINE 1358

ταῦτα   that is why, therefore (adv. usage; LSJ *s.v.* οὗτος C.VIII.1)

δια-φθείρω, aor. pass. -εφθάρην

    destroy, spoil (μή + subjv. in fear clause: S #2221)

<pre>
        ὁδὶ δὲ καὐτός· ἐπὶ σὲ κἄμ' ἔοικε θεῖν.   1360
        ἀλλ' ὡς τάχιστα στῆθι τάσδε τὰς δετὰς
        λαβοῦσ', ἵν' αὐτὸν τωθάσω νεανικῶς,
        οἵοις ποθ' οὗτος ἐμὲ πρὸ τῶν μυστηρίων.
Βδ.   ὦ οὗτος οὗτος, τυφεδανὲ καὶ χοιρόθλιψ,
        ποθεῖν ἐρᾶν τ' ἔοικας ὡραίας σοροῦ.   1365
        οὔτοι καταπροίξει μὰ τὸν Ἀπόλλω τοῦτο δρῶν.
Φι.   ὡς ἡδέως φάγοις ἂν ἐξ ὄξους δίκην.
Βδ.   οὐ δεινὰ τωθάζειν σε, τὴν αὐλητρίδα
        τῶν ξυμποτῶν κλέψαντα;
Φι.   πόθεν; αὐλητρίδα;
</pre>

LINE 1360

θέω	run
ἵστημι	(> aor. act. impv. 2 sing. στῆθι) stand still, stand where you are
δετή, ἡ	(< δέω, bind) pl. δεταί: sticks bound together; <u>torch</u>
τωθάζω, aor. ἐτώθασα	mock, scoff; play joke on
οἵοις	"by such means as <those by which>" = "in the same way"
τὰ μυστήρια	(< μύω, shutting eyes, cf. 92: initiates were to keep eyes closed) the mysteries, e.g., of Demeter at Eleusis, religious initiation rituals that included mockery; πρὸ τῶν μυστ. = "before my initiation," suggests Starkie.

1364–87: Bdel. tries to rescue Dardanis, but Phil. pretends that he is in the company of a torch, not a flute-girl.

LINE 1364

τῦφεδανός, ὁ	(< τῦφος, delusion, nonsense + -δανος, adj. suffix: S #863b1, used of maladies) with cloudy wits, stupid
χοιρόθλιψ, –ιβος, ὁ	(< χοῖρος, pig + θλίβω, squeeze) "twat-rubber" (Somm.) *hapax*
ποθέω	desire (cf. 818)
ἐράω	love (+ gen.)
ὡραῖος (3)	(< ὥρα, season, time) seasonable, fresh; young
σορός, ἡ	coffin. A surprise substitution for κόρη
κατα-προίξομαι	(fut. only; no pres. < κατά + προίξ, for free, with impunity) do something with impunity, escape unpunished (used with suppl. ptcp.)

LINE 1367

ὄξος, τό	vinegar; ἐξ ὄξους "dipped in vinegar"
οὐ δεινά	how dreadful! (take σε as acc. subject of τωθάζειν; ξυμποτῶν is gen. of separation: S #1392)
πόθεν	cf. 1145
αὐλητρίς, –ίδος, ἡ	girl who plays the *aulos* (cf. 1219)

τί ταῦτα ληρεῖc ὥcπερ ἀπὸ τύμβου πεcών;   1370

Βδ.   νὴ τὸν Δί’, αὕτη πού ’cτί coί γ’ ἡ Δαρδανίc.

Φι.   οὔκ, ἀλλ’ ἐν ἀγορᾷ τοῖc θεοῖc δᾷc κάεται.

Βδ.   δᾷc ἥδε;

Φι.   δᾷc δῆτ’. οὐχ ὁρᾷc ἐcχιcμένην;

Βδ.   τί δὲ τὸ μέλαν τοῦτ’ ἐcτὶν αὐτῆc τοὐν μέcῳ;

Φι.   ἡ πίττα δήπου καομένηc ἐξέρχεται.   1375

Βδ.   ὁ δ’ ὄπιcθεν οὐχὶ πρωκτόc ἐcτιν οὑτοcί;

Φι.   ὄζοc μὲν οὖν τῆc δᾳδὸc οὗτοc ἐξέχει.

Βδ.   τί λέγειc cύ; ποῖοc ὄζοc; οὐκ εἶ δεῦρο cύ;

LINE 1370

ληρέω	be silly, speak foolishly
τύμβος, ὁ	tomb
πίπτω, aor.² ἔπεσον	fall. Phil. plays on a proverb, "fall from a donkey."
Δαρδανίς, –ίος, ἡ	(< Dardania, the region around Troy) Dardanis, "Trojan Woman." A good example of an ethnic name given to a slave (cf. 433)

LINE 1372

δήπου	I suppose (cf. 663)
κάω	light on fire; (pass.) burn (cf. 828). A torch burning for gods in the Agora would probably be associated with the sanctuary of the Twelve Gods, suggest B-O.
σχίζω, perf. mid./pass. ἔσχισμαι	split, separate. ἐσχισμένη = wood that has been split, though the reference would also be to her crotch: *MM* p. 147 (cf. 239).

LINE 1374

μέλᾱς, μέλαινα, μέλᾰν	(adj.) black. The dark spot would be her pubic hair. {> *melancholy, melanoma*}
τοὐν	= τὸ ἐν
πίττα, ἡ	pitch. Female secreta are likened to pitch: *MM* p. 145.
κᾱομένης	"when it's hot" (Hend.; gen. abs.: S #2072)
ὄζος, ὁ	knot hole from which a branch springs; here likened to a rump: *MM* p. 201
μὲν οὖν	"On the contrary" (cf. 515)
ἐξ-έχω	stand out, project
εἰμί	(> pres. indic. 2 sing. εἶ) be
δεῦρο σύ	The second σύ in this line is addressed to Dardanis.

Φι.	ἄ ἄ, τί μέλλεις δρᾶν;	
Βδ.	ἄγειν ταύτην λαβὼν	
	ἀφελόμενός ϲε καὶ νομίϲαϲ εἶναι ϲαπρὸν	1380
	κοὐδὲν δύναϲθαι δρᾶν.	
Φι.	ἄκουϲόν νυν ἐμοῦ.	
	Ὀλυμπίαϲιν, ἡνίκ᾽ ἐθεώρουν ἐγώ,	
	Ἐφουδίων ἐμαχέϲατ᾽ Ἀϲκώνδᾳ καλῶϲ	
	ἤδη γέρων ὤν· εἶτα τῇ πυγμῇ θενὼν	
	ὁ πρεϲβύτεροϲ κατέβαλε τὸν νεώτερον.	1385
	πρὸϲ ταῦτα τηροῦ μὴ λάβῃϲ ὑπώπια.	
Βδ.	νὴ τὸν Δί᾽, ἐξέμαθέϲ γε τὴν Ὀλυμπίαν.	

LINE 1379

ἄ	Hey! (in protest)
ἀφ-αιρέω, aor.² -εῖλον	remove; (mid.) deprive acc., ϲε, of acc., ταύτην [= Dardanis] (cf. 884)
ϲαπρός (3)	rotten; worn out (cf. 38). Bdel. begins to take the girl and lead her off.
Ὀλυμπίαϲιν	(< Ὀλυμπία + -ϲι, locative suffix: S #342) at Olympia
θεωρέω	serve as ambassador (cf. 1187). Phil. relates precisely the anecdote Bdel. had told him to at 1191: how old Ephudion fought Askondas!
πυγμή, ἡ	fist {> *pygmy* ("fist-sized" people)}
θείνω, aor.² ἔθενον	strike (Ar. uses this verb only in aor.)
πρέϲβυς, -εως, ὁ	old man (cf. 540; πρεϲβύτης is more common in prose)
πρὸϲ ταῦτα	"wherefore," "the moral is": S #1695.3.c
τηρέω	watch; (mid.) take care that, see to it (a verb of effort introducing an object clause with μή + subjv.: S #2210)
ὑπώπιον, τό	(< ὑπό + ὤψ, eye) the place below the eye; black eye (which appears below eye)

ΑΡΤΟΠΩΛΙϹ	ἴθι μοι παράστηθ᾽,	
	ἀντιβολῶ, πρὸς τῶν θεῶν.	
	ὁδὶ γὰρ ἀνήρ ἐϲτιν ὅϲ μ᾽ ἀπώλεϲεν	
	τῇ δᾳδὶ παίων, κἀξέβαλεν ἐντευθενὶ	1390
	ἄρτουϲ δέκ᾽ ὀβολῶν κἀπιθήκην τεττάρων.	
Βδ.	ὁρᾷϲ ἃ δέδρακαϲ; πράγματ᾽ αὖ δεῖ καὶ δίκαϲ	
	ἔχειν διὰ τὸν ϲὸν οἶνον.	
Φι.	οὐδαμῶϲ γ᾽, ἐπεὶ	
	λόγοι διαλλάξουϲιν αὐτὰ δεξιοί·	
	ὥϲτ᾽ οἶδ᾽ ὁτιὴ ταύτῃ διαλλαχθήϲομαι.	1395
Αρ.	οὔτοι μὰ τὼ θεὼ καταπροίξει Μυρτίαϲ	
	τῆϲ Ἀγκυλίωνοϲ γενομένηϲ καὶ Ϲωϲτράτηϲ,	
	οὕτω διαφθείραϲ ἐμοῦ τὰ φορτία.	
Φι.	ἄκουϲον, ὦ γύναι· λόγον ϲοι βούλομαι	
	λέξαι χαρίεντα.	
Αρ.	μὰ Δία μὴ ᾽μοιγ᾽, ὦ μέλε.	1400

1388–1414: Xanthias's report that Phil. had attacked bystanders is now proven true. Myrtia, a bread seller, accuses Phil. of knocking loaves of bread off of a tray. Phil. insults her and she departs.

LINE 1388

ἀρτοπῶλιϲ, –ιδοϲ, ἡ	(< ἄρτοϲ + πωλέω, sell + –ιϲ, suffix denoting person involved: S #843b2) bread woman. We find at 1396 that her name is Myrtia.
παρ-ίϲτημι, aor.² -έϲτην	
	(παράϲτηθ᾽ = παραϲτῆθι, aor. impv. 2 sing.) make to stand beside; (intrans. aor.²) stand by, help (impv. introduced by ἴθι, cf. 162). Myrtia is addressing Chaerephon, whom she has met on the street.
ἐντευθενί	from here (referring to her tray); cf. 125
ἄρτοϲ, ὁ	loaf of wheat bread
ἐπιθήκη, ἡ	(< ἐπί, on + τίθημι, place) a] addition, increase; additionally (adv. acc.): "[loaves worth] four additional obols"; b] ἐπιθήκη = a cover for the tray: "a tray-cover worth four obols" (thus Wilson)
δεκ᾽ ὀβολῶν	"worth ten obols" (gen. of price: S #1372); for ὀβελόϲ, cf. 52
τέτταρεϲ	four (cf. 260)
ὁτιή	Attic variant of ὅτι (cf. 786, but here conj. for ind. statement)

LINE 1396

τὼ θεώ	(dual) the two goddesses, Demeter and Persephone, commonly invoked by women: LA 189 (cf. 378)
κατα-προίξομαι	escape unpunished from a gen. (cf. 1366)
Ἀγκυλίων, –ωνοϲ, ὁ	the father of Myrtia; a person of that name was ridiculed in fourth-century comedy. The fact that Myrtia names her parents is evidence of her citizen status.
Ϲωϲτράτη, ἡ	the mother of Myrtia
φορτίον, τό	freight, merchandise; (pl.) wares (cf. 66)
χαρίειϲ, –εϲϲα, –εν	charming
ἔμοιγε	"Not to me, at least [though you could tell others]"; limitative γε: GP 122
ὦ μέλε	sir, my friend (only in voc.; colloquial, here sarcastic)

Φι.   Αἴcωπον ἀπὸ δείπνου βαδίζονθ' ἑcπέραc
                 θραcεῖα καὶ μεθύcη τιc ὑλάκτει κύων.
                 κἄπειτ' ἐκεῖνοc εἶπεν, "ὦ κύον κύον,
                 εἰ νὴ Δί' ἀντὶ τῆc κακῆc γλώττηc ποθὲν
                 πυροὺc πρίαιο, cωφρονεῖν ἄν μοι δοκεῖc."   1405

Αρ.   καὶ καταγελᾷc μου; προcκαλοῦμαί c', ὅcτιc εἶ,
                 πρὸc τοὺc ἀγορανόμουc βλάβηc τῶν φορτίων,
                 κλητῆρ' ἔχουcα Χαιρεφῶντα τουτονί.

Φι.   μὰ Δί', ἀλλ' ἄκουcον, ἤν τί cοι δόξω λέγειν.

LINE 1401

Αἴσωπος, ὁ	the fable-teller (cf. 506)
ἑσπέρα, ἡ	evening; (gen.) one evening (cf. 100)
θρασύς, –εῖα, –ύ	bold, insolent (cf. 387, 1031)
μέθυσος (3)	(< μέθυ, wine) drunk with wine, an alcoholic (only used in fem. in classical Attic); cf. 1252
ὑλακτέω	(> imperfect act. 3 sing. ὑλάκτει; augment lengthens υ- to ῡ-) bark at (transitive; contrast 904)

LINE 1403

ἀντί	instead of, in exchange for (+ gen.)
γλῶττα, –ης, ἡ	tongue (cf. 547).
ποθεν	(adv., enclitic) from somewhere or other (cf. 203 and 204)
πῡρός, ὁ	wheat
σωφρονέω	be of sound mind, show some sense (ἄν + inf. after construction with δοκεῖς = σωφρονοίης ἄν: S #1846a); cf. 748
κατα-γελάω	mock, jeer (cf. 515)
προσ-καλέω	summon into court (cf. 1334)

LINE 1407

ἀγορᾱνόμος,	ὁ market regulator. In the fourth century, there were five each in Athens and Piraeus.
βλάβη, ἡ	harm, damage (gen. of crime: S #1375)
φορτίον, τό	load; (pl.) wares, merchandise (cf. 1398)
κλητήρ, –ῆρος, ὁ	witness to serving of summons (cf. 189)
Χαιρεφῶν, –ῶντος	Chaerephon, a friend of Socrates who evidently saw what Phil. had done and will bear witness that a summons has been served
ἤν	= to see if

	Λᾶσός ποτ' ἀντεδίδασκε καὶ Cιμωνίδης·	1410
	ἔπειθ' ὁ Λᾶcοc εἶπεν, "ὀλίγον μοι μέλει."	
Αρ.	ἄληθεc οὗτοc;	
Φι.	καὶ cὺ δή μοι, Χαιρεφῶν,	
	γυναικὶ κλητεύειc ἐοικὼc θαψίνῃ	
	Ἰνοῖ κρεμαμένη πρὸc ποδῶν Εὐριπίδου;	
Βδ.	ὁδί τιc ἕτεροc, ὡc ἔοικεν, ἔρχεται	1415
	καλούμενόc cε· τόν γέ τοι κλητῆρ' ἔχει.	

ΚΑΤΗΓΟΡΟC

	οἴμοι κακοδαίμων. προcκαλοῦμαί c', ὦ γέρον,	
	ὕβρεωc.	
Βδ.	ὕβρεωc; μὴ μὴ καλέcῃ πρὸc τῶν θεῶν·	
	ἐγὼ γὰρ ὑπὲρ αὐτοῦ δίκην δίδωμί cοι,	
	ἣν ἂν cὺ τάξῃc, καὶ χάριν προcείcομαι.	1420

LINE 1410

Λᾶσος, ὁ	Lasus, poet of the sixth century BC; instituted a contest of dithyrambic choruses
ἀντι-διδάσκω	train a rival chorus (cf. 1029)
Cιμωνίδης, –ου, ὁ	Simonides, poet of ca. 556–468; also wrote dithyrambs
μέλει	it is a care (impers. + dat.); ὀλίγον μοι μέλει, "I couldn't care less"; a surprisingly low linguistic register for a high-class poet like Lasos.

LINE 1412

ἄληθες	"Really?" (cf. 1223; adv. acc., in quests.)
κλητεύω	serve a summons, act as a κλητήρ on behalf of a dat., γυναικί (= Myrtia)
θάψινος (3)	(< θάψος, a plant used for yellow dye + -ινος, suffix of *denominative* adj. of material: S #858.12) yellow, pale. Chaerephon was known for his pale complexion.
Ἰνώ, -οῦς, ἡ	Ino, daughter of Cadmus in mythology
κρέμαμαι	hang, hang on to (cf. 298); Chaerephon's trailing after Myrtia seems as undignified as Ino's behavior when, in a Euripidean tragedy, she was hanging on to someone's feet. The dats. Ἰνοῖ κρεμαμένη are governed by ἐοικώς.
Εὐρῑπίδης, ὁ	Euripides (cf. 61). Now it is the feet of Euripides himself that she hangs onto!

1415–49: Another innocent bystander and witness arrive to summon Phil. to court on charges of assault.

LINE 1415

καλούμενος	"to issue a summons" (fut. ptcp. purpose, cf. 1334)
γέ τοι	"And I have a good reason for saying this: . . ." (cf. 912)
κατήγορος, ὁ	accuser. The man arrives with new charges.
ὕβρις, –εως, ἡ	arrogance, violence; charge of assault
δίκην διδόναι	pay restitution, make amends (cf. 453)
τάττω, ἔταξα	order, arrange (subjv. in Pres. Gen. type of condit. rel. clause: S #2567)
χάριν προσειδέναι	owe thanks in addition

Φι.   ἐγὼ μὲν οὖν αὐτῷ διαλλαχθήϲομαι
             ἑκών· ὁμολογῶ γὰρ πατάξαι καὶ βαλεῖν.
             ἀλλ' ἐλθὲ δευρί· πότερον ἐπιτρέπειϲ ἐμοὶ
             ὅ τι χρή μ' ἀποτείϲαντ' ἀργύριον τοῦ πράγματοϲ
             εἶναι φίλον τὸ λοιπόν, ἢ ϲύ μοι φράϲειϲ;   1425
Κα.   ϲὺ λέγε. δικῶν γὰρ οὐ δέομ' οὐδὲ πραγμάτων.
Φι.   ἀνὴρ Ϲυβαρίτηϲ ἐξέπεϲεν ἐξ ἅρματοϲ,
             καί πωϲ κατεάγη τῆϲ κεφαλῆϲ μέγα ϲφόδρα·
             ἐτύγχανεν γὰρ οὐ τρίβων ὢν ἱππικῆϲ.

LINE 1421

μὲν οὖν   "<u>Actually, no</u>; I will settle with him" (cf. 515)

ἑκών, ἑκοῦσα, ἑκόν   voluntarily (cf. 992)

ὁμολογέω   (< ὁμός, same + λόγος, account) agree, acknowledge; admit, confess

πατάϲϲω, ἐπάταξα   beat, strike (cf. 1254)

πότερον . . . ἤ   whether . . . or; "Is it that . . . ? Or . . . ?" (cf. 498)

LINE 1423

ἐπι-τρέπω   entrust (introduces an ind. quest: "whether you will entrust to me <the question of> what money I should <pay> for the trouble <and>, having repaid (ἀποτείϲαντα), to be a friend in the future, or . . .")

ἀπο-τίνω, -έτειϲα   repay (cf. 1255)

φράζω, φράϲω   (< φρήν, cf. 8) consider, decide, indicate; "will you tell me <how much to repay>?" It appears that an informal settlement, without involving the hassles of the court system, will be enough for the plaintiff.

πρᾶγμα, -ατος, τὸ   business, legal trouble (gen. of crime: S #1377); cf. 30

LINE 1427

Ϲυβαρίτης, -ου, ὁ   a man of Sybaris. Phil. tells a Sybaritic fable (cf. 1259), which only insults the accuser further.

ἐκ-πίπτω, aor.² -έπεϲον

                fall out; be driven out, be thrown out

ἅρμα, -ατος, τό   chariot

κατ-άγνῡμι, -έαξα, aor.² pass. -εάγην

                break (for double augment -εάγην: S #434; the part. gen. for "an action that affects the object only in part": "he had a hole knocked <u>somewhere</u> in his head (κεφαλῆς)": S #1341)

τρίβων, -ωνος, ὁ [ῐ]   (adj. < τρίβω, rub, practise) experienced, skilled in something (identical in form with τρίβων [also ῐ], cloak)

ἱππική, ἡ   (< ἵππος, horse + -ικος) the skill of horse riding {> *hippo*drome, *hippo*potamus, Phili*pp*} [< IE *ekwo-, horse; cogn. L. *equus*]

κἄπειτ' ἐπιστὰc εἶπ' ἀνὴρ αὐτῷ φίλοc·   1430
"ἔρδοι τιc ἣν ἕκαcτοc εἰδείη τέχνην."
οὕτω δὲ καὶ cὺ παράτρεχ' εἰc τὰ Πιττάλου.

Βδ.   ὅμοιά cου καὶ ταῦτα τοῖc ἄλλοιc τρόποιc.

Κα.   ἀλλ' οὖν cὺ μέμνηc' οὗτοc ἀπεκρίνατο.

Φι.   ἄκουε, μὴ φεῦγ'. ἐν Cυβάρει γυνή ποτε   1435
κατέαξ' ἐχῖνον.

Κα.   ταῦτ' ἐγὼ μαρτύρομαι.

LINE 1430

ἐφ-ίστημι, aor.² -έcτην

    stand over, present oneself

ἔρδω   do, perform (opt. as impv.: S #1820): the phrase ἔρδοι τιc . . . is proverbial

οἶδα   (> opt. 3 sing. εἰδείη) know (cf. 4)

παρα-τρέχω   run off {> trochee; truck}

Πίτταλοc, ὁ   Pittalos, a doctor; τὰ Πιττάλου would be "Pittalos' property" or "house," where he would have a clinic

LINE 1433

οἱ ἄλλοι τρόποι   "the rest of your behavior"; dat. with ὅμοια = "similar to"

ἀλλ' οὖν   "Well, anyway . . ."; breaks off secondary thought, resumes main issue: *GP* 443 (cf. 1190). The accuser addresses the witness.

ἀπο-κρίνομαι, –εκρινάμην

    ἀπεκρίνατο = ἃ + ἀπεκρίνατο by *crasis*; answer (cf. 964)

κατ-άγνυμι, –έαξα   break (cf. 1427)

ἐχῖνοc, ὁ   (< ἔχιc, snake + suffix –ινοc, "snake-animal," "snake-eater") pot, jug. Evidently Phil. strikes the accuser as he finishes saying this.

μαρτύρομαι, ἐμαρτῡράμην

    call on someone to witness what is happening.

Φι.   οὐχῖνος οὖν ἔχων τιν' ἐπεμαρτύρατο·
        εἶθ' ἡ Cυβαρῖτιc εἶπεν, "αἰ ναὶ τὰν κόραν
        τὰν μαρτυρίαν ταύταν ἐάcαc ἐν τάχει
        ἐπίδεcμον ἐπρίω, νοῦν ἂν εἶχεc πλείονα."   1440

Κα.   ὕβριζ', ἕωc ἂν τὴν δίκην ἄρχων καλῇ.

Βδ.   οὔτοι μὰ τὴν Δήμητρ' ἔτ' ἐνταυθοῖ μενεῖc,
        ἀλλ' ἀράμενοc οἴcω cε—

Φι.   τί ποιεῖc;

Βδ.   ὅ τι ποιῶ;
        εἴcω φέρω c' ἐντεῦθεν· εἰ δὲ μή, τάχα
        κλητῆρεc ἐπιλείψουcι τοὺc καλουμένουc.   1445

Φι.   Αἴcωπον οἱ Δελφοί ποτ'—

Βδ.   ὀλίγον μοι μέλει.

LINE 1437

ἔχων τιν'	having someone; "being with a companion"
ἐπι-μαρτύρομαι	= μαρτύρομαι, but here used to describe the action of another in 3 sing.
Cυβαρῖτιc, ἡ	woman of Sybaris (cf. 1427)
αἰ	= εἰ in Doric, the dialect of Sybaris (a mixed Contrary-to-Fact condit.: aor. indic. prot-asis, ἐπρίω, and imperfect apodosis, εἶχεc, with ἄν)
ναὶ τὰν κόραν	= νὴ τὴν κόρην; young girl, maiden. Doric alpha replaces Attic/Ionic eta. The κόρα is Persephone (cf. 7).
τὰν . . . ταύταν	= τήν . . . ταύτην
μαρτυρία, ἡ	testimony; the business of calling on witnesses (obj. of ptcp. ἐάcᾱc)
ἐάω, εἴᾱσα	allow, leave alone. The aor. augment is actually syllabic; the verb formerly began with a consonant and digamma: σεϝάω: S #431. The -ᾱ- coincidentally lengthens in aor.
τάχος, τό	swiftness; ἐν τάχει = ταχέωc
ἐπίδεσμος, ὁ	(< ἐπί, upon + δέσμος, binding < δέω, bind) bandage
πρίασθαι	(> aor. mid. indic. 2 sing. ἐπρίω) buy

LINE 1441

ὑβρίζω	insult, be insolent (a sarcastic impv.)
ἕως	until (cf. 565)
ἄρχων, ὁ	magistrate (cf. 304)
Δημήτηρ, –τρος, ἡ	(perhaps < Δᾶ-, an old word for "earth" + μήτηρ) Demeter
ἐνταυθοῖ	(adv.) here (indistinguishable from ἐνταῦθα)
αἴρω, ἦρα	(> aor. mid. ptcp. ἀράμενοc) lift up; (mid.) take up for oneself. Bdel. now physically lifts up Phil. and begins to haul him inside. (cf. 51)
ὅ τι	what? (ind. quest. reports dir. quest.; cf. 48 & 793)
ἐντεῦθεν	(adv.) from here (cf. 125)
ἐπι-λείπω, -λείψω	(< ἐπί + λείπω, leave, cf. 583) fail, run out of. That is, there will not be enough witnesses (κλητῆρεc) for the people serving summonses (οἱ καλούμενοι).
Αἴσωπος, ὁ	Aesop (cf. 566).
Δελφοί, –ων, οἱ	Delphi; the people of Delphi

Φι.   φιάλην ἐπῃτιῶντο κλέψαι τοῦ θεοῦ·
      ὁ δ' ἔλεξεν αὐτοῖc ὡc ὁ κάνθαρόc ποτε—
Βδ.   οἴμ' ὡc ἀπολεῖc με τοῖcι coῖcι κανθάροιc.   1449
Χο.   ζηλῶ γε τῆc εὐτυχίαc   [cτρ.
      τὸν πρέcβυν, οἳ μετέcτη
      ξηρῶν τρόπων καὶ βιοτῆc·

LINE 1447

φιάλη, ἡ   sacred bowl (cf. 677)

ἐπ-αιτιάομαι   (< ἐπ-, adding slight intensification: S #1689.4 + αἰτιάομαι, accuse) bring a charge,
                  accuse (+ acc. + inf.)

κάνθαρος, ὁ   beetle. Aesop, when he was unjustly accused and convicted of stealing a sacred bowl
                  from the temple of Apollo at Delphi, told the fable of how a lowly beetle got revenge
                  on an eagle; the moral was that the arrogant Delphians would suffer for the injustice
                  they committed in executing Aesop.

1450–73: The chorus voice their pleasure at the possibility that Phil. will turn his life around and behave with
more dignity.

1450–73: Meter: Iambs and choriambs combined in *strophe* (1450–61) and *antistrophe* (1462–73).

LINE 1450

ζηλόω   rival; be envious of; admire (+ gen. of cause: S #1405), cf. 451
εὐτυχία, ἡ   good fortune
πρέcβυς, –εως, ὁ   old man
οἷ   to where; to what degree of success
μεθ-ίστημι, aor.² -έστην
                  change from (+ gen.)
ξηρός (3)   dry; austere, frugal {> xerox}
βιοτή, ἡ   means of living

ἕτερα δὲ νῦν ἀντιμαθών
ἢ μέγα τι μεταπεϲεῖται
ἐπὶ τὸ τρυφῶν καὶ μαλακόν.   1455
τάχα δ' ἂν ἴϲωϲ οὐκ ἐθέλοι.
τὸ γὰρ ἀποϲτῆναι χαλεπὸν
φύϲεωϲ, ἢν ἔχοι τιϲ ἀεί.
καίτοι πολλοὶ ταῦτ' ἔπαθον·
ξυνόντεϲ γνώμαιϲ ἑτέρων   1460
μετεβάλοντο τοὺϲ τρόπουϲ.
  πολλοῦ δ' ἐπαίνου παρ' ἐμοὶ   [ἀντ.
καὶ τοῖϲιν εὖ φρονοῦϲιν.
τυχὼν ἄπειϲιν διὰ τὴν
φιλοπατρίαν καὶ ϲοφίαν   1465
ὁ παῖϲ ὁ Φιλοκλέωνοϲ.

LINE 1453

ἀντι-μανθάνω	learn instead
ἤ	actually, really; normally the first word in a sentence; here unusually postponed: GP 281
μετα-πίπτω, –πεϲοῦμαι	
	undergo a change
τρυφάω	live luxuriously (τὸ τρυφῶν: attributive neut. sing. ptcp. with art. as a substantive; here, an abstract noun: S #1124)
μαλακόϲ (3)	soft (cf. 738)
ἀφ-ίϲτημι, aor.² -έϲτην	
	remove; (intrans.) stand away from. The art. inf. τὸ ἀποϲτῆναι is the subject of the main clause in a Pres. Gen. rel. construction; because this main clause is a kind of maxim, the opt. ἔχοι, normally in a Past General rel. clause, is allowed: S #2573.
φύϲιϲ –εωϲ, ἡ	nature (cf. 1071)

LINE 1460

ξύν-ειμι	be with, be acquainted with (+ dat.)
μετα-βάλλω, aor.² -έβαλον	
	change

LINE 1462

1462–73: The chorus now turn to praise Bdel.

ἔπαινοϲ, ὁ	(< ἐπί + αἶνοϲ, praise) praise (gen. ἐπαίνου is object of τυχών)
φρονέω	have understanding; οἱ εὖ φρονοῦντεϲ = "those with good sense"
ἄπειμι	(> pres. indic. 3 sing. ἄπειϲι) go away
φιλοπατρία, ἡ	love of father, filial love (or, love of one's country?)

οὐδενὶ γὰρ οὕτως ἀγανῷ
ξυνεγενόμην, οὐδὲ τρόποις
ἐπεμάνην οὐδ' ἐξεχύθην.
τί γὰρ ἐκεῖνος ἀντιλέγων   1470
οὐ κρείττων ἦν, βουλόμενος
τὸν φύσαντα σεμνοτέροις
κατακοσμῆσαι πράγμασιν;
Ξα.   νὴ τὸν Διόνυσον, ἄπορά γ' ἡμῖν πράγματα
δαίμων τις εἰσκεκύκληκεν εἰς τὴν οἰκίαν.   1475
ὁ γὰρ γέρων, ὡς ἔπιε διὰ πολλοῦ χρόνου
ἤκουσέ τ' αὐλοῦ, περιχαρὴς τῷ πράγματι
ὀρχούμενος τῆς νυκτὸς οὐδὲν παύεται
τἀρχαῖ' ἐκεῖν' οἷς Θέσπις ἠγωνίζετο·

LINE 1467

ἀγανός (3)   mild, gentle
ξυγ-γίγνομαι, aor.² -εγενόμην
           be with, meet
ἐπι-μαίνω, aor. pass. -εμάνην
           be mad for (cf. 744)
ἐκ-χέω, aor. pass. ἐξεχύθην
           (< ἐκ + χέω, pour) pour out, melt away; <u>be devoted to, be carried away</u>

LINE 1470

ἀντι-λέγω   contradict, argue; "at what (τί) was he not better in arguing . . . ?"
φύω, ἔφυσα   bring forth; ὁ φύσας = "the father" (cf. 1265)
κατα-κοσμέω, -εκόσμησα
           (< κατά + κόσμος, order, ornament) arrange, equip; adorn

1474–99: Xanthias reports that Phil. has begun dancing and will do so competitively; Phil. describes his dance moves and calls for challengers.

1474–81: Iambic trimeters.

LINE 1474

Διόνῡσος, –ου, ὁ   Dionysus, god of wine and theater (cf. 1046)
ἄπορος (3)   (< ἀ- priv. + πόρος, way, means of achieving, cf. 308) difficult, confusing, unmanageable
δαίμων, –ονος, ὁ   spirit, divinity
εἰσ-κυκλέω, –κεκύκληκα
           wheel in; set awhirl

LINE 1476

πίνω   (> aor. act. indic. 3 sing. ἔπιε) drink
διά   (+ gen.) of intervals; διὰ πολλοῦ χρόνου = "after a long time"
αὐλός, ὁ   *aulos*, "flute," though in fact the music was produced with a reed (cf. 581)
περιχαρής, –ές   (< περί, exceedingly + χαίρω, rejoice) overjoyed
τὰ ἀρχαῖα ἐκεῖνα   those old [dances]
Θέσπις, –ιδος, ὁ   Thespis; said to have been the first tragic playwright in the late sixth century
ἀγωνίζομαι   compete (cf. 993)

	καὶ τοὺς τραγῳδοὺς φησιν ἀποδείξειν Κρόνους	1480
	τοὺς νῦν διορχησάμενος ὀλίγον ὕστερον.	
Φι.	τίς ἐπ’ αὐλείοισι θύραις θάσσει;	
Ξα.	τουτὶ καὶ δὴ χωρεῖ τὸ κακόν.	
Φι.	κλῇθρα χαλάσθω τάδε. καὶ δὴ γὰρ	
	σχήματος ἀρχή—	1485
Ξα.	μᾶλλον δέ γ’ ἴσως μανίας ἀρχή.	
Φι.	—πλευρὰν λυγίσαντος ὑπὸ ῥύμης·	

LINE 1480

τραγῳδός, ὁ	(< τράγος, goat + ἀοιδός, singer) tragic performer
ἀπο-δείκνῡμι, -δείξω	show; show someone to be something (cf. 548); Phil. is subject of φησιν; τραγῳδούς is dir. object of ἀποδείξειν; Κρόνους is pred.
Κρόνος, ὁ	Kronos, father of Zeus; an example of someone hopelessly out of date
οἱ νῦν	contemporaries
δι-ορχέομαι	(< διά, suggesting rivalry: S #1685.3 + ὀρχέομαι, dance) dance a match with someone, dance against (aor. ptcp. can indicate action coincident with the time of the leading verb, here the fut. ἀποδείξειν: S #1872c2)
ὀλίγον ὕστερον	a little later = "very soon"

1482–95: Meter: Anapestic dimeters.

LINE 1482

αὔλειος (3)	(< αὐλή, courtyard, + -ειος, adj. suffix: S #858.2) of the courtyard (cf. 131)
θάσσω	(< θᾶκος, chair) sit (a word more at home in tragedy than comedy; this line may be paratragic). Phil. is calling for the doors to be opened.
καὶ δή	Look! (cf. 492)

LINE 1484

κλῇθρον, τό	(< κλῄς, bar, key + –θρον, suffix denoting an instrument: S #842.2) bar for closing door (cf. 113)
χαλάω, aor. pass. ἐχαλάσθην	
	slacken, let loose; unbolt
σχῆμα, –ατος, τό	(< σχεῖν < ἔχω, the position or posture one "holds" in dance) figure; dance step
μανία, ἡ	madness
λυγίζω, ἐλύγισα	(< λύγος, the vitex, a plant whose stems are flexible and used for weaving + -ιζω) bend, twist (gen. abs., sc. τινος as the subject = "whoever is performing this dance")
ῥύμη, ἡ	(< ῥῦμα, tow, rope, "where crowd presses" < ἐρύω, draw) force, swing; ὑπὸ ῥύμης = "vigorously"

οἷον μυκτὴρ μυκᾶται καὶ
cφόνδυλος ἀχεῖ.

Ξα.   πῖθ᾽ ἐλλέβορον.

Φι.   πτήσσει Φρύνιχος ὥς τις ἀλέκτωρ—   1490

Ξα.   τάχα βαλλήcει.

Φι.   —cκέλος οὐρανίαν ἐκλακτίζων.

πρωκτὸς χάcκει·—

Ξα.   κατὰ cαυτὸν ὅρα.

Φι.   νῦν γὰρ ἐν ἄρθροις τοῖς ἡμετέροις

cτρέφεται χαλαρὰ κοτυληδών.   1495

οὐκ εὖ;

LINE 1488

μυκτήρ, –ῆρος, ὁ	(< μύσσομαι, blow nose, snort) nostril, snout
μῡκάομαι	roar, snort
cφόνδυλος, ὁ	vertebra, backbone [cf. 254 on κόνδυλος]
ἀχέω	(Doric for ἠχέω < ἠχή, noise) make sound; "crack" {> *echo*}
πίνω, aor.² ἔπιον	(> aor. impv. 2 sing. πῖθ᾽ = πῖθι) drink (instead of the expected πῖε Ar. here uses an aor.² –μι inflection: S #687)
ἐλλέβορος, ὁ	(< ἐλλός, fawn + βορά, food) hellebore. A potion made from this plant was thought to cure madness: "drink hellebore" = "you're crazy [and you need the cure]"

LINE 1490

πτήσσω	crouch
Φρύνιχος, ὁ	Phrynichus; here presumably not the politician but the tragedian of the early fifth century (cf. 220)
ἀλέκτωρ, ὁ	rooster (cf. 100; used more in poetry than ἀλεκτρύων: *LA* 100)
βάλλω, fut. βαλλήσω	(fut. mid. 2 sing. βαλλήσει; for mid. with pass. meaning: S #807) you will be hit; "they will stone you" (cf. 222)
cκέλος, τό	leg {> iso*sceles*, a triangle with three equal *legs*}
οὐράνιος (3)	skyward (for fem. acc. οὐρανίαν, cf. 398 κατὰ τὴν ἑτέραν)
ἐκ-λακτίζω	(< ἐκ + λακτίζω, kick < λάξ, adv., with the foot) kick out (cf. ὀδάξ, 164)

LINE 1493

κατὰ cαυτόν	to yourself, regarding yourself
ἄρθρον, τό	joint; hip joint {> *arthritis, arthroscopy*}
cτρέφω	turn; (mid.) turn around, twist
χαλαρός (3)	(< χαλάω, slacken) slack, supple (tr. as pred.)
κοτυληδών, –όνος, ἡ	(< κοτύλη, cup + –δων: S #863b6) socket of the hip-joint. Phil. does not use these words with precision: *LA* 82.

Ξα.	μὰ Δί᾽ οὐ δῆτ᾽, ἀλλὰ μανικὰ πράγματα.
Φι.	φέρε νυν ἀνείπω κἀνταγωνιστὰς καλῶ.
	εἴ τις τραγῳδός φησιν ὀρχεῖσθαι καλῶς,
	ἐμοὶ διορχησόμενος ἐνθάδ᾽ εἰσίτω.
	φησίν τις ἢ οὐδείς;
Ξα.	εἷς γ᾽ ἐκεινοσὶ μόνος. 1500
Φι.	τίς ὁ κακοδαίμων ἐστίν;
Ξα.	υἱὸς Καρκίνου
	ὁ μέσατος.
Φι.	ἀλλ᾽ οὗτός γε καταποθήσεται·
	ἀπολῶ γὰρ αὐτὸν ἐμμελείᾳ κονδύλου.
	ἐν τῷ ῥυθμῷ γὰρ οὐδέν ἐστ᾽.
Ξα.	ἀλλ᾽, ὦζυρέ,

1496–1515: Meter: Iambic trimeter.

LINE 1496

οὐκ εὖ;	"Wasn't that good?"
δῆτα	"No, by Zeus, it *wasn't*"; in a neg. answer, recognizing the surprise the answer may give: *GP* 275
μανικός (3)	(< μανία + –ικος) mad, frantic
ἀν-ειπεῖν	(aor.², no pres.) proclaim, announce (φέρε νυν) with hort. subjv., cf. 5
ἀνταγωνιστής, ὁ	(ἀντί + ἀγών, contest + –της, suffix indicating agency: S #839a1) opponent, rival, competitor
τραγῳδός, ὁ	tragic performer (cf. 1480)
δι-ορχέομαι, -ορχήσομαι	
	dance competitively, against a dat. (cf. 1481)
ἐνθάδε	here (cf. 270)
εἴσ-ειμι	(> pres. impv. 3 sing. εἰσίτω) enter
γε	εἷς γε = "Yes, there is one"; in affirmation

1500–1537: Three sons of Carcinus come out to dance. The play ends as the chorus cheer them all on.

LINE 1500

Καρκῖνος, ὁ	(< καρκῖνος, crab) Carcinus, a tragic playwright
μέσατος (3)	(< a superl. formed from μέσος; a comic intensification: *LA* 243) midmost; the middle of three sons
κατα-πίνω, fut. pass. -ποθήσομαι	
	drink down, swallow; (pass.) "be defeated"
ἐμμέλεια, ἡ	(< ἐν + μέλος, tune) harmony; a dance performed in tragedy
κόνδυλος, ὁ	knuckle; fist (cf. 254)
ῥυθμός, ὁ	(< ῥέω, cf. 126) rhythm, measured motion
οὐδέν ἐστ᾽	"He's no good"
οἰζυρός (3)	(< οἴζω, cry οἴ) miserable (voc. ὦ οἴζυρέ becomes ὦζυρέ by *crasis*; -ῡ- in nom., acc. only)
Καρκῑνίτης, –ου, ὁ	(< καρκῖνος + –ιτης, suffix normally indicates belonging to a city or nationality: S #844.2) a Carcinite

έτερος τραγῳδὸς Καρκινίτης ἔρχεται,   1505
ἀδελφὸς αὐτοῦ.

Φι.   νὴ Δί' ὠψώνηκ' ἄρα.

Ξα.   μὰ τὸν Δί' οὐδέν γ' ἄλλο πλὴν τρεῖς καρκίνους·
προσέρχεται γὰρ ἕτερος αὖ τῶν Καρκίνου.

Φι.   τουτὶ τί ἦν τὸ προσέρπον; ὀξὶς ἢ φάλαγξ;

Ξα.   ὁ πινοτήρης οὗτός ἐστι τοῦ γένους,   1510
ὁ σμικρότατος, ὃς τὴν τραγῳδίαν ποιεῖ.

Φι.   ὦ Καρκίν', ὦ μακάριε τῆς εὐπαιδίας,
ὅσον τὸ πλῆθος κατέπεσεν τῶν ὀρχίλων.
ἀτὰρ καταβατέον γ' ἐπ' αὐτούς μοι· σὺ δὲ

LINE 1506

ἀδελφός, ὁ — (ἀ- copulative + δελφύς, from the same womb) brother

ὀψωνέω, perf. ὠψώνηκα
buy fish and dainties, "buy a tasty meal" (cf. 495)

τουτὶ τί ἦν — "What's this?" (cf. 183)

προσ-έρπω — creep, crawl forward

ὀξίς, -ίδος, ἡ — vinegar cruet; perhaps a name for a scorpion or cray fish

φάλαγξ, -αγγος, ἡ — battle phalanx; a venomous spider. Spiders and cray fish, like crabs, have many legs. {> balcony}

πῖνοτήρης, ὁ — (< πίνη, a bivalve shell + τηρέω, guard) a pinnaguard, a small crab that watched for approaching danger and could scuttle into a shell for protection. This son of Carcinus must have been diminutive.

γένος, -ους, τό — race, family

LINE 1511

τραγῳδία, ἡ — tragedy (cf. 1480)

ποιέω — make; <u>compose</u>

εὐπαιδία, ἡ — fine children (gen. of cause: S #1405)

ὅσον — how great (exclam.)

ὀρχίλος, ὁ — wren, with pun on ὀρχεῖσθαι, dance; "a swarm of <u>dancing birds</u>"

κατα-πίπτω, aor.² -έπεσον
fall down, come to earth, alight

κατα-βαίνω — step down (verbal: S #2149, with dat. agent: S #1488, 2151)

LINE 1514

ἅλμη, ἡ — (< ἅλς, salt) brine (water, or a sauce, for the crabs (τούτοισιν) to be boiled in)

κυκάω — stir up; here perhaps "boil"

ἤν — if; in case

κρατέω — win (cf. 536)

Χο.

ἅλμην κύκα τούτοισιν, ἣν ἐγὼ κρατῶ.　　　　　　　1515

φέρε νυν ἡμεῖς αὐτοῖς ὀλίγον ξυγχωρήσωμεν ἅπαντες,

ἵν' ἐφ' ἡσυχίας ἡμῶν πρόσθεν βεμβικίζωσιν ἑαυτούς.

ἄγ', ὦ μεγαλώνυμα τέκνα τοῦ θαλασσίοιο,　　　　　[στρ.

πηδᾶτε παρὰ ψάμαθον　　　　　　　　　　　　　　1520

καὶ θῖν' ἁλὸς ἀτρυγέτοιο, καρίδων ἀδελφοί·

ταχὺν πόδα κυκλοσοβεῖτε, καὶ τὸ Φρυνίχειον

ἐκλακτισάτω τις, ὅπως　　　　　　　　　　　　　1525

LINE 1516

1516–17: Meter: Anapestic tetrameters, in exhortation as the chorus begins to accompany the dancing.

ξυγ-χωρέω, -εχώρησα proceed, make way together; pull back to make room
ἡσυχία, ἡ quiet; ἐφ' ἡσυχίας, "without interference"
πρόσθεν (prep. + gen.) before
βεμβῑκίζω (< βέμβῑξ, top + -ιζω) set spinning (cf. 1530)

LINE 1518

1518–37: Meter: Archilocheans (× – ◡ ◡ – ◡ ◡ – ◡ – ◡ – ◡ – –); 1520 and 1525 are abbreviated.

μεγαλώνυμος, –ον (< μεγαλ- + ὄνομα, name) with a great name, greatly renowned
τέκνον, τό child. A word rare in comedy, save for paratragedy.
θαλάσσιος (3) of the sea; Carcinus commanded a fleet in 431 (-οιο Homeric gen. sing.: S #230D.1, lending a touch of epic seriousness, as does the substitution of -σσ- for the Attic -ττ-)
πηδάω jump (cf. 227)
ψάμαθος, ἡ sea sand
θίς, θῑνός, ὁ, ἡ beach (cf. 695)
ἅλς, ἁλός, ἡ salt; sea (cf. 1515)
ἀτρύγετος (3) yielding no harvest, barren (epic epithet of the sea; -οιο is an epic gen.)
κᾱρίς, –ίδος, ἡ shrimp

LINE 1524

κυκλο-σοβέω (< κύκλος, circle, cf. 132 + σοβέω, shoo away) whirl around, move in a circle (a *hapax*)
Φρῡνίχειον, τό Phrynichean kick (an internal acc.: S #1567)
ἐκ-λακτίζω kick out (cf. 1492)
ὤζω cry "oh" [< *onomatopoeia* from interjection ὤ, of surprised wonder] (cf. γρύζειν, 373)

ἰδόντες ἄνω cκέλος ὥζωcιν οἱ θεαταί.
cτρόβει· περίβαινε κύκλῳ καὶ γάcτριcον cεαυτόν,
ῥῖπτε cκέλος οὐράνιον· βέμβικες ἐγγενέcθων.   1530
καὐτὸς γὰρ ὁ ποντομέδων ἄναξ πατὴρ προcέρπει
ἡcθεὶς ἐπὶ τοῖcιν ἑαυτοῦ παιcὶ τοῖc τριόρχοιc.
ἀλλ' ἐξάγετ', εἴ τι φιλεῖτ', ὀρχούμενοι, θύραζε   1535
ἡμᾶς ταχύ· τοῦτο γὰρ οὐδείς πω πάρος δέδρακεν,
ὀρχούμενον ὅcτιc ἀπήλλαξεν χορὸν τρυγῳδῶν.

LINE 1527

cτροβέω	twist, make dizzy, whirl
περι-βαίνω	walk around, sidle around
γαcτρίζω, ἐγάcτριcα	
	(< γαcτήρ, stomach + -ιζω) punch in the stomach, slap in the belly
ῥίπτω	hurl, throw
οὐράνιος (3)	skyward. Here, unlike 1492, οὐράνιον modifies a noun: cκέλος.
βέμβιξ, –ῖκος, ἡ	top; pirouette
ἐγ-γίγνομαι, aor.² -εγενόμην	
	occur, happen in place, <u>be included</u>
ποντομέδων, –οντος, ὁ	
	(< πόντος, sea + μέδων, ruler) ruler of the sea, epithet often applied to Poseidon, but here to Carcinus {> *Medusa*}
προc-έρπω	creep forward (cf. 1509)
ἥδομαι, aor. ἥcθην	enjoy
τριόρχης, –ου, ὁ	buzzard; but can be understood as "three dancers" (< τρεῖς, three + ὀρχεῖcθαι, dance)
πάρος	(adv.) earlier, aforetime
ἀπ-αλλάττω	set free, dismiss (cf. 484)
τρυγῳδός, ὁ	performer of comedy; with a play on τραγ-ῳδός (cf. 650).

What was new about leading off a dancing comic chorus? Perhaps they had previously exited singing only, not dancing; or perhaps the chorus were being led off by dancers introduced for this reason—the Carcinus sons.

APPENDIX A
GLOSSARY OF GRAMMATICAL AND RHETORICAL TERMS

The following words are italicized in the body of the commentary.
For purely metrical terminology, consult the Appendices on meter.

Ablaut (German, "sound variety"): a variation of vowels in related word forms, such as λείπω, λέλοιπα, ἔλιπον; πέτομαι, ποτέομαι, πτερόν; δείκνυμι, δίκη. The last of each of these examples is the "zero-grade" in which a vowel between consonants is weaker or absent.

Absolute superlative: a *relative* superlative compares: "the wisest man" (compared with others); an *absolute* superlative simply emphasizes wisdom: "a very wise man" (no comparison is made).

Adherescent (*adhaeresco*, "attach to"): when οὐ precedes a verb, it does not merely negate that verb, but gives it an opposite meaning: οὐ φημί, "I deny" (1023)

Adversative: a conjunction or adverb that expresses the opposition of meanings, for example, *however, nevertheless*; in Greek ἀλλά, "but"; καίτοι, "and yet"; ὅμως, "nevertheless."

Agon (ἀγών, "contest"): the typical Aristophanic protagonist falls into a dispute with another character and/or the chorus. This may begin with a physical altercation but turns to verbal argument. It is organized into recognizable formal components, including pairs of speeches (*epirrhemata*).

Anaphora (ἀναφορά, "carrying back"): repetition of the same word or phrase at the beginning of a clause.

Antistrophe (ἀντιστροφή, "turning back"): at several points, choral odes are presented in two metrically identical stanzas; the *strophe*, followed by *antistrophe*. Conceivably these were accompanied by corresponding "turning" movements in the choral dance. In *Wasps*, these pairs are as follows: 273–280 = 281–90; 291–302 = 303–16; 334–45 = 365–78; 526–45 = 631–47; 729–35 = 743–49; 868–73 = 879–84; 1060–70 = 1091–1101; 1275–82 = 1284–90; and 1450–61 = 1462–73.

Aphaeresis (ἀφαίρεσις, "removal"): the removal of an initial vowel of a word to avoid *hiatus*, for example, μὴ 'ξίη (for ἐξίη, 70).

Asyndeton (ἀσύνδετον, "not bound together"): the omission of conjunctions, resulting in a list of words or phrases.

Causative: a *causative* verb describes not just an action, but what makes the action occur: "get the foot in the shoe," "make it go away," for example, ἀποβιβάζω, "make to step into" (1163).

Conative (*conor*, "attempt"): a *conative* verb indicates that an attempt at the action is (present tense) or was (imperfect tense) being made, for example, ἐκάθαιρε, "trying to purify" (118).

Coronis (κορωνίς, "hook"): a mark resembling a smooth breathing that is placed over a vowel or diphthong that results from a contraction, for example, καταπροὔδοτε (1044).

Correption (*corripio*, "snatch up," "shorten"): the shortening of a long final vowel or diphthong before a word beginning with a vowel or dipthong; internal *correption* is also possible when a long vowel or diphthong precedes a vowel or diphthong.

Crasis (κρᾶσις, "mixture" < κεράννυμι, "mix"): the combination of vowels of two syllables into one long vowel or diphthong, for example, καὶ ἐμοί > κἀμοί.

Deictic (δεικτικός, "demonstrative" < δείκνυμι, "show"): a demonstrative pronoun becomes more emphatic when the deictic suffix –ῑ is added; for example, οὑτοσί. On stage, one can imagine a character pointing.

Deme (δῆμος, "district," "people"): Attica was divided into some 139 administrative districts known as *demes*; most were in the countryside, though city neighborhoods constituted several. The word δῆμος also came to refer to the Athenian people as a whole.

Denominative (*de* + *nomen*, "name," "noun"): a *denominative* verb is one derived from a noun; in Greek this was generally done by adding endings such as –αω, –εω, –οω, –ευω, –αζω, –ιζω, –αινω, and –υνω.

Dissimilation (*dissimilis*, "unlike"): if the same or similar consonants occur twice in the same word, one of those consonants is occasionally dropped, for example, δρύφρακτος becomes δρύφακτος (386).

Elision (*elidere*, "knock out"): the removal of a short vowel at the end of a word to avoid *hiatus*, for example, αὔτ᾽ ἔδρασα, not αὐτό (1002).

Ellipsis (ἔλλειψις, "falling short"): the omission of a word or words that are logically necessary to complete the meaning of a clause or sentence.

Epexegetical (ἐπεξηγέομαι, "explain in detail"): an infinitive following an adverb or adjective can be *epexegetical* in that it further defines the meaning of the adverb or adjective: ἀγαθὸς ὑλακτεῖν, "good at barking."

Epirrhema (ἐπίρρημα, "follow-up speech"): a speech made after a choral song. This was usually paired with an *antepirrhema*, as in the *agon*, where two sides debated; in *Wasps*, the pairs are at 548–619 + 650–718 (*agon*); 1071–90 + 1102–21 (*parabasis*); and 1275–82 + 1284–90 (second *parabasis*).

Euthyna (εὔθυνα, "correction"): when elected officials finished their terms in office, they were required to undergo an audit of their actions; this was known as the *euthynai*.

Factitive (*factitare*, "declare s.o. to be something"): *factitive* verbs, like *choose, elect, declare, name, make*, often take a double acc., in that one thing is made to be another, for example, "He made me angry" (contrast the similar *causative* verbs).

Flectional compound: most compound words originated in a phrase in which the elements had defined syntactic relationships. For example, the word λογογράφος can be derived from λόγον γράφει, wherein λόγον is the acc. dir. object., but the compound word uses only the stem λογο- without inflection. By contrast, θεοισεχθρία (418) retains the dat. ending of θεοίς *within* the compounded form and it is *flectional*.

Frequentative: verbs that describe repeated or habitual actions; for example, φορέω is used of wearing clothes and is thus a *frequentative* of φέρω, carry.

Gnomic aorist (γνώμη, "maxim"): the action described by the aorist is not just once or of the past, but expresses a general truth; what has occurred is typical.

Hapax (ἅπαξ, "once"): this adverb, conventionally used with the participle λεγόμενον, refers to a word that appears only once—either in the corpus of Aristophanic comedy or in all of extant Greek literature.

Hiatus (*hiatus*, "opening"): it was felt in Attic to be awkward if one word ended in a vowel and the next began with a vowel; the result was *hiatus*. To avoid this, writers and speakers would resort to *elision*, the removal of the vowel at the end of the first word, *aphaeresis*, the removal of the vowel beginning the second word, or *crasis*, combining both vowels into one vowel or a diphthong. When possible, the insertion of movable –ν also solves the problem.

Hypocoristic (ὑποκορίζομαι, "call by an endearing name"): a nickname, often in the form of a diminutive.

Inceptive (*incipio*, "begin"): an *inceptive* verb, sometimes ending in –σκω, describes an action that is just beginning.

Iterative (*iteratio*, "repetition"): an *iterative* verb describes an action that is made repeatedly.

Kommation (κομμάτιον, "snippet"): a short introduction to the main *parabasis*.

Litotes (λιτότης, "plainness," "assertion by understatement"): a double negative that implies a strong positive.

Metathesis (μετάθεσις, "change of position"): vowel and consonant exchange places, for example, θάρσος > θράσεως (1031).

Monody (μονῳδία, "solo song"): a song sung by one person only, as opp. to a duet or choral song.

Onomatopoeia (ὀνοματοποιία, "making of a word," "imitation of a sound"): a word formed from a pertinent sound, for example, βόμβος (108) denoting the buzzing of bees.

Orthotone (ὀρθότονος, "with unmodified accent"): a word that is generally enclitic (e.g., ἐστί) is accented under certain conditions; for example, ἔστι receives its accent on the penult when following οὐκ or at the beginning of a sentence, expressing existence or possibility: S #187b.

Parabasis (παράβασις, "stepping forward"): a choral interlude during which the actors withdraw and the chorus are left alone to sing; the chorus directly address the audience, breaking dramatic illusion.

Patronymic (πατρωνυμικός, "derived from father's name"): a name formed from the name of one's father, often with the suffix –ίδης, for example, Κρονίδης (652), that is, Zeus, son of Kronos.

Periphrastic (περίφρασις, "circumlocution"): two or more words are used to convey one verbal expression, for example, using a participle with a form of εἰμί.

Pleonasm (πλεόνασμα, "superfluity"): words that are redundant and unnecessary are inserted into a sentence to add force.

Pnigos (πνῖγος, "choking"): a short passage in the *parabasis* that is spoken in one breath.

Polysyndeton (πολυσύνδετον, "using many conjunctions"): repeated use of conjunctions, like καί, for rhetorical effect.

Prodelision (*pro* + *elidere*): removal of a vowel at the beginning of a word to avoid *hiatus*; Latinate term for *aphaeresis*.

Recitative (Ital. *recitativo*): a term from opera denoting singing but with cadence of speech; similarly, many dialogues and monologues in Greek drama, even if conversational, were in iambic trimeter and remained at root musical.

Resolution: the substitution of two short syllables for a long.

Responsion: the matching metrical schemes of a strophe and antistrophe.

Retained indicative: whereas clauses in secondary sequence often have verbs in the opt., the indic. and subjv. (expected in clauses in primary sequence) are sometimes "retained" for vividness.

Skolion (σκόλιον, cf. 1222): a type of drinking song that would be sung in turns by participants at a symposium.

Sphragis (σφραγίς, a "seal" or "impression"): a short passage sung by the chorus that rounds off the *agon*.

Strophe (στροφή, "turning"): the first of two paired, sung stanzas; cf. *antistrophe* above.

Sycophants (συκοφάντης, "fig-revealers"): the word perhaps derives from a time when exporting figs was illegal and an exporter could be prosecuted; the term came to apply to anyone who used the court system for filing frivolous or vindictive lawsuits.

Syllabic augment: a verb with a syllabic augment generally add ἐ- to the aorist stem, for example, ἔλιπον; by contrast a temporal augment is found on a verb that begins with a vowel, and that vowel is lengthened, for example, ηὗρον (cf. inf. εὑρεῖν).

Syncope (συγκοπή, "beating together"): the deletion of a vowel between two consonants, for example, the gen. θυγατέρος is also found in a syncopated form, θυγατρός.

Syzygy (συζυγία, "yoke together"): originally designating animals yoked together, the term also refers to pairs of speeches that are arranged in conjunction with one another, like *epirrhemata*.

Tmesis (τμῆσις, "cutting"): the separation of a verb from its prefix, for example, instead of ἀναπείθεις, *W.* 784 has ἀνά τοί με πείθεις.

Zero-grade: cf. "ablaut" above.

APPENDIX B
LEGAL PROCEDURE AND LANGUAGE IN CLASSICAL ATHENS AND *WASPS*

(Note: the Athenian court system evolved over time; the reconstruction given here is not an authoritative, historical reconstruction but an illustration of how terminology in *Wasps* was used.)

Imagine that a drunken old man has assaulted an innocent citizen on the street. He has committed a crime (ἀδικεῖν; noun: ἀδίκημα). A bystander, as a witness (μάρτυς), cries out that he has witnessed (μαρτυρεῖσθαι) the crime. The victim, in turn, calls on the bystander to appear as a witness for him (ἐπιμαρτυρεῖσθαι).

The victim then proceeds to prosecute (διώκειν or κατηγορεῖν) and formally issues a judicial summons to court (προσκαλεῖσθαι, generally in middle; noun: πρόσκλησις). A witness to the issuance of the summons (the κλητήρ; his job was to κλητεύειν) would testify that the summons had indeed been served to the defendant. The victim would write up a formal affidavit (ἀντωμοσία) describing the crime that had taken place and would thereby indict (γράφεσθαι, also middle) the accused. The defendant (ὁ φεύγων) might also write an affidavit stating his side of the case.

This would be done in the presence of a presiding magistrate (an ἄρχων, perhaps specifically the θεσμοθέτης), who would decide to bring the case to court (καλεῖν or εἰσάγειν δίκην for a private suit, or γραφήν if it is a criminal prosecution in the interest of the state). There would be a notice publicly posted on a wooden board (σανίς) about the pending trial.

Different courtrooms were located in different parts of Athens, depending on the nature of the crime or jurisdiction. There was one by the Odeion of Athens called "At the Odeion" (ἐν ᾠδείῳ); another was the Eliaea (ἡλιαία; until a few decades ago, this was mistakenly thought to be spelled with an aspirate, ἡλιαία); another was the "New Court" (τὸ Καινόν); yet another the "Court at Lykos" (τὸ ἐπὶ Λύκῳ). At the "Inserted Court" (τὸ Παράβυστον), the "Eleven" (police commissioners, οἱ ἕνδεκα) served as magistrates.

Athenian citizens were eligible to be jurors (δικαστής was a general term; ἡλιαστής could refer more specifically to jurors in the court of the Eliaea; a verb for "being a juror" was ἡλιάζεσθαι). In the fourth century, jurors would undergo a complicated, random selection process, described in the Aristotelian *Athenaion Politeia*, that was a way of insuring that their votes would be impartial. But in the fifth century such safeguards were not yet in place. As jurors filed into the courtroom, there appear to have been opportunities for the defendant to greet and appeal to them personally.

Now it was time to convene the court (καθίζειν τὸ δικαστήριον). The jurors passed by a gate (κιγκλίς) and took their place at a law court railing (δρύφακτος). A water clock (κλεψύδρα) was used to guarantee that the speakers would speak for equal amounts of time.

It was expected that the plaintiff would make his speech on his own, but it would not be unusual to have a legal and rhetorical advisor or advocate (ξυνήγορος) assist him in this. (In *Wasps*, however, the only ξυνήγορος mentioned is a public, state-appointed advocate for public prosecutions.) On some occasions, another person might speak on behalf of (ὑπεραποκρίνεσθαι) one of the parties. The defendant (ὁ φεύγων) would make his speech in defense (ἀπολογεῖσθαι). Many rhetorical techniques were developed over time; one was to charge that your opponent was telling lies and slandering (διαβάλλειν) you.

Finally, it was time to vote (ψηφίζεσθαι), which was done by dropping pebbles (ψῆφοι) or possibly mussel shells (χοιρίναι) into jars (καδίσκοι) that had funnels at their openings (κημοί). There was one jar for acquittal and one for conviction, depending on the juror's decision. A herald would make sure everyone had voted by calling out, "Who hasn't voted? Stand up!" (τίς ἀψήφιστος; ἀνιστάσθω).

A vote against the defendant meant that he was convicted (ἁλίσκεσθαι). Then the jury would decide to punish (κολάζειν) and to impose (τιμᾶν) a penalty or fine (τίμημα or ἐπιβολή). If the juror wanted to be severe, he would draw a long line on a wax tablet and impose the maximum penalty (τιμᾶν τὴν μακράν). If the defendant had been able to persuade (πείθειν) the jurors of his innocence, they would vote to acquit (ἀφίεναι, ἀπολύειν), and being acquitted (ἐκφεύγειν, ἀποφεύγειν, noun: ἀπόφευξις) would be sweet for the defendant.

APPENDIX C
THE STRUCTURE AND METERS OF *WASPS*: AN OVERVIEW

A full metrical analysis would require many pages (for that, see Parker 1996, 214–61); this appendix only provides a brief overview. The terms "ionics," "trochees," "iambs," and "anapests" indicate passages whose verses may have a mixture of meters but are dominated by ionics, etc. Strophe and Antistrophe are marked where response is present for choral parts. Appendix D offers fuller descriptions of prosody and specific meters.

PROLOGUE

1–229: iambic trimeters

PARODOS

230–47: iambic tetrameters catalectic
248–72: iambic tetrameters syncopated

LYRIC DIALOGUE

273–280 Strophe = 281–89 Antistrophe: ionics and dactyloepitrites
290 Cultic cry
291–302 Strophe = 303–16 Antistrophe: ionics
317–33 Monody: choriambs/anapests (317–23) and anapestic dimeters (324–33)

EPIRRHEMATIC AGON

334–45 Strophe = 365–78 Antistrophe: trochees
    346–57: anapestic tetrameters
    358–64: anapestic dimeters
379–402: anapestic tetrameters

SYZYGY

403–19: trochees
420–62: trochaic tetrameters (+ cretics 418–19, 428–29)
463–77: trochees
478–525: trochaic tetrameters

EPIRRHEMATIC AGON

526–45 = 631–47: iambs and choriambs
546–620 = 648–718: anapestic tetrameters
621–30 = 719–24: anapests
725–28 Sphragis: anapestic tetrameters

LYRIC DIALOGUE

729–35 Strophe = 743–49 Antistrophe: iambics and dochmiacs
736–42 = 750–59: anapestic dimeters

DIALOGUE

760–862: iambic trimeters

LYRIC PRAYER

863–67 = 879–84: anapests
868–73 Strophe = 885–90 Antistrophe: iambs (+ 874 cultic cry)
875–78: anapestic tetrameters

DIALOGUE

891–1008: iambic trimeters

1009–1121 PARABASIS

1009–14 Kommation: anapests
1015–50 Parabasis: anapestic tetrameters
1051–59 Pnigos: anapests and trochees

1060–1121
    1060–70 = 1091–1101: trochees
    1071–90 = 1102–21: trochaic tetrameters

DIALOGUE

1122–1264: iambic trimeters
(interrupted by quotations of lyric poems in various meters; see commentary)

"SECOND PARABASIS"

1265–74: trochees
1275–82 = 1284–90: paeonic tetrameters
1283, 1291: trochaic tetrameters

DIALOGUE AND LYRIC VERSES

1292–1325: iambic trimeters
1326–40: trochees and iambs
1341–1449: iambic trimeters

SONG

1450–61 Strophe = 1462–73 Antistrophe: iambs, choriambs

DIALOGUE AND LYRIC DIALOGUE

1474–81: iambic trimeters
1482–95: anapestic dimeters
1496–1515: iambic trimeters

EXODOS

1516–17: anapestic tetrameters
1518–37: archilochean dicola

APPENDIX D
METRICAL SCANSION

PROSODY

The first step toward understanding the meter of a line is to determine whether syllables are long or short.

The syllable is long:

– if it has a vowel that is by nature long (ᾱ, η, ῑ, ῡ, ω)
– if it has a diphthong (αι, αυ, ει, ευ, ηι, ηυ, οι, ου, υι, ωυ)
– if two consonants (or one of the double consonants ζ, ξ, ψ—but not θ or χ, which are merely aspirates of τ and κ) follow the vowel (even if the vowel is by nature short)

The syllable is short:

– if it has a vowel that is short by nature (ᾰ, ε, ῐ, ο, ῠ)
– if a word ending in a long vowel or diphthong is followed by a word beginning in a vowel; thus the final –η is considered short in ὅπῃ ἐγκεκύκλησαι (699), and the final –ει is short in ἕλκει ὁ δ᾽. This is known as *correption* and can even occur internally: the -αι- in φιλαθήναιος is counted short. This applies to the -οι- in ποιήσω, and some editors print ποήσω. (Fifth-century inscriptions often write πο- for ποι-.)
– if a mute consonant (β, δ, γ, π, τ, κ, φ, θ, χ) is followed by a liquid consonant (esp. λ, ρ, sometimes μ, ν), the syllable may be counted as either short or long, though it is usually counted short. Three combinations alone—κλ, κρ and τλ—account for half of these instances in *Wasps*.

Some tips for identifying the length of a syllable. Problems arise when a syllable has an unmarked α, ι, or υ. How can you tell if it is long or short?

– Remember that first-declension nouns whose stems end in -ε, -ι, or -ρ have a final alpha that is long: ὥρᾱ (these are not normally marked in the commentary).
– Note that certain active participles have long vowels: -ᾱ- in λύσᾱς, λύσᾱσα and -ῡ- in δεικνύς, δεικνῦσα; consult S #306 and 308 for the rules.

- The deictic iota is always long: οὑτοσί, ὁδί (but the -ι on οὐχί or νυνί is emphatic, not deictic, and is short).
- A circumflex over a vowel means that it is long: ἆρα (not ἄρα), ὑμῖν.
- Any vowel with a iota subscript counts as long: ᾳ.
- Crasis results in a long syllable: καὶ + ἐμοί > κἀμοί, even if the two vowels were short: ὁ + ἀνήρ > ἁνήρ. (There are multiple clues to the length of -ᾳ- in κᾆτα [< καὶ + εἶτα]: it has a subscript, a circumflex and is the result of crasis.)
- A relatively small number of frequently used words have long ᾱ, ῑ, or ῡ. Students could do worse than to memorize them: ἅπᾱς, ἀπόλλῡμι, ἐάν, θεᾱτής, θῡμός (and ἐπιθῡμέω), ἵημι (and ἀφίημι), κλάω, νεᾱνίας, νῡνί, πῑνω, πῑπτω, σῑγάω, ὑμεῖς, ὑμῶν, ὑμῖν, ὑμᾶς, ψῡχή.
- Other common words have reliably short vowels: ἄν, ἄγε, ἀλλά, ἅμᾰ, ἀπό, γάρ, δῐᾰ, δύο, ἵνα, κᾰλός, θύρα, πᾰτερ, σύ, ὑπέρ, ὑπό, φῐλος.

IAMBIC TRIMETER

This is the usual meter for dialogue, both in comedy and tragedy, and thought to be close to the natural patterns of speech. Slightly more than half of all lines in *Wasps* are in iambic trimeter. The name ἴαμβος originally referred less to the meter than to the genre of early "iambic" poetry, used for mockery and invective; the name is associated with Iambe, who used mockery in the *Homeric Hymn to Demeter*.

The iamb is composed of a short and a long ($\smile$ –); each metron is composed of two iambs ($\times$ – $\smile$ –); a verse has three metra. The first syllable of each metron, however, may be either long or short—this is known as *anceps* (Latin for "two-headed")—and is marked as ×. The final syllable is considered long even if the vowel is short. The three metra of the iambic trimeter may be indicated with this schema:

$$\times - \smile - \times - \smile - \times - \smile -$$

Frequently a word-break and pause, a *caesura*, is found in the middle of the line, such as after the first or third syllables of the second metron, and is marked with a diagonal slash:

$$\times - \smile - \times / - \smile - \times - \smile - \quad \text{or} \quad \times - \smile - \times - \smile / - \times - \smile -$$

The following lines reproduce a straightforward trimeter:

$$\smile - \smile - \smile / - \smile - \smile - \smile -$$

Wasps 17   ἀναρπάσᾱντα τοῖς ὄνυξιν ἀσπίδα

$$\smile - \smile - \smile - / - \smile - \smile -$$

Wasps 729   πιθοῦ πιθοῦ λόγοισι, μηδ' ἄφρων γένῃ

Almost half of Aristophanes' iambic trimeters include *resolution*, the practice of replacing a long syllable with two short syllables, or even replacing a single short with two shorts. Thus any of the first five iambs may be trisyllabic ($\smile\smile \, \smile$ or $\smile\smile \, -$; the second of these constitutes an anapest: $\smile\smile \, -$). Resolution in the last metron is rare, only occurring about once every two pages. Here is an example of a line with a high degree of resolution:

$$- - \smile \smile \smile / \smile \smile \smile \smile \smile - \smile -$$

Wasps 185   Οὗτις σύ; ποδαπός; Ἰθακος Ἀποδρασιππίδου

An even more extreme case of resolution, spoken by a very agitated character:

$$\smile \smile \smile \smile \smile \smile \smile \smile / \smile \smile \smile \smile - \smile -$$

Acharnians 1191   στυγερὰ τάδε γε κρυερὰ πάθεα. τάλᾱς ἐγώ

IAMBIC TETRAMETER CATALECTIC AND SYNCOPATED

The tetrameter is composed of four iambic metra, although the last metron is *catalectic* (καταληκτικός, "incomplete" < καταλήγω, "leave off"), a syllable short.

$$\mathsf{x} - \smile - \mathsf{x} - \smile - \mid \mathsf{x} - \smile - \smile - -$$

The fourth metron always begins with a short syllable. The second and fourth syllables of the first three metra may on occasion be resolved to $\smile\smile$.

Instead of a caesura, this meter has a *diaeresis* (marked here by vertical stroke: |), where there is a sense break, almost always at the end of the second metron. This is a somewhat more rigid meter than the iambic trimeter, used for entrances and exits of the chorus.

At 248–72, we find a "syncopated" version, omitting the ninth syllable (that is, the first anceps of the third metron):

$$\mathsf{x} - \smile - \mathsf{x} - \smile - \mid - \smile - \smile - -$$

ANAPESTIC TETRAMETER

An anapest ($\smile\smile-$) is the basis of the anapestic metron ($\smile\smile- \, \smile\smile-$). Tetrameters (which are catalectic) consist of four metra, as follows:

$$\smile \smile - \smile \smile - \smile \smile - \smile \smile - \smile \smile - \smile \smile - \smile \smile - -$$

227

The last five syllables (– ◡ ◡ – –) never change, but elsewhere an anapest (◡ ◡ –) can be changed into – – or – ◡ ◡. *Wasps* 387 illustrates an unusual possibility: an uninterrupted run of twelve long syllables:

– – – – – – – – – – – – ◡ ◡ – –

Wasps 387   οὐδὲν πείσει· μηδὲν δείσῃς. ἀλλ᾽, ὦ βέλτιστε, καθίει

Anapests have a somewhat measured and deliberate feel; they were felt to be a kind of reverse (ἀνάπαιστος < ἀνά + παίω, "strike back," "rebound") dactyl. Anapests are used in the chorus leader's speeches in the *agon* (546–619, 648–718) and the *parabasis* (1015–50).

TROCHAIC TETRAMETER CATALECTIC

Two trochees (– ◡) constitute a metron (– ◡ – ×); the tetrameter is catalectic, being truncated in the final metron. In six out of seven lines Aristophanes uses a *diaeresis* at the end of the second metron: – ◡ – × – ◡ – × | – ◡ – × – ◡ –

– ◡ – ◡ – ◡ – ◡ | – ◡ – ◡ – ◡ –

Wasps 421   οἷς γ᾽ ἀπώλεσαν Φίλιππον ἐν δίκῃ τὸν Γοργίου

Long syllables may be resolved to ◡◡; for example:

– ◡ ◡ ◡ – – ◡ – – ◡ ◡ – ◡ – ◡ –

Wasps 462   εἴπερ ἔτυχον τῶν μελῶν τῶν Φιλοκλέους βεβρωκότες

Note that the -ο- in Φιλοκλέους is short, since it is followed by mute + liquid (κλ). Proper names tend to be harder to fit into rigid metrical schemata, and to accommodate them resolution may be necessary. Moreover, sometimes ◡ can be resolved into ◡◡.

Trochees (< τροχαῖος, "running") generally convey excitement and are the dominant meter used when the wasps attack Bdelycleon (403–525).

OTHER METERS

The four meters described above account for 80 percent of the lines in *Wasps*. Other passages are based on iambs, anapests, and trochees but are not arranged in trimeters or tetrameters. One finds shorter or irregular runs of these units. Sometimes they are in dimeters (two metra only); sometimes other meters are included, such as dactyloepitrites (– ◡ ◡ – – ◡ ◡ –), choriambs (– ◡ ◡ –), dochmiacs (× – – ◡ –), paeonics (– ◡ ◡ ◡), or archilocheans (cf. 1518).

VOCABULARY

WORDS THAT APPEAR FOUR TIMES OR MORE IN *WASPS*

Included here are positive forms of some adjectives whose comparative and superlative forms also occur in *W.*, and verbs that appear in both compounded and uncompounded forms.

Full principal parts are usually given only for uncompounded forms of verbs.

Words spelled here with Attic -ττ-, such as ἐλάττων, are spelled with -σσ- in LSJ.

References in parentheses are to notes in the commentary that have fuller explanations of meaning, usage, or etymology.

ἀγαθός (3)   good; well-born, gentleman

ἀγορά, ἡ   the Agora, central marketplace of Athens (cf. 35)

ἄγω, ἄξω, ἤγαγον, ἦχα, ἦγμαι, ἤχθην
       lead, drive (cf. 177)

ἀδικέω   do wrong, commit a crime; be guilty; harm, injure

ἀεί   (adv.) always (scanned either ἀεί or ἀεί)

ᾄδω, ᾄσομαι, ᾖσα sing, crow (cf. 100)

αἱρέω, αἱρήσω, εἷλον, ᾕρηκα, ᾕρημαι, ᾑρέθην
       take; convict; (mid.) choose (cf. 330, 355, 668)

αἰσθάνομαι, αἰσθήσομαι, ᾐσθόμην, ᾔσθημαι
       perceive, hear (cf. 176)

αἰτέω   beg, ask for; (mid.) ask for oneself

ἀκούω, ἀκούσομαι, ἤκουσα, ἀκήκοα/ἠκήκοη
       hear (+ gen. of person or thing heard, acc. of the sound); be spoken of (cf. 271, 436)

ἀκροάομαι, ἀκροάσομαι, ἠκροασάμην
       listen to (cf. 391)

ἁλίσκομαι, ἁλώσομαι, ἑάλων
       be caught; be convicted (cf. 355); used as pass. of αἱρέω

ἀλλά   (particle, postpositive) but; anyhow; enough of that; what*ever* (cf. 9, 173, 180, 446)

ἄλλος (3)   other; rest of (cf. 85)

ἄλλως   (adv.) in another way; otherwise; without purpose or reason (cf. 85)

ἅμα	(adv.) at the same time; (prep. with dat.) together with (cf. 246)
ἀνα-βαίνω	step up, climb up, take the witness stand
ἀνα-βάλλω	toss up; throw (cloak) over shoulder, put on
ἄναξ, ἄνακτος, ὁ	lord, master (cf. 143)
ἀνα-πείθω	persuade, bring around to a point of view; seduce, bribe (cf. 103)
ἀνήρ, ἀνδρός, ὁ	man, grown man (cf. 153)
ἀν-ίστημι	make to stand up; (intr. in mid.) stand up, rise, wake up, get out of bed
ἄνθρωπος, ὁ	human being (cf. 168)
ἀντί	(prep. with gen.) instead of; in return for, in exchange for; just like
ἀντιβολέω, -ησω, ἠντεβόλησα, ἠντιβολήθην	
	beg, supplicate; meet with; plead with as supplicant
ἀνύω, ἀνύσω, ἤνυσα	
	accomplish; make haste, hurry up (cf. 30)
ἀπαπαῖ	"oh my!" (cf. 235)
ἅπᾱς, ἅπᾱσα, ἅπᾱν	quite all; (pl.) everyone, everything, all together (cf. 898)
ἄπ-ειμι	go out, go away, exit (cf. 113)
ἀπό	(prep. + gen.) from, out of; after
ἀπο-βάλλω	throw off, lose
ἀπο-δίδωμι	return, give up, pay, yield; (mid.) sell
ἀπο-λογέομαι	make defense, defend self
ἀπ-όλλῡμι, -ολῶ, -ώλεσα, -ολώλεκα	
	kill, destroy, ruin, lose; (mid.) perish, be ruined
ἀπο-λύω	release from, acquit of charge
ἄρα	(particle) so then (marks an inference; cf. 3, 143, 314)
ἆρα	(particle) is it the case . . . ? (signals a question; cf. 4, 217)
ἀργύριον, τό	coin, money (cf. 607)
ἄριστος (3)	best (cf. 11, 304)
ἀρτίως	(adv.) just now, newly (cf. 11)
ἀρχαῖος (3)	ancient, old-fashioned
ἀρχή, ἡ	beginning, onset, initiative; rule, power; magistracy, elected office; empire (cf. 77)
ἄρχω	begin; lead, hold office, rule, rule over (+ gen.)
ἄρχων, -οντος, ὁ	Archon (a magistrate who presided over a court) (cf. 304)
ἀτάρ	(particle) but (cf. 15)
αὖ (adv.)	again, moreover, on the contrary
αὐτός	(pron.) self, he; (with article, ὁ αὐτός = the same) (cf. 63, 119, 255)
ἀφίημι	release, let go; get rid of, remove; send away; adjourn
βαδίζω	walk, proceed (cf. 180)

βαίνω, -βήσομαι, -έβην, βέβηκα
  step, walk; go (cf. 230)
βάλλω, βαλῶ/βαλλήσω, ἔβαλον, βέβληκα
  throw; hit, strike; (intr.) go away, push forward (cf. 19)
βάρβαρος (3)   barbarian, non-Greek; usually the Persians
βίος, ὁ   life; livelihood
βλέπω   look, look at, see; have an eye to; look like
βοάω   cry, shout, shout at (cf. 336)
βούλομαι, βουλήσομαι, βεβούλημαι, ἐβουλήθην
  want, will, wish (contrast ἐθέλω, consent; cf. 41)
γάρ   (particle, postpositive) for, the reason is that, you see; namely (cf. 11,
  158, 269, 836)
γε   (particle, enclitic) emphatic; limitative "at least" (cf. 4, 79, 97, 146,
  216, 890)
γέρων, –οντος, ὁ   old man (cf. 277)
γῆ, ἡ   earth, land
γίγνομαι, γενήσομαι, ἐγενόμην, γέγονα, γεγένημαι
  come into being, be born; be produced; happen; be, become; add up to,
  result in (cf. 24)
γιγνώσκω, γνώσομαι, ἔγνων, ἔγνωκα, ἐγνώσθην
  recognize, know, distinguish; decide, judge (cf. 64, 743)
γνώμη, ἡ   intellect, judgment, good sense; resolution, purpose, idea (cf. 983)
γοῦν   (particle) at any rate; for instance, at least (cf. 262)
γραφή, ἡ   prosecution, indictment; document for indictment
γράφω, γράψω, ἔγραψα, γέγραφα, γέγραμμαι
  write, inscribe; (mid.) note down; indict, prosecute (cf. 97)
γυνή, γυναικός, ἡ   woman; wife (cf. 610)
δαιμόνιος (3)   belonging to a *daimon*; (voc.) dear sir
δάκτυλος, ὁ   finger; toe (cf. 251, 254)
δᾴς, δᾳδός, ἡ   torch
δέ   (particle) but, and
[δείδω], ἔδεισα, δέδοικα
  fear (cf. 109)
δείλαιος (3)   sorry, wretched, pathetic (cf. 40)
δεινός (3)   awesome, terrible; clever, tricky (cf. 26)
δεῖπνον, τό   meal, usually dinner or supper
δεξιός (3)   right (sc. χείρ); smart, skillful (cf. 65)
δεσπότης, –ου, ὁ   master (cf. 67)

δεῦρο   (adv.) to here, hither (cf. 138)

δέχομαι, δέξομαι, ἐδεξάμην
     receive, take up (cf. 669)

δέω, δεήσω, ἐδέησα, ἐδεήθην
     lack, want; (impers. δεῖ) it is necessary; (mid. dep. δέομαι) be in need, require, beg, ask for (+ gen.; cf. 109)

δή   (particle, postpositive) indeed, really (cf. 21, 492)

δῆλος (3)   clear (cf. 442, 734)

δῆμος, ὁ   people, the citizens of Athens; land, district (cf. 34)

δῆτα   (particle) surely (cf. 13, 24, 169)

διά   (prep. + gen.) through; throughout; by means of; (+ acc.) owing to, because of

δια-δύω   slip through, slip by, evade

δι-αλλάττω, διαλλάξω, διηλλάχθην/ -ηλλάγην
     reconcile, settle (cf. 473)

δια-φθείρω, -φθερῶ, -έφθειρα, -εφθάρην
     destroy, ruin, corrupt (cf. 976)

διδάσκω   teach, explain (cf. 2); serve as producer of a drama (cf. 1029)

δίδωμι, δώσω, ἔδωκα, δέδοκα, δέδομαι, ἐδόθην
     give; (in pres.) offer (cf. 52)

δικάζω   judge, serve as juror; pass judgment on, decide between (+ dat.) (cf. 88)

δίκαιος (3)   lawful, just; δικαίως, justly, with reason

δικαστής, -ου, ὁ   juror (cf. 550)

δίκη, ἡ   justice; lawsuit; speech in lawsuit; penalty; ἐν δίκῃ = justly (cf. 88)

δίκτυον, τό   casting net, hunting net (cf. 131)

διώκω, διώξομαι, ἐδίωκα/aor.² ἐδιώκαθον
     chase, pursue; prosecute

δοκέω, δόξω, ἔδοξα, δέδογμαι/δεδόκημαι
     think, have a mind to; seem, appear; seem good, decide, decree (cf. 177, 270)

δουλεία, ἡ   slavery

δράω, δράσω, ἔδρᾱσα, δέδρᾱκα
     act, do, accomplish (cf. 247)

δρύφακτος, ὁ   railing; bar at court room (cf. 386)

δύναμαι, δυνήσομαι   be able (cf. 357)

δύο   two

δύω, δύσω, ἔδῡν, δέδῡκα
     enter; get into, put on (cf. 140)

ἐάν   (conj.) if; in case (usually contracted as ἤν)

ἑαυτοῦ	(refl. pron.) himself
ἐγώ	(pron.) I
ἐθέλω, -ησω	wish (cf. 291)
εἰ	(conj.) if (in condit.); whether (in indir. quest.)
εἰμί, ἔσομαι	be, exist; (impers.) ἔστι, it is possible (cf. 26)
εἶμι	go; will go (cf. 113)
εἴπερ	(conj.) if (cf. 462)
εἰς	(prep. + acc.) into; with respect to; for purpose of (also spelled ἐς)
εἷς, μία, ἕν	one (cf. 595)
εἰσ—άγω	introduce, bring in
εἴσ—ειμι	go in, enter
εἰσ—έρχομαι	enter; come home
εἴσω	(adv.) inside
εἶτα	(adv.) then; next, after that; and so, accordingly (cf. 39)
ἐκ	(prep. + gen.) out of; in view of; after, in consequence of (ἐξ before vowel)
ἐκεῖ	(adv.) there, in that place (cf. 92)
ἐκεῖνος (3)	(demonstrative pron.) that; also of something or someone well known and famous
ἐκ-πορίζω	invent, provide
ἐκ-φεύγω	flee, escape; be acquitted in courtroom (cf. 157)
ἐλάττων, -ον, -ονος	(adj.) less; worse; weaker (cf. 489, 619)
ἐμ-βάλλω	throw in, slide in, insert, dip in
ἐμβάς, –άδος, ἡ	cheap leather shoe (cf. 103)
ἐμός (3)	(poss. adj.) my, mine
ἐμ-πίμπλημι, -πλήσω, -έπλησα, mid. aor.^{2} ἐνεπλήμην	
	fill up; (mid.) have one's fill, stuff self (cf. 424)
ἐν	(prep. + dat.) in, amidst
ἔνδον	(adv.) within, inside
ἐνταῦθα	(adv.) here, there, in this circumstance
ἐξαπατάω	deceive, cheat
ἔοικα	seem, seem like; be fitting to (+ dat.) (cf. 495, 1321)
ἐπεί	(conj., temporal or causal) since
ἐπειδή	(conj., causal) since, seeing that; (temporal) when, after, since
ἔπειτα	(adv.) then, thereupon, thereafter
ἐπί	(prep. + gen.) on, upon, in time of; (+ dat.) at, in addition to, for reason of, in the power of, into, among; (+ acc.) toward, aiming at, against
ἐπι-θῡμέω	desire, set one's heart on (cf. 5)
ἐπίσταμαι, ἐπιστήσομαι	
	understand, know how to (cf. 958)

ἐρέω (ἐρῶ)	s.v. λέγω
ἔρχομαι, εἶμι, ἦλθον, ἐλήλυθα	
	come, go (cf. 104)
ἐσθίω, ἔδομαι, ἔφαγον, ἐδήδοκα	
	eat, devour; bite (cf. 838)
ἕτερος (3)	other, another; one of two; one or the other (cf. 138)
ἔτι	(adv.) still, furthermore
εὖ	(adv.) well
εὐθύς	(adv.) straightaway, immediately, right away (also spelled εὐθέως)
εὑρίσκω, εὑρήσω, ηὗρον, ηὗρηκα, ηὗρημαι, ηὑρέθην	
	find
ἔχω, ἕξω / σχήσω, ἔσχον	
	have; be able; (intrans.) hold oneself, be; (mid.) be close to, touch (cf. 261, 357)
ζάω	live, be alive (cf. 506)
Ζεύς, Διός, ὁ	Zeus (cf. 97)
ζητέω	seek, look for; inquire into; seek to do (cf. 149)
ἤ	(conj.) or, than
ἦ	(particle) affirmative "indeed"; interrogative (cf. 8, 209)
ἤδη	(adv.) already, by this time; just now; now, immediately, right away (cf. 426)
ἡδύς, –εῖα, -ύ	sweet; (adv.) ἡδέως, pleasantly (cf. 272)
ἥκω, ἥξω	arrive, to have come; be present (cf. 214)
ἡμέρα, ἡ	day (cf. 179, 500)
ἡμέτερος (3)	our
ἤν	(conj.) if; in case (contraction of ἐάν)
ἡνίκα	(conj.) when, at the moment when (cf. 236)
ἥρως, –ωος, ὁ	hero (cf. 389)
θεάομαι, θεάσομαι, ἐθεᾱσάμην	
	view, gaze at
θεᾱτής, -οῦ, ὁ	spectator (cf. 54)
θεός, ὁ	god (cf. 378)
θυγάτηρ, –τέρος, ἡ	daughter (also gen. –τρός, 1397)
θῡμός, ὁ	spirit; temper, anger (cf. 5)
θύρα, ἡ	door (cf. 70)
θύραζε	(adv.) to the door
ἵημι, ἥσω, ἧκα, εἷκα, εἷμαι, εἵθην	
	send (cf. 174)
ἵνα	(conj., purpose) that (cf. 70, 113); (local) where (cf. 188)

ἵστημι, στήσω, ἔστησα/ἔστην, ἔστηκα, ἔσταμαι, ἐστάθην
                stand, make to stand; stand still (cf. 39)

ἴσως   (adv.) probably

καθ-εύδω   sleep; lie down to sleep (cf. 67)

κάθ-ημαι   sit (cf. 32)

καθ-ίζω, aor. ἐκάθισα
                cause to sit (cf. 90, 304)

καί   (conj.) and, even; really, actually

καινός (3)   new, fresh (cf. 120)

καίτοι   (particle) and yet (cf. 598, 915)

κακοδαίμων, -ονος   (adj.) possessed by evil spirit; miserable

κακός (3)   evil, bad (cf. 77)

καλέω, καλῶ, ἐκάλεσα, κέκληκα, κέκλημαι
                call; summon up; cite or summon to court (cf. 32)

καλός (3)   beautiful, fair; of fine quality; in good time (cf. 580)

καλῶς   (adv.) well, beautifully

καπνός, ὁ   smoke

κατά   (prep. + gen.) down, down from; down on to, over (+ acc.) at; like, similar to; according to, at a time

κατα-βαίνω   come down, step down, climb down

κατα-κλίνω, -κλινῶ, -έκλῑνα, (aor.² pass.) -εκλίνην
                lay down, put s.o. to bed; (pass.) recline, lie down

κατ-εσθίω   eat up, devour, gobble down

κατ-ηγορέω   speak against, accuse, prosecute

κεῖμαι   lie down (cf. 213)

κελεύω   order, bid, urge (cf. 410)

κεντέω   goad, sting

κέντρον, τό   goad, stinger (cf. 225)

κεφάλη, ἡ   head

κλάω, κλαύσομαι, ἔκλαυσα
                cry, wail, weep; "be sorry"

κλέπτω, ἔκλεψα, ἔκλεψα, κέκλοφα, κέκλεμμαι
                steal (cf. 57)

κλεψύδρα, ἡ   water-clock (cf. 93)

Κλέων, –ωνος, ὁ   Cleon, the politician

κλητήρ, –ῆρος, ὁ   a summoner; a braying donkey (cf. 189)

κολάζω, κολῶμαι, ἐκόλασα
                punish, chastise; (mid.) get a person punished (cf. 244)

κόλαξ, –ακος, ὁ   flatterer, fawner

κόραξ, –ακος, ὁ   raven, crow (cf. 43)

κράζω, ἔκραγον, κέκρᾱγα

     call out for, croak, shriek, clamor

κρατέω, –ήσω   overcome, be master over (cf. 536)

κρείττων, –ον, –ονος

     better, stronger

κρίνω, κρῐνῶ, ἔκρῑνα

     distinguish, judge (cf. 53)

κύκλος, ὁ   circle, ring (cf. 132)

κύων, κυνός, ὁ or ἡ   dog, bitch (cf. 83)

λαμβάνω, λήψομαι, ἔλαβον, εἴληφα, εἴλημμαι, ἐλήφθην

     take; (mid.) take hold of (cf. 122)

λανθάνω, λήσω, ἔλαθον, λέληθα

     escape notice; not be aware (cf. 212)

λέγω, λέξω/ἐρῶ, ἔλεξα/εἶπον, εἴρηκα, λέλεγμαι, ἐλέχθην

     speak, say, tell, recite (cf. 54)

λίθος, ὁ   stone

λόγος, ὁ   word; account, story, fable, plot; argument, thought, theory, rule; pro-posal; financial accounts (cf. 54)

λοιπός (3)   rest, remaining; (adv. acc. λοιπόν) in the future

λύχνος, ὁ   lamp

μά   (particle) in the name of, by (cf. 26)

μακάριος (3)   blessed, happy

μακρός (3)   long (cf. 106)

μάλιστα   (adv.) especially, most

μᾶλλον   (adv.) more, rather

μανθάνω, μαθήσομαι, ἔμαθον, μεμάθηκα

     learn; notice, understand, remember (cf. 251)

μάρτυς, –υρος, ὁ   witness

μάχη, ἡ   battle

μάχομαι, μαχοῦμαι, ἐμαχεσάμην

     fight (+ dat.) (cf. 190)

μέγας, μεγάλη, μέγα

     great, big (cf. 3)

μέλλω   (+ fut. inf.) intend to do, be likely/about to do; (+ pres. inf.) hesitate to, wait to (cf. 403)

μέντοι   (particle) really, you know (cf. 231, 664)

μένω, μενῶ, ἔμεινα   stay (cf. 524)

μετά	(+ gen.) with, among, amidst; (+ acc.) after
μή	(neg. particle) no, not; (conj. fear clause, cf. 109) that
μηδαμῶς	(adv.) not at all
μηδέ	and not, not even
μήν	(particle) in truth (cf. 258, 480, 537)
μιαρός (3)	stained, polluted, impure; abominable, repulsive (cf. 39)
μικρός (3)	small, little (cf. 5)
μιμνήσκω, -μνήσω, -έμνησα, μέμνημαι, ἐμνήσθην	
	remind; (mid.) remember, mention (cf. 354)
μισθός, ὁ	pay, recompense; pay for jury duty (cf. 300)
μόνος (3)	alone; (adv. acc. μόνον) only (cf. 470)
μῦς, μυός, ὁ	mouse (cf. 140)
νέος (3)	new, young (cf. 96)
νεᾱνίᾱς, -ου, ὁ	youth
νεᾱνικός (3)	youthful, typical of young men; vigorous
νή	(+ acc.) by, in the name of (cf. 97)
νομίζω, νομιῶ, ἐνόμισα, νενόμικα, νενόμισμαι	
	do as custom, consider (cf. 467)
νόσος, -ου, ἡ	sickness, illness
νουθετέω	put in mind, advise, warn
νοῦς, νοῦ, ὁ	mind, sense, intention; attention
νῦν	(adv.) now, present time (cf. 30)
νῡνί	(adv.) right now, at this very moment (cf. 232)
νύξ, νυκτός, ἡ	night (cf. 91)
ξίφος, -εος, τό	sword
ξύλον, τό	wood, timber; firewood; wooden bench (cf. 90)
ξυμπότης, -ου, ὁ	symposiast, fellow drinking companion
ξύν	(prep. + dat.) with (for ξυν-/συν-, cf. 72, 233)
ξυνδικαστής, -οῦ, ὁ	fellow juror
ξύν-ειμι	(< εἰμί) be with, be joined with, have dealings with, accompany, be acquainted with
ξυνωμότης, -ου, ὁ	fellow conspirator (cf. 345)
ὀβολός, ὁ	coin, worth 1/6th of a drachma (cf. 52)
ὅδε, ἥδε, τόδε	(demonstrative pron.) this here (cf. 55)
οἶδα, εἴσομαι	know (cf. 4)
οἰκία, ἡ	house, home (cf. 196)
οἴμοι	(interj.) alas; uh-oh! (cf. 24)
οἶνος, ὁ	wine; drinking (cf. 1300)

οἴομαι/οἶμαι	think, suppose (cf. 514)
οἷος (3)	(rel. & exclam. pron.) such as, fit to; what sort of, how; (+ τ᾽ εἰμί) able to
οἴχομαι	go, go away; be gone, dead
ὀλίγος (3)	little, few (cf. 214)
ὅμοιος (3)	like, resembling, similar to (+ dat.)
ὅμως	(conj.) nevertheless, for all that (cf. 92)
ὄνος, ὁ	ass, donkey; a kind of wine vessel (cf. 616)
ὀπή, ἡ	opening, chink; hole in roof; window
ὅπως	(conj.) that (in purpose clauses; exhortations, cf. 212; indir. quests., with superls.)
ὁράω, ὄψομαι, εἶδον, ἑόρακα/ὄπωπα, ὤφθην	
	see, look (cf. 13)
ὀργή, ἡ	temper, anger, wrath (cf. 404)
ὀργίζω, ὀργιῶ, ὤργισα, ὤργισμαι	
	make angry, enrage, vex (cf. 404)
ὀρχέομαι	dance (cf. 1480)
ὅς, ἥ, ὅν	(rel. pron.) who, which
ὅσος, ὅση, ὅσον	(rel. adj.) as much as; (pl.) as many as, everything that
ὅστις, ἥτις, ὅ τι	(rel. pron.) anyone who, whoever
ὅταν	(conj. + subjv.) whenever (cf. 160)
ὅτε	(conj. + indic.) when
ὅτι	(conj.) because; (indir. statement) that; the fact that (cf. 740; for ὅ τι s.v. ὅστις)
οὐ	(neg. particle) no, not
οὐδέ	and not, not even; but not
οὐδείς, οὐδεμία, οὐδέν	
	no one, none, nothing; (adv. acc.) in no way
οὐκέτι	(adv.) no longer
οὔκουν	(particle) therefore not . . ? (cf. 47)
οὖν	(particle) then (cf. 515)
οὕνεκα	(conj. + gen.) because of; on account of, for the sake of (703)
οὐρανός, ὁ	heaven, sky (cf. 22)
οὔτε	nor, and not
οὔτοι	indeed not (cf. 1122)
οὗτος, αὕτη, τοῦτο	(demonstrative pron.) this, that (cf. 1, 142, 176)
οὕτως	so, thus, in this way
παίω	strike, beat (cf. 398)
παῖς, παιδός, ὁ, ἡ	child, boy (cf. 152)
πάλαι	(adv.) long ago; for a long time; recently (cf. 320)

πάλιν   (adv.) back, again (cf. 148)

πάνυ   (adv.) altogether, entirely, very much (cf. 521)

παρά   (prep. + gen.) from; (+ dat.) at; in presence of; in the eyes of; (+ acc.) toward, next to, compared with

πάρ-ειμι   (< εἰμί) be present, be on hand (impers. πάρεστι = it is in my power)

πάρ-ειμι   (< εἶμι) go by, pass by

παρ-έχω   provide, offer, hold beside; move, make way

πᾶς, πᾶσα, πᾶν   (m. & n. gen. sing. παντός) (sing.) the whole, every, any; (pl.) all (cf. 348)

πάσχω, πείσομαι, ἔπαθον, πέπονθα

     suffer; undergo, experience (cf. 1, 328)

πατήρ, πατρός, ὁ   father

παύω   stop, make to cease; (mid.) stop from (+ gen.); (cf. 37 on impv.)

πείθω, πείσω, ἔπεισα/ἔπιθον, πέπεικα, πέπεισμαι, ἐπείσθην

     persuade; (mid.) obey, listen to (cf. 101)

πεντήκοντα   fifty (cf. 490)

πέρδομαι, -παρδήσομαι, -έπαρδον, πέπορδα

     fart (cf. 394)

περί   (gen.) concerning; (+ acc.) about the time of, in defense of

πίνω, πίομαι, ἔπιον, πέπωκα

     drink

πίπτω, πεσοῦμαι, ἔπεσον, πέπτωκα

     fall (cf. 120)

πλείων, πλέον, –ονος

     (comparative of πολύς) more (cf. 662)

πλευρά, ἡ   rib; side, chest; torso (cf. 3)

πλήν   (prep. + gen.) except (also with single words and phrases)

πλῆθος, –ους, τό   the crowd; multitude, majority, common people

ποιέω, ποιήσω, ἐποίησα, πεποίηκα

     do, make; compose (cf. 261)

ποιητής, –οῦ, ὁ   composer; poet

ποῖος (3)   (interrog. pron.) of what sort?

πόλις, –εως, ἡ   city, city-state (cf. 29)

πολύς, πολλή, πολύ   much, many (cf. 260)

πονηρός (3)   toilsome; worthless, good for nothing (cf. 192)

ποτέ   (encl. adv.) at some point, after all, eventually; once upon a time

ποῦ   (interrog. adv.) where?

που   (adv.) somewhere, anywhere; anyway, I suppose

πούς, ποδός, ὁ   foot

πρᾶγμα, –ατος, τό	thing, matter; affair, business, matter at hand, what we are doing; (pl.) trouble, legal problems (cf. 30)
πρίασθαι	buy; s.v. ὠνέομαι (cf. 253)
πρίν	(conj. + subjv., cf. 579) until; (+ inf., cf. 245) before; (adv.) earlier, once
πρό	(prep. + gen.) before, in front of πρός (prep. + gen.) fitting to, characteristic of; on the side of, toward, in the name of; (+ dat.) near, in addition to; (+ acc.) toward, facing, against, with a view to
πρότερος (3)	earlier, sooner (cf. 15)
πρωκτός, ὁ	asshole, bottom, rump (cf. 604)
πρῶτος (3)	first (superl. of which πρότερος is comparative)
πώποτε	ever (cf. 14)
πῶς	(interrog. adv.) how?
πως	(adv.) somehow
ῥᾳδίως	(adv.) easily (cf. 634)
ῥοφέω, ῥοφήσομαι, ἐρρόφησα	
	slurp (cf. 812)
σέμνος (3)	revered, stately, impressive; solemn, pompous (cf. 135)
σῑγάω	be quiet
σμικρός	= μικρός (cf. 5)
σός (3)	(poss. adj.) your
σοφός (3)	wise, "in the know"
συν-	s.v. ξυν-
σφηκιά, ἡ	wasp's nest
σφήξ, σφῆκος, ὁ	wasp (cf. 224)
σφόδρα	(adv.) very much, exceedingly
τάλαντον, τό	a talent, six thousand drachmas (cf. 660); (as a measure of weight) sixty-six pounds
τάττω	order, arrange (cf. 69)
τάχα	(adv.) soon, quickly (=ταχέως); (with ἄν) perhaps
ταχύς, –εῖα, –ύ	fast (superl. τάχιστος)
τηρέω	watch over, guard, observe; (mid.) take care that (cf. 210)
τίθημι, θήσω, ἔηθκα	place; establish (a law) (cf. 96)
τίς, τί	(interr. pron.) who? what? (adv. acc. τί = why?)
τις, τι	(indef. pron.) anyone, anything; someone, something
τοι	(particle) certainly, you know, I tell you (299)
τότε	(adv.) then, at that time
τοίνυν	(particle) well, then (cf. 164, 578)
τοιοῦτος (3)	such as this, like that
τρεῖς, τρία	three (cf. 243)

τρέφω, θρέψω, ἔθρεψα, τέθραμμαι, ἐτράφην
nourish, make grow, breed; support, help, maintain (cf. 110)

τρέχω, θρέξομαι/δραμοῦμαι, ἔδραμον
run (cf. 125, 376, 1432)

τρίβω τρίψω ἔτρῑψα   rub, wear down (cf. 33)

τριώβολον, τό   three-obol wage (cf. 609)

τρόπος, ὁ   way, manner; (of a person, often in pl.) natural bent, temper, character
(cf. 135)

τρώγω, τρώξομαι, ἔτραγον, -τέτρωγμαι
gnaw, chew; eat (cf. 155)

τυγχάνω, τεύξομαι, ἔτυχον
happen; meet up with (+ gen.) (cf. 336)

τυραννίς, –ίδος, ἡ   tyranny

τῡρός, ὁ   cheese (cf. 676)

ὕδωρ, ὕδατος, τό   water; rain (cf. 126)

υἱός, –οῦ, ὁ   son (cf. 134)

ὑπέρ   (prep. + gen.) for sake of, on behalf of

ὕπνος, ὁ   sleep; dream (9)

ὑπό   (prep. + gen.) under; because of; by (agent)

ὑπο-δύω   crawl under, slip under (often in mid.); get into (cf. 182)

ὕστερος (3)   later, too late; latter (cf. 214)

ὑφ-αιρέω, -αιρήσω, -εῖλον
seize underhandedly, filch; (mid.) rob

φαγεῖν   (s.v. ἐσθίω) (cf. 194)

φαίνω, φανῶ, ἔφηνα,
fut. pass. φανήσομαι show; (pass.) seem, appear to be (cf. 124)

φακῆ, ἡ   soup (cf. 811)

φάσκω   say, affirm, assert, promise, claim, allege (cf. 577)

φέρω, οἴσω, ἤνεγκα/ἤνεγκον
bring, carry; receive payment (e.g., juror's pay); pay (tribute); φέρε (cf. 54)

φεύγω, φεύξομαι, ἔφυγον, πέφευγα
flee; be defendant, be prosecuted (ὁ φεύγων = defendant) (cf. 157)

φημί   say (cf. 36)

φιλέω   love; love to, be used to, want to; kiss; cherish

φίλος (3)   dear, beloved

φόρος, ὁ   tribute payment, income (cf. 657)

φράζω, φράσω   point out, show, reveal, declare, explain (cf. 1425)

φυλάττω   guard; (mid.) watch out for, avoid

φωνή, ἡ   voice, speech; sound (cf. 36)

χαίρω, χαιρήσω, κεχάρηκα, κεχάρημαι
                    enjoy (+ dat., + suppl. ptc.); act with impunity (cf. 186)

χαλεπός (3)   difficult, testy

χάρις, –ιτος, ἡ   charm, gratitude, grace; acc. χάριν (prep. + gen.) for the sake of, thanks to (cf. 186)

χάσκω, -χανοῦμαι, ἔχανον, κέχηνα
                    be agape (cf. 342)

χείρ, χειρός, ἡ   hand (cf. 569)

χρή   it is necessary (impers.) (cf. 80)

χρῆμα, –ατος, τό   thing; matter; (pl.) property, money (cf. 799)

χρόνος, ὁ   time (cf. 460)

χωρέω   move, proceed, move on, move forward (cf. 230)

ψῆφος, ἡ   pebble; voting or counting token; vote (cf. 94)

ψῡχή, ἡ   soul, life

ὧδε   in this way; also deictic ὡδί (cf. 688)

ὠθέω, ὠθήσω, ἔωσα
                    push, push open; pile up; thrust; (mid.) push back from oneself

ὠνέομαι, ὠνήσομαι, ἐπριάμην
                    buy (cf. 253)

ὥρα, ἡ   season; time (cf. 346)

ὡς   (conj.) since, because; so that; that; how; like (with superl.) as possible (cf. S #2988–3003)

ὥσπερ   like, just as; (it seems) as if (cf. 395)

ὥστε   (conj.) with the result that (cf. 188)

FURTHER READING

The list of abbreviations preceding the commentary cites editions of *Wasps* referred to in the notes. The Biles-Olson edition (2015) is now the magisterial authority on many matters that a commentary in the OGLCC series is not designed to explore, including detailed discussions of acting, colloquialisms, costuming, culinary questions, discontinuities and inconsistencies in the plot, ellipses, entrances and exits, festivals, iconographical evidence, kitchen utensils, line assignments, linguistic registers, metapoetic references, mythical allusions, political background, props, prosopography, religious allusions, rhetorical figures and strategies, set design, stage directions, technical vocabulary, textual problems, and zoology.

General Works on Aristophanes and Old Comedy

Biles, Zachary. 2011. *Aristophanes and the Poetics of Competition.* Cambridge: Cambridge University Press.

Biles, Zachary, and S. D. Olson, eds. 2015. *Aristophanes: Wasps.* Oxford: Oxford University Press.

Bowie, A. M. 1996. *Aristophanes: Myth, Ritual and Comedy.* Cambridge: Cambridge University Press.

Compton-Engle, Gwendolyn. 2015. *Costume in the Comedies of Aristophanes.* Cambridge: Cambridge University Press.

Csapo, Eric. "Performing Comedy in the Fifth through Early Third Centuries." In Fontaine and Scafuro 2014, 50–69.

Dobrov, Gregory, ed. 2010. *Brill's Companion to the Study of Greek Comedy.* Leiden: E. J. Brill.

Dover, K. J. 1972. *Aristophanic Comedy.* Oxford: Oxford University Press.

Farmer, Matthew. 2017. *Tragedy on the Comic Stage.* Oxford: Oxford University Press.

Fontaine, Michael, and Adele Scafuro, eds. 2014. *The Oxford Handbook of Greek and Roman Comedy.* Oxford: Oxford University Press.

Halliwell, Stephen. 2008. *Greek Laughter.* Cambridge: Cambridge University Press.

Henderson, Jeffrey. 1990. "The Demos and the Comic Competition." In *Nothing to Do with Dionysus?*, edited by J. Winkler and F. Zeitlin, 271–313. Princeton: Princeton University Press.

Hubbard, Thomas K. 1991. *The Mask of Comedy: Aristophanes and the Intertextual Parabasis.* Ithaca: Cornell University Press.

Konstan, David. 1995. *Greek Comedy and Ideology.* Oxford: Oxford University Press.

Lowe, N. J. *Comedy.* Greece & Rome New Surveys in the Classics No 37. Cambridge: Cambridge University Press, 2008.

MacDowell, Douglas. 1995. *Aristophanes and Athens.* Oxford: Oxford University Press.

McLeish, Kenneth. 1980. *The Theatre of Aristophanes.* New York: Taplinger Publishing.

Nelson, Stephanie. 2016. *Aristophanes and His Tragic Muse: Comedy, Tragedy and the Polis in 5th Century Athens.* Leiden: E. J. Brill.

Parker, L. P. E. 1996. *The Songs of Aristophanes.* Oxford: Oxford University Press.

Platter, Charles. 2007. *Aristophanes and the Carnival of Genres.* Baltimore: Johns Hopkins University Press.

Puetz, Babette. 2007. *Symposium and Komos in Aristophanes.* 2nd ed. Warminster: Aris and Phillips.

Reckford, Kenneth. 1979. *Aristophanes' Old-and-New Comedy.* Chapel Hill: University of North Carolina Press.

Revermann, Martin. 2006. *Comic Business: Theatricality, Dramatic Technique, and Performance Contexts of Aristophanic Comedy.* Oxford: Oxford University Press.

Revermann, Martin, ed. 2014. *The Cambridge Companion to Greek Comedy.* Cambridge: Cambridge University Press.

Rosen, Ralph. 2007. *Making Mockery: The Poetics of Ancient Satire.* Oxford: Oxford University Press.

Rothwell, Kenneth S., Jr. 2007. *Nature, Culture and the Origins of Greek Comedy: A Study of Animal Choruses.* Cambridge: Cambridge University Press.

Russo, Carlo. 1997. *Aristophanes: An Author for the Stage.* London: Routledge.

Rusten, Jeffrey, ed. 2011. *The Birth of Comedy: Texts, Documents, and Art from Athenian Comic Competitions, 486–280.* Baltimore: Johns Hopkins University Press.

Segal, Erich, ed. 1996. *Oxford Readings in Aristophanes.* Oxford: Oxford University Press.

Silk, Michael. 2000. *Aristophanes and the Definition of Comedy.* Oxford: Oxford University Press.

Slater, Niall W. 2002. *Spectator Politics: Metatheatre and Performance in Aristophanes.* Philadelphia: University of Pennsylvania Press.

Taaffe, Lauren. 1993. *Aristophanes and Women.* New York and London: Routledge.

Telò, Mario. 2016. *Aristophanes and the Cloak of Comedy: Affect, Aesthetics, and the Canon.* Chicago: University of Chicago Press.

Watkins, Calvert, ed. 2011. *The American Heritage Dictionary of Indo-European Roots*. 3rd ed. Boston and New York: Houghton Mifflin Harcourt.

Whitman, Cedric H. 1964. *Aristophanes and the Comic Hero*. Cambridge, MA: Harvard University Press.

Willi, Andreas. 2003. *Languages of Aristophanes: Aspects of Linguistic Variation in Classical Attic Greek*. Oxford: Oxford University Press.

Studies of Wasps

Beta, Simone. 1999. "Madness on the Comic Stage: Aristophanes' *Wasps* and Euripides' *Heracles*." *Greek Roman and Byzantine Studies* 40(2): 135–57.

Crane, Gregory. 1998. "Oikos and Agora: Mapping the Polis in Aristophanes' *Wasps*." In *The City as Comedy*, edited by G. Dobrov, 198–229. Chapel Hill: University of North Carolina Press.

Crichton, Angus. 1991–93. " 'The Old Are in a Second Childhood': Age Reversal and Jury Service in Aristophanes' *Wasps*." *Bulletin of the Institute of Classical Studies, London* 38(1): 59–80.

Konstan, David. 1985. "The Politics of Aristophanes' *Wasps*." *Transactions of the American Philological Association* 115: 27–46.

MacCary, W. Thomas. 1979. "Philokleon Ithyphallos: Dance, Costume and Character in the *Wasps*." *Transactions of the American Philological Association* 109: 137–47.

McGlew, James F. 2004. " 'Speak on My Behalf': Persuasion and Purification in Aristophanes' *Wasps*." *Arethusa* 37(1): 11–36.

Olson, Stuart Douglas. 1996. "Politics and Poetry in Aristophanes' *Wasps*." *Transactions of the American Philological Association* 126: 129–50.

Purves, Alex. 1997. "Empowerment for the Athenian Citizen: Philocleon as Actor and Spectator in Aristophanes' *Wasps*." In *Griechisch-römische Komödie und Tragödie*, edited by B. Zimmermann, 5–22. DRAMA 5. Stuttgart: Verlag Metzler.

Reckford, Kenneth J. 1977. "Catharsis and Dream-Interpretation in Aristophanes' *Wasps*." *Transactions of the American Philological Association* 107: 283–312.

Rothwell, Kenneth S., Jr. 1994–95. "Aristophanes' Wasps and the Sociopolitics of Aesop's Fables." *Classical Journal* 90(3): 233–54.

Sidwell Keith. 1990. "Was Philokleon Cured?: The νόσος Theme in Aristophanes' *Wasps*." *Classica et Mediaevalia* 41: 9–31.

Slater, Niall W. 1996. "Bringing up Father: Paideia and Ephebeia in the *Wasps*." In *Education in Greek Fiction*, edited by Alan H. Sommerstein and Catherine Atherton, 27–52. Nottingham Classical Lecture Series 4. Bari.

Storey, Ian Christopher. 1995. "*Wasps* 1284–91 and the Portrait of Kleon in *Wasps*." *Scholia* 4: 3–23.

Thorburn, John E. 2005. "Philocleon's Addiction." *Classics Ireland* 12: 50–61.

Vaio, John. 1971. "Aristophanes' *Wasps*. The Relevance of the Final Scenes." *Greek, Roman and Byzantine Studies* 12: 335–51.

Vaio, John. 1997. "Assembling Wasps." In *Griechisch-römische Komödie und Tragödie*, edited by B. Zimmermann, 23–33. DRAMA 5. Stuttgart: Verlag Metzler.

Wright, Matthew. 2013. "Comedy Versus Tragedy in *Wasps*." In *Greek Comedy and the Discourse of Genres*, edited by E. Bakola, L. Prauscello, and M. Telò, 205–25. Cambridge: Cambridge University Press.